Fragile Rights within Cities

Fragile Rights within Cities

Government, Housing, and Fairness

Edited by John Goering

ROWMAN & LITTLEFIELD PUBLISHERS, INC.
Lanham • Boulder • New York • Toronto • Plymouth, UK

ROWMAN & LITTLEFIELD PUBLISHERS, INC.

Published in the United States of America
by Rowman & Littlefield Publishers, Inc.
A wholly owned subsidiary of The Rowman & Littlefield Publishing Group, Inc.
4501 Forbes Boulevard, Suite 200, Lanham, Maryland 20706
www.rowmanlittlefield.com

Estover Road
Plymouth PL6 7PY
United Kingdom

British Library Cataloguing in Publication Information Available

Library of Congress Cataloging-in-Publication Data

Fragile rights within cities : government, housing, and fairness / edited by John Goering.
p. cm.
ISBN-13: 978-0-7425-4735-3 (cloth : alk. paper)
ISBN-10: 0-7425-4735-3 (cloth : alk. paper)
ISBN-13: 978-0-7425-4736-0 (pbk. : alk. paper)
ISBN-10: 0-7425-4736-1 (pbk. : alk. paper)
1. Discrimination in housing—United States. 2. Housing policy—United States.
I. Goering, John, 1950-
HD7288.76.U5F73 2007
363.5'5610973—dc22 2006023822

Printed in the United States of America

∞™ The paper used in this publication meets the minimum requirements of American National Standard for Information Sciences—Permanence of Paper for Printed Library Materials, ANSI/NISO Z39.48-1992.

To

Camille and Marcus Page

May they find a more diverse and tolerant future

Contents

Acknowledgments

The editor thanks Joe Feagin, Todd Richardson, Margery Turner, Marty Abravanel, Stephen Immerwahr, Greg Van Ryzin, and Greg Squires for their helpful advice. Ms. Diane Hammond provided useful editorial advice. Funding for parts of the research reported in this collection has come from the Ford Foundation, the Fannie Mae Foundation, Freddie Mac, and the Office of Research at HUD. Earlier versions of the editor's chapters were presented at the conferences "Anti-discrimination Policy in France and the U.S.: Making a Difference," at Florida State University, Tallahassee, November 23, 2002, and "Field Experiments on Market Place Discrimination," held at Monash University, Prato, Italy, July 6, 2005.

Introduction and Overview

Housing, Justice, and the Government

John Goering

> I urge you again . . . to enact a civil rights law so that we can move forward to eliminate from this nation any trace of discrimination and oppression that is based upon race or color. . . . I appeal to you for your support of legislation that will help to destroy discrimination.
>
> —Lyndon B. Johnson, 1964

> No statutory law can completely end discrimination. Intelligent work and vigilance by members of all races will be required for many years before discrimination completely disappears. . . . To create hope of immediate and complete success can only promote conflict and result in brooding despair.
>
> —William McCulloch, 1964

The racial injustices of America's past—long considered dead and buried—have recently been seen alive and well, reminding us that perpetrators and victims are still among us. The Hurricane Katrina devastation revealed the linked faces of poverty and racial isolation in the city of New Orleans (Dewan and Roberts 2005; Logan 2006). The president of the United States acknowledged that the now-exposed poverty of so many African Americans "has roots in the history of racial discrimination, which cut off generations from the opportunity of America" (Levy 2005: 14). The continuing struggle to rebuild New Orleans is a sign of a broader, troubling lack of commitment to basic rights of citizenship, including the right to be protected from humiliation and abandonment. Blacks and others are familiar with injustice and unfairness, but, Michael Ignatieff (2005: 16) points out, "What was bitter news to them (in New Orleans) was that their claim of citizenship mattered so little to the institutions charged with their protection." A recent investigation using telephone tests confirmed that black families fleeing Katrina, and seeking new housing within several southern states, experienced high levels of housing discrimination. Differences in treatment occurred in 66 percent of the sixty-five tests that were undertaken (National Fair Housing Alliance 2005). Such evidence of racially harmful treatment needs to be seen within the context of an extremely slow and socially and economically costly recovery effort—as of spring 2006 (Katz, Fellowes, and Mabanta 2006; Lee and Fletcher 2006; Warrick 2006).

There were other notable recollections of our racial past in 2005. Official apologies for the racially and class-based mistreatment of their citizens—most of which occurred as long as a half century earlier—were issued by various governmental bodies throughout the United States. In June 2005, for example, the U.S. Senate issued an official apology for its failure to legislate against racial lynchings when such murders were known to be commonplace and federal legislation would have made a difference (Abrams 2005; Loewen 2005: 43). Legislation had been proposed in those years, but the Senate persistently voted it down (Stolberg 2005: 3).

In July 2005, the government of Prince Edward County in Virginia expressed their profound regret for denying blacks and poorer whites their education when the county closed all of its public schools in the 1950s to avoid school racial integration. As a form of reparation, the county offered school vouchers to that sector of the population (Janofsky 2005: 1).

Congress, in fall 2005, honored Rosa Parks, a leader in the civil rights movement, by permitting her body to lie in state in the Capitol Rotunda (Hulse 2005: A19).[1] And in December 2005, the city of Wilmington, North Carolina, released a major report addressing the long-term impacts of racial rioting that had occurred there in 1898 (DeSantis 2005).

Despite such occasional resurrections and remembrances, racial justice and civil rights are not at the top of most Americans' agenda of concerns. This appears especially true at a time when we are at risk of terrorist attacks. At a time when basic human rights, including the right to life itself, seem vulnerable and unprotected, other issues can fade from moral and political centrality.

A central purpose of this book is to remind us that there are connections between civil rights and our broader set of human rights. We argue that the failure to protect one set of rights, those in housing, may plausibly reflect the inability or unwillingness of government agencies to protect more broadly based constitutional and human rights (Fox 2002; Amnesty International 2004; Weiss, Crahan, and Goering 2004; Ignatieff 2005). This book is a reconnaissance of the state of fair housing protections in the United States in the early years of the twenty-first century, which we believe serves as an effective mirror for our larger ability and constraints as a nation to address the broad tapestry of rights' injustices.

The legislative promises that were made when many major civil rights laws were enacted in the 1960s are reminders of what this country committed itself to. Shortcomings in accomplishing these goals, roughly forty years after enactment, cast a deep shadow on our overall rights capabilities. Hubert Humphrey, the Senate floor manager for the critically important 1964 Civil Rights Act, for example, asserted that the law would "make the dream of full freedom, full justice, and full citizenship for every American a reality . . . and it will be remembered to the ending of the world. . . . Let no one doubt the historical significance of this ringing affirmation which we now deliver to the nation and to the world" (Whalen and Whalen 1985: 201, 217). Civil rights were seen as a major moral and political achievement, a key demonstration of distinctive American values. The aging promise of civil rights is still presented decades later as a major basis for measuring the international standing and preeminence of the United States. Schuck (2003: 52–53), for instance, argues that "Blacks" crusade to enforce America's ancient but still unredeemed promises has become the model for other civil and human rights struggles not only in the United States but throughout the world."

Through the Civil Rights Acts of 1964 and 1968 the United States promised that those protected by its laws would be relatively quickly free from discrimination and its harrowing personal and societal consequences. The question for this book is whether we have made sufficient progress toward this goal to justify the judgment that U.S. civil rights enforcement programs are an effective model for others. It will be the conclusion of the book that we have in fact created quite fragile, imperfect rights.

TWO CIVIC AND POLITICAL VIEWS

The expectations for the major Civil Rights Acts were initially different for the two major political parties, as illustrated by the opening quotations from President Johnson and William McCulloch.[2] McCulloch was far more cautious about promising an end to discrimination—to promise its very destruction, to use Johnson's word. The United States then held, and still holds, two largely separate conversations about the race problem. While a majority of Congress voted in support of the civil rights laws, a substantial minority, including many southern Democrats, voted against them (Whalen and Whalen 1985; Loewen 2005). The view of the majority, including that of Johnson, was that injustice had been done and the country needed to abolish discrimination once and for all. A countervailing discourse appeared almost concurrently and argued that government had no need to intervene and that the preferred course would be for blacks to look to themselves for improvements in their lives.

In the contest for mayor of New York in 1965, to cite one countervailing example, a Republican challenger, William F. Buckley, argued for an ideology of racial justice that stressed the duties of blacks. His alternative view, expressed as part of an emerging critique of government action in this area, identified blacks as a key part of their own problem. The political analyst Samuel Lubell observed at the time that Buckley was "giving emotional voice to the many racial discontents among white voters" (Tannenhaus 2005: 106, 114).[3] Such well-known, contrary views of members of Congress and party candidates gave legitimacy to those of like mind who believed that discrimination was a valid personal and policy option. It is the persistence of this contrary view that constitutes a core sociological limit of U.S. civil rights effectiveness.

It is all too easy to find present-day illustrations of the latter argument. The day of the memorial service in Washington, D.C., for Rosa Parks, for example, the *Wall Street Journal* offered the following commentary on the state of racial injustice: "An America where blacks run Merrill Lynch, American Express, and the State Department no longer needs civil rights activism of the Rosa Parks . . . variety, and hasn't for decades. Thanks in large part to their diligence and sacrifices, the battle for legal equality has been fought and won. Blacks face social and economic challenges, but these result mainly from self-inflicted cultural wounds, not a manifestly unjust society" (Riley 2005: W15). This volume will present evidence that this is a misleading portrait of the country's accomplishments in race relations: we will make manifest this country's racial injustices. The scale and obduracy of such views become a critical part of the story of why discrimination has not been, as Johnson and others expected, destroyed. This obduracy is central to another difficult-to-test thesis, namely that civil rights entitlements do not grow linearly. Rather they can and will experience reversion or retrogression depending on either national or local community support or resistance. Rights protections can be marginalized in response to local or national leadership, which can signal varying degrees of tolerance for either ethnic exclusion or inclusion. As the sociological construction of tolerance and support for rights is little understood, this collection hopefully offers insights into its social composition and current meanings.

Many analysts will dismiss commentary about the social marginalization of civil rights by arguing that there has been sufficient observable progress accompanied by little evidence of discontent. While it is undoubtedly true that there have been palpable signs of improvement, a glass half-full is a sign of either progress or of inaction, depending on how carefully we deconstruct the rate and reasons for the cup's relative emptiness. There is nothing embedded in our commitments to civil and human rights that stipulates that half a loaf is sufficient or enduring.

Social scientists have in many ways helped confuse the problem of providing a clear answer to the question of why racial and ethnic disparities continue to exist in the society at large and in housing markets in particular. In the next section we offer a synopsis of the range of replies that social scientists have adopted to the question of how much civil rights progress has been achieved in this country. The range of these views helps to highlight for the reader the evidence that exists and that which is missing in answering the question of whether America's cup of racial progress is emptying or filling—and why.

AMERICAN RACIAL PROGRESS: A CUP HALF FULL?

Three social science viewpoints or types of thinking about the state of race and justice in America can be identified, with three collateral answers to the policy question: to what extent are civil rights laws still needed? While these three arguments are not hard-and-fast schools or camps their research conclusions have distinctive typological formulations.

Viewpoint One: There Has Been Little or No Change

The first line of argument is that things have improved little at all because racism is so structurally embedded and institutionally useful to whites. Civil rights laws, this line of argument holds, have been virtually irrelevant or ineffective. Joe Feagin, for example, argues that "there is only one racialized system, and it was created by whites and applied to all people of color. . . . As a result it maintains the racial hierarchy and its unequal access to resources and privileges. Without these societal structures and their constitutive organizations, racial oppression would not persist and thrive" (Feagin and O'Brien 2004: 8). Race in America is therefore so structurally determined, and so inured to the benefit of whites, that it has become largely immutable.

Another sociologist, Stephen Steinberg (1995: ix), argues analogously: "Through most of its history the United States has 'played ostrich,' failing to address, much less remedy, the racial divisions and inequalities that are the legacy of slavery." While he acknowledges the importance of the civil rights reforms, he nonetheless sees primarily "persistent and widening gaps between blacks and whites in incomes and living standards" (Steinberg 1995: 212). The legal analyst Derrick Bell also is scornful of progress. He argues: "In a nation dedicated to individual freedom, laws that never should have been needed face neglect, reversal, and outright appeal, while the discrimination they were designed to eliminate continues in the same or more sophisticated form" (quoted in Freeman 2000: 574).

Viewpoint Two: There Have Been Major Improvements

Another group of social scientists and social analysts take virtually the opposite view of racial progress. They report on major improvements over the last century including notable progress over the last several decades. The race problem may not have been solved but major cures have been found. McWhorter (2001: 266) is, for example, convinced that not only is "racism quickly receding" but that "to the extent that it still exists today, it is no longer a significant obstacle to black advancement or well-being." For the man in the street the view is simple: "Discrimination ended in the sixties, man" (quoted in Bonilla-Silva 2003: 181).

Another comparable assessment has been made by Thernstrom and Thernstrom (1997: 533), who note the progress that has been achieved in moving from a racial caste system to "a more fluid social order." We have become, they tell us, a nation "no longer separate, much less unequal than it once was, and by many measures, less hostile. Moreover, the serious inequality that remains is less a function of white racism than of the racial gap in levels of educational attainment, the structure of the black family, and the rise in black crime" (Thernstrom and Thernstrom 1997: 534). Not only are we racially better off, but blacks themselves are now causally implicated in their own remaining deficits.

The sociologist Orlando Patterson (1997: 15), while accepting that more must be done, nonetheless also argues: "the achievements of the American people over the past half century in reducing racial prejudice and discrimination and in improving socioeconomic and political conditions of Afro-Americans are nothing short of astonishing."[4] And in an important overview of racial trends, Jaynes and Williams (1989: 67–74) note the progress that has occurred throughout the country. To illustrate this progress, they quote a former Supreme Court justice who described conditions of African Americans living in the South in the early 1950s: "They could not live where they desired; they could not work where white people worked except in menial positions. . . . They could not use the same restrooms, drinking fountains, or telephone booths. They could not eat in the same restaurants, sleep in the same hotels, be treated in the same hospitals. . . . They could not attend the same public schools. . . . They could not vote" (see also Moskos and Butler 1996; Loewen 2005: 41). These signs of progress suggest that the laws intended to provide equality of access have worked.

Viewpoint Three: The Race Problem Has Changed

Other social scientists, however, are convinced by evidence from public opinion surveys that the appearance of racial progress masks persistent underlying problems that older methodologies have ignored or missed entirely. It is, to simplify, limited methodologies that allow us to see surface improvements instead of the necessary deeper institutional change. While things may appear to have improved, in reality an examination of personal opinions and judgments reveals weak commitments to civil rights practice and integration, including on the part of many middle-class African Americans.

A variety of terms have been used to describe these new social-psychological underpinnings of America's racial system including aversive racism, symbolic racism, new racism, and laissez-faire racism. It is these new opinion-based judgments that have supplanted prior forms of racial patterning and have become the principal obstacle to further racial progress. Whites are no longer prejudiced in the manner that traditional, older methods assumed and documented. Overt expressions of bias are no longer used—or used openly—and they have been either supplanted or masked by more carefully framed concerns about the negative behaviors and values of minorities. Whites now "rationalize minorities' contemporary racial status as the product of market dynamics, naturally occurring phenomena, and blacks' imputed cultural limitations" (Bonilla-Silva 2003: 2). In this world of transformed racial norms, whites and blacks have each developed more complex justifications for the racial separateness in their residential lives and the experiences of discrimination they might encounter. "A majority of whites," for example, "frequently think of black America in terms of low-income neighborhoods often seen and stereotyped on news programs" (Feagin and O'Brien 2004: 13).

McConahay (1986: 92), Gaertner and Dovidio (1986: 85–86), and Kinder and Sanders (1996) varyingly note that it is whites' "racial resentment" that negatively affects their support of civil rights policies. Some of this difference is reflected in testing for linguistic bias, which shows that often minorities cannot even get an appointment to see housing because of the complex interweaving of class-cum-race-based speech differences (Fischer and Massey 2004). In this view, it is the cumulative, stacked disadvantages of race, class, and gender that create the worst disadvantages in the search for housing.

Black opinion also diverges from being uniformly supportive of antidiscrimination policies and unqualified believers in integration (DiMaggio, Evans, and Bryson 1996; Schuman, Steeh, Bobo, and Krysan 1997; Bobo 2001). Part of this new form of race reaction is due to blacks' prolonged experiences with discrimination and racial slights, and some part is due to ineptly managed social programs, including school busing for integration. On the former, we find that many minorities experience cumulative, multiple forms of differential treatment or abuse that leads to a deeply ingrained fear of moving into racially atypical neighborhoods. In a survey of New York City residents we conducted, for example, nearly 23 percent (22.7) of the sample reported six or more experiences of biased housing treatment. Social psychologists tell us that such repeated experiences lead to a range of coping mechanisms, some of which include rejecting or distrusting contacts with whites.

There is evidence that anger and resentment at such experiences is a part of the learning experience of many blacks. Others respond to the experience of discrimination by withdrawing or protecting themselves by creating psychological shields. One black woman reported that "for decades, before leaving home she has had to be prepared psychologically and to steel herself in advance for racist insults and acts, to be prepared even if nothing happens on a particular day" (Feagin and Sikes 1994: 295).[5] Others cope with the actual or potential experience of discrimination through the use of ideological buffers to weaken the harmful effects. Sellers and Shelton (2003: 1086) report that for black college students, "a greater endorsement of a nationalist ideology seems to buffer the deleterious influences of perceiving racial discrimination more frequently." At the same time, those respondents who supported a more "humanistic ideology" were less likely to perceive and feel racial biases. Humanists are those who stress the "similarities among individuals of all races and who would, for example, argue that 'Blacks would be better off if they were more concerned with the problems facing all people than just focusing on Black issues'" (Sellers and Shelton 2003: 1083).

Even though their study could not measure the proportions of humanists versus nationalists in the population at large, it is clear that the long history of racial bias in this country has led to some blacks' willingness to engage proactively with white institutions and others to construct justifications for living separately from whites. The relative shares of each of these two groups will undoubtedly, we conjecture, shift according to local circumstances. There is related evidence that minority property managers discriminate against those who are not of their minority group, thus reinforcing discriminatory and segregative patterns (Fox 2002). Choi, Ondrich, and Yinger (2005) report that "discrimination against blacks is higher when the agent [real estate agent] is Hispanic working in a Hispanic neighborhood, when he or she is likely to cater to prejudiced Hispanic customers, than when the agent is white or black or the neighborhood non-Hispanic."

It is, however, not the views and assessments of minorities that matter so critically but rather the views of whites and the institutions managed in alignment with whites' interests (Ellen 2000; Charles 2005). Whites' stereotyped views of blacks, and their fears of living with "too many of them" fundamentally destabilize the demographic balance necessary for more integrated living. In complementary fashion, minorities have simply grown fatigued by decades of frustration at achieving housing parity and residential social mixing (Bobo 2001; Feagin and Sikes 1994; Hochschild 1995; Charles 2005: 74; Loewen 2005: 103; Ihlanfeldt and Scafidi 2001: 384). Closely aligned to these views, antidiscrimination programs in this country are managed by agencies and institutions for whom racial and ethnic justice is either not a paramount priority or that have become a poorly funded stepchild of other interests. Civil rights programmatic entropy can be understood as aligned to the opinions of the white majority by indirectly or through inaction supporting existing patterns of denial and separation. Programs in this view are at the heart of answering the question of whether the cup of racial equity is sufficiently full or filling rapidly enough. We focus then, in the final section of this book, on the social meaning and implementation of the country's fair housing laws.

THE FAIR HOUSING ACT

The term *fair housing policy* refers to those bodies of laws, regulations, programs, and funding that have been allocated over the last forty years to achieving the goal set out in the Civil Rights Acts of 1964 and 1968. The simple aim of the fair housing policy (most specifically Title VIII of the 1968 Civil Rights Act) was to eliminate discrimination in America's housing markets for most categories of housing and mortgage transactions. It established protections for certain groups or protected classes, and the law was then amended substantially in 1988.

The law argues that "It is the policy of the United States to provide, within Constitutional limitations, for fair housing throughout the United States." What this was supposed to say is that it is the policy of this country "to prevent, and the right of every person to be protected against, discrimination on account of race, color, religion, or national origin in the purchase, rental, lease, financing, use or occupancy of housing throughout the nation" (Sidney 2001; Sidney 2003: 34). This latter wording, clearer for the layperson, was stricken from the final bill. The Fair Housing Act, nonetheless, "set the moral and legal authority of the government against housing discrimination" (von Hoffman 1998: 39). But did this new law actually transfer sufficient authority and funding to the federal government to accomplish what we promised?

The partial answer to this question is that it did not, in part because a motivation for the law's enactment was major urban riots following the murder of Martin Luther King on April 4, 1968 (Sidney 2003). The Fair Housing Act was hurriedly enacted on April 11 and the speed led to unfortunate compromises. Congress seemed to take the moral, or at least the political, high ground in passing the act, but it significantly compromised on the enforcement powers granted to the administering agency, the U.S. Department of Housing and Urban Development (HUD). As a result, the first twenty years of the act's implementation involved largely—often solely—the power of "conference, conciliation and persuasion." The enforcing agency, the Department of Housing and Urban Development (HUD), could do virtually nothing more than talk to people and try to convince them to settle. It was a law that—in the words of one observer—was "a beautiful bird without wings to fly" (quoted in Sidney 2001: 182; see also Schill, chapter 7 of this volume).

Central to the compromises was another requirement that any complaints of discrimination filed with HUD had to be passed on to any state or local government office judged to have laws "substantially equivalent" to the federal law. Long before program decentralization became popular in Washington, Republicans in the Senate required that the new Fair Housing Act pass along its duties to the local level rather than entrust them to "the feds" (Whalen and Whalen 1985; Edsall and Edsall 1992; Sidney 2001). Everyone knew that local and state governments would leniently decide whether laws were broken and, if so, what to do about it. This was, simply put, not a reform aimed at revolutionizing the apartheid character of American housing markets.

Amendments to the Fair Housing Act in 1988 (see Schill, chapter 7 of this volume) offered what appeared to be useful improvements in the enforcement tools and penalties. Along with the obligation to take action within 100 days or three months, the government was given powers to issue restraining orders and to take cases to federal court. Penalties were greatly increased, with substantial fines for a first offense and a doubling of them for a subsequent violation. Protection was added for families with children as well as the disabled.[6] Given the importance of the Fair Housing Act, and the changes to it in 1988, do we now know if the law worked as the framers intended? What research is there that can help us assess how well as a society we have met the promises of open housing?

FAIR HOUSING AS A MICROCOSM

This book can then be considered part of the current small wave of retrospective analyses of how just and fair Americans really are, decades after pledges and legal commitments to ensure such rights were enacted by Congress (Loewen 2005).[7] The essays in this volume illustrate one set of rights, those in housing, but do so in the expectation that achievements and shortcomings here imply the achievements and shortcomings of other parts of the U.S. system for ensuring civil rights. The question of concern is whether racial, ethnic, and allied class separation have so spoiled the fabric of U.S. society that such separation remains virtually impervious to moral and legal challenge. Have the institutional roots of discrimination remained unresponsive to the nation's civil rights promises? Put differently, what have our legal commitments to equitable and fair housing achieved?

To answer these questions, the contributors to this volume offer a rich, current analysis of fairness in housing in the United States. They make use of census data, testing studies, surveys, and program evaluation data to offer a clearer portrait of our civil—fair housing—rights achievements and shortcomings. Their research constitutes the best survey of race and housing justice that has been possible in decades.

The study of racial housing inequities is, however, necessarily still incomplete. We lack, for example, a comprehensive view of the personal and institutional sources of the divisions we still encounter in making housing choices and how they are related to other sources of discrimination and denial, say in employment or education. While considerable social science skill has been devoted over the last half-century to developing a picture of individuals' feelings and preferences about race, ethnicity, and housing, this research has been only minimally matched by analyses of the influence on fair housing of institutions like the real estate industry, mortgage lenders, and government agencies (Loewen 2005).

The two faces of the coin of effective analysis of racial division include popular perceptions and choices as well as institutional conduct and influence. We know a good deal about the average American's stated commitments to greater fairness and openness in housing and neighborhoods but all too little about the marginal social groupings and values that continue to sustain racial bias and discriminatory treatment. We know little about forty years of government administration of a civil rights law intended to require real estate agents and rental agents to stop enacting their or their neighbors' biases. We, for example, know what the average American thinks about open housing laws but nothing about how the people charged with implementing these laws feel and judge fairness. We know that the law requires behavior to change in banks and brokerages but have none of the survey and ethnographic detail for the average banker or broker that we have about the average citizen. We know a good deal about how people say they feel about race, in varied hypothetical situations, but next to nothing about how the people who carry out the actual discrimination feel, believe, and choose. Social scientists have by and large stopped with what people say and have not gone the next step to learn if they have put their money—or causal weight—where their opinions are. Have those ostensibly protected by the law and by America's de jure commitment to the principles of freedom of choice actually been helped? If most Americans are only feebly committed to the practice of fair housing justice, how much impact can open housing laws ever have?

We know that local institutions and neighborhood groups can influence open, inclusive communities (Molotch 1973) but have scant national evidence about how effective or constrained these efforts have been over time. Even less is known about institutions and agencies whose intent may be benign but whose practices reflect deeply embedded, institutionalized forms of unfairness (Blank, Dabady, and Citro 2004). We have for decades paid only minimal attention to the causes of persistent or changing patterns of housing denial and choice and to what structural features of our markets create or resist greater housing mixing. As one crucial part of this causal examination, it is especially errant that we have no well-formed evaluations of civil rights program performance to help us know how the law actually affects actions taken in housing transactions.

THERE HAS BEEN MEASURABLE CHANGE—FOR THE BETTER

We learn from chapters in this collection that both segregation and discrimination, for blacks, are declining and that housing integration is increasing. These are critical shifts in the structure and patterning of racial inequalities in our cities. We do not, however, clearly understand why this has happened and what rate of further change we should expect. That is, we do not know whether programs or agency can increase the rate at which such improvement can occur in the future. Have these changes been the result of civil rights laws or merely the by-product of the evanescent demographic composition of this country's population? Are the large numbers of immigrants to this country a key to easing the old black-white frictions and injustices? Should we expect to achieve greater success in open housing as a result of the new waves of families from abroad who know nothing of our forms of discrimination or the biases peculiar to this country's past and who expect fair treatment? The improvements in housing integration shown in Ellen's essay (chapter 6), however, provide reason to worry about improvements for African Americans over time.[8]

The experience of ill treatment on the part of the children of immigrants—in spite of their parents' expectations of fair treatment—means that these children are learning about discrimination from us (Portes and Rumbaut 2001). The experience of discrimination and the expectation of ethnic intergroup conflict are not dissipating, as civil rights theory would lead us to expect, but are rather finding ways to become reinvigorated. The children of immigrants learn not to trust in the promises of a diverse integrated future that their parents arrived with. Portes and Rumbaut (2001: 187) show us some of the corrosive effects of discrimination for the children in their study. They find that "direct experiences of discrimination trigger a reaction away from things American and towards reinforcement of the original immigrant identities. . . . Groups subjected to extreme discrimination and derogation of their national origins are likely to embrace them more fiercely; those received more favorably shift to American identities with greater speed and less pain." So while discrimination has long been technically illegal, it shape-shifts into new forms of resentment by people who came without any such preconceptions. Bias has become part of the process of acculturation to America. We are teaching nonwhite, immigrant children to distrust the promises of a more diverse and tolerant future.[9]

The causal relationship among discrimination, housing choices, segregation patterns, and civil rights program enforcement are, then, complex and only preliminarily understood. The central policy result is that it is impossible to convert much social science argument into policies or ideas of how to best intervene causally into the processes and mechanisms that are sustaining biased housing outcomes. With the exception of research reported within on how programs operate, there is little basis for anticipating which way the causal winds of tolerance will shift and how rapidly patterns of segregation and discrimination may further dissipate.

ABOUT THE BOOK

The research reported in this collection offers the most current overview that we have had for decades of the process and impacts of getting a house fairly. The chapters provide research on the current extent of housing discrimination, segregation, and integration and explore the relative effectiveness of antidiscrimination programs. Two important patterns emerge from this collection. First, there has over time been a modest lessening of racial separation and decline in racial discrimination experienced by blacks in the United States. Hispanics appear currently unaffected by these improvements. Second, given that roughly a quarter or more of those protected by fair housing laws still encounter discrimination, we learn that the law as currently designed and implemented offers limited assistance and relief to most Americans. Most indeed are indifferent to the very existence of their rights to fair housing. Since civil rights laws are not as effective as they were intended to be in eliminating housing discrimination we conclude that the manner of administering justice should be substantially redesigned (Cashin 2004; Schuck 2003). We conclude with a look at the implications of these research findings for fair housing policies and programs.[10]

NOTES

In the epigraphs to this chapter, President Johnson and Representative McCulloch, the Republican House leader, are speaking of Title VI of the Civil Rights Act of 1964. I argue that the political basis for the enforcement of Title VI was fundamental in shaping later enforcement of fair housing (Title VIII of the Civil Rights Act of 1968).

1. Also in 2005, forty years after the murders of three civil rights workers by Ku Klux Klan members, their ringleader was finally found guilty in federal court of negligence and manslaughter (Dewan 2005).

2. There is of course much political willfulness and some sociological naiveté in Johnson's and other Democrats' pledges that the new law would create a rapid change in the social and political construction of opportunities for blacks and others now ostensibly protected by the laws.

3. For historical insight into the origins of blaming blacks when that justifies racial exclusion see Loewen 2005: 37–38.

4. "Only a fool or a bigot would deny that a great deal remains to be done, that indeed in some areas, we have seen intolerable stagnation and even regression" (Patterson 1997: 1).

5. McWhorter (2001: 27, 29) stridently argues that blacks tend to develop a "postcolonial inferiority complex" or experience "culturally based insecurity" and therefore claim they see more racism than is real. I do not take such hyperbole as either serious social science or credible policy analysis.

6. It is also helpful to mention what the Fair Housing Act does not require: it does not mandate diversity or integration in housing or a clear affirmative action program in housing-allocation decisions.

7. The research for this volume was funded by the Ford Foundation, the Fannie Mae Foundation, Freddie Mac, and the Office of Research at HUD. Earlier draft versions of most of these chapters were presented at a national fair housing conference convened jointly by City University of New York and the U.S. Department of Housing and Urban Development and was held in Washington in March 2004.

8. Immigrants, we learn, start here with quite positive views of the prospects for neighborhood diversity and tolerance (Portes and Rumbaut 2001: 94–96). Almost 90 percent (85.9) of adult or parent respondents to a survey of immigrant residents of Miami and San Diego said that their children would not encounter any opposition if in the future they wanted to "move to a white American neighborhood." We learn, how-

ever, that this optimistic story of tolerance changes for their children. When the children of these immigrants were asked some years later about whether they experienced any discrimination, roughly 60 percent (62.2) said they had experienced discrimination; "87 percent . . . agreed that there is racial discrimination in economic opportunities in the United States, 88 percent agree that there is much conflict between ethic and racial groups" (Portes and Rumbaut 2001: 173).

9. There is other research (South and Crowder 1998) that shows a positive, rather than a negative, effect of discrimination on the chance of moving into a whiter community. They report (South and Crowder 1998: 380) that "black movers in areas with greater housing discrimination tend to relocate to tracts that proportionally contain more white residents." Some part of this may be due to real estate agents encouraging whites to move to even whiter areas. The current practice of real estate brokers' allocating—or steering—whites and nonwhites to specific communities appears in this collection to be a major mechanism by which the racial patterning of our cities survives, and does so illegally.

10. Lack of change cannot be treated as the inevitable outcome of conflicted justice in a market-based housing system or to the predictable bureaucratic shortcomings of administering agencies (Tabb and Sawers 1978; Sparrow 2000). They as well reflect and implicate the nature of our societal commitments to the conjoint principles and practice of housing justice.

REFERENCES

Abrams, Jim. 2005. "Senate Notes Its Inaction on Lynchings." *Boston Globe.* June 14: 1.

Amnesty International. 2004. "Threat and Humiliation: Racial Profiling, Domestic Security, and Human Rights in the United States." U.S. Domestic Human Rights Program. New York: Amnesty International.

Blank, Rebecca, Marilyn Dabady, and Constance Citro (eds.). 2004. *Measuring Racial Discrimination*. Washington, DC: National Academy Press.

Bobo, Lawrence. 2001. "Racial Attitudes and Relations at the Close of the Twentieth Century." In *America Becoming: Racial Trends and Their Consequences*, vol. 1, ed. Neil Smelser, William Julius Wilson, and Faith Mitchell, 264–301. Washington, DC: National Academy Press.

Bonilla-Silva, Eduardo. 2003. *Racism without Racists: Color-bland Racism and the Persistence of Racial Inequality in the United States*. New York: Rowman & Littlefield.

Cashin, Sheryll. 2004. *The Failures of Integration: How Race and Class Undermine the American Dream*. New York: Public Affairs.

Charles, Camile Zubrinsky. 2005. "Can We Live Together? Racial Preferences and Neighborhood Outcomes." In *The Geography of Opportunity: Race and Housing Choice in Metropolitan America*, ed. Xavier de Souza Briggs, 45–80. Washington, DC: Brookings Institution Press.

Choi, Seok, Jan Ondrich, and John Yinger. 2005. "Do Rental Agents Discriminate against Minority Customers: Evidence from the 2000 Housing Discrimination Study." *Journal of Housing Economics*. 14:1–26.

DeSantis, John. 2005. "North Carolina City Confronts Its Past in Report on White Vigilantes." *New York Times*, December 19.

Dewan, Shaila. 2005. "Former Klansman Guilty of Manslaughter in 1964 Deaths." *New York Times*, June 22: A1.

Dewan, Shaila, and Janet Roberts. 2005. "Louisiana's Deadly Storm Took Strong as Well as the Helpless." *New York Times,* December 18: A1, 46.

DiMaggio, Paul, John Evans, and Bethany Bryson. 1996. "Have Americans' Social Attitudes Become More Polarized?" *American Journal of Sociology* 102:690–755.

Edsall, Thomas, and Mary Edsall. 1992. *Chain Reaction: The Impact of Race, Rights, and Taxes on American Politics*. New York: W.W. Norton.

Ellen, Ingrid Gould. 2000. *Sharing America's Neighborhoods: The Prospects for Stable Racial Integration*. Cambridge: Harvard University Press.

Feagin, Joe, and Eileen O'Brien. 2004. *White Men on Race: Power, Privilege, and the Shaping of Cultural Consciousness*. Boston: Beacon.

Feagin, Joe, and Melvin Sikes. 1994. *Living with Racism: The Black Middle Class Experience*. Boston: Beacon.

Fischer, Mary, and Douglas Massey. 2004. "The Ecology of Racial Discrimination." *City & Community* 3(3): 221–41.

Fox, Robin. 2002. "Human Rights and Foreign Policy." *National Interest* 68:118–21.

Freeman, Alan. 2000. "Derrick Bell—Race and Class: The Dilemma of Liberal Reform." In *Critical Race Theory: The Cutting Edge*, ed. Richard Delgado and Jean Stefancic, 573–78. Philadelphia: Temple University Press.

Gaertner, Samuel, and John Dovidio. 1986. "The Aversive Form of Racism." In *Prejudice, Discrimination and Racism*, ed. John Dovidio and S. Gaertner, 61–89. New York: Academic Press.

Hochschild, Jennifer. 1995. *Facing up to the American Dream: Race, Class, and the Soul of the Nation*. Princeton, NJ: Princeton University Press.

Hulse, Carl. 2005. "New Honor for Rosa Parks." *New York Times*, October 28: A19.

Ignatieff, Michael. 2005. "The Broken Contract." *New York Times Magazine*, September 25: 15–17.

Ihlanfeldt, Keith, and Benjamin Scafidi. 2001. "Black Self-Segregation as a Cause of Housing Segregation: Evidence from the Multi-City Study of Urban Inequality." *Journal of Urban Economics* 51:366–90.

Janofsky, Michael. 2005. "A New Hope for Dreams Suspended by Segregation." *New York Times*, July 31: 1.

Jaynes, Gerald, and Robin Williams (eds). 1989. A *Common Destiny: Blacks and American Society.* Washington, DC: National Academy Press.

Katz, Bruce, Matt Fellowes, and Mia Mabanta. 2006. *Katrina Index: Tracking Variables of Post-Katrina Reconstruction*. Metropolitan Policy Program, March 2. Washington, DC: Brookings Institution.

Kinder, Donald, and Lynn Sanders. 1996. *Divided by Color: Racial Politics and Democratic Ideals*. Chicago: University of Chicago Press.

Lee, Christopher, and Michael Fletcher. 2006. "Katrina Report urges Retooled Disaster Plans." *Washington Post*, February 24: A1.

Levy, Clifford. 2005. "Post-Katrina: Bricks and Mortals." *New York Times*, September 18.

Loewen, James. 2005. *Sundown Towns: A Hidden Dimension of American Racism.* New York: The New Press.

Logan, John. 2006. "The Impact of Katrina: Race and Class in Storm-Damaged Neighborhoods." Department of Sociology, Brown University, January.

McConahay, John. 1986. "Modern Racism, Ambivalence, and the Modern Racism Scale." In *Prejudice, Discrimination, and Racism*, ed. John Dovidio and Samuel Gaertner, 91–125. New York: Academic Press.

McWhorter, John. 2001. *Losing the Race: Self-Sabotage in Black America*. New York: Perennial.

Molotch, Harvey. 1973. *Managed Integration: Dilemmas of Doing Good in the City.* Berkeley: University of California Press.

Moskos, Charles, and John Sibley Butler. 1996. *All that we Can Be: Black Leadership and Racial Integration the Army Way*. New York: Basic.

National Fair Housing Alliance. 2005. *No Home for the Holidays: Report on Housing Discrimination against Hurricane Katrina Survivors*. December 20. Washington, DC: National Fair Housing Alliance.

Patterson, Orlando. 1997. *The Ordeal of Integration: Progress and Resentment in America's "Racial" Crisis*. Washington, DC: Civitas Press.

Portes, Alejandro, and Ruben Rumbaut. 2001. *Legacies: The Story of the Immigrant Second Generation*. New York: Russell Sage.

Riley, Jason. 2005. "When the Leaders of Civil Rights Were Civilized." *Wall Street Journal*, October 28: W15.

Schuck, Peter. 2003. *Diversity in America: Keeping Government at a Safe Distance.* Cambridge, MA: Belknap Press.

Schuman, Howard, Charlotte Steeh, Lawrence Bobo, and Maria Krysan. 1997. *Racial Attitudes in America: Trends and Interpretations*. Cambridge, MA: Harvard University Press.

Sellers, Robert, and J. Nicole Shelton. 2003. "The Role of Racial Identity in Perceived Racial Discrimination." *Journal of Personality and Social Psychology* 84: 1079–92.

Sidney, Mara. 2001. "Images of Race, Class, and Markets: Rethinking the Origins of U.S. Fair Housing Policy." *Journal of Policy History* 13(2): 181–214.

———. 2003. *Unfair Housing: How National Policy Shapes Community Action.* Lawrence: University of Kansas Press.

South, Scott, and Kyle Crowder. 1998. "Housing Discrimination and Residential Mobility: Impacts for Blacks and Whites." *Population Research and Policy Review* 17:369–87.

Sparrow, Malcolm. 2000. *The Regulatory Craft: Controlling Risks, Solving Problems, and Managing Compliance*. Washington, DC: Brookings Institution.

Steinberg, Stephen. 1995. *Turning Back: The Retreat from Racial Justice in American Thought and Policy*. Boston: Beacon.

Stolberg, Sheryl Gay. 2005. "The Senate Apologizes, Mostly." *New York Times*, June 19: 3.

Tabb, William, and Larry Sawers. 1978. *Marxism and the Metropolis: New Perspectives in Urban Political Economy*. New York: Oxford.

Tannenhaus, Sam. 2005. "The Buckley Effect." *New York Times Magazine*, October 2: 67–116.

Thernstrom, Stephan, and Abigail Thernstrom. 1997. *America in Black and White: One Nation, Indivisible*. New York: Simon and Schuster.

von Hoffman, Alexander. 1998. *Like Fleas on a Tiger? A Brief History of the Open Housing Movement*. Working Paper W98-3, August. Cambridge, MA: Joint Center for Housing Studies.

Warrick, Joby. 2006. "Multiple Layers of Contractors Drive up Cost of Katrina Cleanup." *Washington Post*, March 20: A1.

Weiss, Thomas, Margaret Crahan, and John Goering (eds.). 2004. *Wars on Terrorism and Iraq: Human Rights, Unilateralism, and U.S. Foreign Policy*. New York: Routledge.

Whalen, Charles, and Barbara Whalen. 1985. *The Longest Debate: A Legislative History of the 1964 Civil Rights Act*. New York: New American Library.

1

An Overview of Key Issues in the Field of Fair Housing Research

John Goering

This is the first time in roughly the last half-century that significant analytic attention has been focused on the patterns and causal influences of racial disadvantage and separation in America's housing markets. This collection includes time-series and current research on why whites, blacks, and other ethnic minorities remain separate from and hostile to each other. The research addresses the question of how well the United States is doing in its commitment to end housing market discrimination.

This volume references four broad types of evidence. The first measures discriminatory behavior through the use of audits. Research using the testing, or audit, method is critical in answering the question of whether racial practices remain unchanged or have improved over time. The second examines racial separation through measures of housing segregation and integration. The major data source is the Bureau of the Census covering the periods from 1980 up to 2000 for the analyses of segregation and integration.[1]

Research on housing discrimination has for thirty years been heavily influenced by auditing funded by the U.S. Department of Housing and Urban Development (HUD) to assess the actual behavior of actors in housing and credit markets (Heckman and Siegelman 1993; Fix and Turner 1998). Drawing on the experiences of local fair housing enforcement groups, economists recommended in 1974 that HUD make use of formalized methods of testing, or auditing, to gather systematic evidence about the behavior of real estate actors and agents (Saltman 1978). In 1976 HUD issued a contract for roughly $1 million to do the first national audit.[2] Included was a pilot test of discrimination against Hispanics in the Dallas rental housing market. In 1988 a national estimate of black discrimination was repeated, along with the first national estimate of discrimination against Hispanics.

The most recent and third wave of auditing was the Housing Discrimination Study 2000, or HDS2000. It has provided national estimates for discrimination against blacks and Hispanics and local area testing for discrimination against Asians, American Indians, and the disabled. The last of the reports was released in the summer of 2005. The total cost for all stages of HDS2000 was roughly $16 million.[3]

The third type of evidence is national surveys of the American public conducted in 2001 and 2005 on their knowledge of and attitudes toward fair housing law and discrimination. A survey focused on a comparable set of questions was also administered to a sample of New Yorkers in 2005 (the methodology for this survey is provided in an appendix at the conclusion of chapter 11).[4] The final type of evidence we present addresses the question of what programs have worked to make us less racially divided. Have public policies designed to address housing unfairness worked as designed and intended by Congress, and have they been effective in causing changes for the better?

Virtually all of the information presented in this collection is new or newly synthesized. It draws upon both research data recently commissioned by HUD as well as the work of individual researchers. Information on program effects has been gathered from federal agencies as well as from nonprofit groups.[5]

The combination of these sources of information help us understand both the trajectories of racial differences in housing and whether programs aimed at housing justice have worked to reduce racially disparate forms of treatment in housing markets. Since roughly $40 to $50 million in program funding is allocated by the federal government annually for fair housing enforcement programs, do we know whether such allocations are worth it? Have the programs been effective? The core concern for this collection then is what has changed during the nearly forty years since the enactment of the Fair Housing Act of 1968 and has public policy helped change it?

PERSISTENCE, CHANGE, AND RESISTANCE

While it is difficult to get reliable historical data on the practice of discrimination by major institutions such as banks, realtors, public agencies, and jurisdictions (Blank, Dabady, and Citro 2004: 77–89), two types of quantitative evidence help to illustrate the extent to which the country is standing still, moving ahead, or failing to cope with the mutating forms of racial obstruction in housing. Evidence from data on housing segregation, integration, and discrimination are key sources. The second includes evidence of practical rather than just abstract agreement with the tenets of housing justice. This includes whether Americans are willing to put some opinion-based "'teeth'" into their support for housing equity. We briefly summarize the main lines of this evidence to highlight the questions: have we made progress and, if so, do we know why this may have happened?

Measuring Housing Segregation and Integration

Analysts of the city and of race have wondered for decades why the much-praised civil rights laws enacted in the 1960s appear to have bypassed poor blacks in most of our cities. Some have argued that "failure in American racial policy is most easily summarized by the phrase 'inner cities'" (Hochschild 1996: 7). Persistent racial ghettos in the United States appear to signal the failure of civil rights law as a curative for black isolation. The increase (36 percent) in the number of blacks living in urban ghettos in the decade between 1980 and 1990 appeared especially jarring (Jargowsky 1997).

Many inner-city areas obviously contain densely populated neighborhoods of very poor families, many of which are black or Hispanic, and it is these concentrated problems that many whites and African Americans typically use to measure progress. Race relations in the United States can therefore appear inextricably linked to systemic racial and economic separation (Wilson 1987; Massey and Denton 1993; Loewen 2005). Indeed, housing segregation in the United States, or the extent to which whites and nonwhites live in mixed or integrated communities, has for decades seemed to only minimally decline. The reasons offered have included official governmental policies and systematic patterns of violence and intimidation that have forced or scared blacks away from towns that have declared themselves to be only all-white (Jackson 1985; Loewen 2005). Many analysts, including Cutler, Glaeser, and Vigdor (1999: 457), have reported that up through the 1970s a form of "centralized racism" existed in which whites used "legal, quasi-legal, or violent, illegal barriers to keep blacks out of white neighborhoods."

This has now changed, they argue, into "decentralized racism," in which only the preferences of whites for living with "members of their own race," accompanied by their willingness to pay a high price for such isolation is the driving force behind contemporary patterns of urban separation. The era of illegal barriers has ended, they say, and whites' preference to live among their own kind has become the touchstone for less policy-relevant racial patterning.[6] Cutler, Glaeser, and Vigdor (1999: 461, 471), tell us that from 1970 to 1990 segregation levels began a steady decline. "Between 1970 and 1990, both dissimilarity and isolation fell by 17 percentage points." This trend toward declining segregative living has meant that there are now fewer all-white neighborhoods.

In 2000, Iceland tells us (chapter 5, this volume), the index of segregation for blacks declined again to roughly 64. Blacks and whites as a result today live in more integrated communities than they did ten or twenty years earlier. Not only has the level of racial segregation declined for blacks, there has also been an accompanying decadal decline in the proportion of deeply poor communities in U.S. cities, reflecting a surprising change in the urban morphology of race and poverty (Jargowsky 2003). Importantly, segregation levels for the country's fast-growing Hispanic population have not declined, running at roughly 50 percent since 1980.

Analyses of housing integration have typically accompanied regular census-based segregation studies.[7] Low scores on a segregation measure imply, as suggested by Reardon and Firebaugh (2002) and Reardon and O'Sullivan (2004), diversity or integration (Bradburn, Sudman, and Gockel 1971). Time-series comparisons distinguish temporarily mixed areas from those with decade-long stability in their mixing. This approach has been followed by Ingrid Ellen (2000) in her analysis of 1980–1990 data as well as in chapter 6 of this volume using 2000 census data.[8]

Ellen's research also reveals progress toward increased racial mixing during the 1990s. She finds that while 25.5 percent of tracts were totally integrated in 1980 this proportion grew to 36 percent by 2000. The share of majority white neighborhoods as a proportion of the total has then declined over the past twenty years, although the bulk of Americans still live within relatively homogeneous communities. But there has been notable growth over the last decades in the number or stability of racially mixed communities. Importantly, a good deal of this integration is between whites and nonblack minorities.

The causes of these changes are uncertain, however. The suggestion by Cutler, Glaeser, and Vigdor that illegal forms of exclusion have ended appears an overly optimistic reading of partial data (Emerson, Yancey, and Chai 2001; Dawkins 2004; Maly 2005). Some of the change that has occurred has been due to economic improvements for minorities, changing white preferences for expensive forms of racial isolation, desegregation and fair housing litigation, and some to the efforts of local neighborhood organizations (Cutler, Glaeser, and Vigdor 1999; Schuck 2003; Dawkins 2004; Logan, Stutts, and Farley 2004; Fischer et al. 2004). Evidence of persistent, and possibly increasing, levels of racial steering suggest that more "coerced," discriminatory forces are still relevant to our understanding of why we remain so residentially apart (Acorn-NJ 2005; Loewen 2005).[9]

We do not then have a good answer to the question of why we are becoming less segregated and more integrated. We do not know why blacks or Hispanics selectively benefit from such changes. Most importantly we do not have any clear evidence about whether it has been government-driven or private market forces that have been major causes for these changes. We do not know, for example, whether programs to encourage less bias and more tolerance have affected the rate at which we are desegregating our cities.

Measuring Support for Open Housing

One way to learn whether Americans would choose more than token support for housing justice is to ask for their support for legislation banning bias in the housing market. If a world of decentralized or "new" racism exists, there might be support for the abstract principle of equity but not for a specific law banning discriminatory conduct, since it would be assumed unnecessary (Blank, Dabady, and Citro 2004: 183–85). A survey question used for decades illustrates support for an actual law enforcing open housing.[10] The responses come from the General Social Survey of whites and blacks taken since 1978 (see table 1.1).

In 1978, ten years after the enactment of the federal fair housing law, fewer than four in ten white Americans, and only seven of every ten blacks, agreed that an antidiscrimination law was the correct option. Whites, however, have become somewhat more supportive of a law on antidiscrimination since 1978, with a nearly thirty-percentage-point increase from 1978 to 2001, and continuing improvements in support to 2005.[11] By 2005, support by whites for a hypothetical fair housing law had increased to its highest level in nearly thirty years to 77 percent, although these percentages are higher than those reported by Abravanel for his 2005 survey.

Black support for such a law appears to have at first increased from a level of seven out of ten who supported the law in 1978 to a high support level of

Table 1.1. White, Black, and Hispanic Support for Hypothetical Open-Housing Law, 1978–2005

	1978	*1989*	*1996*	*2001*	*2004*	*2005*
% Owner Can't Refuse						
Whites	37	57	67	66	65.4	77
Blacks	71	88	84	74	74.5	78
Hispanics	—	—	—	77	—	79
% Owner Can Decide						
Whites	63	43	33	27	34.6	23
Blacks	29	12	16	12	22.5	22
Hispanics	—	—	—	5	—	21

NORC staff indicated that this question was not used in either their 2000 or 2002 GSS surveys. The 2004 GSS number is derived only from a one-third sample suggesting a higher level of potential sample bias/variance. The 2001 and 2005 results are from national probability samples; Abravanel (2001; 2005).

89 percent in 1989, immediately following the passage of major amendments to the federal fair housing act. Indeed, support grew more sharply for open housing than it had for most other major policy issues reflected in the General Social Survey (Davis 1997). By 2005, however, black support had declined by nearly ten percentage points to 78 percent, converging with the responses expressed by whites and Hispanics. This convergence in both support and opposition to a local fair housing ordinance is unexpected and the increase in opposition by both blacks and Hispanics as of 2005 is not readily explainable.

The option that respondents have to express opposition to such a law has also become robust and consistent over time. While 63 percent of whites in 1978 openly expressed support for landowners' rights to discriminate, by 2001 only roughly one-third (27 percent) still held this view. By 2005, this figure declined again to less than one-quarter (23 percent) of white Americans stating that it is legal to deny housing. For blacks, there is a fairly consistent if low level of support for allowing owners to do with their property whatever they wish: 16 percent in 2001 increasing to 22 percent in both the 2004 and 2005 surveys.

The 2001 survey also asked the same question of Hispanics. In that year, they indicated a higher level of support, with 77 percent saying they would vote for a local open-housing ordinance. By 2005, support among Hispanics increased slightly to 79 percent. Again, there has been a convergence in opposition to a fair housing law, with slightly over 20 percent of all three groups supporting owners' rights to decide for themselves to whom they should sell their units, with Hispanic support for such an option increasing notably from only 5 percent in 2001.

A citywide probability survey conducted in New York in the summer of 2005 reveals distributions comparable to those found in the last GSS survey. Roughly three-quarters of New Yorkers (74.2 percent) would support an open-housing law while 26 percent (25.8) would oppose it. Among white New Yorkers, a proportion slightly above that found nationwide, or nearly 30 percent (28.2), support the right of owners to deny housing to anyone they feel appropriate. For blacks, the opposition to an open-housing law is ten percentage points lower, at 18 percent, while 22 percent of Hispanics would not support such a law. Support for open housing is the flip side of these proportions: nearly two-thirds (64.8 percent) of whites and three-quarters of blacks support an open-housing law, percentages that are just slightly below the 2005 national averages for the entire U.S. population; 71.4 percent of Hispanic respondents would support an open-housing statute.

Interestingly, foreign-born residents of New York City express greater support for an open-housing law (75.2 percent) than do those born here. We find a statistically significant relationship between being native or foreign born and support for the right to deny housing. Nearly 30 (29) percent of those who are native-born residents of the city, compared with 16 percent of foreign-born, would support a law allowing them to discriminate. Curiously, it is also those with lower incomes who are more likely to vote to deny open housing.

In the New York City survey, we asked an additional question to probe people's assessment of the federal government's obligation to fair housing: "Some people think the Federal government has a special obligation to help groups that have historically experienced discrimination in housing. Others do not believe the government has such an obligation. What do you think?" Although 71 percent support federal engagement, a nontrivial 21 (20.7) percent oppose any federal role. The remainder was undecided. White support for a federal role was slightly lower than that expressed by nonwhites; 67 to 74.5 percent. Again, we find solid support for federal engagement to solve this issue, with greater support among minorities. A sizable minority disagrees.

So roughly forty years after enactment, a substantial majority of Americans would support an open-housing law for their community. Nearly 80 percent of whites, blacks, and Hispanics are at least nominal fair housing supporters, and this number has in general increased over the last quarter-century (DiMaggio, Evans, and Bryson 1996; Davis 1997). Conversely, roughly 20 percent of blacks, whites, and Hispanics now say they would oppose a local law that restricts the right of a property owner to rent or sell in a laissez-faire manner. In New York City, 30 percent of whites say the federal government should have no role in addressing this concern. Transposing this level of dissent onto the national population of whites suggests that there are roughly 70 million to 75 million whites who would oppose a local open-housing law and perhaps another 5 million to 6 million African Americans who, for less clear reasons, also would not support the enactment of a local open-housing law.

This resistant one-fifth of the U.S. population appears to be a persistent if not necessarily politically mobilized source of opposition to efforts at housing inclusion.[12] The persistence of such oppositional attitudes makes it risky, if not imprudent, to agree with Cutler, Glaeser, and Vigdor (1999: 496) that we need to wait for "greater change in attitudes towards racial integration" to occur before we can expect segregation levels to decline. Attitudes of the resistant quarter may never change given that the law has been in place for four decades. Or they may require a level of intervention that has been, so far, beyond the scope of existing governmental initiatives.

Such hypothetical survey questions have a necessarily abstract character, since they can never pick up the local nuances of racial ambivalence, resentment, antiracism, or anger that can emerge in response to local circumstances (Feagin and O'Brien 2003: 239–46). Central to any fuller test of Americans' ambivalence or "new racist" character would be questions that describe what punishments and investigative regime would be associated with the law's enforcement, including how much monetary benefit complainants could gain if they succeeded in pressing their claims of discrimination. A law that proposes stringent financial or criminal penalties for violations might well receive a more unfavorable response from the real estate community and whites who oppose government meddling in general. There could be enthusiastic support from most minorities if they believed it would make a real difference in their treatment. Alternatively, a law that included only weak penalties, limited governmental enforcement powers, and an option for local areas to intervene in the administration of the law might be welcomed by all except those who believed themselves victims of discrimination.

The absence of any recent national debate about the *content* of civil rights enforcement since the 1960s means that people are supportive of a law with little potential agreement on what law enforcement actually requires. Chapter 4 of this volume, by Abravanel, reports the results of two national surveys taken in 2001 and 2005 that reveal low to modest levels of awareness of what federal law actually prohibits.

TOWARD AN EFFECTIVE OPEN-HOUSING LAW?

An actual local open-housing law, rather than the hypothetical one referred to above, makes important assumptions about how individuals and the housing system will respond. Table 1.2 outlines the assumptions of how such a law becomes implemented by both the individual and by the agencies responsible for administering the law. Statutes, of course, require regulatory and administrative administration to transform what Congress says into a usable program available to the public (Sparrow 2000). There is an approximate correspondence between the requirements for the individuals experiencing housing discrimination and requirements facing the managers of the administrative system.

The critical question we ask here is: is there evidence concerning whether these idealized stages of the enforcement processes, shown in table 1.2, actually occur for either individuals or concerned agencies? Do people in fact follow this trajectory from awareness to complaining to some degree of satisfaction following their complaint? Do we know how well agencies are doing in meeting the requirements associated with helping individuals get relief from any housing injustices they encounter?

Table 1.2. Requirements for Individuals and System Managers for Fair Housing Enforcement

Individuals	*System Managers*
1. Housing consumers are aware of their legal rights.	1. Agencies routinely advertise and educate public about FHA purposes, processes, and outcomes.
2. Individuals are aware they have been victims of discrimination.	2. Testers provided to ensure discrimination evidence is credible.
3. Willingness to report discrimination to an official agency.	3. Intake offices widely available to accept complaints; agencies seen as germane and effective.
4. Ability and patience to pursue claim through enforcement process.	4. Clients provided support and information on the timely processing of cases.
5. Satisfaction with remedy or relief.	5. Adequate penalties imposed; evidence used to obtain effective relief.
6. Informs others of effectiveness of relief.	6. Success of case used to promote law's benefits.
Costs: Individual's time; humiliation.	Costs: Public or private resources made available for each step above.
Outcome: Discrimination eliminated in single transaction for consumer.	Outcome: Marketplace discrimination and segregation incrementally reduced.

Source: Adapted from Briggs (2005: 248).

Knowledge of the Law

The data garnered from the survey about a hypothetical open-housing law has been supplemented by the surveys conducted by Abravanel aimed at answering the questions posed above (see chapter 4 within).[13] The answers are surprising.

Americans have a correct idea only about some parts of the law but imprecise and often wrong ideas about many other parts. Large numbers of Americans say that they do not know what the law requires, or that "it depends"; anywhere from 15 to 46 percent of people do not know whether the law mandates certain protections. Another nontrivial group, ranging from 4 to 16 percent, gives wrong answers (Abravanel and Cunningham 2002: 11).

In general, Americans have only a solid understanding that *racial* discrimination in housing is illegal; more than 80 percent of the public for example knows that it is illegal for real estate agents to limit the sale of homes to whites only. However, only 54 percent are aware that it is also illegal to use race to steer clients. In New York City a larger proportion, 61 percent, knows that this is illegal. Slightly less than three-quarters know that real estate agents should not charge a higher fee or price because of ethnicity or race. However, when asked whether a "real estate agent should be able to decide to focus a housing search on all-white areas," 26 percent of New Yorkers argue that this should be legal.

Nearly 80 percent (78) of Americans also say they are aware that it is illegal to discriminate in rental housing because of religion, but only 38 percent know aware that it is illegal to deny housing to a family because there are children included. In the New York City sample, however, 71 percent knew that it was illegal to limit access to families with children. In both the national survey as well as in our 2005 New York City study, large percentages incorrectly believe that it is legal to deny a person a housing unit because of their housekeeping habits. In New York, for example, nearly one-quarter (23.7 percent) state that it is legal under federal law to deny a person a housing unit because of their housekeeping standards.

Knowledge of fair housing law typically increases with income and education and generally declines with age. It is not, however, the case that those youngest have a better grasp of these laws, with people under age thirty-four being less likely to have a high level of awareness of the provisions of the law compared to older-age cohorts. The young are not going to approach housing issues better informed than those who went before them; there has not been a collectively improved learning curve (Abravanel and Cunningham 2002: 14).

One of the protected groups about which there is the lowest level of knowledge or awareness of their protections is the handicapped. Protections for this population were first enacted nationwide in 1988, but only a little more than half of Americans know that the law protects those with mental illnesses as well as those in wheelchairs (57 and 56 percent respectively). Since 1988, or in seventeen years, then, educational efforts have not succeeded in informing the average American of what the law requires.[14]

The lack of knowledge may be partly the cause of the discrimination experienced by the handicapped when testers were used in 2005 in Chicago. Testing results covering both wheelchair users and those hard of hearing found some of the highest levels of housing discrimination that have been measured in the Housing Discrimination Study series. The deaf experienced adverse treatment nearly 50 percent of the time, with the lower-bound estimate being 27 percent. Those in wheelchairs had a lower-bound level of differential treatment of over 30 percent, not counting the fact that roughly one-third of the advertised rental units in Chicago were already off limits and inaccessible to a person in a wheelchair (Turner et al. 2005). People know less about the laws banning discrimination against the handicapped, and—possibly causally linked—the level of mistreatment of this group is the highest measured in the most recent wave of testing research.

There of course need be no perfect correlation between average citizens' knowledge of the law and the measured level of discrimination because much of the differential treatment is practiced by rental and sales agencies and not the average person. Knowledge of the law by the regular citizen may simply set the approximate value context or communitywide expectations as to what forms of housing equity would be tolerated. Concomitantly, brokers would have some sense of what they can get away with in a locality in which most people do not know or care about fair housing issues or may actually oppose such laws. We have the sense from surveys of real estate agents done in the 1970s that sales agents know more about the law than those who rent apartments, but there is no current data. There is an absence of any national study of the knowledge and attitudes toward open housing among real estate industry actors, including their assessment of how local community support influences their conduct and choices. We are missing a core part of a sensible social science and policy understanding of the behavioral and attitudinal foundations for just treatment in housing and mortgage market transactions.

Some brokers may of course act legally on their own volition (see Galster and Godfrey 2005). We also know that they knowingly break the law. Real estate agents who know that the law prohibits them from racially steering whites and minorities to different areas have told testers that they nonetheless feel compelled to tell the white housing seeker that they really want a whiter area. A broker in the HDS 2000 audits felt it permissible to say, "It is not the neighborhood in which you want to buy a home; too many Hispanics living there" (Galster and Godfrey 2005: 10). An unknown proportion of agents consciously breaks the law and facilitates race-based home shopping. This form of differential treatment is the one most aligned with sustaining segregated living and obstructing any natural support for racially and ethnically mixed housing options. The fact that such behavior increased over the last ten years suggests that forms of mistreatment can morph into more carefully hidden patterns of selective treatment, which are much harder to detect than simply telling a black person that an apartment is unavailable (Loewen 2005: 131). In our New York study, only 54.6 percent of whites knew that steering to white areas was illegal, while roughly 66 percent of both black and Hispanic residents knew that this was illegal. Conversely, this means that over 30 percent of minorities and roughly 45 percent of whites gave an incorrect answer to the question on steering. Again, even in a city like New York, over one-quarter of city residents felt it was perfectly legal to steer families to all-white areas, despite the fact that many knew it was illegal.

If the goal of the 1968 Fair Housing Act was to authorize a set of rights that would be known to most if not all Americans, then it has failed for many provisions and succeeded for some, mostly those covering racial mistreatment. There is an uneven patchwork of understanding of what Congress has said is the law of the land in housing transactions, and this understanding is not getting better with time.

We are also left with a clearer picture of a rights-resistant core, which includes those who support the practice of housing discrimination, often knowing it is illegal. One in five Americans (21 percent) approves of unlawful conduct while not knowing the conduct is illegal. It is not clear if they would continue supporting the conduct were they told of what the law requires. Some of them might join the 13 percent of the population that knows full well that the conduct is illegal but nonetheless supports discriminatory actions (Abravanel and Cunningham 2002: 23). Nearly 35 percent of Americans, therefore, are actual or potential supporters of fair housing misconduct. If the goal of the Fair Housing Act was to convince most but not all Americans that they should learn a little about the law, and to support it marginally, then the law has succeeded. But one suspects that if 35 percent of Americans were tax cheats or bank robbers this would be classified as an epidemic of misconduct warranting immediate governmental action. As this survey was the first ever done of these matters, we lack insight as to whether these proportions of fair housing law resisters and supporters are malleable. We have no appreciation of whether educational campaigns have had a measurable impact on people's knowledge and support of the law, including the views of real estate industry actors.

Experiencing Discrimination

One of the centerpieces of the perceptual "reality" of race is that people disagree about whether and how much discrimination exists. Most whites, for example, believe that racial discrimination no longer constitutes a major problem for minorities. Whites also believe that blacks and other minorities have made substantial progress over the last decade or more; lower-income whites are the most convinced that blacks have made lots of progress.[15] Most surveys tell us, then, that whites typically think there is little discrimination and it is diminishing, while most minorities feel there is a lot of it and that it has hardly declined at all (Feagin and Sikes 1994; Delgado 1994; Hacker 1992).[16]

The survey by Abravanel and Cunningham (2002: 26) specifically asked whether respondents had actually ever experienced discrimination in trying to rent or buy a home ("Do you think you have ever been discriminated against when you were trying to buy or rent a house or apartment.") It is, of course, recognized that such opinion data may either over- or understate the actual level of mistreatment, with the judgment from social science experts that blacks will on average have a better understanding of how much discrimination exists than will whites (Blank, Dabady, and Citro 2004: 170–71).[17]

The survey findings from 2001 indicate that 28 million people, or 14 percent of the U.S. population, said yes they had experienced discrimination in housing: 13 percent of whites, 24 percent of blacks, and 22 percent of Hispanics. In 2005, the figure rose to 17 percent, but many of those complaints, they discovered upon probing, would not have been illegal under federal law. The estimate is that roughly 9 percent of Americans experienced forms of discrimination prohibited under federal law.

In the New York survey, roughly 15 percent of whites (14.8), 32.3 percent of blacks, and 22 percent of Hispanics report that they have experienced some housing discrimination in their lives. About equal proportions of foreign- and native-born city residents report an experience of housing mistreatment; 23.8 percent of those born in the United States and 22.6 percent of those born outside this country say they have encountered housing mistreatment. When asked about the frequency of such experiences, roughly one-third of the sample had one or two race-based encounters; the remaining 63.8 percent report three or more apparent violations.

There is, then, a credible minority proportion of the population that believes they have experienced at least one instance of discrimination in the housing market. As we will see in the next section, blacks' perception of housing discrimination in the rental and sales markets of our largest cities is close to tester-based measurements.

TESTING RESULTS IN SUMMARY

Four results emerge from the testing research done in recent years that are central to answering the question of whether there has been any change, for better or worse, in discrimination in the United States (see chapter 2 within by Turner et al.). First, the level of discrimination experienced by blacks over the last decade has lessened, suggesting that racial misconduct in the housing market is not intransigent. The major finding of the 2000 study results, when compared with 1988 data, is that discriminatory treatment against minority home seekers declined roughly 25 percent for blacks and Hispanics. For blacks the level declined from 29 percent to 17 percent. For Hispanics the decline was from 27 to 20 percent (figure 1.1).

Second, despite the decline for blacks, discrimination still occurs roughly 20–30 percent of the time whenever a person who is black, Hispanic, Asian,

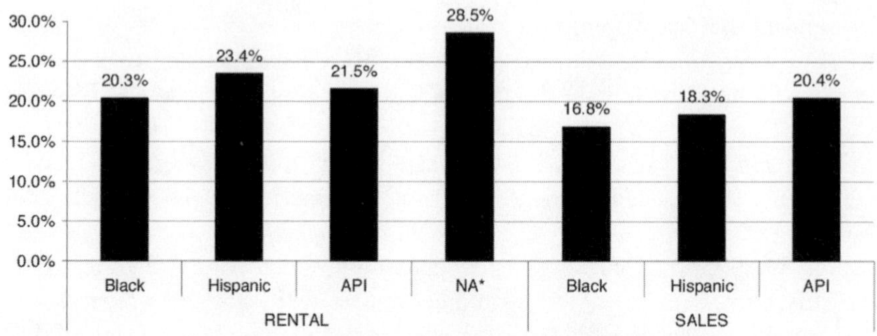

Figure 1.1. Levels of Discrimination in Rental and Sale Housing, 2000.

Native American, or disabled searches for a housing unit. Third, discrimination against nonblack minority groups appears higher than that against blacks, with testing for the first time revealing higher levels for Asians, American Indians, and the disabled.[18] The fourth major finding is that racial steering, a critical factor in supporting residential separation, has increased over time (Dawkins 2004: 396).

Minorities, then, appear to provide an accurate assessment of the actual amount of housing mistreatment (roughly a quarter) while whites significantly underestimate its presence. If there were a means to translate these experimental estimates of housing discrimination onto the population of protected-class members actually searching for a housing unit, using newspaper adds as the starting point, we would then have an actual measure of the incidence of real housing discrimination comparable to that generated experimentally in HDS2000. It would be a number in the millions. But how many of those who felt they experienced housing abuse, out of this million or more, actually go to the next step, stage three, and formally complain? How many of the 20 to 30 percent mistreated in their housing search actually make use of their civil right to complain?

Complaining about Discrimination

A key assumption in constructing a story of American civil rights justice is to assume that people who experience, and know they have experienced, mistreatment will take action. They would no longer have to stand mutely as their housing options were mistreated by those in charge of real estate opportunities. They could feel enabled to make use of existing civil rights laws enacted for their protection and relief.

However, just as we have only a dim understanding of how race identity is constructed, so too we know little about the psychological processes associated with the claiming and use of civil rights. Some, as we noted in the introduction, react to the experience of discrimination by growing resentful and angry, some by withdrawing into a defensive sense of blackness, and some number elect to use their rights. Among the many adaptations to American-style racial practices is the use of official channels and law suits. As Feagin and Sikes (1994: 275; 290–93) comment: "There has been a significant increase in the number of African Americans with the professional and financial resources to fight discrimination, often directly." Thus of the 15 to 20 million Americans who stated that they were discriminated against in housing at some point in their lives the key question is: how many turned to civil rights laws for help?

The surprising and policy-troubling answer is very few. Of those who thought of themselves as a victim of housing discrimination, over 80 (83) percent in 2001 and 2005 told interviewers they would "do nothing about it." Only 16 percent said they would take some form of action; 6 percent out of the 16 percent in 2001 said they would bring their complaint back to the same people who discriminated against them, apparently because they either felt they had no other option or because that seemed the most practical and fastest route to getting the housing unit that was denied them (Abravanel and Cunningham 2002: 27). A comparable response occurred in 2005. Only roughly 5 percent of people who experienced housing discrimination said they would file a complaint with an agency or attorney. Many of the reasons given for their inaction or indifference to fair housing legal options include the sense that it was not worth the time and trouble. The overwhelming majority of Americans—believing they have been treated unfairly—feel it would be too costly or time consuming, or that complaining would not solve anything.[19]

After roughly forty years of civil rights funding and programs, only tiny numbers of Americans believe or are aware they have a usable right to claim governmental help in getting the housing illegally denied them. Most of those who could use this right have little or no confidence it would be of help. Having described the intent of this volume and outlined key patterns of evidence, the next chapters provide the detailed analytic and methodological examination of the state of housing and racial disjunctures early in the twenty-first century. This research helps frame the question that is central to the final section of the book, namely, do we know whether federal programs aimed at ending illegal housing practices are working effectively? The answer, as you will soon see, is that they largely are not.

NOTES

1. See chapters 5 and 6 of this volume by Iceland and Ellen, respectively. Also a useful overview of other methods appears in chapter 3 by Massey and Blank. Data on the fair housing enforcement processing of cases was provided by HUD, the Justice Department, and the National Fair Housing Alliance (2005). This new information is referred to in chapter 7, by Schill, and chapter 8, by Ross and Galster.

2. The HUD director of this effort in 1974 was Dr. Fred Eggers, who convinced senior HUD officials in the Ford administration of the need for significant funding for this first-ever national discrimination audit. He also ensured that the project was not canceled when that possibility arose later on (interview with Fred Eggers on September 27, 2005).

3. This research has been analyzed by a variety of research institutes and academics (see, for example, Yinger et al. 1979; Yinger 1995; Galster and Godfrey 2005).

4. *How Much Do We Know: Public Awareness of the Nation's Fair Housing Laws*, released April 2002; 2001 national telephone sample survey; 1,001 adults; 2005 national sample of 1,029 adults, with oversampling; see chapter 4 by Abravanel, this volume. New York sample of 375 adults.

5. The following list suggests the progression of that research between 1974 and 2005:

- 1974: HUD Research Design Competition (Advocacy Group Precedent)
- 1977: The Housing Market Practices Survey (forty metropolitan areas; 3,264 tests; blacks and whites only)
- 1977: Rental market, Mexican-Americans/Chicanos, Dallas only
- 1989: The Housing Discrimination Study (twenty-five metropolitan areas; 3,200 tests; blacks and Hispanics)
- 2002: All Other Things Being Equal: A Paired Testing Study of Mortgage Lending Institutions (250 tests; blacks and Hispanics; Chicago and Los Angeles)
- 2000–2005: "The Housing Discrimination Study 2000" (forty-six metropolitan statistical areas; 7,000 tests; blacks, Hispanics, Asians, Native Americans, the disabled). Discrimination against Persons with Disabilities, 2005; 200 tests; Chicago metropolitan statistical area. See also the study: Multifamily Building Conformance with Fair Housing Act Accessibility Guidelines; report produced 2003, released 2005; 988 engineering surveys of a sample of 397 newly constructed multifamily building projects; interviews with twenty developers or architects.

6. While segregation levels were relatively low in the 1800s and through 1910, by 1940 the city-level index of dissimilarity began to move rapidly higher, reaching 85 and rising to 87 by 1950 (Loewen 2005: 81). By 1980, the index of dissimilarity was roughly 73 and was 67 ten years later (see Farley and Frey 1994: 30). Index of dissimilarity numbers for 1940, 1950, and 1960 taken from the Kerner Commission Report, p. 247. Data for 1970, 1980, and 1990 are from Massey and Denton (1993: 222). The sample of cities/MSAs used for these of course varied, so there is only an approximate trend.

7. "'Racial integration,' . . . is a term that is widely used in both popular and academic literature but is rarely defined precisely. In part, this lack of specificity is due to the fact that most researchers exploring racial patterns of settlement have focused not on evaluating integration, but on measuring segregation." (Ellen 2000: 14).

8. The Urban Institute has also released a report on stable neighborhood integration covering the same twenty-year period (Rawlings, Harris, and Turner 2004).

9. There have been some modest attempts to promote racial and economic mixing through programs such as the Chicago Gautreaux Program, the Moving to Opportunity demonstration, and a variety of housing desegregation cases that have been prosecuted over the last quarter-century. The localized and uneven execution of such efforts could not, however, have substantially altered national trends or attitudes. For some analysts (Schuck 2003: 319), such racial mixing should only be the consequence of market forces and people's ability to afford new, more diverse communities and not from governmental actions. Briggs (2005: 100) too has written skeptically about whether policy actions have been helpful, noting that "Our responses to spatial segregation have been episodic, fragmented across a patchwork of public agencies and private actors, inconsistent in content and objectives, misunderstood, highly localized in the details, hotly contested, and often forced to compete with other policy objectives or public ideals."

10. Survey/opinion data provide only a potential lower-bound estimate of actual, true levels of bias. "Asking white Americans whether they intend to discriminate or whether they support discriminatory policies is unlikely to provide a good indication of the prevalence of racial discrimination in American society" (Blank, Dabady, and Citro 2004: 164). Respondents have been asked to choose either a law banning discrimination or a law allowing sellers to do as they wish with their property, including discriminating: "Suppose there is a community-wide vote on the general housing issue. There are two possible laws to vote on. One law says that a homeowner can decide for himself who to sell his house to, even if he prefers not to sell to (blacks). The second law says that a homeowner cannot refuse to sell to someone because of their race."

11. The 2004 survey question on this issue (RACOPEN) was only asked of roughly one-third of the full sample, so there are only replies from 685 whites and 102 blacks. These smaller sample sizes, although weighted, may introduce some unreliability into the sample estimates. Because of a reduced sample size, or split one-third sample for this question by GSS in 2004, the replies in that year may be an anomaly.

12. Cutler, Glaeser, and Vigdor (1999: 488) also note that 25 percent of the population agrees that "White people have the right to keep blacks out of their neighborhood if they want to," pointing to a consistently resistant quarter of the U.S. population.

13. Abravanel and Cunningham 2002. The study, using a national probability telephone survey of 1,001 adults, was conducted for HUD in forty-eight states in December 2000/January 2001.

14. However, of the sample population in New York, 65 percent (65.5) knows it is illegal to deny a housing unit to a person with a history of mental illness.

15. See Gallup Poll Social Audit (1997); also Morin (1995).

16. Jennifer Hochschild (1995: 55) summarized this evidence: "African Americans (and other minorities) increasingly believe that racial discrimination is worsening and that it inhibits their race's ability to participate in the American dream; whites increasingly believe that discrimination is lessening and that blacks have the same chance to participate in the dream as whites."

17. Social scientists also caution that the "willingness to report discriminatory treatment may depend on the ease of reporting and the vigor with which an agency deals with complaints" (Blank, Dabady, and Citro 2004: 174).

18. Estimates for the disabled might of course only reflect the Chicago rental market.

19. "Almost two out of every five people in this situation believed there was no point in responding, that it would not have solved the problem or, in some instances, that it could have made the problem worse" (Abravanel and Cunningham 2002). Importantly, others knew that the housing they wanted was perishable; 9 percent said that other housing was easier to find. Some simply did not know their rights: 14 percent felt that they did not know what to do, another 3 percent said they "didn't know their personal rights," and another 2 percent said there were no equal housing laws in existence at the time.

REFERENCES

Acorn-NJ. 2005. *A Tale of Two Cities: Rental Housing Discrimination, Racial Steering Create Segregated Neighborhoods in Jersey City and Hoboken*. September 21. Newark, New Jersey: Acorn-NJ.

Abravanel, Martin. 2005. "Do We Know More Now? Trends in Public Knowledge, Support and Use of Fair Housing Law." Office of Policy Development and Research. Washington, DC: HUD.

Abravanel, Martin, and Mary Cunningham. 2002. *How Much Do We Know? Public Awareness of the Nation's Fair Housing Laws*. Washington, DC: The Urban Institute. http://www.huduser.org/publications/fairhsg/hmwk.html.

Blank, Rebecca, Marilyn Dabady, and Constance Citro (eds.). 2004. *Measuring Racial Discrimination*. Washington, DC: National Academy Press.

Bradburn, Norman, Seymour Sudman, and Galen Gockel. 1971. *Side by Side: Integrated Neighborhoods in America*. Chicago: Quadrangle.

Briggs, Xavier de Souza. 2005. "Conclusion: Desegregating the City." In *Desegregating the City: Ghettos, Enclaves, and Inequality*, ed. David Varady, 233–57. Albany: State University of New York Press.

Cutler, David, Edward Glaeser, and Jacob Vigdor. 1999. "The Rise and Decline of the American Ghetto." *Journal of Political Economy* 107(3): 455–506.

Davis, James. 1997. "The GSS-Capturing American Attitude Change." *Public Perspective* 8:31–34.

Dawkins, Casey. 2004. "Recent Evidence on the Continuing Causes of Black-White Residential Segregation." *Journal of Urban Affairs* 26: 379–400.

Delgado, Richard. 1994. "Rodrigo's Eighth Chronicle: Black Crime, White Fears—On the Social Construction of Threat." *Virginia Law Review* (March): 503–48.

DiMaggio, Paul, John Evans, and Bethany Bryson. 1996. "Have Americans' Social Attitudes Become More Polarized?" *American Journal of Sociology* 102:690–755.

Ellen, Ingrid Gould. 2000. *Sharing America's Neighborhoods: The Prospects for Stable Racial Integration*. Cambridge, MA: Harvard University Press.

Emerson, Michael, George Yancey, and Karen Chai. 2001. "Does Race Matter in Residential Segregation? Exploring the Preferences of White Americans." *American Sociological Review* 66:922–35.

Farley, Reynolds, and William Frey. 1994. "Changes in the Segregation of Whites from Blacks in the 1980s: Small Steps toward a More Integrated Society." *ASR* 59 (February): 23-45.

Feagin, Joe, and Eileen O'Brien. 2003. *White Men on Race: Power, Privilege, and the Shaping of Cultural Consciousness*. Boston: Beacon.

Feagin, Joe, and Melvin Sikes. 1994. *Living with Racism: The Black Middle Class Experience*. Boston: Beacon.

Fischer, Claude, Gretchen Stockmayer, Jon Stiles, and Michael Hout. 2004. "Distinguishing the Geographic Levels and Social Dimensions of U.S. Metropolitan Segregation, 1960–2000. *Demography* 41:37–59.

Fix, Michael, and Margery Turner (eds.). 1998. *A National Report Card on Discrimination in America: The Role of Testing*. Washington, DC: Urban Institute.

Gallup Organization. 1997. "Black/White Relations in the United States: 1997." Gallup Poll Social Audit, June.

Galster, George, and Erin Godfrey. 2005. "By Words and Deeds: Racial Steering by Real Estate Agents in the U.S. in 2000." *Journal of the American Planning Association* 71:1–19.

Hacker, Andrew. 1992. *Two Nations: Black and White: Separate, Hostile, Unequal*. New York: Charles Scribner's.

Heckman, James, and Peter Siegelman. 1993. "The Urban Institute Studies: Their Methods and Findings." In *Clear and Convincing Evidence*, ed. Michael Fix and R. Struyk, 187–258. Washington, DC: Urban Institute Press.

Hochschild, Jennifer. 1995. *Facing up to the American Dream: Race, Class, and the Soul of the Nation*. Princeton, NJ: Princeton University Press.

———. 1996. "You Win Some, You Loose Some . . . : Explaining the Patterns of Success and Failure in the Second Reconstruction." Paper Presented at the annual meetings of the American Sociological Association, New York, August 19.

Jackson, Kenneth. 1985. *Crabgrass Frontier: The Suburbanization of the United States*. New York: Oxford University Press.

Jargowsky, Paul. 1997. *Poverty and Place: Ghettos, Barrios, and the American City*. New York: Russell Sage.

———. 2003. *Stunning Progress, Hidden Problems: The Dramatic Decline of Concentrated Poverty in the 1990s*. Center for Urban and Metropolitan Policy, May 19. Washington, DC: Brookings Institution.

Logan, John, Brian Stutts, and Reynolds Farley. 2004. "Segregation of Minorities in the Metropolis: Two Decades of Change." *Demography* 41:1–22.

Loewen, James. 2005. *Sundown Towns: A Hidden Dimension of American Racism.* New York: The New Press.

Maly, Michael. 2005. *Beyond Segregation: Multiracial and Multiethnic Neighborhoods in the United States*. Philadelphia: Temple University Press.

Massey, Douglas, and Nancy Denton. 1993. *American Apartheid: Segregation and the Making of the Underclass.* Cambridge, MA: Harvard University Press.

Morin, Richard. 1995. "A Distorted Image of Minorities: Poll Suggests that What Whites Think They See May Affect Beliefs." *Washington Post*, October 8: Al.

National Fair Housing Alliance. 2005. *2005 Fair Housing Trends Report*. April 5. Washington, DC: National Fair Housing Alliance.

Rawlings, Lynette, Laura Harris, and Margery Turner. 2004. *Race and Residence: Prospects for Stable Neighborhood Integration*. March. Washington, DC: The Urban Institute.

Reardon, Sean, and G. Firebaugh. 2002. "Measures of Multi-Group Segregation." *Sociological Methodology* 32:33–68.

Reardon, Sean, and David O'Sullivan. 2004. "Measures of Spatial Segregation." Working Paper 04-01, January. Population Research Institute, Pennsylvania State University.

Saltman, Juliet. 1978. *Open Housing: Dynamics of a Social Movement*. New York: Praeger.

Schuck, Peter. 2003. *Diversity in America: Keeping Government at a Safe Distance.* Cambridge, MA: Belknap Press.

Sparrow, Malcolm. 2000. *The Regulatory Craft: Controlling Risks, Solving Problems, and Managing Compliance*. Washington, DC: Brookings Institution.

Turner, Margery, et al. 2005. *Discrimination against Persons with Disabilities: Barriers at Every Step*. May. Washington, DC: The Urban Institute. This report is available at http://www.huduser.org/publications/hsgspec/dds.html.

Wilson, William Julius. 1987. *The Truly Disadvantaged: The Inner City, The Underclass, and Public Policy.* Chicago: University of Chicago Press.

Yinger, John. 1995. *Closed Doors: Opportunities Lost: The Continuing Costs of Housing Discrimination*. New York: Russell Sage.

Yinger, John, George Galster, Barton Smith, and Fred Eggers. 1979. "The Status of Research into Racial Discrimination and Segregation in American Housing Markets: A Research Agenda for the Department of Housing and Urban Development." In *Occasional Papers in Housing and Community Affairs*, vol. 6. Washington, DC: U.S. Department of Housing and Urban Development.

2

Housing Discrimination in Metropolitan America

Unequal Treatment of African Americans, Hispanics, Asians, and Native Americans

Margery Austin Turner, Todd M. Richardson, and Stephen Ross

The Fair Housing Act of 1968 outlawed what was then a common occurrence—discrimination by landlords, real estate agents, property owners, and managers based on a home seeker's race or ethnicity. Housing discrimination denies minorities free and full access to homes and apartments they can afford, raises the costs of housing search, creates barriers to homeownership, and contributes to the perpetuation of racial and ethnic segregation (Yinger 1995). Most Americans know that discrimination based on race or ethnicity is illegal, and agree that it should be. But 14 percent believed, in 2001, that they had been the victim of housing discrimination at some time (see chapter 4, by Abravanel, and Abravanel and Cunningham 2003). How much progress has our country made since 1968 in combating discriminatory practices in sales and rental markets?

BACKGROUND

Since the 1970s, the U.S. Department of Housing and Urban Development (HUD) has pioneered the development and use of *paired testing* to systematically and rigorously measure discrimination in the nation's housing markets. In a paired test, two individuals—one white and one minority—pose as equally qualified home seekers and separately visit real estate or rental offices to inquire about the availability of homes or apartments that have recently been advertised. Because their inquiries and their qualifications are the same, the two partners should receive comparable information about housing availability and terms.

HUD recognized the potential of the paired-testing methodology as a research tool at a time when it was just emerging as an investigative and enforcement strategy. The 1977 Housing Market Practices Study provided powerful evidence of the prevalence of discrimination against African American home seekers (Wienk et al. 1979), and helped build the case for strengthening the enforcement of federal fair housing protections in the 1988 Fair Housing Act Amendments. The 1989 Housing Discrimination Study extended those initial national estimates to cover Hispanics, and concluded that overall levels of adverse treatment against African Americans had remained essentially unchanged since 1977 (Turner, Struyk, and Yinger, 1991). Over the subsequent decade, this evidence played an important role in building public knowledge about the persistence of housing discrimination, making the case for more enforcement resources, and suggesting areas where heightened enforcement efforts may be needed.

In 2000, HUD commissioned the Urban Institute to launch the third and most ambitious of its national paired-testing studies, HDS2000. This study was designed to measure change in the incidence of discrimination against African Americans and Hispanics, to document the extent of discrimination against Asian home seekers nationwide, and to produce the first rigorous estimates of discrimination against Native Americans seeking housing outside of Native Lands. From the summer of 2000 through the spring of 2003, local fair housing organizations in forty-five metropolitan areas nationwide conducted over seven thousand paired tests, directly comparing the treatment that African Americans, Hispanics, Asians, and Native Americans receive to the treatment that whites receive when they visit real estate or rental offices to inquire about available housing. Findings from HDS2000 provide the most complete and up-to-date information available about the persistence of housing market discrimination against minority home seekers in the United States today and about the progress we have made in combating discrimination over the last decade.

METHODS—CHALLENGES AND CHOICES

Although the paired-testing methodology is quite simple in concept, designing a rigorous testing study that provides consistent measures of discriminatory treatment and is representative of metropolitan housing markets nationwide poses numerous methodological challenges and choices. This section provides a brief overview of the HDS2000 methodology, and then highlights key choices that are essential for understanding study findings.

The Basics—Standardized Visits to Randomly Selected Providers

Housing search is a complex process (Farley 1996; Newburger 1995), and no study can capture all of its components or all of the points at which discrimination may occur. HDS2000, like most paired-testing studies, focuses on the initial encounter between a home seeker and a rental or sales agent. But it is possible that some forms of discrimination may occur earlier, preventing this encounter from happening. For example, some housing providers may limit their advertising so that minorities are unlikely to find out about certain properties (Galster, Freiberg, and Houk 1987). And additional incidents of adverse treatment may occur later in the housing transaction, when a renter submits an application or negotiates lease terms, or when a home buyer makes an offer on a particular unit or applies for mortgage financing.

Given this basic caveat, the goal of a national paired-testing study is to capture the ways in which a *typical* or *representative* housing provider treats minority customers compared to the treatment of comparable white customers. To accomplish this goal, one would ideally select a random sample from a master listing of all real estate agents and rental housing providers. Advertisements for homes and apartments that are available for sale or rent provide the most complete and up-to-date source for such a listing. Therefore, for each phase of HDS2000, random samples of advertised housing units were drawn from newspapers and other advertising sources on a weekly basis, and testers visited the sampled offices to inquire about the availability of these advertised units. This approach is by no means perfect. Not all housing units for sale or rent are advertised, not all real estate and rental agents use newspaper advertising to attract customers, and not all home seekers rely upon newspaper advertisements in their housing search. Nonetheless, using advertisements to generate a sample of real estate and rental agents offers the advantage of reflecting differences that qualified whites and minorities experience when they inquire about housing that has been publicly advertised as available.

Both minority and white partners were assigned income, assets, and debt levels to make them equally qualified to buy or rent the advertised housing unit. Test partners were also assigned comparable family circumstances, job characteristics, education levels, and housing preferences. During their test visits, testers followed tightly standardized protocols,[1] inquiring about the availability of the advertised housing unit that prompted their visit, similar units (same size and price) that might be available, and other units that might meet their housing needs. They tried to inspect at least three housing units, making return visits or appointments with an agent if necessary, and in sales tests they recorded the address, size, and price of any other units that were recommended to them. In response to questions from the real estate or rental agent, testers provided information about their (assigned) household composition, financial characteristics, employment, and housing needs. They were trained to express no preferences for particular amenities or geographic locations, and they did not submit formal applications, agree to credit checks, or make offers to rent or buy available units.

In conjunction with these basic testing protocols, testers were also trained to be convincing in the role of an ordinary home seeker, obtain as much information as possible from the housing provider about available housing, and take notes in order to remember key information about what occurred during the test and what information was provided by the housing provider. Following each test, the testers filled out detailed reporting forms, documenting their experiences and the treatment and information they received. Only those tests where both testers correctly implemented the required protocols and fully reported on their treatment were included in the analysis sample. Moreover, test partners did not compare their experiences with one another or record any conclusions about differences in treatment; each simply reported the details of the treatment he or she experienced as an individual home seeker. Instead, the treatment of white and minority partners was systematically compared by analysts to produce estimates of the incidence and forms of differential treatment.

Replication or Innovation?

One of the most important methodological choices addressed in the design of HDS2000 was whether to *replicate* the basic testing protocols implemented in the 1989 HDS in order to yield comparable measures of differential treatment or to *update* these protocols to reflect evolving market conditions and practices. Replicating the testing protocols and sampling procedures that were used in 1989 would make it possible to directly compare results from the two national testing studies and produce statistically rigorous estimates of change in consistent measures of discrimination against African Americans and Hispanics. The 1989 HDS did *not* replicate all of the testing and sampling protocols from the 1977 Housing Market Practices Study, because so much had been learned over the intervening decade about how to conduct effective research testing. As a result, researchers were not able to say with any certainty whether levels of discrimination had changed between the two studies. The most researchers could say in 1989 was that they saw no evidence of significant reductions in discrimination since 1977.

HUD policy makers and Urban Institute researchers all saw strong arguments in favor of designing HDS2000 to more closely replicate the 1989 study. In particular, many policy makers wanted to assess the effectiveness of the Fair Housing Act Amendments, which were passed in 1988 to substantially strengthen enforcement of federal fair housing protections by HUD and the Justice Department. Moreover, members of the design team felt strongly that, given the resources invested in measuring housing market discrimination over three decades, it was essential to be able to report to the public and policy makers whether progress was being made in reducing the levels of adverse treatment experienced by African Americans and Hispanics.

However, there are also valid arguments to be made *against* replication. If the form of discrimination changes over time, then a methodology that keeps measuring the same types of treatment may seriously understate the levels of discrimination actually occurring in the market. Opponents of replication in HDS2000 argue in particular that real estate and rental agents increasingly use telephone screening to avoid even meeting with home seekers they think are minorities. In addition, some have argued that real estate and rental agents may now treat minority customers more equally during the initial phases of the transaction, postponing discriminatory treatment until after an application has been completed or financing has been preapproved. These forms of differential treatment were not captured in the 1989 HDS, and would similarly be overlooked if HDS2000 implemented the same testing protocols.

Appointment Calls or In-Person Visits?

In the 1989 HDS, testers generally tried to "drop in" for sales tests as well as rental tests. However, practitioners familiar with market practices in many of the testing sites indicated that this practice would not be feasible for HDS2000. According to these practitioners, real estate agents increasingly expect customers to make appointments, and "drop-in" visits would raise suspicions and potentially lead to disclosure of the testing effort. This represents the only significant deviation from 1989 protocols that was implemented in HDS2000.

The decision to make appointment calls raises the possibility that some rental and real estate agents may "screen" potential phone customers at the telephone inquiry or appointment stage, and avoid ever meeting with home seekers whom they believe to be minority. In the years since 1989, the use of telephone message systems appears to have become much more widespread. And the decision to have testers make appointments rather than simply "dropping in" for sales tests meant that minority testers might be unable to get appointments to even inquire about some available units. One option would be to include in the new estimates of discrimination tests where only the white partner was able to get an appointment. Although there is a growing body of evidence that some accents and speech patterns are readily identifiable as black or Hispanic (Massey and Lundy 2001), it is less clear that all black and Hispanic testers would be clearly identifiable. In other words, analysts could not be certain that housing providers knew the race or ethnicity of callers. Therefore, an HDS2000 test did not officially begin until both the minority and the white tester was able to appear in person at a real estate or rental office.[2]

Differences in Treatment or Discrimination?

A paired test can result in any one of three basic outcomes for each measure of treatment: (1) the white tester is favored over the minority; (2) the minority tester is favored over the white; or (3) both testers receive the same treatment (which may be either favorable or unfavorable). The simplest measure of adverse treatment is the share of all tests in which the white tester is favored over the minority. This *gross incidence* approach provides very simple and understandable indicators of how often whites are treated more favorably than equally qualified minorities. However, there are instances in which minority testers receive better treatment than their white partners. Therefore, when reporting gross measures, we report both the incidence of white-favored treatment and the incidence of minority-favored treatment.

Although these simple *gross measures* of white-favored and minority-favored treatment are straightforward and easily understandable, they may overstate the frequency of systematic discrimination.[3] Specifically, adverse treatment may occur during a test not only because of differences in race or ethnicity, but also because of random differences between the circumstances of their visits to the real estate agency. For example, in the time between two testers' visits, an apartment might have been rented, or the agent may have been distracted by personal matters and forgotten about an available unit. Or one member of a tester pair might meet with an agent who is unaware of some available units. Gross measures of white-favored and minority-favored treatment include some random factors, and therefore provide *upper-bound estimates* of systematic discrimination.[4]

One strategy for estimating systematic discrimination, that is, to remove the cases where nondiscriminatory random events are responsible for differences in treatment, is to subtract the incidence of minority-favored treatment from the incidence of white-favored treatment to produce a *net measure*. This approach essentially assumes that all cases of minority-favored treatment are attributable to random factors—that systematic discrimination never favors minorities—and that random white-favored treatment occurs just as frequently as random minority-favored treatment.

Based on these assumptions, the net measure subtracts differences due to random factors from the total incidence of white-favored treatment. However, it seems unlikely that all minority-favored treatment is the result of random factors; sometimes minorities may be systematically favored on the basis of their race or ethnicity. For example, a minority landlord might prefer to rent to families of his or her own race, or a real estate agent might think that minority customers need extra assistance. Other instances of minority-favored treatment might reflect a form of race-based steering, in which white customers are discouraged from considering units in minority neighborhoods or developments. Therefore, the net measure subtracts not only random differences but some systematic differences, and therefore probably understates the frequency of systematic discrimination. Thus, net measures provide *lower-bound estimates* of systematic discrimination, and they reflect the extent to which the differential treatment that occurs (some systematically and some randomly) is more likely to favor whites than minorities.[5]

It is essential to recognize that HDS2000 was designed to measure the extent to which minority home seekers experience adverse treatment when they look for housing in urban areas nationwide. The tests conducted for this study were not designed to assemble evidence of discrimination in individual cases. The question of when differential treatment warrants prosecution and the related question of whether sufficient evidence is available to prevail in court can only be resolved on a case-by-case basis, which might also consider other indicators of treatment than those reported here. Even when no statistical pattern of race-based differential treatment is observed, individual cases of discrimination may occur. Specifically, even if the gross incidence of white favored treatment is statistically insignificant, this does not mean that discrimination never occurred, but only that the number of cases was too small to draw any conclusions about systematic patterns across the sample as a whole. Similarly, for variables where the net measure is close to zero, there may in fact be instances of race-based discrimination, even though the overall pattern does not systematically favor one group.

It is possible to adapt the basic paired-testing methodology to directly observe how often random differences in treatment occur. Specifically, in two metropolitan areas, HDS2000 conducted three-part tests. In these tests, a white tester was followed by two minorities or a minority tester was followed by two whites, all following the same protocols. Comparing the treatment of the two same-race testers provides a direct estimate of random (non-race-based) differential treatment. This exploratory triad testing effort suggests that most, if not all, minority-favored treatment is random; it provides no convincing evidence that minority-favored treatment systematically exceeds differences in treatment of same-race testers. However, because these results are based on a relatively small number of tests in only two metropolitan areas, and because net measures of discrimination for these metros were atypically low, they should be viewed as preliminary and require further confirmation.

Forms of Treatment: Do Some Matter More Than Others?

A visit with a rental or sales agent is a complex transaction and may include many forms of favorable or unfavorable treatment. HDS2000 reports results for a series of individual treatment indicators that reflect important aspects of the housing transaction. Indicators of adverse treatment in rental housing transactions address four critical aspects of the interaction between a renter and a landlord or rental agent: housing availability, inspections, costs, and agent encouragement. Indicators of adverse treatment in sales housing transactions fall into five categories: housing availability, inspections, geographic steering, assistance with financing, and agent encouragement.

But in addition to presenting results for individual treatment indicators, HDS2000 combined these individual indicators to create *composite measures* for categories of treatment (such as housing availability or housing costs) as well as for the transaction as a whole.[6] The first type of composite replicates the approach implemented in 1989. Specifically, tests are classified as white-favored if the white tester received favorable treatment on one or more individual items, while his or her partner received *no* favorable treatment. Tests are classified as "neutral" if one tester was favored on some individual treatment items and his or her partner was favored on even one item. This approach has the advantage that it identifies tests where one partner was *consistently* favored over the other. But it may incorrectly classify tests as neutral when one tester received favorable treatment on several items, while his or her partner was favored on only one. This approach also classifies tests as neutral if one tester was favored on the most important item while his or her partner was favored on items of lesser significance.

Therefore, HDS2000 introduced a set of *hierarchical* composites that take into account the relative importance of individual treatment measures to determine whether one tester was favored over the other. For each category of treatment measures (and for the overall test experience), a hierarchy of importance was established *independent* of analysis of the testing results. For example, in the *availability* category, if the white tester was told that the advertised home was available, while the minority was told it was no longer available, then the white tester was deemed to be favored overall, even if the minority was favored on less important items.

These hierarchical composites offer the advantage of reflecting important differences in the treatment of minorities and whites. But because random differences on a single treatment indicator may cause a test to be classified as white-favored or minority-favored, the gross composite measures certainly overstate the incidence of systematic discrimination. However, under the unlikely assumption that whites are never discriminated against, subtracting the minority-favored overall hierarchical score from the white-favored hierarchical score provides a net estimate that is a clear lower-bound estimate of the level of discrimination. Therefore, in the findings below for an overall level of discrimination we report the lower-bound estimate of systematic discrimination with the net *hierarchical* estimate along with the estimate of the percent of cases where the white tester was *consistently* favored over their minority partner. As a lower-bound estimate, the net hierarchical estimate is unimpeachable evidence that minorities are systematically receiving less favorable treatment than whites in the housing market simply because of race. Because the lower-bound estimate almost certainly understates the level of discrimination, the consistency estimate is provided as the currently accepted measure of the actual level of discrimination against minorities.

FINDINGS—GRADUAL PROGRESS, BUT PERSISTENT DISCRIMINATION

HDS2000 produces two major sets of social sciences findings, both of which offer important lessons for public policy. First, the study provides rigorous estimates of the change since 1989 in discrimination against African Americans and Hispanics in metropolitan housing markets nationwide, offering insight on the extent to which the nation is making progress in the fight against discrimination. In addition, HDS2000 provides up-to-date estimates of the incidence of discrimination, including the first national estimates of discrimination against Asians and Pacific Islanders and the first rigorous estimates of discrimination against Native Americans searching for housing outside of Native Lands. These results tell us how far we still have to go to eliminate housing discrimination and how enforcement and education efforts might best be directed.

Evidence of Progress

Between 1989 and 2000, the incidence of discrimination against African Americans declined significantly, in both rental and sales markets nationwide. The incidence of discrimination against Hispanic home buyers also declined, but no significant change occurred for Hispanic renters. Figure 2.1 shows changes in levels of discrimination for blacks and Hispanics in the rental market using our two composite measures—the lower-bound estimate

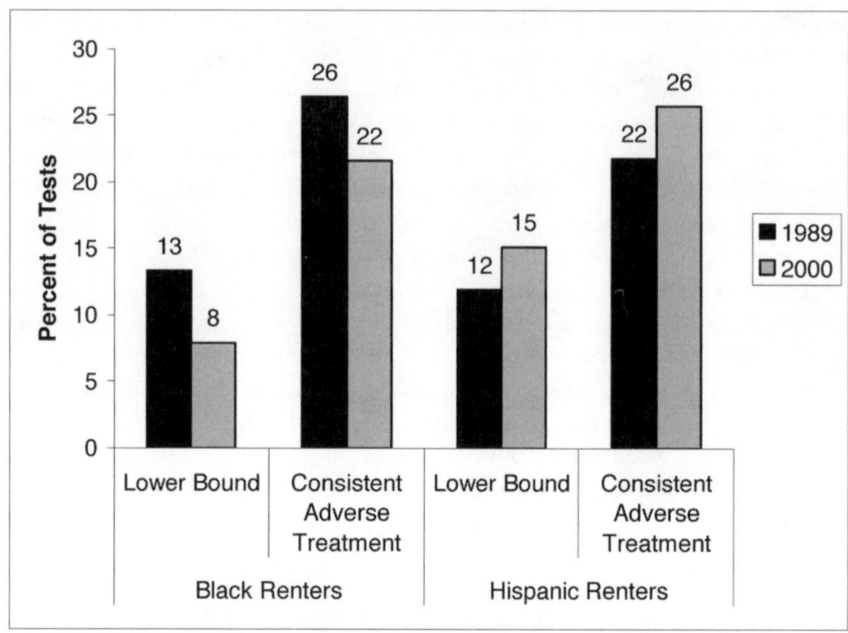

Figure 2.1. Rates of Discrimination, 1989–2000.

and the consistency measure. Although the lower-bound estimate is substantially lower than the consistent adverse treatment measure, the patterns of change are the same. Over time, the level of discrimination experienced by African Americans in the rental market has declined markedly, but discrimination against Hispanics has not (the small increase shown in the figure is not statistically significant).

The overall decline in adverse treatment against black renters reflects the fact that blacks are now much more likely to be told about the same number of available units as comparable white renters, and to be able to inspect the same number of units. Hispanics appear no better off than in 1989 on these indicators and are now more likely than in 1989 to be quoted a higher rent compared to non-Hispanic whites when asking about the same unit. On the other hand, agents are more likely than in 1989 to encourage Hispanics to apply by asking them to complete an application and/or make future contact.

In metropolitan sales markets, both African Americans and Hispanics have experienced quite dramatic declines in discrimination since 1989 (see fig. 2.2). Specifically, the rate of consistent adverse treatment dropped from 29 percent in 1989 to 17 percent in 2000 for African American home buyers and from 27 percent to 20 percent for Hispanic home buyers. As growing numbers of blacks and Hispanics enter the homeownership market, they are sub-

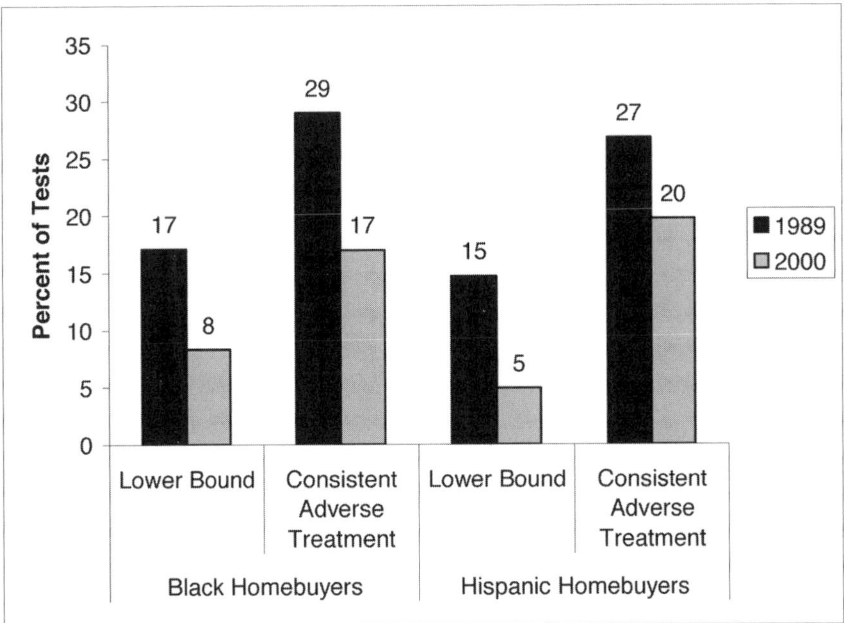

Figure 2.2. Changing Levels of Discrimination in Metropolitan Sales Housing Markets, 1989 to 2000.

stantially more likely to receive treatment from real estate agents that is comparable to what whites experience. This is an extraordinary achievement for the nation, especially since evidence from previous studies did not show evidence of such a decline between 1977 and 1989.

The overall reductions in sales market discrimination reflect more complex changes in patterns of discrimination on individual treatment measures. For African Americans, the decline in adverse treatment is largest with respect to housing availability; black home buyers are more likely to be told about the same number of available homes as whites than they were in 1989. However, black home buyers are also more likely to be steered to racially mixed neighborhoods (while comparable whites are steered to predominantly white neighborhoods) compared to 1989. In other words, they may find out about just as many homes as comparable whites, but not necessarily in the same neighborhoods.

Hispanic home buyers are also much more likely now than in 1989 to be told about and to inspect the same number of available homes as non-Hispanic whites. They are also more likely to receive equal levels of follow-up contact from real estate agents. However, over the course of the 1990s, agents appear to have expanded the assistance and information about financing that they provide to white customers, but not Hispanics, leading to an increase in the level of adverse treatment experienced by Hispanics on measures of financing assistance.

What can we conclude from these trends? Although analytic efforts to link fair housing education and enforcement efforts to the changing level of discrimination has not provided robust supporting evidence, we still hypothesize that the education and enforcement efforts of HUD, the Justice Department, and fair housing groups are likely contributors to declines in discrimination against African American renters and against both African American and Hispanic home buyers. Clearly, real estate agents in the sales market have significantly changed their behavior since 1989. Many agents have learned to meet the standard of equal treatment in terms of telling minority buyers about available units. But as agents have become more willing to work with African Americans, they have increased their proclivity toward steering African Americans toward more racially mixed or minority neighborhoods. Similarly, agents seem more willing to work with Hispanic buyers, a very fast-growing segment of the home-buying public. It is unclear, however, why agents are less willing to help Hispanic buyers with obtaining financing than their comparable white customers.

The lack of progress for Hispanic renters may be a consequence of the changing demographics of the renter population and some resistance from landlords toward this changing demographic. For example, one housing forecast estimates that by 2020, minority households will constitute 51 percent of all renter households, an increase from the 2000 rate of 39 percent and the 1980 rate of 27 percent (Masnick and Di 2003). This increase stems both from a projected decline in the total number of non-Hispanic white renter households of 3.4 million and a projected increase of minority renter households of 4.9 million, 2.9 million of which are projected to be Hispanic households (Masnick and Di 2003).

Persistence of Discrimination

Despite the significant progress since 1989, levels of discrimination against African American and Hispanic home seekers remain unacceptably high. Moreover, HDS2000 shows (for the first time) that Asians and Pacific Islanders face comparable levels of adverse treatment nationwide, and that Native American renters may face even higher rates of discrimination than other groups (based on evidence from three states). Figures 2.3 and 2.4 present current estimates of overall levels of discrimination in metropolitan rental and sales markets, respectively.[7]

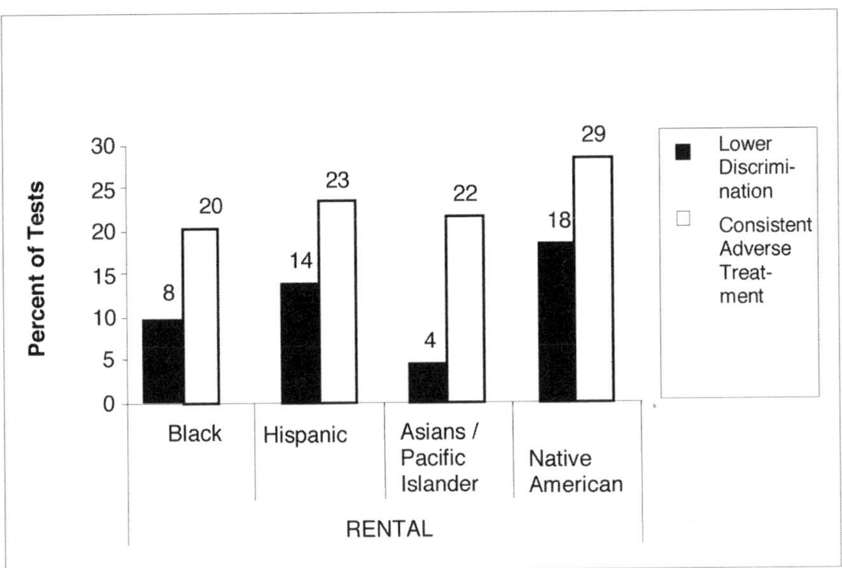

Figure 2.3. Discrimination in Metropolitan Rental Housing. The Native American estimates are based on three states only, Montana, Minnesota, and New Mexico. The Asian and Pacific Islander lower-bound estimate is not statistically different from zero.

In the rental market, lower-bound estimates of discrimination vary quite substantially by race and ethnicity—from a high of 18 percent for Native Americans to 14 percent for Hispanics, 8 percent for African Americans, and a level for Asians that is not significantly different than zero. In contrast, the consistent adverse treatment measure yields relatively similar results across racial/ethnic groups, ranging from 29 percent for Native Americans to 20 percent for blacks.

In the sales market, the lower-bound estimates of discrimination again reflect much greater variation across racial/ethnic groups than the consistency measure. Specifically, the lower-bound estimate is twice as high for Asians (20 percent) than for blacks (8 percent) or Hispanics (7 percent). Levels of consistent adverse treatment, on the other hand, range from 17 percent for African Americans to 20 percent for Asians.

The fact that the lower-bound estimates are statistically significant (for all but Asian renters) indisputably confirms that systematic discrimination based on race and ethnicity persists in both rental and sales markets nationwide.

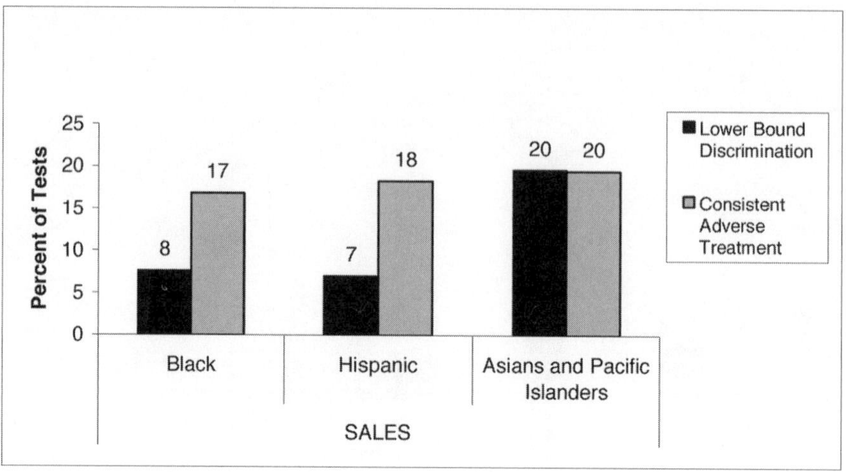

Figure 2.4. Discrimination in Metropolitan Sales Housing Markets.

And both measures, but particularly the measure of consistent adverse treatment, indicate that discrimination still occurs with alarming frequency for all of the racial/ethnic groups studied.

It is puzzling, however, that the lower-bound estimate and consistent adverse treatment measure are not more consistent across racial/ethnic groups and tenure categories. One possible explanation is that real estate professionals have different stereotypes about specific racial and ethnic groups, which result in different patterns of adverse treatment. If this is the case, the use of a single hierarchy of treatment measures for all groups to create the lower-bound estimate of overall discrimination may not be appropriate. Moreover, although random differences in treatment have the biggest impact on the hierarchical composite measures, they can also affect the consistency measures, particularly in situations where the level of systematic discrimination is low relative to inevitable random differences.

Patterns of Discriminatory Treatment

Although overall composite measures are useful for estimating how big the problem of discrimination is, policy makers and practitioners should focus on individual treatment measures to develop strategies for reducing discrimination. Tables 2.1 and 2.2 present the lower-bound estimates of systematic discrimination for individual treatment measures and for categories of treatment, by racial/ethnic group, in the rental and sales market respectively. A positive indicator reflects the extent to which the percentage of tests with white-

Table 2.1. Net Adverse Treatment in the Rental Market by Treatment Category

	Blacks	*Hispanics*	*Asians*	*Native Americans*
Availability	**+5**	**+12**		**+16**
Advertised Unit Available?	+4	+6		+6
Similar Units Available?				+10
Number Units Available	+6	+10		+13
Inspection	**+7**	**+8**		
Advertised Unit Inspected?	+6	+4		
Similar Units Inspected?				
Number Units Inspected	+7	+7		
Cost		**+4**		
Rent for Advertised Unit		+5		
Rental Incentives Offered?	+3	+3		
Amount of Security Deposit				
Application Fee Required?	−3			
Encouragement				
Follow-up Contact from Agent?			+3	
Asked to Complete Application?				
Credit Check Required?			−10	
Arrangement for Future?			+8	

Note: Results for Native Americans are for three states, Minnesota, Montana, and New Mexico. Entries represent the difference between white-favored and minority-favored treatment, where these are significantly different from zero at a 90 percent confidence level.

favored treatment exceeds the percentage of tests with minority-favored treatment (the lower-bound estimate of adverse treatment). A negative indicator reflects the extent to which minority-favored treatment exceeds white-favored treatment. Only estimates that are statistically significant (at a 90 percent confidence level) are reported in these tables.

In the rental market, the most frequent form of discrimination against blacks, Hispanics, and Native Americans is denial of information about available housing units. This is a critically important form of discrimination because it so clearly limits the options from which minority home seekers can choose. The opportunity to actually inspect available units also represents an extremely damaging form of discrimination, and lower-bound estimates of discrimination against blacks and Hispanics are also statistically significant on this measure. For Asian renters, lower-bound estimates of discrimination are generally not statistically significant. Where they are—in the area of agent encouragement—the direction sometimes points toward more favorable treatment of Asians than whites.

Patterns of discrimination look quite different in metropolitan sales markets. African American home buyers still face some discrimination with respect to

Table 2.2. Net Adverse Treatment in the Sales Market by Treatment Category

	Blacks	*Hispanics*	*Asians*
Availability			**+11**
Advertised Unit Available?			
Similar Units Available?		+5	+7
Number Units Recommended	+9	+7	
Inspection	**+6**		**+19**
Advertised Unit Inspected?			+6
Similar Units Inspected?	+5	+4	+9
Number Units Inspected	+9		+14
Steering—Homes Recommended	+5		
Steering—Homes Inspected	+4	+4	
Financing Assistance	**+5**	**+13**	**+15**
Help with Financing Offered?		+12	+15
Agent Prequalified Tester?	+5	+6	
Lenders Recommended?		+8	
Encouragement	**+6**		
Follow-up Contact from Agent?			
Prequalification Required?	+6		+8
Told Qualified?	+8	+4	+9
Arrangement for Future?	−2		

Note: Entries represent the difference between white-favored and minority-favored treatment, where these are significantly different from zero at a 90 percent confidence level.

information about available homes and opportunities to inspect homes. In addition, agents steer black customers to homes in less predominantly white neighborhoods, provide less information and assistance with financing, and offer less encouragement overall. Hispanic home buyers also face some discrimination with respect to information about available homes, but the major obstacle they face appears to be the lack of assistance with financing compared to equally qualified white testers. Finally, lower-bound estimates of discrimination against Asian home buyers are shockingly high, particularly given the mixed pattern observed in the rental market. Asian home buyers face high levels of discrimination with respect to information about available homes (11 percent), opportunities to inspect homes (19 percent) and assistance with financing (15 percent).

Summary of Findings

Over the last decade levels of discrimination against African Americans have declined significantly, in both rental and sales markets nationwide. Hispanic home buyers have also experienced significant reductions in overall levels of discrimination, but not Hispanic renters. Despite this encouraging evidence of progress, levels of discrimination against both African Americans and Hispanics remain disturbingly high, limiting the information they receive about available homes and apartments as well as the assistance they need to complete a rental or sales transaction. Moreover, although overall levels of discrimination against black and Hispanic home buyers are declining, some forms of discriminatory treatment are on the rise. Specifically, black home buyers now appear *more* likely than in the past to be steered away from predominantly white neighborhoods, and Hispanic home buyers are more likely than in the past to be denied information that comparable whites receive about the mortgage financing process.

In addition, HDS2000 expands our understanding of racial and ethnic discrimination in metropolitan housing markets by providing estimates for Asians and for Native American renters. This new information indicates that Asian home buyers face levels of discrimination as high or higher than African Americans and Hispanics, and that Native American renters face extremely high levels of discrimination, primarily due to denial of information about available units, when they search for housing outside of Native Lands.

WHERE DO WE GO FROM HERE?

Like the two previous national studies of housing market discrimination, HDS2000 is helping to inform ongoing fair housing enforcement and public education efforts. For example, the study has highlighted the lack of improvement in levels of discrimination against Hispanic renters, and HUD is allocating more attention and resources to outreach and enforcement in the Hispanic community. Study results can be used to inform the general public and real estate professionals about the persistence and forms of housing discrimination. The findings from this study dispel two competing myths about housing discrimination—first, that discrimination hardly occurs any more, and second, that discrimination cannot be eliminated. Americans of all races and ethnicities need to know more about fair housing protections and about the persistence of unfair practices. But they also need to know that by standing up against discrimination and filing complaints, they can contribute to ongoing reductions in the level of discrimination. Moreover, fair housing training for real estate and rental agents needs to be informed about the specific forms of adverse treatment that are still being practiced, whether intentionally or as a result of unacknowledged stereotypes.

As we pass the half-way point of the first decade in the twenty-first century, it makes sense to start thinking about a fourth decennial study of housing discrimination in the nation's rental and sales markets. Despite significant progress over the last decade, discrimination clearly still persists. Should HUD launch a fourth national paired-testing study in 2010? And should it again replicate the protocols implemented in 1989 and 2000?

Such a study could yield a wealth of valuable information. It would enable HUD to again produce statistically rigorous estimates of changes in discrimination against African Americans and Hispanics, and to track any changes that might be occurring in national levels of discrimination against Asians. Rigorous change measures of this kind would help assess the efficacy of ongoing public education and enforcement efforts. For example, is discrimination against African American renters and home buyers continuing to decline? Is the new attention now being focused on discrimination against Hispanic renters paying off with results in that area? Does the downward trend in discrimination apply to Asians and Pacific Islanders as well? Moreover, a fourth national housing discrimination study could expand testing for discrimination against Native Americans to more states and metropolitan areas, possibly even producing national estimates for both renters and home buyers.

However, such a study would be extremely expensive, probably costing in excess of $20 million. And, as discussed earlier, replication has serious shortcomings. There are good reasons to believe that housing market practices may be undergoing substantial change, making the 1989 and 2000 testing protocols less applicable by 2010. For example, more and more Americans may be relying on the Internet for the early stages of their housing search, assembling information about available homes and apartments, and even viewing available units on line. Real estate and rental agents may be changing their advertising practices as well. In addition, some fair housing practitioners have reported that a growing share of sales agents expect serious home buyers to be prequalified for mortgage financing before they begin visiting available homes. Discriminatory practices may be changing as well, with more adverse treatment occurring either *before* a conventional paired test begins (through phone screening) or *after* a conventional test ends.

An alternative approach for 2010 would focus on using the power of paired testing to learn about evolving forms of discrimination and to investigate new segments of the market. HUD has experience with this more exploratory approach to research testing. Over the last decade, innovative studies have extended the paired-testing methodology to measure discrimination against minority neighborhoods by home insurance providers (Wissoker, Zimmerman, and Galster 1998), discrimination against minority home buyers by mortgage lending institutions (Turner et al. 2002), discrimination against Native Americans searching for housing outside of tribal lands (as discussed here), and discrimination against persons with disabilities inquiring about rental housing

(Turner et al. 2005). All of these studies focused on a small number of sites (typically two or three), developed new testing strategies, and produced statistically rigorous results about patterns of discrimination about which little was previously known.

The same exploratory and innovative approach could be applied to a number of other, underinvestigated forms of discrimination, stages of the transaction, or segments of the housing market. Possible candidates include:

- Measuring discrimination at the telephone inquiry or appointment stage based on speech patterns and accent
- Capturing levels and forms of discrimination that occur when housing search is conducted (or initiated) on the Internet
- Testing for discrimination in rural housing markets, including mobile home developments
- Structuring tests to capture discrimination by rental agents
- Measuring the extent and forms of discrimination against home seekers who do not speak fluent English

All of these possibilities would involve modifications to existing testing protocols and sampling procedures, and would provide new information about dimensions of housing market discrimination that are not yet well understood.

Although pilot testing studies of this kind would not yield an updated set of national estimates or estimates of change in the level of discrimination, experience indicates that they could be used to educate the public and policy makers effectively. Pilot testing studies conducted in the past, when combined with a proactive dissemination strategy, have proven to be effective in informing the public and policy makers about the role that discrimination plays in limiting options for minority home seekers. In addition, targeted research testing of this kind can be implemented in conjunction with enforcement testing to build local capacity in new areas and to raise awareness among housing practitioners about the importance of providing equal treatment to minority and white home seekers. And exploratory testing strategies that focus on new segments of the market or new forms of discrimination can generate protocols and tools that are of value to enforcement practitioners as well.

Findings from the national paired-testing studies conducted in 1977, 1989, and 2000 have contributed in important ways to ongoing efforts to educate the public and policy makers about the persistence of housing market discrimination, about the need for effective enforcement tools and resources, and about how these resources should be targeted as market conditions evolve.

Thus, there are strong arguments for planning a fourth national housing discrimination study for 2010. However, there is also room for disagreement about how this study should be designed. Now is the time to start working together to resolve these disagreements and to craft the framework of a study that will provide the greatest value to policy makers and practitioners.

NOTES

1. The protocols implemented in HDS2000 were designed to yield consistent data that could be aggregated across thousands of tests. The same protocols would not be appropriate for investigatory or enforcement testing, which often requires much more flexible approaches tailored to particular complaints or following up on particular patterns of treatment.
2. The results of appointment calls by testers were recorded and are available for analysis.
3. We use the term "systematic discrimination" to mean differences in treatment that are attributable to a customer's race or ethnicity, rather than to any other differences in tester characteristics or test circumstances. This term is not the same as "intentional" discrimination.
4. Note that it is conceivable that random factors might *reduce* the observed incidence of white-favored or minority-favored treatment, so that the gross-incidence measure is technically not an absolute upper-bound estimate for systematic discrimination.
5. Ondrich, Ross, and Yinger (2000) examine a structural approach to closing the gap between the upper and lower bounds provided by the net and gross measures, but their approach only reduced the bounds by a small amount.
6. Again, it is important to emphasize the difference between methods used for the statistical analysis of paired-testing results and methods used to assemble or assess evidence of unlawful conduct in an individual case. No predetermined set of decision criteria can substitute for case-by-case judgments about test results.
7. Note that the lower-bound and consistent adverse treatment levels for 2000 in figures 2.1 and 2.2 differ slightly from the totals in figures 2.3 and 2.4. This is because figures 2.3 and 2.4 reflect a national sample that included Baltimore and Miami testing results while figures 2.1 and 2.2 show change over time and do not include those metropolitan areas because those areas were not included in the 1989 sample.

REFERENCES

Abravanel, Martin, and Mary Cunningham. 2003. *How Much Do We Know? Public Awareness of the Nation's Fair Housing Laws*. Washington, DC: U.S. Department of Housing and Urban Development.

Farley, Reynolds. 1996. "Racial Differences in the Search for Housing: Do Whites and Blacks Use the Same Techniques to Find Housing?" *Housing Policy Debate* 7(2): 367–86.

Fix, Michael, and Raymond J. Struyk. 1992. *Clear and Convincing Evidence: Testing for Discrimination in America*. Washington, DC: Urban Institute Press.

Galster, George, Fred Freiberg, and Diane Houk. 1987. "Racial Differences in Real Estate Advertising Practices: An Exploratory Case Study." *Journal of Urban Affairs* 9:199–215.

Harris, David R. 2000. "What's the Internet Got to Do with It? Housing Discrimination in the Twenty-first Century." *Focus* 21(2): 63–64.

Kingsley, G. Thomas, Maris Mikelsons, and Carla Herbig. 1996. *Housing Problems and Needs of American Indians and Alaska Natives*. Washington, DC: U.S. Department of Housing and Urban Development.

Masnick, George S., and Zhu Xiao Di. 2003. "Projections of U.S. Households by Race/Hispanic Origin, Age, Family Type, and Tenure to 2020: A Sensitivity Analysis." In *Issue Papers on Demographic Trends Important to Housing*. Washington, DC: U.S. Department of Housing and Urban Development.

Massey, Douglas S., and Garvey Lundy. 2001. "Use of Black English and Racial Discrimination in Urban Housing Markets: New Methods and Findings." *Urban Affairs Review* 36:470–96.

Newburger, Eric C. 1999. "Computer Use in the United States." In *Current Population Reports*, P20-522. Washington, DC: U.S. Bureau of the Census.

Newburger, Harriet. 1995. "Sources of Difference in Information Used by Black and White Housing Seekers: An Exploratory Analysis." *Urban Studies* 32(3): 445–70.

Ondrich, Jan, Stephen L. Ross, and John Yinger. 2000. "How Common Is Housing Discrimination? Improving on Traditional Measures." *Journal of Urban Economics* 47:470–500.

Roth, K. 2000. *The 2000 National Association of Realtors Profile of Home Buyers and Sellers*. Report of the National Association of Realtors. http://www.nar.realtor.com/research/images/668prof.pdf.

Turner, Margery, John Edwards, and Maris Mikelsons. 1991. *Housing Discrimination Study: Analyzing Racial and Ethnic Steering*. Washington, DC: U.S. Department of Housing and Urban Development.

Turner, Margery, Raymond Struyk, and John Yinger. 1991. *Housing Discrimination Study: Synthesis*. Washington, DC: U.S. Department of Housing and Urban Development.

Turner, Margery, and Ron Wienk. 1993. "The Persistence of Segregation in Urban Areas: Contributing Causes." In *Housing Markets and Residential Mobility*, ed. T. Kingsley and M. Turner. Washington, DC: Urban Institute Press.

Turner, Margery, et al. 2002. *All Other Things Being Equal: A Paired Testing Study of Mortgage Lending Institutions*. Washington, DC: U.S. Department of Housing and Urban Development.

Turner, Margery, et al. 2005. *Discrimination against Persons with Disabilities: Barriers at Every Step*. Washington, DC: U.S. Department of Housing and Urban Development.

Wienk, Ron, Cliff Reid, John Simonson, and Fred Eggers. 1979. *Measuring Racial Discrimination in Housing Markets: The Housing Market Practices Study*. Washington, DC: U.S. Department of Housing and Urban Development.

Wissoker, Douglas, Wendy Zimmerman, and George Galster. 1998. *Testing for Discrimination in Home Insurance.* Washington, DC: Urban Institute Press.

Yinger, John. 1995. *Closed Doors: Opportunities Lost: The Continuing Costs of Housing Discrimination*. New York: Russell Sage.

3

Assessing Racial Discrimination

Methods and Measures

Douglas S. Massey and Rebecca M. Blank

Race remains a salient cleavage in American society at the dawn of the twenty-first century. Despite the passage of laws during the 1960s and 1970s to end legalized segregation in the South, to outlaw racial exclusion in the provision of public and private services throughout the land, and to ban racial discrimination in all U.S. markets, large gaps remain between blacks and whites on many dimensions of well-being, including earnings (Altonji and Blank 1999), wealth (Oliver and Shapiro 1995), housing (Massey and Denton 1993), health (Smedley, Smith, and Nelson 2003), education (Hallinan 2001), and criminal justice (Tonry 1995). There is similar concern about the differential outcomes faced by Native Americans, by Hispanics, or by Asian Americans, especially recently arrived immigrants. The color line continues to divide American society in multiple ways (Smelser, Wilson, and Mitchell 2001a, 2001b).

Although racial disparities with respect to social and economic outcomes are well documented, the means by which these differentials are produced remain a matter of considerable debate. On the one hand are those who argue that the civil rights legislation of the 1960s and 1970s was successful in reducing racial bias in American institutions; lingering differentials stem from market mechanisms operating in race-neutral fashion on past disadvantages following the associational preferences of different racial and ethnic groups (Thernstrom and Thernstrom 1997). On the other hand are those who see racism as deeply ingrained within the values, practices, and institutions of American society, which absent some intervention will continue to reproduce racial inequality in manifold ways (Feagin 2000).

Whatever viewpoint one adopts, adjudicating between them requires accurate information on the extent of racial discrimination in various domains of

American life. To the extent that discrimination is low and declining, the former view is supported; to the extent that it is high and persistent, the latter view gains currency. Because differential treatment on the basis of race is against the law, however, when it does occur it is often subtle, publicly justified on other grounds, and, hence, inherently difficult to observe and measure. After the civil rights era, social scientists were compelled to develop a set of indirect methodologies to measure racial discrimination and to model statistically its causes and consequences.

The methods they developed are not without controversy, however, and many serious questions have been raised about their relative performance and validity in different circumstances (Fix and Struyk 1993; Fix and Turner 1998). In order to bring some order to the debate and to offer an authoritative assessment of measurement issues, the National Research Council in 2001 constituted the Panel on Methods for Assessing Discrimination. The panel was funded by a consortium of institutions that included the Ford Foundation, the Mellon Foundation, the U.S. Department of Agriculture, and the U.S. Department of Education. The panel was chaired by Rebecca M. Blank, Henry Carter Adams Professor of Public Policy, professor of economics, and dean of the Gerald R. Ford School of Public Policy at the University of Michigan. The panel membership was deliberately structured to represent the various subfields of social science, including criminology (Alfred Blumstein), demography (Douglas Massey), economics (Joseph Altonji, Glenn Loury), law (John Donohue), psychology (Susan Fiske), sociology (Lawrence Bobo, Samuel Lucas, Roberto Fernandez), and statistics (Stephen Fienberg, Janet Norwood, John Rolph). Marilyn Dabady provided staff support from the National Research Council, and Connie Citro also assisted the panel in their deliberations.

The panel was charged with four tasks: to provide new tools for assessing the extent to which racial discrimination continues in American society; to evaluate current methodologies for measuring discrimination in different circumstances; to consider other sources of data that might contribute to research on this topic; and to recommend further research and data collection to supplement existing studies. Given the inherent difficulty of inventing new methodologies on command, especially by committee, the panel was more successful in fulfilling the latter three charges than the first. The panel's final report reviews existing approaches and methods for measuring discrimination, evaluates their relative costs and benefits, and suggests promising avenues for future development; it does not offer new methods per se.

In order to meet its responsibilities, the panel sponsored a variety of intellectual endeavors. In addition to meeting several times per year over the course of two years, the panel held a "Workshop on the Measurement of Racial Disparities and Discrimination in Elementary and Secondary Education" in July 2002. It also commissioned nine external academic experts to prepare background papers on various subjects related to the measurement and analysis of discrimination, and it heard testimony from seven stakeholders in federal agencies involved in civil rights enforcement, plus presentations from two additional academic experts. The information generated by these papers and presentations, together with the expertise and knowledge of the panel members themselves, provided the basis for the panel's conclusions and recommendations. The final report (see Blank, Dabady, and Citro 2004) begins by clarifying key conceptual issues—the meaning of race, the definition of discrimination, and a review of theories of discrimination—before presenting an evaluative discussion of specific methods and procedures of measurement.

CONCEPTUAL ISSUES

Although discrimination may arise with respect to factors such as gender, ethnicity, religion, or disability, the panel was explicitly asked to focus on the issue of race and the appropriate ways to measure discrimination based on race within various social and economic domains of the United States. The panel conceptualized race as a social rather than a biological construct. Although various human subpopulations may be distinguished from one another in terms of visual genetic markers, it is the way that these differences are treated socially, economically, culturally, and politically that determines the meaning of race. Panel members defined race as a subjective social construct involving both achieved and ascribed characteristics that have acquired social significance over time in response to shifts in immigration, public policy, economic organization, social structure, and cultural perceptions.

The fact that race is defined by social context does not mean it is unimportant, for as the sociologist W. I. Thomas (1966) has noted, things that are perceived as real are real in their consequences. Given recent efforts to prevent government agencies from collecting data tabulated on the basis of race, the panel felt obliged to reaffirm the importance of race as a social indicator and to state that "despite measurement problems, data on race and ethnicity are necessary for monitoring and understanding evolving differences and trends in outcomes among groups in the U.S. population." The panel further recommends that "the federal government and, as appropriate, state and local governments, should continue to collect data on race and ethnicity" (Blank, Dabady, and Citro 2004: 3).

In compiling data on race, however, the panel noted that government statisticians must be sensitive to changes in the social meaning of race over time and to adapt methodologies accordingly. Of course, statisticians must balance the need for definitional change against the competing need for continuity in measurement, an adjudication that is difficult and not always clear. The panel therefore advocated additional research on how relevant variables (e.g., format of data collection, location of interview, characteristics of respondent, question wording, question order, etc.) affect racial identification and the perceived role of race. As a general rule, the panel suggested employing multiple measures in research and assessment whenever feasible.

Given the panel's consensus that race is a social fact whose expression in society is worthy of serious study, the next conceptual issue it faced was the definition of discrimination. The panel concluded that discrimination occurs whenever one or both of two basic criteria were satisfied: "*differential treatment on the basis of race that disadvantages a racial group; and treatment on the basis of inadequately justified factors other than race* that disadvantages a racial group" (Blank, Dabady, and Citro 2004: 39, emphasis in original). In the legal literature, these two criteria are generally discussed as "disparate treatment" and "disparate impact" definitions of discrimination, although the panel's discussion was not limited to the measurement of discrimination that is considered illegal under the law. The report discusses a variety of situations that could result in differential racial treatment and outcomes and that are of interest to social science researchers even though they may not be explicitly unlawful.

In a world where differential treatment on the basis of race is legally proscribed in public settings, persons of color are no longer routinely told: "We don't serve, rent, or sell to people of your race. Now go away." Instead, other actions are taken to prevent transactions, discourage exchanges, or skew interactions to the disadvantage of minority racial groups. As a result, panel members stated, "discriminatory behavior is rarely observed directly [and] researchers *must infer* its presence by trying to determine whether an observed adverse outcome for an individual would have been different had the individual been of a different race" (Blank, Dabady, and Citro, 2004: 5, emphasis added).

Any attempt at making such an inference necessarily rests on an underlying theory of how and why discrimination occurs. In the research literature, discrimination has been discussed in terms of four ontological processes (Allport 1954). The first is *intentional and explicit discrimination*, which occurs whenever a person harbors animus against some particular racial group and engages in one of a series of behaviors of escalating severity to express that animus. *Verbal antagonism* is the most basic kind of explicit discrimination. It includes racial slurs and disparaging comments made in or out of the target group's presence. *Avoidance* involves people selectively choosing interaction with members of their own group over interaction with members of another. *Segregation* occurs when one racial group actively excludes members of another group from the allocation of resources or from access to societal institutions. *Physical attacks*, commonly discussed as "hate crimes," involve a direct assault on the person or possessions of an individual of a particular racial group, with the intent to harm on the basis of race. Finally, *extermination*, also labeled *genocide*, involves the mass killing of a members of a particular racial group simply because they belong to that group.

While explicit or intentional discrimination has not disappeared, it is far less prevalent than in the past because it has been criminalized. Given that explicit discrimination is illegal, it cannot be openly practiced and is therefore no longer responsible for as much racial disadvantage as in the past.

More common in the contemporary United States is a second process of discrimination known as *subtle, unconscious, or automatic discrimination*. Even though overt acts of racial discrimination are deemed publicly unacceptable by respectable citizens, many people still have prejudicial feelings that stem from the nation's long history of racial construction. Furthermore, to the extent people think in terms of racial categories, the simple self-definition of "belonging" to one racial group can result in subtle discrimination toward other racial groups. A sense of racial prejudice or racial difference continues to condition and shape individual actions and behaviors in subtle, often unconscious, and frequently automatic ways, wherein people avoid, segregate, and antagonize members of other groups without even consciously realizing they are doing it. The persistence of unconscious discrimination has been amply documented by experiments conducted by psychologists in laboratory settings and, to a lesser extent, in field studies (Fiske 1998).

A third process of discrimination has been labeled *statistical discrimination*. Here, individuals or institutions may not harbor animus toward a particular racial group but nonetheless employ the average characteristics of that group to make judgments that adversely affect the interests of individual group members (Arrow 1973). It is an empirical fact, for example, that blacks are more likely to have a criminal record than whites. Other things equal, therefore, if an employer wishes to avoid hiring someone with a criminal background, he can "statistically" discriminate by routinely eliminating all black applicants from the hiring pool, thus guaranteeing a lower average rate of criminality among the remaining applicants. Of course, despite higher rates of black criminality, the vast majority of African Americans have not committed any crime, but they are denied access to employment irrespective of their own individual traits or abilities. Although statistical discrimination may appear "rational" for an employer seeking to avoid hiring criminals, it is nonetheless illegal and just as injurious to African Americans as if the discrimination were motivated by pure racial animus.

The final process of discrimination is known as *structural discrimination*, and it occurs within social organizations and institutions that adopt rules and procedures that, though neutral on the surface, still produce differential racial outcomes (Sidanius and Pratto 1999). Structural discrimination follows from the fact that many contemporary organizations evolved during an era when racism was prevalent and open, causing racially exclusive practices to become embedded, formally and informally, within institutional operations and procedures. Absent a deliberate attempt to change these institutional practices, inertia will prevail and they will continue to replicate racial inequality in manifold ways throughout the social structure. In the contemporary United States, for example, patterns and processes of structural discrimination have been amply documented within institutions associated with labor markets, schools, housing markets, banking, criminal justice, and health care (Blank, Dabady, and Citro 2004: 67).

METHODS FOR ASSESSING DISCRIMINATION

Establishing whether racial discrimination did or did not occur within a particular setting requires the investigator to make a causal inference. In an ideal setting, the investigator can ask the counterfactual, "How would the outcome have differed if the race of the subject were different?" In asking this classic causal question with regard to race, there is the inherent problem that race cannot be "switched." One can only observe different individuals of different races, and cannot change race for the same individual. This is a common problem of inference in social science and affects causal inferences about questions relating to any largely invariant characteristic such as gender or ethnic identity as well as race.

In the absence of direct counterfactual evidence, causality is generally inferred by answering a more complex counterfactual question, "Would the observed association between race and the outcome remain after accounting for potential confounding factors?" The various methodological approaches to measuring discrimination are differentiated from one another in how they eliminate confounding factors while trying to measure racial differentials. Perhaps the most fundamental distinction between methodologies is the degree of control exercised by the investigator—whether confounding factors are eliminated as competing explanations by design (ruled out because of the way the study was set up) or held constant statistically (ruled out because the potentially confounding variable was directly measured and included in a regression model predicting the outcome).

After reviewing the methods and procedures used in the past to infer whether discrimination has occurred, the panel concluded that "no single approach to measuring racial discrimination allows researchers to address all the important measurement issues or to answer all the questions of interest. Consistent patterns of results across studies and different approaches tend to provide the strongest argument [so that researchers] should embrace a multidisciplinary, multi-method approach to the measurement of racial discrimination and seek improvements in all major methods employed" (Blank, Dabady, and Citro 2004: 88–89). The panel then considered the relative strengths and weaknesses of four basic approaches to the measurement of racial discrimination.

Laboratory Experiments

The experiment remains the "gold standard" in research to sustain an inference of causality. In the classic experimental design, subjects are randomly assigned to treatment and control groups; an instrument is applied to measure baseline performance on some outcome of interest; an experimental treatment is then administered to those assigned to the treatment group but not those in the control group; and, finally, a new round of measurement is undertaken to determine final performance on the outcome (Campbell and Stanley 1963). If the two groups were randomly chosen they will be identical at baseline. If the change in pretest and posttest outcomes is different for the experimental and control groups, then the investigator is justified in inferring that the experimental variable caused this difference, and that the difference between the two scores represents the estimated size of the causal effect.

This kind of controlled setting is most readily achieved within the laboratory, where the investigator directly manipulates the timing of measurements, the administration of treatments, and the conditions of the experimental environment. Laboratory experiments have been central in documenting the existence of unconscious implicit discrimination and determining which situational and individual factors affect its expression (Fiske 1998). The control exercised by the investigator over the design and implementation of the experiment yields a very high degree of internal validity—confidence that the experimental variable was indeed responsible for the presumed causal effect.

A classic example of a laboratory experiment documenting implicit racial discrimination is the study by Word, Zanna, and Cooper (1974). White subjects were instructed by the investigators to "interview" black and white high school students "for a team to plan a marketing campaign." The "applicants" were confederates of the experimenter, the first of whom was always white, followed by black or white applicants presented in a randomly counterbalanced order. Judges unaware of the study's hypotheses were trained to observe the encounter behind a one-way mirror and code the nonverbal behavior of the subject interviewers.

When the judges' ratings were tallied, investigators found that white interviewers evinced greater seating distance, shorter interviews, more speech errors, more discomfort, and less warmth toward black applicants than white applicants. In a second phase of the study, white confederates of the investigator were trained to behave exactly the same as white interviewers had behaved toward black applicants during the first round of the study. When these trained interviewers displayed these nonverbal behaviors toward white subjects (now applicants) during a second round of "interviews," white subjects displayed more speech errors, greater seating distance, performed worse in the interview, and judged the interviewer to be less friendly compared with untrained interviewers. In other words, they behaved as blacks had behaved on the first round, thus confirming the power of unconscious discrimination to shape behavior.

Although laboratory experiments may produce data essential to a full understanding of discriminatory processes, the panel noted that laboratory studies done to date have focused more on attitudes than behavior, and that the artificial nature of most laboratory settings inevitably raises issues about the real world generalizability, or external validity, of the results. In light of these observations, the panel recommended that researchers give greater priority to analyses of behavior as well as attitudes, and that they attempt to replicate well-established results from laboratory studies in field settings. The latter recommendation led directly to a consideration of designs covered in the next section.

Field Experiments

Field experiments share many features in common with laboratory experiments except that the experimental manipulation is carried out in a real-world, non-laboratory setting. In shifting from the laboratory to the field, typically some internal validity is sacrificed but external validity is enhanced (Campbell and Stanley 1963). In a field experiment, people within a particular environment (a school, a welfare office, a pool of applicants) are randomly assigned to treatment and control groups, the experimental manipulation is then undertaken, and a measurement instrument applied to measure performance on some outcome. Two challenges to the internal validity of field experiments are that real-world settings often preclude administration of a baseline measurement, and that the investigator lacks control over the experimental environment. In this case, the experimental effect is estimated to be the difference between outcome measures rather than the differential change between pretest and posttest measures. As a result, extraneous events that occur in tandem with the experimental manipulation in the field may become confounded to affect the outcome, thus biasing the estimated causal effect.

In measuring discrimination, the classic field experiment is a "housing audit study," which is based on a paired-testing methodology where black and white auditors under the control of the investigator contact rental or sales agents to inquire about the availability of housing identified in real estate advertisements. Auditors are randomly assigned to pairs (one from each racial group); they are matched on equivalent characteristics, credentials, expressed tastes, and market needs; they are trained to dress and act in similar fashion; and they are randomly assigned to contact a real estate agent either first or second. After the encounter with the agent is over, auditors fill out forms detailing their experience, collecting information on variables such as the number of callbacks, number of units described, number of units shown, number of units offered, location of units, terms of rental or sale, size of deposit required, and so on.

Across a range of such encounters, the average experience of black and white auditors with respect to various outcomes is determined by the investigator and compared to determine whether black auditors received systematically worse treatment and gained access to fewer units than whites, thereby sustaining an inference of racial discrimination. The first nationwide housing audit was implemented by the U.S. Department of Housing and Urban Development in 1977 (Wienk et al. 1979) and was replicated in 1989 (Yinger 1995) and again in 2000 (Turner et al. 2002). Audit studies have also been used to study discrimination in labor markets (Turner, Fix, and Struyk 1991), sales markets (Ayers and Siegelman 1995), lending markets (Ross and Yinger 2002), and insurance markets (Wissoker, Zimmerman, and Galster 1997).

Audit studies have been criticized because they are not true experiments (race cannot be randomly assigned) and they are difficult to run in double-blind fashion, where the auditors are unaware of the purposes of the study. Hence, unobserved characteristics of the auditor, including their own expectations of discrimination, may become confounded with the experimental variable of race (Heckman 1998). Recent studies have made design improvements in response to these criticisms, and the panel thus concluded that "nationwide field audit studies of racially based housing discrimination, such as those implemented by the U.S. Department of Housing and Urban development in 1977, 1989, and 2000 provide valuable data and should be continued" and that researchers and funding agencies should attempt to conduct audit studies more widely in markets besides housing (Blank, Dabady, and Citro 2004: 117).

Observational Data

The weakest platform for inferring causality is observational data—information collected for administrative purposes, through field observations or survey questionnaires. Administrative data are typically generated as a by-product of administrative operations, yielding statistics in the form of court records, complaint files, and registration lists. Since they were compiled to serve administrative rather than research purposes, such observational data often lack information on the full range of variables relevant to the determination of discrimination and are often characterized by haphazard reporting with considerable missing information. Typically they come in a cumbersome format that is ill-suited to analysis, thus requiring extensive preprocessing and cleaning before any estimation can be undertaken.

Data gathered through field observations are generally quite costly to compile, as they typically require a field worker to spend a considerable amount of time living and interacting within a specific social setting, a style of research known as ethnography. The resulting data are rich and often informative about the micro-social mechanisms of discrimination, but because gathering them is so time- and resource-intensive, sample sizes are generally small and the data are qualitative, thereby limiting external validity. Moreover, because field workers are typically unable to observe the counterfactual—how would a person have been treated if he or she were of a different race—field observations suffer from serious limits on internal validity as well.

Although survey questionnaires likewise cannot observe or measure counterfactual outcomes, they are less expensive per person interviewed and can yield a large number of cases at a relatively low cost per person and in a timely fashion. Because they can be applied according to various mathematically well-understood sampling designs, surveys yield representative data with a high degree of external validity, in that precise statements can be made about the degree to which estimates may be generalized to a broader population of interest. Establishing internal validity is thus the principal challenge of survey-based research.

Although survey researchers are unable to administer any sort of "experiment," they can, within limits, determine which variables are collected, offering the possibility of statistical control as a substitute for the direct elimination of confounding effects through control of the experimental environment. To achieve statistical control, a regression or other equation is typically estimated to predict outcomes for blacks and whites using the same set of predictor variables. Using equations estimated in this fashion, a statistical decomposition analysis is then performed to divide an observed racial differential into an "explained" component that is attributable to racial differences in demographic or skill characteristics, and an "unexplained" component associated with race and any unmeasured factors correlated with it. If the process by which the outcome is determined has been correctly modeled and all relevant variables have been measured accurately and included in the equation, then the unexplained portion of the racial difference may legitimately be attributed to some form of discrimination (Oaxaca and Ransom 1999).

The problem, of course, is that knowing whether a social process has been modeled correctly requires satisfying two additional criteria: having a valid theory of the social behavior in question and possessing the technical ability to measure all of the variables it specifies as relevant. As the panel noted, the estimation of statistical models requires not just appropriate methods and data, but "a sufficient understanding of the process being studied to justify the necessary assumptions" (Blank, Dabady, and Citro 2004: 159). Inclusion of an incomplete set of predictor variables in a regression equation yields a specification error, whereas the inability to measure theoretically important variables produces selection bias because unobserved heterogeneity associated with the outcome is uncontrolled. Given such errors, an investigator could mistakenly conclude that black-white differentials stem from discrimination, when in fact they might partially or wholly reflect some other unmeasured difference between the two groups.

Despite the difficulty of making causal inferences about discrimination using observational data, the panel nonetheless concluded that "the statistical decomposition of racial gaps in social outcomes using multivariate regression and related techniques is a valuable tool for understanding the sources of racial differences" (Blank, Dabady, and Citro 2004: 158). It cautioned, however, that many datasets commonly used for this purpose (such as the Decennial Census or the Current Population Surveys) lack a sufficient number and depth of variables to be of much use in making causal attributions about racial discrimination.

The highest quality observational data generally come from longitudinal surveys, wherein a representative sample of respondents is interviewed to create a baseline of data and then reinterviewed at regular intervals over some extended period of time. The panel felt that surveys such as the Panel Study of Income Dynamics and the various National Longitudinal Surveys held considerable promise for more accurate inferences about the presence of racial discrimination in certain social domains. It also noted the value of detailed studies of black and white achievement within specific social settings (such as firms, schools, or other institutions) to generate knowledge and data necessary for investigators to specify more accurate statistical models (Blank, Dabady, and Citro 2004: 159–60).

One final kind of observational study highlighted by the panel is the natural experiment, which takes advantage of administrative or survey data gathered before and after some exogenous policy change has occurred, such as the implementation of a consent decree on minority hiring or the outlawing of certain hiring practices. In this case, the policy change is analogous to an experimental manipulation in the sense that some actors (organizations or individuals) experience the change while others do not, typically yielding a time-series or multiple time-series design (Campbell and Stanley 1963).

A good example is Goldin and Rouse (2000), who studied hiring outcomes among U.S. symphony orchestras. In response to allegations of gender bias in hiring, during the late 1970s and early 1980s many orchestras changed their method of auditioning potential musicians. Instead of having aspiring orchestra members perform directly in front of judges, musicians entered the room silently behind a screen, thus preventing judges from knowing whether the person trying out was male or female, black or white.

In this case, the investigators focused on gender discrimination and compiled data on the number of men and women advanced from one round to the next for nine symphony orchestras. They estimated a binary regression model to predict advancement and discovered that the introduction of the screen led to the advancement of significantly more women, enabling them to conclude that significant discrimination on the basis of gender had prevailed among American symphony orchestras before the new auditioning procedures were introduced. Heckman and Payner (1989) undertook a similar analysis of black versus white wages before and after the instigation of federal antidiscrimination enforcement efforts in South Carolina and found strong evidence for widespread racial discrimination before the policy shift.

These and other examples of natural experiments led panelists to conclude that "despite limitations, natural experiments—in which a legal change or some other change forces a reduction in or the complete elimination of discrimination against some groups—can provide useful data for measuring discrimination prior to the change and for groups not affected by the change." In keeping with this conclusion, the panel went on to recommend that "public agencies should assist in the evaluation of natural experiments by collecting data that can be used to evaluate the effect of antidiscrimination policy changes on groups covered by the changes, as well as groups not covered" (Blank, Dabady, and Citro 2004: 60).

Self-Reports of Discrimination

Survey data have also been employed to develop direct estimates of discrimination based on self-reports of personal experiences of adverse treatment. The trouble with self-reports, of course, is that what is being reported is the *perception* of discrimination, not the discrimination itself. Not only are individual perceptions inherently subjective, but they are singularly subject to the absence of a counterfactual. Members of a minority racial group who suspect they have been victimized by discrimination cannot observe how a white person would have been treated in the same circumstances. Such self-reports can be biased up or down; individuals may not be aware of discrimination when it affects them and may attribute what they observe to other factors, or they may suspect discrimination at times when other factors are actually operating.

Survey questionnaires have been used more often to assess prejudice than discrimination itself (Schuman et al. 1997). Although self-reports of prejudicial attitudes and sentiments may not be limited by an inability to observe the counterfactual, they are beset by social desirability bias—the tendency to underreport thoughts and behaviors perceived by respondents to be socially inappropriate. Given that it is no longer publicly acceptable to espouse racist sentiments, prejudicial attitudes toward blacks are likely to be underreported by whites. Measures of explicit racism are therefore best viewed as a lower-bound estimate on the prevalence of racial prejudice in the population.

An additional problem with self-reported prejudice stems from the aforementioned fact that people often are not aware of their own racist sentiments, as they are unconsciously held. Under these circumstances, rather than being expressed explicitly, prejudice is more likely to be expressed symbolically in coded form by positions taken with respect to various public issues with racial overtones, such as crime, busing, and welfare. In recognition of the shift from explicit to symbolic racism (Kinder and Sears 1981), McConahay (1986) developed a Scale of Modern Racism that has been validated and been shown to be associated reliably with other attitudes and behaviors in numerous studies (Kinder and Sanders 1996).

Despite the foregoing limitations and problems, which are inherent in observational data, the panel concluded that in order "to understand changes in racial attitudes and reported perceptions of discrimination over time, public and private funding agencies should continue to support the collection of rich survey data." The panel singled out the General Social Survey, in particular, "which since 1972 has been the leading source of repeated cross-sectional data on trends in racial attitudes and perceptions of racial discrimination" and encouraged the addition of questions on perceived discrimination and prejudice to ongoing longitudinal surveys such as the Panel Study of Income Dynamics and the National Longitudinal Survey of Youth (Blank, Dabady, and Citro 2004: 181).

NEEDED DATA AND RESEARCH

Having reviewed prior work on the assessment of racial discrimination in the United States, the panel found that, under appropriate circumstances and given certain caveats, all methods contributed something of value to scientific understanding of the issue. In closing its report the panel considered needs for additional data and research.

Collection of Data on Race by the U.S. Government

One issue central to understanding racial discrimination is the measurement of race itself. In order to place current concepts and measures into a broader perspective, the panel reviewed the history of government attempts to measure race from 1790 to the present. The panel found that changes in how race was measured historically by the U.S. Bureau of the Census were linked to the shifting meaning of race in American society and to changes in the social and political status of African Americans, providing concrete evidence that race is a social construction rather than a physical fact.

The contemporary conceptualization of race in the United States appears to be in a state of flux owing to massive immigration from Asia, Latin America, and the Caribbean, as well as rising rates of intermarriage between whites, on the one hand, and Asians and Latinos, on the other. Rates of black-white intermarriage, though higher than they were before the civil rights era, remain relatively low. In recognition of the rising importance of interracial marriage, the U.S. Census Bureau in 2000 offered respondents the opportunity to select more than one racial identifier. Only 2.4 percent of the population chose more than one racial category, though 5.5 percent said they were some "other race" besides white, black, Amerindian, Asian, or Pacific Islander. All told, 75.1 percent of all Americans reported themselves as white, 12.3 percent said they were black, and 3.6 percent said they were Asian. Some 12.5 percent of all Americans reported themselves to be of Hispanic origin, though the latter could be of any race (Blank, Dabady, and Citro 2004: 213).

Immigration has the potential to reshape American racial identities in two ways. First, immigration from Asia and the Americas increases the diversity of racial categories well beyond the traditional black-white divide that has historically characterized the United States, dramatically increasing the number and range of phenotypes present in U.S. society. Second, immigrants from

Latin America and the Caribbean, in particular, typically do not conceive of race as a dichotomy and have resisted this way of thinking, thus pushing U.S. society toward a more fluid conceptualization of race.

Whereas the United States both formally and informally came to define race according to a "one drop rule," which classified people with any detectable African ancestry as "black," Latin Americans and Caribbeans have traditionally viewed race as a continuum ranging from black to white and composed of various admixtures of European, African, Asian, and Amerindian ancestries. As the American conceptualization of race itself shifts in response to immigration and social change, the panel advises that "data collectors, researchers, and others should be cognizant of the effects of measurement methods on the reporting of race and ethnicity, which may affect the comparability of data for analysis" and that they should "collect and analyze longitudinal data to measure how reported perceptions of racial identification change over time for different groups" (Blank, Dabady, and Citro 2004: 222).

Measuring the Cumulative Effects of Discrimination

Most research to date has sought to measure the incidence and severity of racial discrimination within particular domains of social and economic life, and to a lesser extent to model the determinants of discriminatory behavior. The panel found that considerably less attention has focused on the consequences of discrimination for individuals and society at large. This state of affairs is unfortunate because the consequences are ultimately what determine the importance of the phenomenon. If discrimination were a neutral social fact that harmed no one, then society would have little interest in its eradication. It is because racial discrimination is presumed to have serious negative consequences for individuals and society that laws prohibiting it were enacted. As the panel concluded, "measures of discrimination from one point in time and in one domain may be insufficient to identify the overall impact of discrimination on individuals" (Blank, Dabady, and Citro 2004: 246).

The key to comprehending discrimination's full effect lies with the concept of cumulative discrimination. According to the panel, "by cumulative discrimination we mean a dynamic concept that captures systematic processes over time and across domains. . . . Measures that focus on episodic discrimination at a particular place and point in time provide very limited information on the effect of dynamic, cumulative disadvantage. . . . Current legal standards do not adequately address issues of cumulative discrimination. . . . The effects of cumulative discrimination can be transmitted through the organizational and social structures of society" (Blank, Dabady, and Citro 2004: 225–26).

Discrimination and the disadvantages it causes become cumulative because discrimination at one point in time and in one domain influences the resources that an individual brings to performance at later points in time and in other domains, thus affecting outcomes in a context entirely apart from that within which the discrimination originally occurred. Moreover, the process by which disadvantage is cumulated over time and across domains may not simply be additive, but multiplicative, owing to the possibility of feedback effects, whereby past discriminatory events increase the incidence and severity of future discrimination, yielding larger and larger disparities over time. In the domain of education, for example, past discrimination against African Americans clearly inhibited their educational achievement (Lieberson 1980), which made them appear to be less successful than otherwise, lowering the expectations of white teachers in a way that undermines the performance of black students today and yields a self-fulfilling prophecy (Rosenthal 2002).

Thus discrimination at one time and place does much more than simply harm the transitory interests of one person. Discrimination not only accumulates over time and across domains within a single lifetime, but is instrumental in perpetuating racial inequality across the generations. Housing offers a particularly clear example. When mass markets for the sale of owned housing were created with government support during the 1930s and 1940s, the private policies of the real estate industry and the public policies by which the federal government underwrote mortgage lending both explicitly discriminated against blacks (Massey and Denton 1993).

Owing to institutionalized discrimination, it was almost impossible for African Americans to purchase housing except in existing black neighborhoods or in adjacent residential areas undergoing purposeful racial transition managed by the real estate industry. Moreover, because of a government-initiated and privately popularized policy of "redlining," black and transitional neighborhoods were systematically cut off from inflows of investment capital, not only for the purchase and construction of homes, but from lending for maintenance, improvement, or expansion (Jackson 1985). As a result, aspiring middle-class black families bought into neighborhoods that, bereft of meaningful investment, quickly went downhill. The stagnation and at times absolute decline of property values made it exceedingly difficult for black families to build wealth in the form of home equity, and as a result, today black families have accumulated a small fraction of the financial assets of white families. Although the gap between white and black earnings narrowed following the civil rights era, the wealth gap did not and the net financial assets of blacks today stand at less than 10 percent of the assets of whites; half of this huge racial gap is accounted for by differences in home equity (Yinger 1995).

In addition to the transmission of cumulative disadvantage through housing markets, the panel explored other potential mechanisms of cumulative disadvantage occurring through other domains such as criminal justice, public health, education, and labor markets. To the extent that racial discrimination occurs in each of these domains, the negative effects on the life chances of Americans of color will not only cumulate, but reinforce one another to create durable racial inequalities that will be resistant to change. This potentially accounts for the pervasive racial differentials that continue to characterize the United States, despite the end of legalized segregation and the banning of open discrimination in most markets. In the panel's view, therefore, "further research is needed to model and analyze longitudinal and other data and to study how effects of discrimination may accumulate across domains and over time in ways that perpetuate racial inequality" (Blank, Dabady, and Citro 2004: 246).

A principal reason why relatively few attempts have been made to model and understand cumulative disadvantage is because it is difficult to do so. Measuring the cumulative effect of discrimination makes three formidable demands on researchers: they need a valid theory of how cumulative disadvantage operates over time and across generations; they need longitudinal data to measure these diachronic effects; and they need credible indicators of when exposure to discrimination has occurred. The first hurdle must be met by social scientists themselves, but the latter two require the assistance of governmental and private funding agencies.

The panel thus specifically recommended that "major longitudinal surveys . . . merit support as data sources for studies of cumulative disadvantage across time, domains, generations, and population groups. Furthermore, consideration should be given to incorporating into these surveys additional variables or special topical modules that might enhance the utility of data for studying the long-term effects of past segregation . . . [including indicators] that would help researchers identify experiences of discrimination and their effects" (Blank, Dabady, and Citro 2004: 246).

The persistence of large racial inequalities on numerous dimensions of social and economic well-being, noted at the outset of this chapter, demands scientific explanation. Many explanations have been posited, ranging from the debilitating effects of government welfare programs (Wilson 1987); but at least as plausible is the persistence of significant levels of racial discrimination in key domains of American life and their mutually reinforcing effects over time and across the generations. The work of the NRC Panel on Methods for Assessing Discrimination confirms that, despite the epistemological and methodological problems common to social science, valid techniques for the measurement and analysis of racial discrimination do exist, but to date they have been underutilized and ineffectively combined. We hope that the panel's report will contribute to more and better research on racial discrimination and lead to the formulation of policies that will help to overcome the legacy of racial division in the United States.

REFERENCES

Allport, Gordon. 1954. *The Nature of Prejudice*. Reading, MA: Addison Wesley.

Altonji, Joseph G., and Rebecca M. Blank. 1999. "Race and Gender in the Labor Market." *Handbook of Labor Economics* 3:3143–59.

Arrow, Kenneth. 1973. "The Theory of Discrimination." In *Discrimination in Labor Markets*, ed. Orley Ashenfelder and Albert Rees. Princeton, NJ: Princeton University Press.

Ayers, I., and P. Siegelman. 1995. "Race and Gender Discrimination in Bargaining." *American Economic Review* 85:304–21.

Blank, Rebecca M., Marilyn Dabady, and Constance F. Citro, eds. 2004. *Measuring Racial Discrimination*. Washington, DC: National Academy Press.

Campbell, Donald T., and Julian C. Stanley. 1963. *Experimental and Quasi-Experimental Designs for Research*. Chicago: Rand McNally.

Feagin, Joe R. 2000. *Racist America: Roots, Current Realities and Future Reparations*. New York: Routledge.

Fiske, Susan T. 1998. "Stereotyping, Prejudice, and Discrimination." In *The Handbook of Social Psychology*, 4th edition, ed. Daniel Gilbert, Susan T. Fiske, and Gardner Lindzey. New York: McGraw-Hill.

Fix, Michael, and Raymond J. Struyk, eds. 1993. *Clear and Convincing Evidence: Measurement of Discrimination in America*. Washington, DC: Urban Institute Press.

Fix, Michael, and Marjorie A. Turner. 1998. *A National Report Card on Discrimination in America: The Role of Testing*. Washington, DC: Urban Institute Press.

Goldin, Claudia, and Cecilia Rouse. 2000. "Orchestrating Inequality: The Impact of 'Blind' Auditions on Female Musicians." *American Economic Review* 90:715–41.

Hallinan, Maureen T. 2001. "Diversity Effects on Student Outcomes: Social Science Evidence." *Ohio State Law Journal* 59:733–54.

Heckman, James J. 1998. "Detecting Discrimination." *Journal of Economic Perspectives* 12:101–16.

Heckman, James J., and B. S. Payner. 1989. "Determining the Impact of Federal Anti-Discrimination Policy on the Economic Status of Blacks: A Study of South Carolina." *American Economic Review* 79:138–77.

Jackson, Kenneth T. 1985. *Crabgrass Frontier: The Suburbanization of the United States*. New York: Oxford University Press.

Kinder, Donald R., and Lynn M. Sanders. 1996. *Divided by Color: Racial Politics and Democratic Ideals*. Chicago: University of Chicago Press.

Kinder, Donald R., and D. O. Sears. 1981. "Prejudice and Politics: Symbolic Racism Versus Racial Threats to the Good Life." *Journal of Personality and Social Psychology* 40:414–31.

Lieberson, Stanley. 1980. *A Piece of the Pie: Blacks and White Immigrants Since 1880*. Berkeley: University of California Press.

Massey, Douglas S., and Nancy A. Denton. 1993. *American Apartheid: Segregation and the Making of the Underclass*. Cambridge, MA: Harvard University Press.

McConahay, J. B. 1986. "Modern Racism, Ambivalence, and the Modern Racism Scale." In *Prejudice, Discrimination, and Racism*, ed. John F. Dovidio and S. L. Gaertner. San Diego, CA: Academic Press.

Murray, Charles A. 1984. *Losing Ground: American Social Policy, 1950–1980*. New York: Basic Books.

Oaxaca, Ronald L., and Mark R. Ransom. 1999. "Identification in Detailed Wage Decompositions." *Review of Economics and Statistics* 81:154–57.

Oliver, Melvin T., and Thomas M. Shapiro. 1995. *Black Wealth, White Wealth: A New Perspective on Racial Inequality*. New York: Routledge.

Rosenthal, Robert. 2002. "The Pygmalion Effect and its Mediating Mechanisms." In *Improving Academic Achievement: Impact of Psychological Factors on Education*, ed. Joshua Aronson. San Diego, CA: Academic Press.

Ross, Stephen M., and John Yinger. 2002. *The Color of Credit: Mortgage Discrimination, Research Methodology, and Fair-Lending Enforcement*. Cambridge, MA: MIT Press.

Schuman, Howard, Charlotte Steeh, Lawrence Bobo, and Maria Krysan. 1997. *Racial Attitudes in America: Trends and Interpretations*. Cambridge, MA: Harvard University Press.

Sidanius, Jim, and F. Pratto. 1999. *Social Dominance: An Intergroup Theory of Social Hierarchy and Oppression*. New York: Cambridge University Press.

Smedley, Brian D., Adrienne Y. Smith, and Alan R. Nelson, eds. 2003. *Unequal Treatment: Confronting Racial and Ethnic Disparities in Health Care*. Washington, DC: National Academy Press.

Smelser, Neil J., William Julius Wilson, and Faith Mitchell. 2001a. *America Becoming: Racial Trends and Their Consequences, Volume I*. Washington, DC: National Academy Press.

———. 2001b. *America Becoming: Racial Trends and Their Consequences, Volume II*. Washington, DC: National Academy Press.

Thernstrom, Stephen, and Abigail Thernstrom. 1997. *America in Black and White: One Nation, Indivisible*. New York: Simon and Schuster.

Thomas, William Isaac. 1966. *W. I. Thomas on Social Organization and Social Personality*. Chicago: University of Chicago Press.

Tonry, Michael. 1995. *Malign Neglect: Race, Crime, and Punishment in America*. New York: Oxford University Press.

Turner, Marjorie A., Michael Fix, and Raymond J. Struyk. 1991. *Opportunities Denied, Opportunities Diminished: Racial Discrimination in Hiring*. Washington, DC: Urban Institute Press.

Turner, Marjorie A., Stephen L. Ross, George C. Galster, and John Yinger. 2002. *Discrimination in Metropolitan Housing Markets: A Paired Testing Study of Mortgage Lending Institutions*. Washington, DC: U.S. Department of Housing and Urban Development.

Wienk, Ronald, C. E. Reid, J. C. Simonson, and F. J. Eggers. 1979. *Measuring Racial Discrimination in American Housing Markets: The Housing Practices Survey*. Washington, DC: U.S. Department of Housing and Urban Development.

Wilson, William Julius. 1987. *The Truly Disadvantaged: The Inner City, the Underclass, and Public Poverty*. Chicago: University of Chicago Press.

Wissoker, D. A., Wendy Zimmerman, and George Galster. 1997. *Testing for Discrimination in Home Insurance*. Washington, DC: Urban Institute Press.

Word, C. O., M. P. Zanna, and Joel Cooper. 1974. "The Nonverbal Mediation of Self-Fulfilling Prophesies in Interracial Interaction." *Journal of Experimental Social Psychology* 120:109–20.

Yinger, John. 1995. *Closed Doors, Opportunities Lost: The Continuing Costs of Housing Discrimination*. New York: Russell Sage Foundation.

4

Paradoxes in the Fair Housing Attitudes of the American Public, 2001–2005

Martin D. Abravanel

Effective enforcement of the Fair Housing Act of 1968, as amended in 1988, is largely dependent on individual housing consumers recognizing or suspecting they have been victims of illegal discrimination.[1] Typically it is only after an alleged victim files a complaint with either the U.S. Department of Housing and Urban Development (HUD) or a designated state or local agency or nonprofit group that such an allegation is investigated, conciliation sought, a formal charge filed, and, if successful, a remedy obtained (see chapter 7 by Schill; see also HUD, *Fair Housing*; *Housing Laws*). For the process to work effectively, therefore, housing consumers must know what types of treatment or behavior the act considers to be illegal, what categories of persons it protects, and what actions on their part are necessary to help them get relief. When consumers feel they have been treated unjustly, they need to understand they have a right to get help and where to turn, and trust that an appropriate outcome is attainable.

For over a decade now researchers have known that compared to the ten thousand or fewer cases of suspected housing discrimination filed annually with HUD, auditing or testing studies have revealed an incidence of discriminatory practices that is far greater (see Fix and Struyk 1993; Turner and Herbig 2005; Turner et al. 2002; see also chapter 2 by Turner, Richardson, and Ross). This disparity between complaints filed and measured discrimination raises substantial social science, policy, and programmatic questions. What explains the difference is the core curiosity motivating this chapter. Is it due to limitations in the public's knowledge of what constitutes discrimination under the Fair Housing Act? Are people unwilling to take action when faced with what they consider to be discrimination, and if so, why? Are some forms of discrimination simply not recognizable to consumers, regardless of their level of knowledge or willingness to take action? And, is there anything programmatically that can be done to change the situation?

Evidence about consumer perceptions, attitudes, and behavior related to fair housing law had been relatively rare until recently, when two national, cross-sectional surveys of the adult population of the United States were conducted. They were sponsored by HUD in 2000–2001 and again in 2005, and reveal several paradoxes. One such paradox is that some groups perceive less discrimination than objective evidence would indicate actually exists. A second is that while the public's support for fair housing law has improved and continues to improve over time, public knowledge of what actually constitutes illegal discrimination is uneven and has generally not improved in recent years. A third is that considerably more people assert, in advance, they would do something if they were discriminated against than, in reality, do so after the fact. As a result, and despite the putative benefits of civil rights legislation, violations often go unchallenged and protections regularly go unrealized.

From a social science perspective, understanding the causal dynamics underlying the disjuncture between reality and perception, and between attitudes and behavior, is essential. Yet, from a programmatic perspective, simply recognizing there are such paradoxes, even if not fully understanding them, is also of considerable importance. To be effective, efforts to enhance consumer knowledge and action need to be built on empirical evidence about such matters, which the surveys offer for the first time. They are by no means the last word, however. As they provide fresh evidence and insights, they also raise questions that will require additional research and policy assessment.

CONSUMERS' PERCEPTIONS OF HOUSING DISCRIMINATION

The first fair housing survey, conducted during December 2000 and January 2001, sampled 1,001 adults living in the nation's forty-eight contiguous states and the District of Columbia. It was designed by the Urban Institute and administered by telephone by the University of Michigan's Survey Research Center as an adjunct to its monthly consumer confidence survey (Abravanel and Cunningham 2002; Abravanel 2002). The second survey, involving 1,029 adults, was designed to replicate the methodology of the first one. Administered by Morris Davis and Associates between January 28 and May 1, 2005, it also included supplemental samples of African Americans, Hispanics, and individuals in either families with children less than eighteen years of age or households with persons with disabilities—to permit special analyses of those groups (Abravanel 2006).[2]

The surveys inquired about the fair housing attitudes and behavior of the American public and, among other issues, asked consumers if they believed they had ever experienced unfair treatment in a housing transaction. Although housing discrimination may occur in various contexts, such as when a landlord fails to accommodate the needs of an existing tenant with a disability, the surveys explicitly inquired about the point at which discrimination most frequently occurs, that is, when people are looking to buy a house or rent an apartment. If respondents stated they had experienced such discrimination, they were asked follow-up questions that had not previously been attempted in national surveys, including what actions if any they had taken in response.

Beyond the surveys' value in examining what consumers do when faced with discrimination, the initial question as to whether or not a person had been discriminated against allows estimation of the rate of alleged housing discrimination across the nation. In the 2000–2001 survey, that rate represented the proportion of all respondents who said they had experienced some form of housing discrimination, but the definition of discrimination was determined by each respondent and not otherwise defined in the survey. The 2005 survey, however, went a step further by asking those who perceived discrimination what it consisted of, why they believed it had occurred, and when it had occurred in order to get a better appreciation of the nature and timing of such incidents. That information provided an opportunity to estimate the rate of perceived discrimination based on more consistent criteria related to the practices and bases that are, in fact, prohibited under law.

With respect to the incidence of perceived discrimination that does not take into account its basis or timing, the findings of the two surveys are similar (Abravanel 2006). Since, however, the 2005 survey is somewhat more expansive than its predecessor, the observations in this section will draw primarily from it.

Responses given to short-answer questions asked over the telephone are, of course, insufficient for making an administrative or judicial determination as to the merits of any specific allegation. Nonetheless, they allow a basic distinction to be made between experiences that more or less plausibly fall within the terms of the federal Fair Housing Act and those that do not.[3] Indeed, when asked if they had ever experienced discrimination, many of those who thought they had said the bias related to characteristics or attributes protected under the law—involving race, color, national origin, religion, sex, familial status, or disability. But others believed they had been discriminated against for reasons not covered under existing federal law. These included the fact that they were students or lacked sufficient employment, income, or credit history. Yet others identified their age, receipt of welfare, appearance (such as having tattoos), (nonassistance) pet ownership, or criminal history as reasons for their differential treatment. Also, some of the alleged discrimination occurred prior to enactment of the Fair Housing Act or its amendment and would not, therefore, have been illegal under federal law at the time it occurred.[4]

Although 17 percent of the public claimed to have experienced some type of housing discrimination at one point or another, when the descriptions, bases, and dates of the perceived discrimination are taken into account, approximately 8 percent of the general public surveyed in 2005 believed they had experienced housing discrimination that could reasonably have been illegal under federal law when it happened.[5] About 70 percent of such persons were attempting to rent and 26 percent were attempting to purchase. Owners or representatives of apartment buildings constituted a plurality of those accused of discriminating (32 percent) followed, in frequency, by homeowners (26 percent), real estate agents (19 percent), and loan officers or lenders (8 percent).

Asked why they thought they had been discriminated against, respondents provided one or more reasons—the most frequent of which was race (58 percent). Familial status (27 percent), ethnicity (17 percent), sex (7 percent), and religion (4 percent) were also alleged bases.[6] Despite the fact that discrimination based on disability is among the most common complaints received by HUD, less than 1 percent of respondents indicated disability as a reason they believed they had suffered discrimination when buying or renting a home or apartment.

Considering demographic characteristics, one-fifth of all African Americans believed they had at some point experienced discriminatory treatment because of their race. This proportion corresponds quite closely to the results of the latest national audit study (see chapter 2 by Turner, Richardson, and Ross). It is also considerably higher than that for other groups: only 6 percent of Hispanics perceived discrimination as a result of their ethnicity; 4 percent of persons in households with children perceived discrimination as a result of their familial status; and less than 1 percent of persons in households with a disabled individual perceived discrimination as a result of disability status.[7] These latter proportions do not comport with more objective evidence from either testing studies or incidence reports of complaints filed with HUD, which suggest higher rates of discrimination for such groups than is apparently perceived (see Turner et al. 2003, 2005).

To the extent that there is a difference between objective and subjective indications of discrimination, it is not clear whether this is due to discriminatory practices not otherwise observable to consumers or to consumers not knowing what practices are unlawful. The surveys could not address the former, but allowed examination of the nature and extent of consumer knowledge of fair housing law. They did so by posing to respondents a series of hypothetical scenarios describing housing practices, each based on different home buyer or renter attributes or characteristics. Most of the scenarios described practices and bases that were discriminatory under the Fair Housing Act, but none involved blatantly prejudicial or mean-spirited motives. Respondents were asked whether, in their judgment, the practices were legal or illegal under federal law.

Compared to asking the question, "Is it legal or illegal when renting an apartment to discriminate on the basis of race?" the use of scenarios involving descriptions of situations, actions and bases, and explanations as to why the actions were taken, provide a more nuanced and authentic way to assess how well the general public understands what the nation's fair housing law bans or permits. Figure 4.1 describes the procedure, while the exact wording of the unlawful scenarios appears in the appendix.

Brief scenarios describing the actions listed below were read to respondents.

- A landlord:
  - Assigning families with children to a particular building
  - Excluding families with children from a particular building
  - Disapproving construction of a wheelchair ramp
  - Disapproving a rental based on mental illness
  - Disapproving a rental based on religion
  - Advertising a religious preference for an apartment.
- A real estate agent limiting a buyer's housing search based on neighborhood racial composition.
- An owner, working through a real estate agent, restricting a home sale based on race.
- A mortgage lender requiring a higher down payment based on ethnicity

Respondents were asked, separately, if they: (a) agreed with them and (b) believed them to be legal under Federal law.

To protect against the scenarios and questions appearing too test-like, obvious, or patterned, a number of precautions were taken. Respondents were asked whether they agreed with the actions (where there are no right or wrong answers) before being asked whether the actions were legal, to avoid the appearance of simply testing them. The wording of the scenarios included justifications or intentions for each action that did not involve blatant prejudice, which could have biased respondents' opinions or more obviously signaled the illegality of the actions—all of which were illegal regardless of the motivations involved. Finally, two questions that did not depict illegal actions were also included to help avoid the occurrence of a response "set" where respondents might sense a pattern or strive for consistency as opposed to giving their best answer.

Figure 4. 1. Method for measuring consumer fair housing knowledge.

Although the 2005 survey posed nine scenarios depicting illegal practices, the 2000–2001 survey posed only eight of them—it did not contain the scenario describing exclusion of families with children from a rental building. Because the 2005 data are compared with those of 2000–2001 later in this chapter, only the eight that were in both surveys are used in this analysis at this point. In addition, it should be noted that respondents were also asked about two lawful practices, one involving an apartment building owner disapproving a rental because an applicant did not have good housekeeping habits and the other involving a mortgage denial to an African American applicant who did not have a steady job or enough income to pay a monthly mortgage payment. Responses to those questions are reported elsewhere, but not here (Abravanel and Cunningham 2002; Abravanel 2006).

Results from the 2005 survey, as shown in table 4.1, confirm what was found in 2000–2001 with respect to variation in consumer understanding: awareness of fair housing law ranged from substantial to modest, depending on the practices and bases in question. The scenario about which there was the greatest knowledge of the law deals with home selling prohibitions involving race. Other scenario depictions that were better understood involved ethnicity or religion, and included both home buying and rental transactions. Less-well-understood scenarios concerned advertising a religious preference, real estate steering based on race, and rental bias based on mental disability. Finally, practices least well understood as unlawful involved differential treatment of renter families with children and opposition to construction of a wheelchair ramp for a renter with a disability.

Notable in table 4.1 is the fact that between 19 and 56 percent of the public, as of 2005, were not aware of one or another aspect of what the law prohibits or what treatment is required. Equally relevant is the observation that some affected populations—such as individuals in households with children or with disabled persons—are often no more likely than the general population to be aware that certain practices that could affect them are illegal.

In sum, there are clearly aspects of the law where the public needs further information, and these data suggest that lack of awareness could be part of the explanation for lower rates of perceived, as opposed to actual, discrimination. Nonetheless, awareness is generally widespread enough such that lack of knowledge, alone, is unlikely to be the primary explanation.

Public Responses to Suspected Discrimination

While all persons suspecting they have experienced housing discrimination have the option of filing a formal complaint, the fact is that four of every five

Table 4.1. Awareness of Illegal Practices by Scenario

Percent Correctly Identifying the Practice as Illegal

Scenarios Depicting Illegal Discrimination	*Total**	*African Americans***	*Hispanics***	*Households with Families with Children***	*Households with Persons with Disabilities***
Assigning families with children to a particular building	44%	50%	55%***	44%	43%
Excluding families with children from a particular building	61%	65%	74%***	63%	64%
Disapproving construction of wheelchair ramp	54%	53%	55%	57%	58%
Limiting housing search based on neighborhood racial composition	58%	67%***	68%***	60%	60%
Disapproving rental based on mental illness	60%	57%	71%***	64%	64%
Advertising a religious preference for an apartment	62%	68%	68%	61%	61%
Requiring higher down payment for a home loan based on ethnicity	70%	68%	87%***	81%	77%
Disapproving rental to a person based on religion	77%	79%	94%***	88%	88%
Restricting home sale to white buyers only	81%	85%	88%***	85%	82%
Number of Respondents	1,029	404	399	404	475

*Includes the national sample only.
**Includes respondents from the national sample plus a supplemental sample of this subgroup.
***The chi-square test of differences between subgroup and the total population is significant at $P \leq 0.05$.

Table 4.2. Responses to Perceived Discrimination

Responses to Perceived Discrimination	*Percent*
Did nothing	80%
Complained to the person discriminating	9
Complained to someone else	3
Talked to/hired a lawyer/filed a lawsuit	2
Sought help from/filed complaint with a fair housing/other group	1
Filed a complaint with a government agency	1
Did something else	6
Don't know/not sure/no answer	1
Total	103%*
Number of respondents	78

*Multiple responses were permitted.

persons who perceived discrimination took no action at all in response—a proportion that is virtually identical to the 83 percent obtained in the 2000–2001 survey. Of the minority of persons who did act, the predominant response was not to file a complaint with the federal government but to complain to the person thought to be discriminating or to someone else. (See table 4.2.)

Only 4 percent of the actions taken in response to perceived discrimination involved talking to or hiring a lawyer, or seeking help from or filing a complaint with a fair housing group, another group, or a government agency. Since that is fundamental to the enforcement process, it is important to ask why the complaint-filing rate is so small and marginal.

Possible Reasons for Not Taking Action

Inasmuch as the 2000–2001 fair housing survey had revealed a low rate of consumer response, the 2005 survey sought to learn more about this intriguing pattern of inaction. As possible explanations, the survey inquired about consumer knowledge of the fair housing complaint system and the extent of consumer optimism regarding the benefits of filing a complaint with the federal government.

Most members of the general public have had no firsthand experience with the fair housing complaint system, yet some basic conception of that system is a logical prerequisite to taking formal action (see chapter 11 by Goering). This includes having some idea, or being able to deduce, where to go for help, how to file a complaint, knowing if there is any cost to doing so, and appreciating how long it might take to resolve a complaint. Knowing what kind of judgment or relief could be expected could also be a normal part of the motivation to file a complaint. Lack of understanding or misinformation about such matters would likely impede consumer responses and help to explain the low proportion of filed complaints.

The survey reveals that consumer impressions of the fair housing complaint system are uneven, although there is considerable recognition of the basics. Over three-fourths of the public acknowledges they could go to a lawyer or to a state or local government agency for assistance in dealing with housing discrimination. Over 60 percent understand they can go to a private nonprofit group or the federal government for help. While there is some confusion as to which federal agency has responsibility for investigating housing discrimination (indeed, some believe the Departments of Commerce, Homeland Security, and Agriculture have such responsibility), the large majority (90 percent) recognizes HUD as having enforcement authority. At most, therefore, inaccurate or limited knowledge regarding where to go for help can only partially explain a failure to take action.

Although consulting with a private attorney on housing discrimination issues could potentially be expensive, there is no cost to filing a housing discrimination complaint with HUD or other fair housing agencies. This is not universally known, however. Compared to 35 percent of the public who believe it would cost nothing to complain, 55 presumed there would be at least some monetary cost involved, including 26 percent who supposed it would cost a considerable amount of money.[8] While the latter individuals, in particular, might well decide not to file a complaint based on that misinformation, the proportion of the population thinking costs would be very high is not itself sufficient to explain the minuscule rate of complaint filing.

Finally, believing it would take a long time to resolve a complaint could also be a disincentive to filing one (see chapter 7 by Schill).[9] Public estimates as to how long the process would take vary widely, with many expecting it to take quite some time (see table 4.3). Roughly 60 percent believe it could take

Table 4.3. Anticipated Time Respondents Think It Would Take to Get a Fair Housing Complaint Resolved if Filed with a Federal Agency

Anticipated Time	*Total Sample*
A week	2%
A month	7
One to 6 months	20
More than 6, to 12 months	31
More than 12 months	32
Don't know/no answer	8
Total	100%
Number of Respondents	1029

Table 4.4. Respondent Expectation of Likelihood of Accomplishing Good Results if Filing a Fair Housing Complaint with a Federal Agency

Likelihood of Accomplishing Good Results	*Total Sample*
Very likely	13%
Somewhat likely	55
Not likely	19
Maybe/possibly/it depends/don't know/no answer	13
Total	100%
Number of Respondents	1029

more than six months to over a year to achieve a final resolution, a belief that could certainly dissuade some persons.

Consumer Expectations about the Likely Benefits of Filing a Complaint

Aside from any effects that consumer understanding of the complaint system may have on behavior, failure to respond to perceived discrimination could also be a function of the anticipated results of taking action. On this score the evidence is extraordinary: only 13 percent of the public thinks good outcomes would *very* likely happen from filing a fair housing complaint with the federal government; the majority believes good results to be only *somewhat* likely (see table 4.4).[10] African Americans and Hispanics are somewhat more optimistic than the public at large in this respect, but still, only about one in five such persons assumes good results would be *very* likely. Presumably, such low expectations dampen consumer inclination to take action.

Self-expressed Reasons for Not Taking Action

Having established that response rates to perceived discrimination are extremely low, and having considered whether this might be explained by lack of consumer understanding of the fair housing complaint system or pessimistic expectations regarding results, it is important to know how consumers themselves explained their inaction. As in the 2000–2001 survey, many respondents to the 2005 survey attributed it to an expected low benefit to them.

As table 4.5 shows, a typical reason for not taking action involved expectations regarding results—that it would not have been worth it or helped: nearly two-thirds of all responses were in this category. Other reasons involved perceived attributes of the complaint system: 11 percent of the re-

Table 4.5. Respondents' Self-expressed Rationale for Not Taking Action in Response to Perceived Housing Discrimination

Reasons for Not Responding	*Percent of Responses*
Expectations regarding results:	
• Not worth it	49%
• Would not help	15
Understanding of the fair housing complaint system:	
• Didn't know where to complain	11
• Thought it would cost too much	5
• Might take too much time	4
Personal reasons:	
• Too busy	5
• Afraid of being retaliated against	8
Unsure whether discrimination occurred	2
Other reasons	23
Total	122%*
Number of Respondents	63

*Multiple responses were permitted.

sponses indicated consumers did not know where to file a complaint, for example. Some said they were too busy to take action, and others feared there would be some retaliation against them. Two percent of the responses indicated uncertainty as to whether discrimination had occurred as a reason for inaction. That, conceivably, reflected either a lack of understanding of the law or the fact that the discrimination was not practiced in a way that was directly observable or easily recognizable by consumers.

IMPROVING CONSUMER RESPONSE TO HOUSING DISCRIMINATION

To this point, the 2005 fair housing survey in conjunction with other evidence allows two important observations: there is a higher rate of housing discrimination against some groups, such as Hispanics and persons with disabilities, than there are subjective perceptions of discrimination on the part of such persons; and, overall, there are fewer housing discrimination complaints filed than there are subjective perceptions of housing discrimination. Having considered some of the reasons for the latter and also having learned that public awareness of fair housing law is uneven, it is reasonable to ask what might be done to improve consumer response—especially filing complaints. Logical

Table 4.6. Respondents' Expectation of the Likelihood They Would Take Action in Response to Future Housing Discrimination

Likelihood of Responding	*Total Sample*
Very likely	41%
Somewhat likely	25
Not likely	24
Maybe/possibly/depends	5
Don't know/no answer	5
Total	100%
Number of Respondents	1,029

possibilities would be to raise public expectations about the likely results of taking action, to deal with the second observation, and to enhance public awareness of fair housing law, to deal with both of them. Although these are desirable objectives, evidence regarding the extent to which raising expectations or awareness will pay off in terms of consumer behavior is mixed.

The 2005 survey offers empirical support for the presumption that persons would be more predisposed to take action, such as filing a complaint with a government agency, if they believed its outcome would likely be positive. Initially, at any rate, this suggests the value of raising public expectations. The data shown in tables 4.6–4.8 indicate what all respondents, regardless of whether or not they had experienced housing discrimination in the past, said they would do if they faced discrimination in the future.

In sharp contrast to the small proportion of persons who took action when treated unfairly in the past, two-thirds of the public claimed they would take some action in the future if confronted with biased treatment; indeed, 41 percent said they would be *very* likely to take action (table 4.6).[11] Of those *somewhat* or *very* likely to take action, the majority claimed they would consult with a lawyer, file a lawsuit, seek help from a (fair housing) group, or seek help from or complain to a government agency (table 4.7). All of these actions go beyond simply complaining to the person thought to be discriminating, which was the predominant action taken by those perceiving discrimination in the past. And, fully two-thirds of those who expected that filing a complaint would have a good outcome said they would *very* likely take some action, compared to less than one-fourth of those who did not anticipate such results (table 4.8).

Do these findings mean that if expectation of good results were more prevalent, consumers would be more inclined to take action when faced with housing discrimination? Possibly, but the connection is apparently not that simple. Not only are there contradictions between the proportions of persons

Table 4.7. Respondents' Anticipated Responses to Future Housing Discrimination, by Likelihood of Responding to Future Housing Discrimination

Anticipated Responses to Future Housing Discrimination	*Likelihood of Responding to Future Housing Discrimination*	
	Very Likely	*Somewhat Likely*
Complain to person thought to be discriminating	28%	31%
Consult a lawyer/file a lawsuit	44	28
Seek help from a (fair housing) group	17	17
Seek help/file complaint with government agency	26	18
Other	16	14
Total*	131%	108%
Number of Respondents	424	256

*Total equals more than 100 percent because multiple responses were permitted.

who claimed they would take future action and those having taken past action, and between the kinds of actions they said they would take and the kinds actually taken, but some 46 percent of those reporting they *had* experienced discrimination *and had done nothing about it* also assert they would *very* likely take action in the future. For many people, there appears to be an inconsistency between what they say they would do in response to perceived discrimination and what they actually do when faced with it, suggesting that the former is not a particularly reliable predictor of the latter (see table 4.9). Although the evidence is not entirely compelling because of the small number of respondents to the 2005 survey who perceived discrimination, the

Table 4.8. Respondents' Expectation of the Likelihood They Would Take Action in Response to Future Housing Discrimination, by Expected Likelihood that Filing a Complaint Would Accomplish Good Results*

Self-expressed Likelihood of Responding to Future Housing Discrimination	*Expectation that Filing a Complaint Would Accomplish Good Results***		
	Very Likely	*Somewhat Likely*	*Not Likely*
Very likely	66%	46%	23%
Somewhat likely	16	29	21
Not likely	11	19	46
Maybe/possibly/it depends/don't know/no answer	8	6	11
Total	101%**	100%	101%**
Number of Respondents	133	570	200

*The chi-square test is significant at $P \leq 0.05$.
**Percentage does not total to 100 due to rounding error.

Table 4.9. Respondents' Likelihood of Responding to Future Housing Discrimination, by Response to Past Perceived Discrimination*

Likelihood of Responding to Future Housing Discrimination	*Response to Past Perceived Discrimination*	
	Did Something	*Did Nothing*
Very likely	(62%)	46%
Somewhat likely	(13)	16
Not likely	(17)	31
Maybe/possibly/depends	(8)	6
Don't know/no answer	—	1
Total	(100%)	100%
Number of Respondents	15	63

*The difference is not significant at $P \leq 0.05$.

same conclusion applies when examining the relationship between consumer expectations about results and actual behavior. There is no statistically significant difference with respect to whether action was taken between those expecting good results from filing a complaint and those not (see table 4.10).[12]

In sum, while both consumer predisposition to take action and consumer confidence that doing so will result in good outcomes seem to be logical precursors to action, the survey evidence suggests that neither is especially predictive of whether action is actually taken. Therefore, while efforts to improve both the complaint process and public confidence in its results are desirable, these may not by themselves be sufficient to motivate the kind of consumer response enabled and envisaged by the Fair Housing Act.

Table 4.10. Responses to Perceived Discrimination, by Respondents' Expectation that Filing a Complaint Would Accomplish Good Results

Responses to Perceived Discrimination	*Expectation that Filing A Complaint Would Accomplish Good Results**	
	Very Likely	*Not/Somewhat Likely*
Did something	(24%)	17%
Did nothing	(71)	83
Don't Know	(5)	—
Total	(100%)	100%
Number of Respondents	14	60

*The difference is not significant at $P \leq 0.05$.

Implications of Improving Consumer Awareness of Fair Housing Law

Is improved public knowledge of the law likely to stimulate more consumer action, presumably by allowing at least observable discriminatory practices to be spotted? And, what are the prospects for improving awareness?

Data from both the 2000–2001 and 2005 surveys speak to these questions by allowing for measurement of the level of consumer awareness of fair housing law and comparison of awareness levels with both consumer predisposition to take action and consumer behavior. They also permit examination of changes in awareness over time. The data are somewhat encouraging with respect to the relationship between awareness and behavior, but less so with respect to prospects for improving awareness.

To measure the level of consumer awareness, responses to questions about the legality of practices in the scenarios described above were combined into an index showing how many illegal actions each respondent could identify.[13] In 2005, about one-half of the public recognized that at least six of eight unlawful practices were illegal, indicative of a higher level of knowledge in comparison to 16 percent who recognized only two or fewer instances.[14]

With respect to the relationships between level of awareness and both consumer predisposition to take action and actual behavior, persons with higher levels of knowledge were somewhat more likely than others to say they would take assertive action, and also somewhat more likely to have taken action when faced with discrimination (Abravanel 2002). While the small sample size of persons perceiving discrimination warrants treating the latter relationship as only suggestive, better informed persons were over two and one-half times as likely to have taken action in response to perceived discrimination than those who were less well informed. But, even among those with high levels of fair housing knowledge, less than one in four persons took any kind of action (Abravanel 2002). It is because of these types of associations, in addition to the sensible notion that housing consumers ought to be well informed about fair housing law, that fair housing agencies and advocates have been working to improve consumer knowledge of the law, and that HUD has provided funding for this purpose.

Efforts to enhance public awareness were under way well before the 2000–2001 survey and have continued since that time, including a variety of outreach and education programs conducted by state and local fair housing entities. Beyond those, the nonprofit Ad Council, in conjunction with the Leadership Conference on Civil Rights Education Fund, the National Fair Housing Alliance, and HUD, initiated a substantial public service advertising campaign in 2003 to try to improve public sensitivity to fair housing issues. The council aired a series of fair housing ads on television, cable, and radio over one million times in English and over twelve thousand times in Spanish as well as placed ads in the print media, equivalent to $38 million in advertising costs.

One of the ads, "Accents," depicted a man making multiple phone calls inquiring about the availability of an advertised apartment—using different names and accents for each call to indicate he was, variously, Hispanic, Indian, African American, Chinese, Vietnamese, and so on. Each time he was told the apartment was not available. Then, when using a name and accent suggesting he was white, he was told the apartment was still available. A second ad, "Do You Still Like Me?" involved a man saying he had a good job, salary, and credit history, and asking, "Would you rent your place to me?" Then he asks, "What if I have an accent, or a last name that sounds foreign? What if I have a disability? What if I am a single parent? Would you steer me away? Would you close the door?"[15] Tracking surveys indicated that 18 percent of the public recalled having seen, heard, or read something about reporting housing discrimination during and immediately following the campaign, suggesting reasonably wide coverage.[16]

While the ad campaign did not attempt to improve the level of public knowledge of fair housing law as such, it was a major part of the fair housing education effort that occurred between the 2000–2001 and 2005 surveys, and the only effort that sought a wide audience across the nation. It is reasonable, then, to ask if public knowledge of the law improved between 2000–2001 and 2005—whether as a function of the ad campaign, other educational efforts, or other "inputs."

As measured by the two surveys' awareness questions and the indexes derived from them, the evidence is somewhat mixed and not especially encouraging. Although a larger proportion of the public in 2005 than in 2000–2001 knew both that a real estate agent could not restrict a client's search for housing based on neighborhood racial composition, and that an apartment owner could not treat families with children differently from others, a smaller proportion knew that advertising a tenant preference based on religion was illegal (see table 4.11). No statistically significant differences are observed between 2000–2001 and 2005 for the remaining five scenarios or for the awareness indexes (see table 4.12).

In both surveys the median index score was six, meaning that one-half of the public knew the law with respect to six or more of the scenario depictions and that the level of public awareness had not changed since 2000–2001. Of interest, also, is the fact that in 2005 there is no statistically significant difference in awareness level between persons who recalled having seen or heard an ad dealing with housing discrimination and those who had not.[17]

Table 4.11. Respondents' Awareness of Illegal Practices, by Scenario and Year

Scenarios Depicting Illegal Discrimination	*2000–2001*	*2005*
Assigning families with children to a particular building	38%	44%*
Disapproving construction of wheelchair ramp	56%	54%
Limiting housing search based on neighborhood racial composition	54%	58%*
Disapproving rental based on mental illness	57%	60%
Advertising a religious preference for an apartment	67%	62%*
Requiring higher down payment for a home loan based on ethnicity	73%	70%
Disapproving rental to a person based on religion	78%	77%
Restricting home sale to white buyers only	81%	81%
Number of Respondents	1,001	1,029

*The chi-square test is significant at $P \leq 0.05$.

Lack of improvement in fair housing knowledge is somewhat paradoxical in light of the fact that public *support* for fair housing law has slowly but steadily improved over time, including between 2000–2001 and 2005. For example, survey respondents were asked if they approved or disapproved of the (unlawful) practices posed in the various scenarios—disapproval constituting support for fair housing law. On an individual, scenario-by-scenario basis, support increased between 2000–2001 and 2005 in five of the eight scenarios (see table 4.13). Indeed, it increased by as much as nine percentage points with respect to opposing restrictions of home sales based on race, and eight percentage points in the case of real estate agents limiting a client's home search based on neighborhood racial composition. Smaller, yet statistically significant increases occurred with respect to differential treatment of families with children, advertising a religious preference for an apartment, and rental discrimination based on religion.[18]

When the individual items are combined into an index measuring the extent of public support, the share of the public expressing support in six or more of

Table 4.12. Extent of Public Awareness of Fair Housing Law, by Year*

Extent of Awareness	*2000–2001*	*2005*
Low	16%	15%
Medium	33	35
High	51	50
Total	100%	100%
Number of Respondents	1001	1029

*The chi-square test is not significant at $P \leq 0.05$.

Table 4.13. Public Attitudes about Fair Housing Law—Percent Supporting Each Provision, by Scenario and Year

	Percent Indicating Support	
Scenarios Depicting Illegal Discrimination	*2000-2001*	*2005*
Placement of renter families with children in a particular building	36%	42%*
Limiting real estate search for a white buyer to white-only areas	63%	71%*
Opposing construction of wheelchair ramp for a renter with disabilities	67%	64%
Disapproval of a rental to a person with mental illness	62%	64%
Advertising "Christians preferred" for a rental	58%	63%*
Requiring a higher down payment for a home loan based on ethnicity	84%	85%
Disapproval of a rental to a person based on religion	84%	87%*
Restricting a home sale to white buyers only	79%	88%*
Number of Respondents	1,001	1,029

*The chi-square test is significant at $P \leq 0.05$.

the hypothetical scenarios changed from 66 percent in 2000–2001 to 73 percent by 2005 (see table 4.14). The median score also increased from six to seven, meaning that by 2005 about one-half of the public supported the law in seven or more of the scenario depictions as compared to six in 2000–2001.[19]

There are additional indications that increased support for fair housing law between 2000–2001 and 2005 is part of a long-term trend. A question repeatedly asked since the early 1970s on the National Opinion Research Center's General Social Survey (GSS) dealing with the acceptability of open-housing laws as applied to home sales revealed that about six in ten white Americans would not support such laws in the 1970s compared to about three in ten by the late 1990s (Abravanel and Cunningham 2002; see chapter 11 by Goering). And, a similar item included in the fair housing surveys show results consis-

Table 4.14. Extent of Public Support for Fair Housing Law, by Year*

Extent of Support	*2000–2001*	*2005*
Low	6%	3%
Medium	28	24
High	66	73
Total	100%	100%
Number of Respondents	1001	1029

*The chi-square test is significant at $P \leq 0.05$.

tent with this trend (Abravanel, 2006).[20] While the GSS survey dealt specifically with home sales based on the race of the buyer, the fair housing surveys expanded the question to include sales based on religion and nationality as well. The surveys show a statistically significant three-percentage-point decline between 2000–2001 and 2005 in the acceptance of discriminatory home sales practices (from 24 percent to 21 percent of the adult public), and a comparable increase in support for nondiscriminatory prohibitions (from 67 percent to 70 percent).

Interestingly, of respondents who were able to recall something specific about a housing discrimination ad they had recently seen, heard, or read, 82 percent supported an open-housing law, compared to 68 percent for those who were not able to recall any such ad. This difference is statistically significant.[21] That the Ad Council's campaign could have had a positive impact on this aspect of public support for fair housing law is certainly a possibility, although it is also possible that those who supported open-housing laws were more likely than others to be inclined to recall an ad supporting nondiscrimination in housing.

CONCLUSION

The fair housing surveys conducted in 2000–2001 and 2005 were the first to examine systematically the attitudes of the public regarding a wide range of fair housing law and law-enforcement-related issues. They not only describe the status of public knowledge and support for the law but, also, crucially identify some paradoxes or puzzles that are relevant for fair housing analysis and policymaking. The surveys highlight the need to better understand the intersection of fair housing enforcement, public attitudes, and the role of fair housing education programs.

A central limitation with respect to fair housing enforcement is the low rate of filing complaints. Testing research has shown higher levels of disparate treatment in housing markets than there are fair housing complaints, suggesting either consumer unawareness of the disparate treatment or victim passivity when discrimination is suspected. The surveys show that the latter is not an insignificant part of the explanation and suggest some core reasons for inaction—involving consumer understanding of the fair housing complaint system, predilections with respect to taking action, and expectations about the probable results of doing so. The survey data also imply that there are critical doubts about the relevance of the consumer-initiated enforcement process and its potential helpfulness on the part of many alleged victims of housing discrimination and, as well, on the part of the public at large. As such, the results provide both new insights into the perceived utility of civil rights law as well as useful information for considering how to motivate a better consumer response.

Equally useful from a programmatic perspective is the observation that public support for fair housing law continued to improve while overall awareness of the law did not improve between 2000–2001 and 2005. Knowing that awareness outcomes were unchanged following a reasonably energetic public service advertising campaign, albeit one not designed to enhance awareness in the way it is measured by the fair housing surveys, signals that a different strategy may be necessary for increasing consumer knowledge than for boosting public support. These findings suggest that serious attempts to improve consumer knowledge of the fair housing complaint system, and confidence in its use, are likely to require significant resources as well as a more coordinated, focused, and sustained education program than is currently under way.

Future research evaluating fair housing enforcement should continue to survey the public to track trends in knowledge, support, and behavior. It should also include additional methods to learn more about consumers' reasoning when faced with housing discrimination, including the choices considered and rationale for action or inaction. And such research should more rigorously evaluate the efficacy of national and local fair housing education programs to ensure the funds and energies spent on them are producing desired results.

APPENDIX: SURVEY SCENARIOS DEPICTING ILLEGAL PRACTICES UNDER FEDERAL LAW

#	Scenario	Wording
1	Assigning families with children to a particular building	An apartment building owner who rents to people of all age groups decides that families with younger children can only rent in one particular building, and not in others, because younger children tend to make lots of noise and may bother other tenants.
2	Excluding families with children from a particular building	An owner of an apartment complex containing three large buildings has rented to families with children in all three buildings for many years. Recently, at one of the buildings, several tenants without children complained that children in the building were too loud. They asked the owner not to rent to any more families with children in that building. The owner agreed, saying he would not rent to families with children from that point on. Later, when a family with children contacts the owner to

#	Scenario	Wording
		find out if any apartments are available for rent, the only vacant apartment is in that building. So, the landlord replies that there is nothing for them to rent at the time.
3	Disapproving construction of a wheelchair ramp	An apartment building owner is renting to a tenant who uses a wheelchair. The building is old and does not have a wheelchair ramp, and the tenant wants a small wooden ramp constructed at the building door to more easily access the building. He asks the owner if it is okay to build the ramp. The tenant says he will pay all the costs and agrees to have the ramp removed at his own expense when he leaves. The owner, however, believes such a ramp will not look good on his building and decides he does not want it constructed on his property.
4	Advertising a religious preference for an apartment	An apartment building owner places a notice on a community bulletin board to find a tenant for a vacant apartment. This notice says, "Christians preferred."
5	Disapproving rental based on mental illness	In checking references on an application for a vacant apartment, an apartment building owner learns that the applicant has a history of mental illness. Although the applicant is not a danger to anyone, the owner does not want to rent to such a person.
6	Disapproving rental to a person based on religion	An apartment building owner learns that an applicant for a vacant apartment has a different religion than all the other tenants in the building. Believing the other tenants would object, the owner does not want to rent to such a person.
7	Restricting home sales to white buyers only	The next question involves a family selling their house through a real estate agent. They are white, and have only white neighbors. Some of the neighbors tell the family that, if a nonwhite person buys the house, there would be trouble for that buyer. Not wanting to make it difficult for a buyer, the family tells the real estate agent they will sell their house only to a white buyer.
8	Limiting a housing search based on neighborhood racial composition	A white family looking to buy a house goes to a real estate agent and asks about the availability of houses within their price range. Assuming the family would only want to buy in areas where white people live, the agent decides to show them only houses in all-white neighborhoods, even though there are many houses in their price range in other parts of the community.

(*continued*)

#	Scenario	Wording
9	Requiring a higher down payment for a home based on ethnicity	A Hispanic family goes to a bank to apply for a home mortgage. The family qualifies for a mortgage but, in that bank's experience, Hispanic borrowers have been less likely than others to repay their loans. For that reason, the loan officer requires that the family make a higher down payment than would be required of other borrowers before agreeing to give the mortgage.

NOTES

1. The act prohibits discrimination with respect to most kinds of housing transactions—including rentals, home sales, mortgage lending, home improvement, and zoning—based on race, color, national origin, religion, sex, familial status, and disability. It confers primary authority and responsibility for administering as well as enforcing its provisions on the Secretary of HUD. HUD (or a state agency in cases where state or local laws are substantially equivalent to the federal Fair Housing Act) investigates allegations of discrimination. If conciliation efforts are not successful following a complaint and the investigation indicates that reasonable cause exists to believe a discriminatory practice has occurred, HUD (or a state agency, if the matter is brought under substantially equivalent laws) can file formal charges resulting in an administrative hearing or trial at no cost to the complainant. Either a HUD attorney (when the HUD process is pursued) or a state representative (when a case is filed with the state) represents the complainant in a hearing before one of HUD's administrative law judges or the equivalent state process. Prevailing complainants could be entitled to injunctive relief, compensatory damages, or punitive damages. Within the HUD process, a complainant or respondent may elect to have the case heard in federal district court, where the U.S. Department of Justice (DOJ) represents the complainant. The Fair Housing Act also permits the HUD secretary to initiate an action where information suggests that a discriminatory housing practice may have occurred, and authorizes the U.S. Department of Justice to file a civil action in cases where there is a pattern or practice of discrimination or an issue of general public importance. In such circumstances, injunctive relief may be obtained but not monetary damages or penalties of any kind. Decisions of administrative law judges and the federal district court are subject to a review by the U.S. court of appeals. Beyond the Fair Housing Act of 1968, other fair housing protections derive from the Civil Rights Act of 1866, Title VI of the Civil Rights Act of 1964, the Age Discrimination Act of 1975, Executive Order 11063 (Nondiscrimination), Executive Order 12892 (Equal Opportunity in Housing), Executive Order 12898 (Environmental Justice), Section 504 of the Rehabilitation Act of 1973 (as amended), Title II of the Americans with Disabilities Act of 1990 (ADA), the Equal Credit Opportunity Act, and the Architectural Barriers Act of 1968.

2. Unless otherwise indicated, the data reported in this chapter rely on the cross-sectional survey and not the supplemental samples.

3. While some states and localities provide for additional protected classes beyond those included in the Fair Housing Act, this analysis considers only bases defined by the federal act.

4. In some instances, the Civil Rights Act of 1866 or Title VI of the Civil Rights Act of 1964 may cover discrimination that took place prior to enactment of the Fair Housing Act; that was also taken into account.

5. The comparable figure for the 2000–2001 survey was 14 percent, but the difference between the two surveys is not statistically significant at $P \leq 0.05$.

6 Since multiple responses were permitted, the sum of responses is 133 percent ($n = 78$), including 2 percent of respondents who did not answer the question and 18 percent of responses consisting of reasons not covered by the Fair Housing Act. While respondents in this group gave at least one response involving bases enumerated in the act, some also gave other reasons as well. This is either because they perceived multiple reasons for the unfair treatment, only some of which fell within the terms of the law, or because they believed they had experienced discrimination multiple times. Although asked to describe only the most recent such experience, it is conceivable they provided reasons that covered multiple occurrences.

7. These data are based on the randomly drawn national sample plus supplemental samples of each of the subgroups. Persons perceiving discrimination based on familial status or disability that occurred prior to 1990 are excluded from these figures.

8. Ten percent were not sure or did not answer when asked about the costs of filing a complaint.

9. The Fair Housing Act requires HUD to investigate complaints within 100 days of filing unless it is impracticable to do so. After such an investigation is completed, HUD determines if there is either "reasonable cause" or "no reasonable cause" to believe that discrimination has occurred. If reasonable cause is established, it is at that point that HUD issues a formal charge of discrimination and brings the complaint before an administrative law judge on behalf of the complainant.

10. The question was, "How likely do you think it is that filing such a complaint would accomplish good results?"

11. The question was, "Suppose, in the future, you believed you were being discriminated against when you went to buy or rent a house or apartment. How likely is it that you would do something about it?"

12. At $P \leq 0.05$, using the chi-square test.

13. As indicated, the 2005 survey included nine such scenarios, but one of them had not previously been asked in 2000–2001. Therefore, the data examined here use eight scenarios.

14. HUD's FY 2004 Annual Performance Plan (APP) established as a goal for the year 2006 raising the level of public awareness of fair housing law beyond the level observed in the 2000–2001 survey (HUD 2003b). Although it established a performance target, subsequent years' APPs continued to seek improvement but did not include a target (HUD 2004: 2–97). Likewise, improvement in public awareness of fair housing law is one of HUD's strategic objectives (HUD 2003a: 35).

15. Also, in April 2005, during the time in which the 2005 survey was being conducted, the Ad Council launched a new series of radio and print ads involving more than fifteen thousand outlets, which donated in excess of $50 million in advertising time and space for the campaign. It features the tagline, "Fair Housing. It's not an option. It's the law."

16. Awareness of the ads increased over time from 4 percent to 23 percent for one of the ads, "Accents," and from 3 percent to 17 percent for another, "Do You Still Like Me?" Also, awareness of the Fair Housing Act increased from 67 percent to 74 percent between the pre- and post-ad period, and those who saw or heard the ads were more likely than those who did not to be aware of the Act—87 percent versus 70 percent. Likewise, 19 percent of adults contacted for the 2005 fair housing survey recalled having heard or seen an "advertisement about housing discrimination" over the past year or so, with 80 percent of this group able to say something specific about what they had heard (Millward Brown 2004).

17. At $P \leq 0.05$, using the chi-square test.

18. There was no difference in support between 2000–2001 and 2005 with respect to opposition to construction of a wheelchair ramp, opposition to renting to a person with mental illness, or charging a higher down payment due to ethnicity.

19. The chi-square test is significant at $P \leq 0.05$. While it is conceivable that the Ad Council's public service advertisements helped to increase the level of support for fair housing law, there is no statistically significant difference in support levels between persons who recalled having seen or heard such ads and those who did not.

20. The question asked in the fair housing surveys, similar to that used in the GSS surveys, was: "Suppose there's a community-wide vote on housing issues, and there are two possible laws to vote on. One law says that homeowners can decide for themselves whom to sell their house to, even if they prefer not to sell to people of a certain race, religion, or nationality. Another law says that homeowners cannot refuse to sell to someone because of their race religion, or nationality. Which law would you vote for?"

21. At $P \leq 0.05$, using the chi-square test.

REFERENCES

Abravanel, Martin D. 2002. "Public Knowledge of Fair Housing Law: Does it Protect against Housing Discrimination?" *Housing Policy Debate* 13:3.

Abravanel, Martin D. 2006. *Do We Know More Now? Trends in Public Knowledge, Support and Use of Fair Housing Law*. Washington, DC: U.S. Department of Housing and Urban Development.

Abravanel, Martin D., and Mary K. Cunningham. 2002. *How Much Do We Know? Public Awareness of the Nation's Fair Housing Laws*. Washington, DC: U.S. Department of Housing and Urban Development.

Fix, Michael, and Raymond J. Struyk. 1993. *Clear and Convincing Evidence: Measurement of Discrimination in America*. Washington, DC: Urban Institute Press.

Galster, George C. "The Evolving Challenges of Fair Housing since 1968: Open Housing, Integration, and the Reduction of Ghettoization," *Cityscape* 4:24–138.

HUD. 2003a. *Strategic Plan: FY 2003-FY 2008*. March. Washington, DC: U.S. Department of Housing and Urban Development.

HUD. 2003b. *FY 2004 Annual Performance Plan (APP)*. April. Washington, DC: U.S. Department of Housing and Urban Development.

HUD. 2004. *Performance and Accountability Report, FY 2004*. November. Washington, DC: U.S. Department of Housing and Urban Development.

HUD. 2005. *Fiscal Year 2006 Annual Performance Plan*. June. Washington, DC: U.S. Department of Housing and Urban Development.

HUD. N.d. *Fair Housing—It's Your Right*. Washington, DC: U.S. Department of Housing and Urban Development. www.hud.gov/offices/fheo/FHLaws/yourrights.cfm.

HUD. N.d. *Fair Housing Laws and Presidential Executive Orders*. Washington, DC: U.S. Department of Housing and Urban Development. www.hud.gov/offices/fheo/FHLaws/index.cfm.

Millward Brown. 2004. *Housing Discrimination Post Wave Tracking Report*, September. Santa Monica, CA: Millward Brown.

Turner, Margery Austin, and Carla Herbig. *Closing Doors on Americans' Housing Choices*, September 18, 2005. www.urban.org/url.cfm?ID=900853.

Turner, Margery Austin, Carla Herbig, Deborah Kaye, Julie Fenderson, and Diane Levy. 2005. *Discrimination against Persons with Disabilities: Barriers at Every Step*. Washington, DC: U.S. Department of Housing and Urban Development.

Turner, Margery Austin, and Stephen Ross. 2003. *Discrimination in Metropolitan Housing Markets, Phase 2, Asians and Pacific Islanders*. Washington, DC: U.S. Department of Housing and Urban Development.

Turner, Margery Austin, Stephen L. Ross, George C. Galster, and John Yinger. 2002. *Discrimination in Metropolitan Housing Markets: National Results from Phase I of HDS 2000: Final Report*. Washington, DC: U.S. Department of Housing and Urban Development.

5

Racial and Ethnic Residential Segregation and the Role of Socioeconomic Status, 1980–2000

John Iceland

Racial and ethnic residential segregation is a topic of wide concern, as residential patterns are both a cause and reflection of persisting racial divisions and inequalities in U.S. society. The 1980s and 1990s saw mixed patterns of change in racial and ethnic residential segregation. On the one hand, the segregation of blacks from whites decreased moderately over the period, suggesting decreasing levels of racial polarization. On the other hand, segregation of Hispanics and Asians from whites did not decline, and even increased slightly according to some measures. Researchers are still in the midst of disentangling the forces driving these patterns. Thus, the goal of this chapter is twofold. First is to describe in some detail the residential segregation of African Americans, Hispanics, Asians, and, to a lesser extent, American Indians from whites in U.S. metropolitan areas using the dissimilarity index. Second is to draw comparisons in patterns across these groups over time and by socioeconomic and demographic characteristics in order to provide insight into causes of the trends witnessed over the 1980 to 2000 period. I conclude with a brief discussion of alternative measures of segregation.

This analysis indicates that while racial divisions still tend to drive high levels of residential segregation between blacks and whites in particular, socioeconomic differences in residential patterns of all groups also play some role. In addition, high levels of immigration also have an effect on observed patterns of Asian and Hispanic residential segregation, suggesting an ongoing process of spatial assimilation.

BACKGROUND

Racial and ethnic residential segregation refers to the differential distribution of groups across space and is usually thought of in terms of the degree to which various groups reside in different neighborhoods. Two broad theoretical perspectives have been used to explain patterns and trends in residential segregation: spatial assimilation and place stratification (Charles 2003). According to the spatial assimilation model, which is often used to explain settlement patterns of immigrants or migrants, newcomers often settle in fairly homogeneous racial/ethnic enclaves within a given metropolitan area. This may be due to migrants feeling more comfortable with and welcomed by fellow ethnics, and the fact that minority members may simply not be able to afford to live in the same neighborhoods as more affluent whites (Pascal 1967; Clark 1986, 1988; Alba and Logan 1991; Massey and Mullan 1984). According to this model, individuals eventually convert socioeconomic gains over time into better housing, and this leads to higher levels of integration with whites.

In contrast to the spatial assimilation model, the place stratification perspective holds that a group's residential patterns and integration into society depends on the group's position in the social hierarchy (Charles 2003; White and Glick 1999). The dominant group—non-Hispanic whites—is at the top of the hierarchy, and other groups follow in some order, depending on prejudices and preferences of society at large. Negative stereotypes, for example, reduce openness to integration with certain groups (Bobo and Zubrinsky 1996; Farley et al. 1994), and blacks tend to be perceived in the most unfavorable terms (Bobo and Zubrinsky 1996; Farley et al. 1994; Charles 2000, 2001; Alba and Logan 1991; Zubrinsky and Bobo 1996).

Thus, many have argued that the spatial assimilation model simply does not hold for all groups, especially blacks, in part because prejudices lead not only to avoidance of particular groups but also to racial discrimination (Massey and Denton 1993; Yinger 1995; Meyer 2000; Goering and Wienk 1996; Massey and Mullan 1984; Alba and Logan 1991, 1993; Galster 1988), even if housing discrimination has declined modestly in recent years (Ross and Turner 2005). Discriminatory practices include racial steering by real estate agents, unfair mortgage lending patterns, and even in some cases physical attacks when moving into white neighborhoods.

Both theoretical perspectives have received some support from past research (e.g., Denton and Massey 1988; Massey and Fischer 1999; Iceland et al. 2005; Iceland and Lake 2005; Darden and Kamel 2000; St. John and Clymer 2000; Alba et al. 2000; Clark and Blue 2003; Fischer et al. 2004; White and Sassler 2000; Farley 1977). This study builds on previous ones in this area by comparing residential patterns of several race groups simultaneously using the most recent data available (the 2000 census) from all metropolitan areas in the U.S. and looking at change over a two-decade period. When examining socioeconomic differences, this analysis also uses a variety of measures of class—income, education, and occupation—and analyzes the role of nativity in 2000. Before moving on to the detailed examination of patterns and trends in segregation, the next section discusses the data and measures used in this study.

DATA AND METHODS

The data for this analysis were drawn from the 1980, 1990, and 2000 censuses. I calculated basic segregation indexes by race using census short-form data. For more detailed indexes that incorporated socioeconomic characteristics of groups, I used long-form data. Both datasets come from restricted (non-public-use) census files.

Residential segregation indexes usually measure the distribution of different groups across units within a larger area. This study, following the lead of most others, uses metropolitan areas as reasonable approximations of housing markets and uses census tracts as the unit of analysis (e.g., Iceland et al. 2002; Logan et al. 2004). Metropolitan areas are defined as having a large population center (sometimes two or more) with a high degree of economic and social integration with adjacent communities.[1] They generally contain at least fifty thousand people. Census tracts, which typically have between fifteen hundred and eight thousand people, with an average size of about four thousand people, are defined with local input and were designed to represent neighborhoods.

This study uses the dissimilarity index to measure residential patterns. The dissimilarity index is a measure of evenness, and it is also the most widely used segregation index. Dissimilarity, which ranges from 0 (complete integration) to 1 (complete segregation), measures the percentage of a group's population that would have to change residence for each neighborhood to have the same percentage of that group as the metropolitan area overall. A common rule of thumb is that dissimilarity scores over 0.6 are high, those from 0.3 to 0.6 are moderate, and those below 0.3 are low.

Measuring residential housing patterns usually requires choosing a reference group against which the housing patterns of other groups can be compared. In this analysis non-Hispanic whites are the reference group—a common selection (e.g., Iceland et al. 2002; Massey and Denton 1988), although not the only one possible. For 2000 data, when individuals could report more than one race, this analysis defines this group as consisting of individuals who designated white alone as their racial classification, and did not choose Hispanic as their ethnicity. For each of the other racial groups in the analysis, the indexes are calculated using anyone who designated a racial or ethnic group alone or in combination with another group (or groups).[2] Indexes are calculated for African Americans, Hispanics, Asians and Pacific Islanders, and American Indians and Alaska Natives. Asians and Pacific Islanders were combined into a single group in this analysis because of the very small number of Pacific Islanders in most metropolitan areas.

TRENDS IN RESIDENTIAL SEGREGATION BY RACE, 1980–2000

In 2002, the Census Bureau released a report entitled *Racial and Ethnic Residential Segregation in the United States: 1980–2000*. I was the lead author of that report for which the major findings were that:

1. Declines in African American segregation over the 1980 to 2000 period occurred across the various dimensions of segregation considered.
2. Despite these declines, residential segregation was still higher for African Americans than for the other groups across all measures. Hispanics were generally the next most highly segregated, followed by Asians and Pacific Islanders (API), and then American Indians and Alaska Natives (AIAN).
3. Asians and Pacific Islanders, as well as Hispanics, tended to experience increases in segregation. Increases were generally larger for Asians and Pacific Islanders than for Hispanics.

Figure 5.1 helps illustrate these findings. First, we see that the average dissimilarity score for African Americans declined from 0.727 in 1980 to 0.640 in 2000.[3] The 0.640 figure can be interpreted as indicating that about 64 percent of one group would have to move for all neighborhoods in the metropolitan area to have an equal proportion of African Americans. Dissimilarity for Hispanics increased very slightly from 0.502 to 0.509 over the same period, while the scores for Asians likewise increased slightly from 0.405 to 0.411. Dissimilarity scores for American Indians were the lowest for all groups and also decreased over the period, from 0.373 in 1980 to 0.333 in 2000.

Figure 5.2 illustrates findings in a different way by showing experiences of specific metropolitan areas. Only shown are metropolitan areas with at least 3 percent of 20,000 or more of the minority group in question as of 1980.

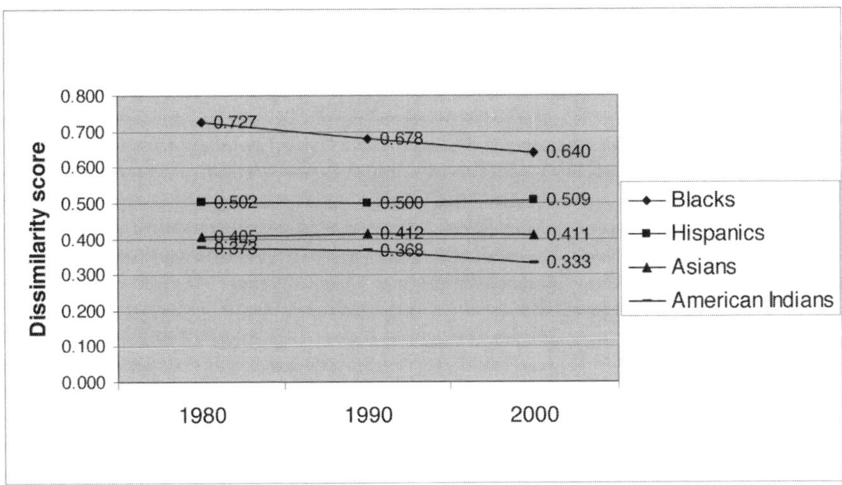

Figure 5.1. Dissimilarity Scores by Race, Hispanic Origin, and Year: 1980–2000. Source: Iceland et al. (2002). Scores represent weighted averages for all metropolitan areas.

Each symbol in figure 5.2 represents a dissimilarity score for a particular group in a particular metropolitan area. Symbols that lie below the 45-degree line are metropolitan areas that experienced decreases in segregation from 1980 to 2000. The figure again shows that segregation tended to be higher for African Americans than other groups, though African American scores tended to decline over the period while those of other groups often did not.

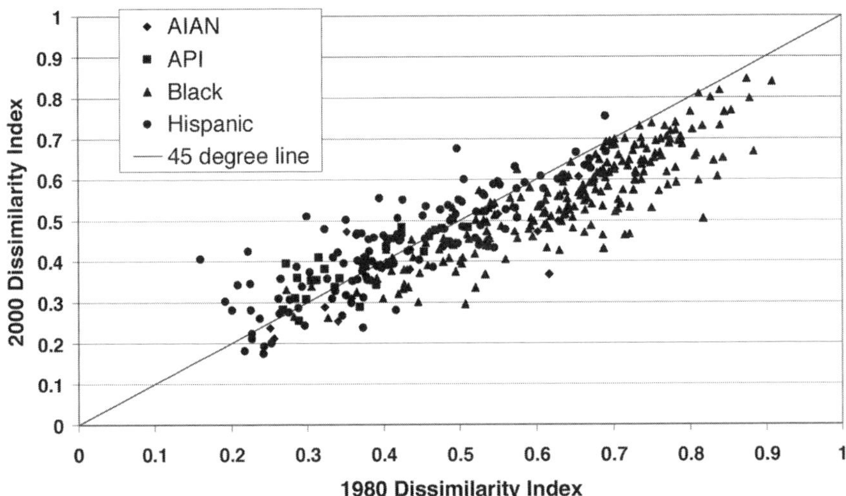

Figure 5.2. Dissimilarity Index (Evenness) for Selected Metropolitan Areas: 2000 by 1980. Source: Iceland et al. (2002).

A question remains whether these results indicate both decreasing polarization between whites and blacks and increasing racial/ethnic polarization between whites and Hispanics and Asians. The alternative explanation is that increasing levels of segregation for the latter groups are in part a function of the fact that continued immigration translates into a growth in ethnic enclaves, at least in the short run, as some research suggests (Portes and Rumbaut 1996; Iceland and Lake 2005; Iceland 2004). If so, the spatial assimilation model would predict that segregation is lower for both the native born of these groups and for those with greater socioeconomic resources who can translate their status into better—and perhaps more integrated—housing. These are the issues examined next.

RESIDENTIAL SEGREGATION BY SOCIOECONOMIC STATUS AND NATIVITY

The analysis here focuses on differing patterns of residential segregation across socioeconomic status categories (income, education, and occupation) and nativity using the dissimilarity index in 2000.[4] Education is split into four groups: less than high school, high school graduate, some college, and college graduate. Occupations are also split into four general categories: managerial, professional, and technical; sales and administrative; service occupations; and farming, precision crafts, and operators. Income is represented by approximate household income quartiles.[5] Finally, I also examine segregation by nativity, as these may play a role in the residential patterns of Asians and Hispanics in particular.[6]

When comparing black residential patterns to those of all non-Hispanic whites (figure 5.3), we find that segregation was highest for African Americans in the lowest income quartiles, those with less education, and for African Americans in service occupations. While the differences are moderate, the findings do lend support to the argument that socioeconomic status does play at least some role in black segregation from whites. For example, the dissimilarity score of African Americans in the lowest household income quartile (0.697) is significantly higher than the score in the highest income quartile (0.597). The foreign born are also more segregated (0.678) than the native born (0.617). However, it is important to point out that even among high SES groups and native-born African Americans, segregation is still high in absolute terms—the dissimilarity score is above 0.6 for all but three subgroups.

Figure 5.4 shows corresponding dissimilarity scores for Hispanics by socioeconomic status. As with African Americans we see lower segregation vis-

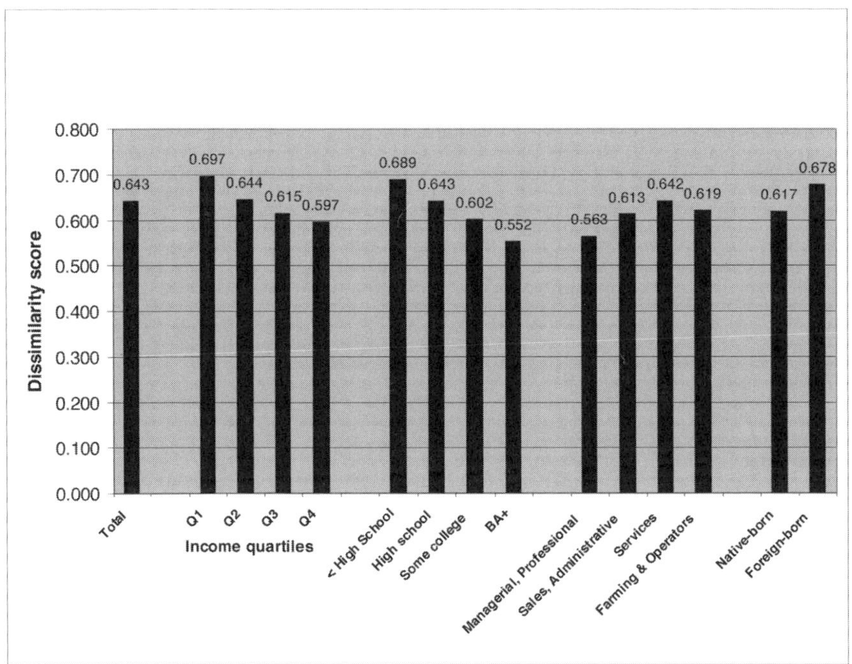

Figure 5.3. Dissimilarity for African Americans by Socioeconomic Characteristics and Nativity: 2000. Source: Tabulations of Census 2000 long-form data.

à-vis non-Hispanic whites among higher SES groups. For example, the dissimilarity score among Hispanics with less than a high school education was high at 0.621. For those with a BA or more the score was only 0.360. Among Hispanic managers, professionals, and technicians, the dissimilarity score was 0.369, well below the score among farmers and operators (0.590). Thus, we see that differences between high and low-SES Hispanics are larger than the difference observed among blacks. This suggests that the spatial assimilation model is better at explaining Hispanic patterns of segregation from non-Hispanic whites than African American patterns. In this vein, we also see that native-born Hispanics (0.469) are substantially less segregated than foreign-born Hispanics (0.588).

In figure 5.5 we see many of the same patterns for Asians and Pacific Islanders as we saw for Hispanics. Higher SES groups are less segregated from whites than lower SES groups, and the native born are less segregated (0.378) than the foreign born (0.454). Those with a college education, for example, have a dissimilarity score of 0.411, considerably lower than the 0.575 figure for those with less than a high school education. Those in the highest household income quartile (0.432) are likewise less segregated from non-Hispanic

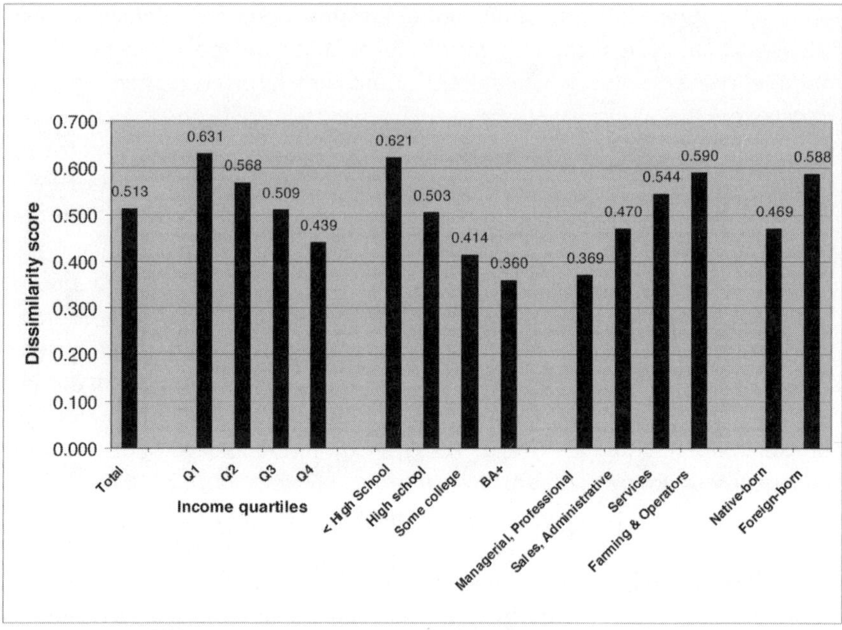

Figure 5.4. Dissimilarity for Hispanics by Socioeconomic Characteristics and Nativity: 2000. Source: Tabulations of Census 2000 long-form data.

whites than those in the lowest quartile (0.603). The differences in segregation between SES groups may not be quite as large for Asians as for Hispanics, but the results nevertheless support the spatial assimilation model in that those with higher socioeconomic status are significantly more likely to be evenly distributed across neighborhoods than others.

DISCUSSION: SEGREGATION MEASURES

The measurement of the spatial patterning of the urban populations in U.S. cities has evolved considerably over the past several decades. There is increasing focus upon multiple, complementary measures, such as the nineteen that the Census Bureau used in its 2002 report (Iceland et al. 2002) that mirrored social science practice (Massey and Denton 1988). There has been some recent discussion and debate about the utility of dissimilarity and isolation measures, as well as the practice of using non-Hispanic whites as the key reference group in such analyses. This debate became localized, for example, in the series of articles on this topic that appeared in the *Milwaukee Sentinel* in 2003 after the Census Bureau monograph on residential segregation re-

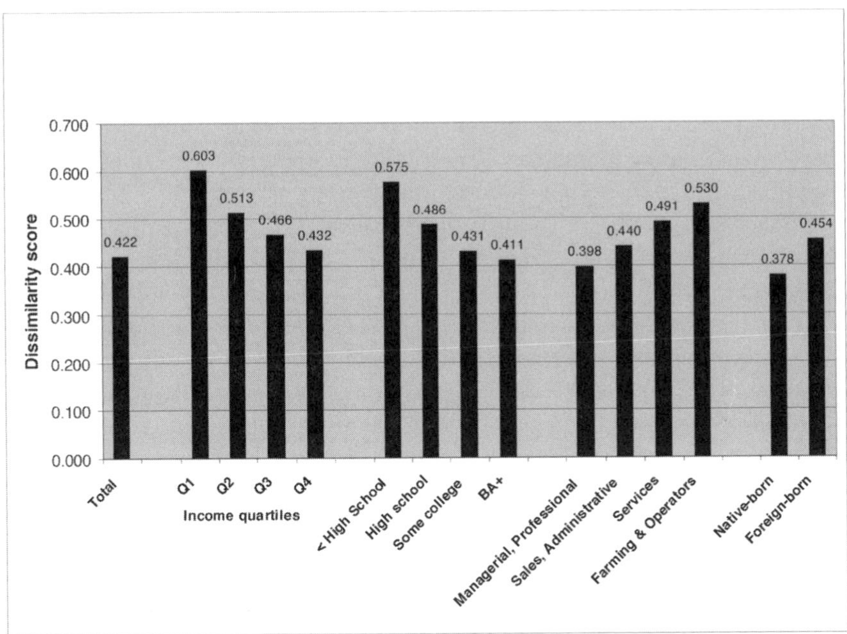

Figure 5.5. Dissimilarity for Asians and Pacific Islanders by Socioeconomic Characteristics and Nativity: 2000. Source: Tabulations of Census 2000 long-form data.

ported that Milwaukee was the most segregated large metropolitan area in the United States for African Americans.

In response, the Census Bureau organized a peer-review of its methodology and summarized the findings of this group.[7] The group generally affirmed the U.S. Census Bureau's methodology and offered constructive feedback concerning future directions for segregation measurement (see U.S. Census Bureau 2005). There was agreement that using multiple measures was preferable to a reliance on any single measure, given the multidimensional character of residential segregation. There was also support for replicating Massey and Denton's 1988 study with 2000 census data to empirically gauge whether it is reasonable to group segregation measures into five dimensions (evenness, exposure, concentration, centralization, and clustering). At least one recent study has suggested that there are two primary conceptual dimensions to spatial segregation rather than five, consisting of spatial exposure and spatial evenness (Reardon and O'Sullivan 2004).

Along these lines, there is increasing interest in *spatial* measures of segregation. The most commonly used measures of segregation—dissimilarity and isolation—are "aspatial" in that they do not account for the spatial relationships among census tracts (Reardon and O'Sullivan 2004; White 1983; Wong

1993, 2002). That is, while dissimilarity measures the distribution of the population across census tracts (or other smaller units, such as blocks), it does not use information on whether particular tracts (or blocks) are in close proximity to each other or not. One drawback of spatial measures of segregation is that they are generally more complicated to calculate than dissimilarity and isolation. However, with increasing computational power available to researchers, along with advances in GIS software, it has and will likely continue to become somewhat easier to calculate spatial segregation measures in the future.

Those who peer-reviewed the Census Bureau report also supported calculating segregation indexes for non-Hispanic whites, who have traditionally been used mainly as the reference group in the calculation of "African American," "Hispanic," or "Asian" segregation indexes (U.S. Census Bureau 2005). Implementing this sensible recommendation involves calculating additional indexes (perhaps supplementing traditional indexes) for all groups with alternative reference groups—such as all people not in the group of interest. That is, segregation indexes could be calculated for non-Hispanic whites vis-à-vis all others, non-Hispanic blacks vis-à-vis all others, and so forth, for all groups.

There is also growing interest in *multigroup* segregation measures that allow researchers to consider multiple racial and ethnic groups, geographic levels (e.g., metropolitan area or regions) or dimensions (race, class, age) simultaneously (e.g., Reardon and Firebaugh 2002; Iceland 2004; Fischer et al. 2004; Fischer 2003; Wong 2003). This is in contrast to the most common methods of implementing the dissimilarity and isolation indexes, which measure the differential distribution of only two groups at a time. Especially with the growing diversity of the U.S. population—in the wake of increasing immigration from Asia and Latin America over the past few decades—it is likely that multigroup measures will become more popular in the coming years. A different, but related issue is that there will likely be growing interest in the residential patterns of multiracial individuals. While only 2.4 percent of the population reported more than one race in the 2000 Census, this proportion is likely to increase in the coming years.

Finally, there will likely be growing interest in measures of "integration" or "diversity" calculated at the neighborhood level. While segregation measures typically measure the distribution of groups across neighborhoods within a metropolitan area, diversity measures focus on the composition of smaller area units (such as census tracts), and perhaps summarizing this information at the metropolitan level. Diversity measures include the entropy score, which is calculated in the derivation of the entropy index (Theil 1972; Reardon and Firebaugh 2002), the Diversity Index (Maly 2000), or Simpson's D (or Herfindahl-Hirschman) index (see also Galster's commentary in U.S.

Census Bureau [2005] for a description of these measures). Other possible measures of diversity are possible, such as classifying neighborhoods as being multiracial if they meet some sort of compositional criteria (e.g., Frey and Farley 1996; Fasenfest et al. 2004; Quinn and Pawasarat 2003), though there is little agreement in the literature of what such criteria should be.

CONCLUSION

The 1980 to 2000 period saw moderate declines in black-white segregation, though blacks continued to be highly segregated and more segregated from non-Hispanic whites than other groups. In contrast, Hispanic-white and Asian-white segregation levels were somewhat lower, but they did not decline over the period.

Socioeconomic differences played a role in explaining patterns and trends for all groups, providing at least some support for the spatial assimilation model. Lower SES groups—when considering income, education, and occupation—were more highly segregated from whites than lower SES groups. The SES differences were greater among Hispanics and Asians in particular, suggesting that SES plays a larger mediating role for these groups. Moreover, the native born were less segregated than the foreign born for all groups, again providing support for the spatial assimilation model. Thus, this suggests that the slight increases in segregation for Hispanics and Asians over the 1980–2000 period were in part driven by continued immigration and socioeconomic differences. Nevertheless, race clearly plays a large role in producing observed residential segregation patterns, especially for African Americans, where levels of segregation were high for all socioeconomic groups.

In short, this analysis has provided moderate support for the spatial assimilation model but also documents persistently high levels of racial separation. There is a need for additional research focused on causal patterning, such as through multivariate modeling that measures the relative effect of race versus class on residential patterns with recent data (e.g., Massey and Denton 1985; Clark and Ware 1997; Freeman 2000). Research on the residential patterns of immigrants also needs to continue (e.g., Alba et al. 1997; Freeman 2002; White and Glick 1999; White and Sassler 2000; Iceland and Lake 2005), as the immigrant population in the United States is growing rapidly. We need a greater understanding not only of how this growth is affecting segregation patterns for particular racial and ethnic groups, but also how segregation varies across the immigrant groups themselves. For example, when we look at specific groups of the foreign born, do we see that more recent arrivals are indeed more segregated than those who have been in the

United States longer? Do these patterns hold over time in successive censuses?

Finally, research should continue on improving segregation measures. In recent years several suggestions have received attention, including using multiple measures of segregation, explicitly incorporating spatial information—such as distance between neighborhoods of various compositions—in measurement, producing segregation indexes for non-Hispanic whites and experimenting with alternative reference groups, using multigroup measures of segregation rather than traditional dual-group ones, and finally looking at "integration" and "diversity" of neighborhoods within metropolitan areas and not just the segregation of groups across neighborhoods. Research using these alternative methods will likely provide a more nuanced picture of the residential patterns of the U.S. population in the coming years.

NOTES

1. In this analysis, the nation's metropolitan areas (MAs) were based on Metropolitan Statistical Areas (MSAs) and Primary Metropolitan Statistical Areas (PMSAs) as defined by the Office of Management and Budget on June 30, 1999. Minor Civil Division–based MSAs and PMSAs were used in New England (this represents the most common way such metropolitan areas were defined in Census publications until new metropolitan area definitions were issued after the 2000 census).

2. Other work has shown that adopting a race definition where a person is considered in a group if he or she chooses only that particular group has little effect on African American segregation calculations and a modest effect on Asian segregation calculations (Iceland et al. 2002, appendix A). The similarity of scores across group definitions results, in large part, from the fact that the proportion of people who marked two or more race groups in the 2000 census was small (2.4 percent). This specific issue does not affect Hispanic indexes since Hispanic origin is asked in a separate question.

3. All segregation scores in the tables are weighted by the size of the minority group in question. The scores therefore represent the experience of the average minority group individual rather than the average metropolitan area.

4. Using the isolation index produces the same general conclusions as when using the dissimilarity index, with some exceptions. See Iceland et al. (2005) for further discussion of this issue.

5. For the education segregation indexes, only people aged twenty-five and over were included in the analysis. For the occupation indexes, only workers were included. Household income indexes omit people in group quarters. The household income quartiles in 2000 were: under $19,999, $20,000–$44,999, $45,000–$74,999, and $75,000 and over.

6. Overall group scores differ slightly in this section from those in the previous section because the data here come from the census long-form (a one-in-six sample

of U.S. households) rather than from the census short-form. Long-form data contain detailed information about income, education, and the other characteristics examined in this section. Differences in overall segregation scores are larger for the smaller groups, as might be expected.

7. The peer reviewers included George Galster, John Goering, Douglas Massey, Lois Quinn, and Michael White.

REFERENCES

Alba, Richard D., and John Logan. 1991. "Variations on Two Themes: Racial and Ethnic Patterns in the Attainment of Suburban Residence." *Demography* 28(3): 431–53.

———. 1993. "Minority Proximity to Whites in Suburbs: An Individual-level Analysis of Segregation." *American Journal of Sociology* 98(6): 1388–1427.

Alba, Richard D., John Logan, and Kyle Crowder. 1997. "White Ethnic Neighborhoods and Assimilation: The Greater New York Region, 1980–1990." *Social Forces*, 75(3): 883–912.

Alba, Richard D., John Logan, and Brian J. Stults. 2000. "How Segregated are Middle-Class African Americans?" *Social Problems* 47(4): 543–58.

Bobo, Lawrence, and Camille Zubrinsky. 1996. "Attitudes Toward Residential Integration: Perceived Status Differences, Mere In-Group Preference, or Racial Prejudice?" *Social Forces* 74(3): 883–909.

Charles, Camille Z. 2000. "Neighborhood Racial-Composition Preferences: Evidence from a Multiethnic Metropolis." *Social Problems* 47(3): 379–407.

———. 2001. "Processes of Residential Segregation." In *Urban Inequality: Evidence from Four Cities*, ed. Alice O'Connor, Chris Tilly, and Lawrence D. Bobo. New York: Russell Sage Foundation.

———. 2003. "Dynamics of Racial Residential Segregation." *Annual Review of Sociology* 29(1): 167–207.

Clark, William A. V. 1986. "Residential Segregation in American Cities: A Review and Interpretation." *Population Research and Policy Review* 5:95–127.

———. 1988. "Understanding Residential Segregation in American Cities: Interpreting the Evidence, a Reply to Galster." *Population Research and Policy Review* 7:113–21.

Clark, William A. V., and Sarah A. Blue. 2003. "Race, Class and Segregation Patterns in U.S. Immigrant Gateway Cities." Paper presented at the annual meetings of the Population Association of America, Minneapolis, MN, May 1–3.

Clark, William A. V., and Julian Ware. 1997. "Trends in Residential Integration by Socioeconomic Status in Southern California." *Urban Affairs Review* 32(6): 825–43.

Darden, Joe, and Sameh Kamel. 2000. "Black Residential Segregation in the City and Suburbs of Detroit: Does Socioeconomic Status Matter?" *Journal of Urban Affairs* 22(1): 1–13.

Denton, Nancy, and Douglas S. Massey. 1988. "Residential Segregation of Blacks, Hispanics, and Asians by Socioeconomic Status and Generation." *Social Science Quarterly* 69:797–817.

Farley, Reynolds. 1977. "Residential Segregation in Urbanized Areas of the United States in 1970: An Analysis of Social Class and Racial Differences." *Demography* 14(4): 497–518.

Farley, Reynolds, Charlotte Steeh, Maria Krysan, Tara Jackson, and Keith Reeves. 1994. "Stereotypes and Segregation: Neighborhoods in the Detroit Area." *American Journal of Sociology* 100(3): 750–80.

Fasenfest, David, Jason Booza, and Kurt Metzger. 2004. *Living Together: A New Look at Racial and Ethnic Integration in Metropolitan Neighborhoods, 1990–2000*. The Brookings Institution Center on Urban and Metropolitan Policy, The Living Cities Census Series. http://www.brookings.edu/dybdocroot/urban/pubs/20040428_fasenfest.pdf.

Fischer, Claude S., Gretchen Stockmayer, Jon Stiles, and Michael Hout. 2004. "Geographic Levels and Social Dimensions of Metropolitan Segregation." *Demography* 41:37–60.

Fischer, Mary J. 2003. "The Relative Importance of Income and Race in Determining Residential Outcomes in U.S. Urban Areas, 1970–2000." *Urban Affairs Review* 38(5): 669–96.

Fong, Eric, and Rima Wilkes. 1999. "The Spatial Assimilation Model Reexamined: An Assessment by Canadian Data." *International Migration Review* 22:594–620.

Freeman, Lance. 2000. "Minority Housing Segregation: A Test of Three Perspectives." *Journal of Urban Affairs* 22(1): 15–35.

———. 2002. "Does Spatial Assimilation Work for Black Immigrants in the U.S.?" *Urban Studies* 39(11): 1983–2003.

Frey, William H., and Reynolds Farley. 1996. "Latino, Asian, and Black Segregation in U.S. Metropolitan Areas: Are Multiethnic Metros Different?" *Demography* 33:35–50.

Galster, George. 1988. "Residential Segregation in American Cities: A Contrary Review." *Population Research and Policy Review* 7:93–112.

Goering, John M., and Ron Wienk (eds.). 1996. *Mortgage Lending, Racial Discrimination and Federal Policy*. Washington, DC: Urban Institute Press.

Iceland, John. 2004. "Beyond Black and White: Metropolitan Residential Segregation in Multi-ethnic America." *Social Science Research* 33:248–71.

Iceland, John, and Cynthia Lake. 2005. "Immigrant Residential Patterns in U.S. Metropolitan Areas, 1990–2000." Paper presented at the 2005 Population Association of America meetings in Philadelphia, PA, March 31–April 2.

Iceland, John, Cicely Sharpe, and Erika Steinmetz. 2005. "Class Differences in African American Residential Patterns in U.S. Metropolitan Areas: 1990–2000." *Social Science Research* 34:252–66.

Iceland, John, Daniel H. Weinberg, and Erika Steinmetz. 2002. *Racial and Ethnic Residential Segregation in the United States: 1980–2000*. U.S. Census Bureau, Census Special Report, CENSR-3. Washington, DC: U.S. Government Printing Office.

Logan, John, Brian Stults, and Reynolds Farley. 2004. "Segregation of Minorities in the Metropolis: Two Decades of Change." *Demography* 41(1): 1–22.

Maly, Michael. 2000. "The Neighborhood Diversity Index." *Journal of Urban Affairs* 22(1): 37–47.

Massey, Douglas S., and Nancy Denton. 1985. "Spatial Assimilation as a Socioeconomic Outcome." *American Sociological Review* 50(1): 94–106.

———. 1988. "The Dimensions of Residential Segregation." *Social Forces* 67(2): 281–315.

———. 1993. *American Apartheid: Segregation and the Making of the Underclass*. Cambridge, MA: Harvard University Press.

Massey, Douglas S., and Mary J. Fischer. 1999. "Does Rising Income Bring Integration? New Results for Blacks, Hispanics, and Asians in 1990." *Social Science Research* 28:316–26.

Massey, Douglas S., and Brendan P. Mullan. 1984. "Processes of Hispanic and Black Spatial Assimilation." *American Journal of Sociology* 89:836–73.

Meyer, Stephen Grant. 2000. *As Long As They Don't Move Next Door: Segregation and Racial Conflict in American Neighborhoods*. Lanham, MD: Rowman and Littlefield.

Pascal, Anthony. 1967. *The Economics of Housing Segregation*. Santa Monica: RAND.

Portes, Alejandro, and Ruben G. Rumbaut. 1996. *Immigrant America: A Portrait*. Berkeley, CA: University of California Press.

Quinn, Lois M., and John Pawasarat. 2003. "Racial Integration in Urban America: A Block Level Analysis of African American and White Housing Patterns." University of Wisconsin—Milwaukee Employment and Training Institute Research Report. http://www.uwm.edu/Dept/ETI/integration/integration.htm.

Reardon, Sean F., and Glenn Firebaugh. 2002. "Measures of Multigroup Segregation." *Sociological Methodology* 32(1): 33–67.

Reardon, Sean, and David O'Sullivan. 2004. "Measures of Spatial Segregation." *Sociological Methodology* 34(1): 121–62.

Ross, Stephen L., and Margery Austin Turner. 2005. "Housing Discrimination in Metropolitan America: Explaining Changes between 1989 and 2000." *Social Problems* 52(2): 152–180.

St. John, Craig, and Robert Clymer. 2000. "Racial Residential Segregation by Level of Socioeconomic Status. *Social Science Quarterly* 81(3): 701–15.

Theil, Henry. 1972. *Statistical Decomposition Theory*. New York: American Elsevier.

U.S. Census Bureau. 2005. *Peer Review of "Racial and Ethnic Residential Segregation in the United States: 1980–2000."* Released on the Internet in January. http://www.census.gov/hhes/www/housing/resseg/peer_review.html.

White, Michael J. 1983. "The Measurement of Spatial Segregation." *American Journal of Sociology* 88:1008–18.

White, Michael J., and Jennifer E. Glick. 1999. "The Impact of Immigration on Residential Segregation." In *Immigration and Opportunity*, ed. Frank D. Bean and Stephanie Bell-Rose, 345–72. New York: Russell Sage Foundation.

White, Michael J., and Sharon Sassler. 2000. "Judging Not Only by Color: Ethnicity, Nativity, and Neighborhood Attainment." *Social Science Quarterly* 81(4): 997–1013.

Wilkes, Rima, and John Iceland. 2004. "Hypersegregation in the Twenty-First Century." *Demography* 41(1): 23–36.

Wong, David S. 1993. "Spatial Indices of Segregation." *Urban Studies* 30:59–72.

———. 2002. "Spatial Measures of Segregation and GIS." *Urban Geography* 23:85–92.

———. 2003. "Spatial Decomposition of Segregation Indices: A Framework Toward Measuring Segregation at Multiple Levels." *Geographical Analysis* 35(3): 179–94.

Yinger, John. 1995. *Closed Doors, Opportunities Lost: The Continuing Costs of Housing Discrimination*. New York: Russell Sage Foundation.

Zubrinsky, Camille, and Lawrence Bobo. 1996. "Prismatic Metropolis: Race and Residential Segregation in the City of Angels." *Social Science Research* 25:335–74.

6

How Integrated Did We Become during the 1990s?

Ingrid Gould Ellen

On the fiftieth anniversary of the Supreme Court decision in *Brown v. Board of Education*, the popular press has been filled with stories lamenting the unfulfilled promise of the case. One article after another describes how segregated our schools remain along ethnic and racial lines. But while we've seen little progress in school integration in recent decades, neighborhoods in the United States have been quietly and steadily growing more integrated. I use the term "quietly" because most of the attention paid to neighborhoods, like schools, highlights their extremely high level of segregation (Mumford Center 2001). Although levels of residential segregation remain undeniably high, this emphasis on segregation can obscure the fact that integrated communities do exist and, as one of the key findings here demonstrates, are becoming more, not less, common.

In a book published in 2000, I described the status of racial integration during the 1970s and 1980s, focusing on neighborhoods shared by whites and blacks (Ellen 2000). The aim of this chapter is to update this account and to incorporate a more explicit analysis of neighborhoods shared by whites and nonblack minorities. In particular, this chapter presents an empirical overview of the extent of racial integration in the United States in the year 2000 and documents changes in integration during the 1990s. The chapter starts with some definitions and then moves on to address five research questions. First, how prevalent are racially integrated neighborhoods? Second, how has this prevalence changed in recent years, particularly during the 1990s? How does the answer vary for neighborhoods shared by whites and blacks and those shared by whites and other minorities? Third, how stable are racially integrated neighborhoods? Are these integrated neighborhoods merely transitional—neighborhoods that are in the process of moving from all white to all black or Hispanic? Fourth, have integrated neighborhoods become more stable during the 1990s?

Finally, the chapter ends by examining the characteristics of households who live in integrated communities and exploring why we have seen growing integration in our neighborhoods but not in our schools. A better understanding of who is choosing to live in integrated communities should help to shed light on the causes of America's continuing segregation.

PAST LITERATURE: A BRIEF REVIEW

Until the past few decades, few researchers examined the stability of racial integration, since racial tipping or succession (that is, rapid transition to majority minority community) was considered to be the norm. This began to change in the 1980s, when several studies were published on the topic (Taub, Taylor, and Dunham 1984; Lee 1985; Lee and Wood 1990; Denton and Massey 1991; Lee and Wood 1991). Focusing on the decade of the 1970s, these studies questioned the inevitability of racial succession and began to examine the factors correlated with stability. Nevertheless, stable, racially integrated communities continued to be viewed as the exception.

Research focused on the 1980s uncovered more integration (Ellen 1998; Ellen 2000; Nyden, Maly, and Lukehart 1997) and found a marked increase in both the prevalence and stability of neighborhood integration as compared to earlier decades. While not the norm, stable, integrated neighborhoods could no longer be considered an anomaly.

The question for this chapter is what happened during the 1990s. Did the trend toward integration continue? A few recent studies have examined this question. Rawlings et al. (2004) study integration in sixty-nine metropolitan areas and find an increase in the number of neighborhoods shared by blacks and whites. They also find that many of these neighborhoods appear to remain stably integrated over time. Fasenfast, Booza, and Metzger (2004) consider other racial/ethnic groups in addition to blacks and whites and also find an increase in racial mixing during the 1990s. Their study, however, covers only the ten largest metropolitan areas.

This chapter builds on these two studies but should provide a broader overview of integration patterns during the 1990s, as it examines the full set of metropolitan areas in the United States. Because they focus only on large metropolitan areas, which tend to be more racially and ethnically diverse, these two earlier studies may overstate the extent of integration and may get an inaccurate picture of changes. Another point of departure from earlier work is that this chapter focuses more explicitly on comparing patterns evident in black-white and other types of integrated communities. Finally, it also departs from these other studies by beginning to explore the characteristics of residents who live in integrated neighborhoods.

DEFINITIONS

There is no single, accepted definition of an integrated neighborhood. Thus, before presenting any empirical results, this section lays out some definitions. In particular, the paragraphs below discuss such terms as *neighborhood*, *racial integration*, and *stability*.

Most people probably have a sense of the boundaries of their own neighborhood but would have a difficult time expressing more generalizable rules. This chapter, like most research on neighborhoods in the United States, relies on census tracts to approximate neighborhoods. Census tracts typically include between twenty-five hundred and eight thousand people (and on average include about four thousand). Some have argued that census tracts are too large and may conceal pockets of segregation within them; they have advocated studying segregation at the block level instead (Farley and Frey 1994; Jargowsky 1997). Surely, census tracts are hardly perfect representations of neighborhoods, and segregation would undoubtedly appear somewhat higher if examined at the level of the individual block. Nonetheless, census tracts are probably closer in size to what most people envision as a neighborhood, and moreover, far more data is available at the tract level.

Racial integration is also a term that requires some discussion. This chapter uses two basic definitions (though I have experimented with many others and the basic conclusions presented here hold for them as well). Following most of the literature on integration, the first definition focuses on the integration of blacks and defines as integrated any neighborhood in which the proportion of blacks lies between 10 and 50 percent. As discussed in Ellen (1998), this definition balances the idea that integration should be about sharing on relatively equal grounds and the fact that blacks made up just 13 percent of the U.S. population in the year 2000.

The second definition takes into account a more multiethnic world—one not only with whites and blacks, but also with Hispanics and Asians and Native Americans. Here an integrated neighborhood is one that is shared by non-Hispanic whites and at least one minority racial group. The presence of whites is required since it is whites who have historically excluded (and avoided) members of minority groups. Thus, while a neighborhood shared by blacks, Hispanics, and Asians may be wonderfully diverse, it is not considered integrated for the purposes of this chapter. Instead, it is labeled mixed minority. More specifically, a neighborhood is considered integrated if non-Hispanic whites comprise 40 percent or more of the population and at least one minority group comprises at least 10 percent of the population.[1] Note that for ease of presentation, the term *white* is used throughout the chapter, rather than *non-Hispanic white*.

We consider nine different neighborhood types:

- homogenous white
- homogenous black
- homogenous Hispanic
- homogenous other
- integrated, white-black
- integrated, white-Hispanic
- integrated, white-other
- integrated, white–multiple minority
- mixed minority

Note that the "other" category is not monolithic. Most individuals in this group are Asian (roughly 75 percent), but the category also includes non-Hispanic individuals who identify as a member of a racial group other than black, white, or Asian, such as Native American.[2]

Because these groups are mutually exclusive, they assume that we can classify every person living in a tract as a member of a single racial/ethnic group. In reality, however, people can place themselves into more than one category. Most notably, Hispanic origin is not considered to be a racial category—the Census Bureau defines Hispanic or Latino as "a person of Cuban, Mexican, Puerto Rican, South or Central America, or other Spanish culture or origin, regardless of race" (Grieco and Cassidy 2001). Households, in other words, are asked what racial group they belong to *and* whether or not they are Hispanic. In this chapter, individuals who self-identify as both black and Hispanic are classified as black. Anyone who is not black and who self-identifies as Hispanic, however, is considered to be Hispanic.[3]

A second issue is how to handle respondents who listed more than one race on the 2000 Census, since in contrast to earlier years, the 2000 Census allowed respondents to select more than one racial group, and just over 2 percent of respondents did so. I use the bridging method developed by Jeffrey Passel at the Urban Institute to categorize these multiracial respondents (GeoLytics 2002). Specifically, anyone who selects black as one of their racial groups is considered black (this is essentially the one-drop-of-blood rule). Anyone who lists Asian (but *not* black) is categorized as Asian. Anyone who self-identifies as white (but does *not* also list black, Asian, or Pacific Islander) is considered to be white.

To some extent, this bridging method may overstate the number of blacks relative to earlier years, since some individuals who list black as one of their racial groups might not have self-identified as black if only allowed to select a single ethnic/racial group. Thus, I also replicated analyses with an alternative approach, which counts as black only those households who identify as black and not as any other racial group. The results were largely unchanged when using this alternative.

Neighborhood change is measured in several ways, but in general, the chapter focuses on the change in the proportion of whites in a community. This approach is consistent with theories of racial change, which tend to emphasize white household behavior in the face of racial integration (Ellen 2000; Schelling 1972). Moreover, a shrinking white population is typically considered to be the greatest threat to integration (see Denton and Massey 1991; Ellen 2000; Galster 1990).

DATA

This study relies on the Neighborhood Change Database (NCDB) developed by GeoLytics and the Urban Institute.[4] The NCDB draws on census tract data for 1970, 1980, 1990, and 2000, taken from the decennial censuses in those years. It covers all census tracts in the United States. In addition to individual files for each of these four census years, the NCDB also includes a longitudinal file of census tracts with fixed boundaries, in which 1970, 1980, and 1990 census tract data are remapped to Census 2000 tract boundaries. Thus, the NCDB is particularly useful for examining changes over time in census tracts.

The first empirical section of the chapter describes the extent and nature of racial integration in U.S. metropolitan areas in the year 2000. The second section then compares how integration in the year 2000 compares to that in earlier decades. For these analyses, I rely on the individual 1970, 1980, 1990, and 2000 census tract files. In each year, the sample covers census tracts in the full set of metropolitan areas as they were defined in that year. Census tracts are omitted if they have fewer than two hundred residents.

The rest of the chapter considers changes in neighborhoods over time, and thus the longitudinal, fixed-boundary file is used. Note that I have not used the fixed-boundary file when simply comparing levels of integration across years, since it could lead to biased assessments of changes in the extent of integration over time.[5]

Table 6.1. Distribution of Census Tracts and Population by Percentage Black, 2000
Universe: All Metropolitan Areas

Percent Black in Neighborhood	*Percentage of Census Tracts*	*Percentage of White Population*	*Percentage of Black Population*
< 1% Black	20.7	25.8	0.7
1–10% Black	46.1	54.4	13.9
10–50% Black	21.8	18.1	35.8
> 50% Black	11.4	1.7	49.6
N	*50,956*	*150,509,503*	*31,329,056*

Note: White refers in this table, and in all tables, to non-Hispanic whites only.
Source: Data from Neighborhood Change Database.

THE EXTENT OF INTEGRATION IN 2000

Table 6.1 presents an overview of the extent of integration in U.S. metropolitan areas in the year 2000, using the first definition of integration, which focuses on the integration of blacks. Neighborhoods, or census tracts, are classified into four categories: less than 1 percent black, 1–10 percent black, 10–50 percent black, and at least 50 percent black. The first column shows that 20.7 percent of metropolitan census tracts had virtually no blacks, 46.1 percent had some blacks (1–10 percent black), 21.8 percent were integrated, or 10–50 percent black, and 11.4 percent were majority black. Using the first definition of integration, in other words, just over one in five census tracts was integrated in the year 2000.

Since these neighborhood categories are defined simply by their share of blacks, it is possible that some of the 11,000 neighborhoods identified here as integrated (10–50 percent black) may in fact be mixed minority communities—that is, neighborhoods shared largely by blacks and Hispanics or Asians. Further analysis shows that in three-quarters of all 10–50 percent black neighborhoods, the proportion of whites is at least 40 percent. Most of these 10–50 percent black neighborhoods, that is, also contain a significant share of whites. Moreover, the second and third columns show that nearly a fifth of all metropolitan whites and over a third of all metropolitan blacks live in 10–50 percent black census tracts.

The second definition of integration allows for a distinction between mixed-minority neighborhoods and integrated neighborhoods shared by whites and minorities. Using the second definition, in which integrated neighborhoods can be white-black, white-Hispanic, white-other, or white-multiethnic, table 6.2 shows that over one-third of neighborhoods—or some 17,400 census tracts—were racially integrated in some manner in the year 2000. While many might wish this proportion to be higher, this is certainly not a trivial number.

Table 6.2. Distribution of Census Tracts by Neighborhood Type, 2000
Universe: All Metropolitan Areas

Neighborhood Type	*Percent of Census Tracts*
White	42.7
Black	8.6
Hispanic	4.4
Other	0.5
Subtotal, Homogenous	*56.2*
White-Black	11.4
White-Hispanic	10.0
White-Other	4.3
White-Multiethnic	8.4
Subtotal, Integrated	*34.1*
Mixed Minority	9.6
Subtotal, Mixed Minority	*9.6*
N	*50,956*

Source: Data from Neighborhood Change Database.

As for the other neighborhoods, 9.6 percent of metropolitan census tracts were mixed minority—in other words, they included at least two minority groups but few whites. Just over half (56 percent) were racially homogenous—that is, only one racial or ethnic group was present in significant numbers.

Looking in more detail at the integrated group, we see that the most common type of integrated neighborhood is one shared by whites and blacks, followed by those shared by whites and Hispanics. These two types of neighborhoods account for 11.4 and 10 percent of all neighborhoods respectively. Another 8.4 percent of neighborhoods are shared by whites and multiple minority groups. Roughly 70 percent of these integrated, multiple-minority neighborhoods included a significant presence of blacks (at least 10 percent of the population was black), while 88 percent included a significant share of Hispanics.

CHANGES IN EXTENT OF INTEGRATION, 1970–2000

The second key question for this chapter is how this distribution of neighborhoods—and in particular how the prevalence of integration—has changed in recent decades. Table 6.3 presents the distribution of metropolitan census tracts by percentage black from 1970 to 2000 and reveals a few notable trends.[6]

First, and perhaps most striking, the proportion of neighborhoods with no black residents has fallen dramatically over the past thirty years. In 1970,

Table 6.3. Distribution of Census Tracts by Percentage Black, 2000
Universe: All Metropolitan Areas

	Percentage of Census Tracts			
Percent Black in Neighborhood	*1970*	*1980*	*1990*	*2000*
< 1% Black	59.9	39.8	29.7	15.4
1–10% Black	20.3	34.0	40.5	51.3
10–50% Black	10.9	14.5	17.7	21.8
> 50% Black	8.9	11.7	12.1	11.5
N	*34,128*	*45,524*	*44,159*	*50,956*

Source: Data from Neighborhood Change Database.

more than half of metropolitan neighborhoods were less than 1 percent black; by 2000, only one in five neighborhoods was less than 1 percent black. Second, as the number of neighborhoods with no black residents has dwindled in number, the number of integrated neighborhoods has correspondingly increased. The share of 10–50 percent black neighborhoods has climbed steadily and consistently over the past three decades, from just 12 percent in 1970 to 15 percent in 1980 to 18 percent in 1990 and 22 percent in 2000.

As noted above, because neighborhoods that are between 10 and 50 percent black do not necessarily include a significant number of whites, the growing number of these neighborhoods might simply reflect a growth in the number of neighborhoods shared by blacks and other minorities, rather than indicating any increase in integration with whites. Table 6.4 demonstrates that this is not the case: the proportion of whites living in 10–50 percent black neighborhoods has in fact increased steadily over this period, from 9.9 percent in 1970 to 18.1 percent in 2000. The proportion of blacks living in such neighborhoods has meanwhile increased too, from 23.5 percent in 1970 to 35.8 percent in 2000.

When using the second definition of integration, the story is similar, though here the analysis extends back only to 1980.[7] Again, we see a decline in homogenous neighborhoods and a growth in those that are integrated. More specifically, Table 6.5 shows that the proportion of racially homogenous

Table 6.4. Percentage of Black and White Population Living in 10–50 Percent Black Tracts, 1970–2000
Universe: All Metropolitan Areas

	1970	*1980*	*1990*	*2000*
Percentage of Black Population	23.5	26.7	30.4	35.8
Percentage of White Population	9.9	11.8	14.4	18.1

Source: Data from Neighborhood Change Database.

Table 6.5. Distribution of Census Tracts by Percentage Black, 1980–2000
Universe: All Metropolitan Areas

	Percentage of Census Tracts		
Neighborhood Type	*1980*	*1990*	*2000*
White	60.9	53.1	42.7
Black	8.9	9.1	8.6
Hispanic	2.1	2.7	4.4
Other	0.4	0.4	0.5
Subtotal, Homogenous	*72.3*	*65.3*	*56.2*
White-Black	12.0	12.2	11.4
White-Hispanic	8.1	8.6	10.0
White-Other	1.0	2.6	4.3
White-Multiethnic	3.1	5.5	8.4
Subtotal, Integrated	*24.2*	*28.9*	*34.1*
Mixed Minority	3.5	5.9	9.6
Subtotal, Mixed Minority	*3.5*	*5.9*	*9.6*
N	*42,524*	*44,159*	*50,956*

Source: Data from Neighborhood Change Database.

neighborhoods has in fact fallen steadily—from over 72 percent in 1980 to 56 percent in the year 2000.

The share of integrated neighborhoods has meanwhile risen from 24 percent in 1980 to 34 percent in 2000. Significantly, the table suggests that the increase has been driven largely by an increase in the number of neighborhoods shared by whites and Hispanics or other nonblack minorities. In fact, there appears to have been a slight decrease in the proportion of neighborhoods housing *only* blacks and whites during the 1990s. Looking at neighborhoods lived in only by blacks and whites is somewhat misleading, however. A more meaningful measure is the proportion of neighborhoods in which both blacks and whites are present (but in which other racial groups, such as Hispanics and Asians, might also reside). When considering all neighborhoods shared by blacks and whites, we see that the proportion has in fact increased from 14.2 percent in 1980 to 15.7 percent in 1990 and 17.1 percent in 2000.[8]

In short, the answer to our second question is that neighborhood integration has been growing steadily and consistently over the past few decades, though less rapidly in the case of neighborhoods shared by whites and blacks. This is perhaps not surprising, given that the growth in the Asian and Hispanic populations far outpaced that of the black and white population during the 1980s and 1990s. Between 1980 and 2000, the Hispanic and Asian populations rose by 142 percent and approximately 200 percent respectively. By contrast, the white population increased by less than 8 percent, and the black population rose by 37 percent.[9]

STABILITY OF INTEGRATION

The conventional view of integration is perhaps best captured by the famous words of Saul Alinsky, in which he described neighborhood integration as merely the "time between when the first black moves in and the last white moves out." Do Alinsky's words hold true today? Are neighborhoods identified here as integrated merely transitory communities, in the process of moving from majority white to majority minority? This section addresses this question, using the fixed-boundary file of the NCDB. The fixed-boundary file follows 49,304 metropolitan census tracts.

As noted already, there are many ways to measure stable integration. One approach is to consider the share of integrated tracts that remain integrated ten years later. Using this metric, the 10–50 percent black neighborhoods appear quite stable. Eighty percent of census tracts that were integrated (10–50 percent black) in 1990 remained integrated in 2000.

While this seems to suggest a fair degree of stability, 10–50 percent black is a broad category, and thus this measure could conceal considerable change. Thus, perhaps a better approach is to calculate the share of tracts in which the percentage of non-Hispanic whites remains within ten percentage points of its original level. This metric suggests that among the 8,574 tracts that were integrated in 1990, 47 percent remained stable during the 1990s. Just over half (50.6 percent) lost whites, while 2.4 percent gained whites.

Using the alternative definition of integration, table 6.6 suggests reasonable stability too—though integrated neighborhoods are generally not as stable as racially homogenous neighborhoods. Roughly 77 percent of tracts that were all white in 1990 remained all white in 2000 and 90 percent of all-black neighborhoods remained all black in 2000. By contrast, 63 percent of neighborhoods that were shared by blacks and whites in 1990 remained black-white in 2000, while 58.6 percent of Hispanic-white neighborhoods remained Hispanic-white in 2000.

Of course some of these neighborhoods that have changed may have shifted to become a different type of integrated community. If one's concern is primarily the departure, or disappearance, of whites from these integrated neighborhoods, then the last column of table 6.6 is potentially more telling, and it suggests somewhat more stability. It shows the percentage of tracts in the given category in 1990 that ended the decade as some type of integrated community. This column suggests considerably more stability. Nearly 80 percent of the neighborhoods that were white-black or white-Hispanic in 1990 ended the decade as integrated. (Many of these neighborhoods shifted to become white–multiple minority communities.)

Table 6.6. Racial Change by Type of Neighborhood, 1990–2000
Universe: All Metropolitan Areas
Standardized Boundary File

	Number of Tracts in 1990	*Percent of Tracts Remaining in Same Category in 2000*	*Percent of Tracts Ending as Integrated Neighborhood*
White	26,449	77.0	22.8
Black	3,959	88.3	2.0
Hispanic	1,480	91.3	2.1
Other	166	92.2	2.4
White-Black	5,743	63.0	77.9
White-Hispanic	4,696	58.6	77.0
White-Other	1,246	66.1	89.0
White-Multiethnic	2,718	43.6	51.7
Mixed Minority	2,847	89.0	1.8

Source: Data from Neighborhood Change Database.

Table 6.6 illustrates some interesting differences among integrated neighborhoods. In particular, among the integrated neighborhoods, those that are shared by whites and other nonblack, non-Hispanic minorities appear to be the most stable, and those that are shared by whites and multiple minority groups are the least stable. Consider that 89 percent of those that started the decade shared by whites and other minorities remained integrated in the year 2000. By contrast, roughly 77 percent of neighborhoods shared by whites and blacks or Hispanics and just 52 percent of those shared by whites and multiple minority groups ended up as integrated ten years later.[10]

Interestingly, while this table suggests little difference between the change occurring in black-white and Hispanic-white neighborhoods, the pattern of change was in fact different. In particular, in the average black-white neighborhood, the loss in white population was driven by an absolute decline in the number of whites between 1990 and 2000. In the average Hispanic-white neighborhood, the absolute number of whites actually increased between 1990 and 2000. The reduction in percent white that occurred in Hispanic-white neighborhoods was driven by a rapid growth in the Hispanic population, in other words, not by any absolute decline in the number of white residents. This would seem to suggest that white households are more wary of, and more likely to avoid, living in neighborhoods with blacks than they are living in neighborhoods with Hispanics.

Finally, the last column of the table also offers some insight into how neighborhoods become integrated. Integrated neighborhoods are far more likely to arise from minorities moving in and integrating an all-white neighborhood than they are to originate from an all-minority neighborhood that attracts whites. In fact, 97 percent of all the neighborhoods that became integrated during the 1990s began the decade as predominantly white neighborhoods. In this sense, Alinsky's comment rings true—integration does tend to come about as minorities move into all-white communities. Integration through gentrification is far less common. But in contrast to Alinsky's description, these integrated communities do not seem to be merely on their way to becoming predominantly minority communities; a good number are staying integrated for many years.

DID INTEGRATION BECOME MORE STABLE DURING THE 1990S?

Past research has documented that racially integrated neighborhoods (defined as 10–50 percent black) were more stable during the 1980s than during the 1970s (Ellen 2000). During the 1990s, by contrast, there appears to have been little change. Consider neighborhoods that started the decade as 10–50 percent black. The proportion of neighborhoods that remained 10–50 percent black ten years later rose from 62 percent during the 1970s to 78 percent during the 1980s and then rose very slightly to 80 percent during the 1990s. We saw a fairly dramatic increase in stability between the 1970s and 1980s, in other words, and little change in stability between the 1980s and 1990s.

When using the second definition of integration, there actually appears to be a decline in stability during the 1990s, as compared to the 1980s. Table 6.7 shows that the average loss in percent white in integrated tracts was 13.1 percentage points during the 1990s as compared to 10.1 percentage points during the 1980s. In fact, the loss in percent white was higher in every type of integrated neighborhood during the 1990s than during the 1980s. This simple comparison is misleading, however, since the overall proportion of whites in metropolitan areas fell more rapidly during the 1990s than during the 1980s. Consider that the mean loss in percent white in all census tracts in the sample was 5.4 percentage points during the 1980s and 7.4 percentage points during the 1990s. The ratio of white loss in integrated tracts to the white loss in all tracts is roughly the same in both decades (in fact, it is slightly lower during the 1990s than during the 1980s). Controlling for the overall rate of white loss in metropolitan areas, in other words, integrated tracts appear to be just as stable during the 1990s as they were during the 1980s. Thus, the fact that integrated neighborhoods lost more whites during the 1990s would seem to be more a function of larger demographic shifts than reflecting any underlying change in the viability of integration.

**Table 6.7. Mean Change in Percent White, by Neighborhood Type
Comparing 1990s and 1980s**

	Mean Percentage Point Change in % White	
	1980–1990	*1990–2000*
White	−3.8	−5.4
White-Black	−7.4	−11.7
White-Hispanic	−12.4	−14.0
White-Other	−8.4	−10.4
White-Multiethnic	−13.5	−15.9
Total, Integrated	**−10.1**	**−13.1**
Total, All Tracts	−5.4	−7.4

Source: Data from Neighborhood Change Database.

In summary, while the 1990s witnessed an increase in the prevalence of integrated neighborhoods, these neighborhoods appear to be no more (and no less) stable than they were during the 1980s.

WHO LIVES IN INTEGRATED COMMUNITIES?

This section briefly explores the characteristics of the households who live in integrated communities. Learning who lives in integrated communities (and more critically, perhaps, who does not) can deepen our understanding of integrated neighborhoods and also help to shed light on who resists integration and why.

Table 6.8 compares the characteristics of households living in integrated and segregated neighborhoods. For black and Hispanic households, the key difference seems to be status. Black and Hispanic households living in mixed areas have higher incomes and more education on average than their counterparts living in largely black and Hispanic communities. Given the typically higher incomes of white households, this result is not surprising. Black households living in integrated areas also appear somewhat more likely to be married and to have children than their counterparts in largely black areas, but this is not true for Hispanic households.

The findings for white households show a greater contrast. White households living in neighborhoods with blacks and Hispanics tend to be less educated and less affluent than their counterparts living in predominantly white environments. Interestingly, white households living in neighborhoods with

Table 6.8. Characteristics of Households by Neighborhood Type, 2000

	Black-White	*Hispanic-White*	*White-Other*	*White*	*Black*	*Hispanic*
White Households						
Homeownership rate, 2000	65.0%	66.3%	65.8%	77.2%	NA	NA
% Households with kids, 2000	27.3%	28.6%	28.5%	31.8%	NA	NA
% Households that are married	48.3%	50.5%	53.7%	58.7%	NA	NA
% Adults with some college	53.2%	58.5%	73.7%	59.0%	NA	NA
Mean household income	$52,515	$58,572	$88,860	$69,176	NA	NA
Black Households						
Homeownership rate, 2000	46.8%	NA	NA	NA	46.4%	NA
% Households with kids, 2000	41.6%	NA	NA	NA	36.3%	NA
% Households that are married	35.5%	NA	NA	NA	27.7%	NA
% Adults with some college	46.5%	NA	NA	NA	37.5%	NA
Mean household income	$41,587	NA	NA	NA	$37,027	NA
Hispanic Households						
Homeownership rate, 2000	NA	51.6%	NA	NA	NA	47.4%
% Households with kids, 2000	NA	53.5%	NA	NA	NA	56.6%
% Households that are married	NA	57.9%	NA	NA	NA	58.7%
% Adults with some college	NA	37.1%	NA	NA	NA	21.4%
Mean household income	NA	$49,473	NA	NA	NA	$39,289
Total Tracts	5,805	5,118	2,194	21,772	4,362	2,265

Source: Data from Neighborhood Change Database.

Asians and other (nonblack, non-Hispanic) minorities actually appear to be higher status than those living in largely white communities.

The table also provides some support for the neighborhood racial stereotyping hypothesis (Ellen 2000). This hypothesis, which aims to explain white reluctance to share neighborhoods with blacks, argues that whites avoid integrated neighborhoods because they assume that such neighborhoods are inevitably on their way to becoming all black and experiencing the decline in public services and neighborhood conditions that they associate with such largely black neighborhoods. Previous work focused on the 1980s found evidence to support this theory (Ellen 2000). For instance, white homeowners and households with children were the white households most averse to racial mixing, most likely because of concerns about property values and school quality in integrated communities. But this hypothesis has only been tested on the 1980s and only on neighborhoods shared by whites and blacks.

The data here suggest that racial stereotyping continues to be relevant in understanding white avoidance of integrated neighborhoods. First, the neighborhood racial stereotyping hypothesis suggests that white homeowners will be more wary of integration as compared to white renters. Table 6.8 shows that the homeownership rate among whites was significantly lower in black-white and Hispanic-white communities as compared to predominantly white areas.

Second, white households with children should be the least likely white households to choose integrated neighborhoods because of their fears about school quality in such neighborhoods. And sure enough, the proportion of white households with children is lower in black-white and Hispanic-white communities as compared to predominantly white areas. In fact, the proportion of white households with children declines monotonically with the proportion of blacks in the neighborhood in 2000. The proportion of white households with children is 32 percent in neighborhoods that are less than 1 percent black, 30 percent in 1–10 percent black neighborhoods, 27 percent in 10–50 percent black neighborhoods, and 19 percent in neighborhoods that are majority black. The pattern is similar, though less dramatic, when examining the proportion of Hispanics in a neighborhood. The proportion of white households that have children is 29 percent in neighborhoods that are less than 1 percent Hispanic as compared to 22.5 percent in neighborhoods that are majority Hispanic.

These data certainly do not prove the neighborhood racial stereotyping hypothesis, but at the very least they are consistent with it. More support comes when comparing the characteristics of stable integrated neighborhoods and those that lost whites during the 1990s. The racial stereotyping hypothesis predicts that white households should be more open to integrated neighborhoods when those neighborhoods have been racially stable in the past and therefore seem less likely to transition in the future. Thus, neighborhoods that had a larger share of blacks in 1980 (and therefore experienced more modest racial change during the 1980s), should be more stable during the 1990s than those integrated neighborhoods that lost whites during the 1980s. This is shown strongly in the data for black-white neighborhoods and also holds, though to a much lesser extent, in Hispanic-white communities.

Meanwhile, in contrast to the conventional wisdom, the data do not suggest that whites are more apt to leave integrated neighborhoods when the minorities living there are of lower social and economic status. In fact, the poverty rate among black households living in stable, integrated neighborhoods is significantly higher than the poverty rate among black households living in integrated neighborhoods that lost whites during the 1990s. Similarly, black households living in stable, integrated neighborhoods were less likely to be college-educated than their counterparts in transitional neighborhoods.

CONCLUSION

This chapter offers a mixed report. As was true in the 1980s, a growing number of neighborhoods are integrated, and not just fleetingly, but typically over many years. And meanwhile, the number of exclusively white neighborhoods continues to fall fairly rapidly. Integrated neighborhoods appear to be an increasing fact of metropolitan life.

That said, there have been some limits to this development. First, much of the increase in integration that we've seen (especially during the 1990s) has been between whites and nonblack minority groups—that is, Asians and Hispanics. There has been far less change in the prevalence of neighborhoods shared by blacks and whites. On the whole, black households remain extremely racially segregated in U.S. metropolitan areas.

Second, while integrated neighborhoods became more stable during the 1980s than they were during the 1970s, there was little change in the stability of these neighborhoods during the 1990s. Racially integrated neighborhoods were as likely to lose whites during the 1990s as they were during the 1980s.

Third, the evidence here suggests that certain types of white households are particularly resistant to racial integration, a fact that takes us back to the anniversary of the *Brown v. Board of Education* decision. In the fifty years since that landmark decision, we've made enormous strides in integrating many aspects of U.S. society—public spaces, the workplace, even our residential neighborhoods. But we've seen the least progress in the very area on which the decision focused, public schools. This relative lack of progress on the schools front is to a large degree predicted by the neighborhood racial stereotyping hypothesis. If, as suggested here, a key reason why many white households, especially those with children, avoid integrated neighborhoods is that they harbor stereotypes about the quality of public services delivered in these neighborhoods (the most critical service being the local public schools), then it's not surprising that these white households also avoid sending their children to integrated schools.

In summary, metropolitan areas in the United States have become more integrated during the 1990s. But a particular set of white households—homeowners and those with children—are still resisting this trend. To make further progress in the coming decades in integrating both our schools and our neighborhoods, we not only need to target discrimination by landlords and realtors but also need to pay closer attention to the neighborhood racial stereotypes that many white households rely on when choosing new neighborhoods and schools.

NOTES

1. The threshold for presence of non-Hispanic whites is higher because non-Hispanic whites represent a significantly larger share of the overall population.

2. These racial groups are grouped under a single "other" category to keep the number of neighborhood types to a manageable number.

3. Black Hispanics are placed in "black" category since past research suggests that the settlement patterns of black Hispanics are closer to those of blacks than to those of other Hispanics (see Denton and Massey 1989).

4. The long-form release is used.

5. When using the fixed-boundary file, neighborhood population in the standardized tracts tends to be smaller in earlier years. Thus, these neighborhoods may appear to be more segregated.

6. Note that the number of census tracts increases in each decade, since metropolitan areas have grown larger over time and the total number of metropolitan areas has grown as well.

7. Differences in the definition of *Hispanic* used in 1970 make comparisons between 1970 and later census years problematic.

8. These percentages add together the proportion of white-black, white-black-Hispanic, white-black-other, and white-black-Hispanic-other neighborhoods.

9. This figure counts the number of blacks in 2000 as all individuals who list black as one of their racial groups. If we count as black only those individuals who list black and no other racial group, then the 1980–2000 growth in the black population would be 31 percent.

10. Given the fact that the white-multiethnic neighborhoods were at least 20 percent minority (since at least two minority groups had a presence of at least 10 percent), it is

likely that the proportion of non-Hispanic whites was actually lower to start with in these multiethnic census tracts.

REFERENCES

Denton, Nancy, and Douglas Massey. 1989. "Racial Identity Among Caribbean Hispanics: The Effect of Double Minority Status on Residential Segregation." *American Sociological Review* 54:790–808.

——. 1991. "Patterns of Racial Transition in a Multiethnic World: U.S. Metropolitan Areas, 1970–1980." *Demography* 28:41–63.

Ellen, Ingrid Gould. 1998. "Stable, Racial Integration in the Contemporary United States: An Empirical Overview." *Journal of Urban Affairs* 20(1): 27–42.

——. 2000. *Sharing America's Neighborhoods: The Changing Prospects for Stable Racial Integration.* Cambridge, MA: Harvard University Press.

Farley, Reynolds, and William Frey. 1994. "Changes in the Segregation of Whites from Blacks during the 1980s: Small Steps Toward a More Integrated Society." *American Sociological Review* 59:23–45

Fasenfast, David, Jason Booza, and Kurt Metzger. 2004. *Living Together: A New Look at Racial and Ethnic Integration in Metropolitan Neighborhoods*. Center for Urban and Metropolitan Policy. Washington, DC: Brookings Institution. http://ww.brook.edu/urban/publications/20040428_fasenfest.htm.

Galster, George C. 1990. "Neighborhood Racial Change, Segregationist Sentiments, and Affirmative Marketing Policies." *Journal of Urban Economics* 27:334–61.

Galster, George, and Heather Keeney. 1993. "Subsidized Housing and Racial Change in Yonkers, New York." *Journal of the American Planning Association* 59:172–81.

GeoLytics, 2002. *User Guide, CensusCD Neighborhood Change Database (NCDB) 1970–2000*. East Brunswick, NJ: GeoLytics.

Grieco, Elizabeth, and Rachel Cassidy. 2001. *Overview of Race and Hispanic Origin*. Census 2000 Brief. Washington, DC: U.S. Bureau of the Census.

Jargowsky, Paul. 1997. *Poverty and Place: Ghettos, Barrios, and the American City*. New York: Russell Sage Foundation.

Lee, Barrett. 1985. "Racially Mixed Neighborhoods during the 1970s: Change or Stability?" *Social Science Quarterly* 66:346–64.

Lee, Barrett, and Peter Wood. 1990. "The Fate of Residential Integration in American Cities: Evidence from Racially Mixed Neighborhoods, 1970-1980." *Journal of Urban Affairs* 12: 425-436.

Lee, Barrett, and Peter Wood. 1991. "Is Neighborhood Racial Succession Place-Specific?" *Demography* 28:21–39.

Logan, John R., and Mark Schneider. 1984. "Racial Segregation and Racial Change in American Suburbs, 1970–1980." *American Journal of Sociology* 89:874–88.

Mumford Center. 2001. *Ethnic Diversity Grows, Neighborhood Integration Lags Behind*. Lewis Mumford Center. Albany: State University of New York Press. http://mumford1.dyndns.org/cen2000/WholePop/WPreport/MumfordReport.pdf.

Nyden, Philip, Michael Maly, and John Lukehart. 1997. "The Emergence of Stable Racially and Ethnically Diverse Urban Communities: A Case Study of Nine Cities," *Housing Policy Debate* 8(2): 491–534.

Rawlings, Lynette, Laura Harris, and Margery Austin Turner. 2004. "Race and Residence: Prospects for Stable Neighborhood Integration." Washington, DC: The Urban Institute. http://www.urban.org/UploadedPDF/310985_NCUA3.pdf.

Schelling, Thomas. 1972. "The Process of Residential Segregation: Neighborhood Tipping." In *Racial Discrimination in Economic Life*, ed. Anthony Pascal, 157–84. Lexington, MA: D. C. Heath.

Taeuber, Karl, and Alma Taeuber. 1965. *Negroes in Cities: Residential Segregation and Neighborhood Change*. Chicago: Aldine Publishing Company.

Taub, Richard, D. Garth Taylor, and Jan Dunham. 1984. *Paths of Neighborhood Change*. Chicago: University of Chicago Press.

7

Implementing the Federal Fair Housing Act

The Adjudication of Complaints

Michael H. Schill

Over three decades ago, Congress enacted the landmark Fair Housing Act of 1968 (the "Fair Housing Act"), which outlawed private as well as public discrimination in housing. Twenty years later, Congress passed the Fair Housing Amendments Act of 1988 (the "1988 Amendments Act"), a law that significantly expanded the scope of the original legislation and strengthened its enforcement mechanisms. Like most important pieces of federal legislation, the Fair Housing Act and the 1988 Amendments Act embody a series of careful compromises crafted by members of Congress.

Among the most controversial issues faced by Congress in its deliberation and passage of the 1988 Amendments Act was the forum that would adjudicate claims of housing discrimination. Once the United States Department of Housing and Urban Development (HUD) investigators and attorneys had determined that reasonable cause existed to believe that housing discrimination had taken place, some body would have to decide whether liability existed and, if so, what remedies would be forthcoming. In the end, the machinery created by the 100th Congress allows either party to elect to proceed in federal district court before a judge and jury. If neither party makes this "election," the case will be heard by an administrative law judge (ALJ).

This chapter represents one of the first attempts to systematically examine how the 1988 Amendments Act has been implemented. Data on HUD's enforcement efforts from 1989 through 2003 are analyzed to show how patterns of complaints and HUD investigations have evolved over the fifteen-year period. In addition, I describe results from a survey of 161 complainants and 126 respondents that was undertaken in 1999. The responses from these litigants provide unique insights into the successes and failures of the 1988

Amendments Act and the enforcement machinery that has evolved to implement its provisions.

In the first part of this chapter, I describe the enforcement provisions of the 1988 Amendments Act. To place the legal machinery in context, a short legislative history is presented that describes both the state of the law prior to 1988 and contemporaneous views of members of the legislative and executive branches of government regarding the need for a new enforcement regime. A summary of existing literature on Fair Housing enforcement is also provided. In the second part, I describe the data utilized in this chapter as well as the research methodology employed. In the chapter's third section, I offer a description of HUD's enforcement efforts from 1989 through 2003. In section four, I analyze the survey of complainants and respondents, each of whom had a case that progressed beyond HUD to be adjudicated by the HUD ALJs or federal district courts. The chapter concludes with a short discussion of the implications of these empirical findings as well as an examination of the types of research that still need to be done to gain a more complete understanding of the Fair Housing Act enforcement process.

THE ENFORCEMENT PROVISIONS OF THE FAIR HOUSING ACT OF 1968 AND THE FAIR HOUSING AMENDMENTS ACT OF 1988

Title VIII of the Civil Rights Act of 1968, commonly known as the Fair Housing Act, was passed by Congress on April 10, 1968. The act made it illegal to discriminate in the sale or rental of housing on the ground of race, color, religion, or national origin.[1] Despite the fact that several states and localities had already adopted laws forbidding discrimination in privately owned housing, Title VIII was the product of several years of contentious legislative debate. Indeed, the difficulty the sponsors had in amassing sufficient votes to overcome a Senate filibuster is reflected in several compromises throughout the act.

Perhaps the legislative compromise that would have the most profound impact on the Fair Housing Act's efficacy in fighting housing discrimination was its enforcement provisions. The original bill sponsored by Senator Walter Mondale in 1967 contained provisions that would have empowered HUD to investigate complaints of discrimination, hold evidentiary hearings, and issue enforcement orders.[2] After several successful filibusters, Senator Everett Dirksen introduced an amendment in 1968 that stripped the bill of most of its enforcement provisions (Dubofsky 1969). Under the Fair Housing Act, persons who felt that they had been discriminated against could file complaints with HUD, but the agency only had the power to investigate and seek conciliation. If efforts to achieve voluntary settlements failed, as they often did, the complainant would be left to file a private lawsuit. Private litigants could seek actual damages and injunctive relief, but punitive damages were capped at $1,000. The Fair Housing Act also provided for the payment of legal fees, but only in instances where the complainant could not afford to pay his or her own attorney. Although HUD had little power to enforce the law, the Department of Justice (DOJ) was given the authority to bring lawsuits under the act when it uncovered a pattern or practice of discrimination.

Over the next twenty years, despite the fact that housing discrimination remained endemic in the United States, the federal government was either powerless or unwilling to take major steps to enforce the act. HUD's conciliation efforts often were fruitless and politics frequently constrained the DOJ from aggressively pursuing pattern and practice cases.[3] Indeed, in legislative debates over the 1988 Amendments Act, the consensus for change was bipartisan and widespread. One of two cosponsors of the bill in the Senate, Edward Kennedy, characterized the Fair Housing Act as a "toothless tiger" (Kennedy 1988). Former HUD secretary Patricia Roberts Harris was quoted as saying that filing a complaint was a "useless task" (Henderson 1987) and her successor, Secretary Samuel Pierce, cited the lack of effective HUD enforcement power as the "most glaring deficiency in Title VIII" (Pierce 1987).

Efforts to bolster federal enforcement powers date back to the late 1970s. Congress repeatedly considered legislation that would have given HUD the power to enforce the statute subject to judicial review in federal courts of appeal. Despite significant support in Congress for amending the law, deep disagreements surfaced over the scope of power to be accorded to HUD and its administrative law judges. The major source of concern was whether Congress had the authority to vest sole jurisdiction over discrimination complaints in HUD administrative law judges. A 1974 Supreme Court case, *Curtis v. Loether* (1974), had interpreted the Seventh Amendment to the Constitution to provide respondents with the right to jury trial when they were sued for damages under the act. In addition, the Reagan administration questioned whether administrative judges would be as efficient and cost-effective as proponents suggested (Reynolds 1987).

The Fair Housing Amendments Act of 1988

The logjam in crafting a new enforcement mechanism was broken in 1988 by Representative Hamilton Fish of New York State. Fish, working in cooperation with civil rights groups and the National Association of Realtors, devised a compromise that sidestepped the constitutional issue. Upon the filing of a complaint alleging housing discrimination, HUD simultaneously seeks to achieve conciliation and to investigate the claim. If the complaint comes from a state or locality whose law has been deemed by HUD to be substantially equivalent to the Fair Housing Act, it must be referred to that state's human rights agency. For complaints over which it retains jurisdiction, in cases where mediation is impossible, HUD must make a determination as to whether reasonable cause exists to believe that the complainant has been discriminated against. If such a cause finding is made, HUD files a charge with the Office of Administrative Law Judges in HUD.

Either party can, within twenty days, elect to have the case adjudicated in federal district court rather than by an administrative law judge (ALJ). If no election takes place, an administrative law judge hears the case and issues a ruling. In election cases, the DOJ represents the interests of the complainant and the government in federal district court; in cases before the HUD ALJs the complainant is represented by an attorney from HUD's Office of General Counsel. The complainant may also choose to retain counsel and intervene in the case to protect his or her interests in the event that those interests diverge from the government's interests.[4] Complainants also have the option of filing claims directly in federal district court, thereby bypassing the federal administrative enforcement apparatus altogether.[5]

Remedies available to successful complainants vary depending on the forum in which their claims are adjudicated. HUD ALJs are empowered to grant compensatory damages, injunctive relief, and civil penalties of up to $50,000 in the case of three offenses within a seven-year period. Federal district court judges and juries may award punitive damages in lieu of civil penalties.[6]

Although inferring legislative intent is seldom clear-cut, it seems that members of Congress had certain expectations at the time the 1988 Amendments Act was passed about how the legislation would work out in practice. Under the preexisting law, there was little incentive for respondents to conciliate discrimination claims because HUD had no power to penalize recalcitrant or culpable parties. Private litigation was, for the most part, an empty threat because it took too long for matters to be resolved and cost too much money. Therefore, several members of Congress, including the chairman of the House Committee on the Judiciary, Peter Rodino, expressed the view that the strengthened enforcement provisions would make parties take HUD's conciliation efforts more seriously and thereby promote settlements (Rodino 1987).[7]

It also seems likely that congressional sponsors of the 1988 Amendments Act expected that most cases that did not settle and were not transferred to state and local agencies would be heard before the HUD ALJs. The election provision was added to the bill fairly late in the legislative debate on the floor of the House of Representatives. The reason given by its author, Representative Fish, for introducing the amendment was that the provision would insulate the legislation from constitutional challenges. Members of Congress repeatedly emphasized the need for an inexpensive and effective remedy, and there was virtually no debate over the ability of the DOJ to handle the increased caseload from elections.

HUD's Enforcement Operations and their Effectiveness: Recent Studies

Since the mid-1990s, a handful of reports have described HUD enforcement efforts, typically concluding that they were plagued by delay and relatively low rates of reasonable-cause findings. For example, the United States Commission on Civil Rights (1994) examined the first four years of experience under the 1988 Amendments Act. According to the commission, through 1993, HUD had closed 23,007 cases. Of these cases, 4,461 were conciliated and charges were issued in 619 cases. The majority of charges involved claims based on familial status (61 percent), followed by race (16 percent), and disability (14 percent). Of the 619 cases in which HUD found reasonable cause to believe that an act of discrimination had occurred, one or more parties elected to proceed in federal district court in 369 cases. In a majority of these cases, the party who elected was the respondent or defendant.

Although earlier reports had identified the absence of coercive power as the main reason for HUD's complaint processing backlog, the commission found that delays remained even after the 1988 Amendments Act. Under the statute, HUD is supposed to make its reasonable-cause determination within 100 days unless it is impracticable to do so. According to the Commission on Civil Rights, in 1993 the average time for HUD to close a case was 151 days, an improvement of 55 days over 1991, but still far from conformity with the standards set by Title VIII. The commission further found that HUD's procedures were "deficient" and that the agency "lacked a systematic approach to processing complaints" (U.S. Commission on Civil Rights 1994).

In 2001, the National Council on Disability (NCD) published *Reconstructing Fair Housing*, a report that analyzed data on complaints filed between 1989 and 2000. The report showed that over the eleven-year span, complaints alleging discrimination based on disability had overtaken the other categories of complaints to become the most common basis of discrimination. Beginning in 1996, no-cause findings increased to 45 percent of all closures. The NCD also reported that the number of cause findings "declined dramatically" between 1994 and 2000 from 325 cases to only 96. The NCD report found that delays in closing complaints mushroomed over time. Instead of inspections being resolved within the statutory 100-day period, the average time from filing to date of closure by HUD rose from 96 days in 1989 to 137 days in 1992 and reached 497 days in 2000.

Although much less comprehensive than the NCD and Civil Rights Commission reports, every two years the Citizens' Commission on Civil Rights, a private civil rights advocacy organization, issues a report on civil rights enforcement. A report covering the period through the end of the Clinton administration (Relman 2002) is extremely critical of HUD's enforcement efforts:

> At the conclusion of the Clinton Administration, the harsh reality sadly remains that, notwithstanding [Secretary] Cuomo's success in winning budget increases for the agency, HUD's dismal record in processing fair housing complaints shows no signs of improvement. . . . The trend is in the opposite direction. HUD fair housing enforcement actions have, on a relative scale, declined across the board since 1997. (Relman 2002, 100)

Among the issues identified by Relman were increased delays in complaint processing, declining compensation obtained for settlements, and a decrease in reasonable-cause findings. Relman notes that the reasons for this deterioration in performance included the choice by former secretary Cuomo to emphasize high-profile cases that "produced more spin than substance," and the failure to monitor effectively state and local Fair Housing Assistance Program (FHAP) agencies.

The most recent report on HUD enforcement activities was produced by the United States General Accounting Office (GAO) in 2004. The GAO examined complaints filed between 1996 and 2003 and its findings include the following:

- In 2001, the proportion of investigations that were completed within 100 days increased from 14 percent in 2000 to 41 percent.
- Regional differences in outcomes of investigations were prevalent, with some HUD offices much more likely to make no-cause determinations than others.
- HUD staffing has fluctuated over time and new hires have frequently lacked the skills necessary to conduct thorough and effective investigations.
- Reliable data on intake and outcomes of Fair Housing cases does not exist.
- Fundamentally HUD has failed over the last three decades to undertake a systematic nationwide review of the enforcement practices of federal and FHAP agencies.

Thus, the first eighteen years of experience under the Fair Housing Amendments Act of 1988 have not been free from controversy. Prior studies are rife with criticism that the act has not achieved its objective of creating a streamlined process for persons who believe they have been discriminated against to achieve a resolution of their complaints. Yet even more glaring has been the absence of any systematic analysis by HUD of how the law has worked in practice.

DATA AND SURVEY METHODOLOGY

Whether the 1988 Amendments Act has fulfilled the expectations of its sponsors is a question that has received very little attention. Studies of the Fair Housing Act enforcement process have been hampered by the fact that enforcement responsibilities have been vested in three separate agencies: (1) HUD, (2) the Office of ALJs in HUD, and (3) the DOJ. Each of these agencies maintains a separate database to track cases that is incompatible with the other two.

HUD's TEAPOTS Database

In this chapter, I make use of HUD's Title Eight Automated Paperless Office Tracking System ("TEAPOTS"). TEAPOTS was made operational by HUD in the mid-1990s to track the progress of all Fair Housing cases (including those investigated by FHAP agencies). An extract of the database was made available to the author in which all names and addresses were expurgated.

Unfortunately, the data included in TEAPOTS has not been consistently reported since 1989. From 1989 to the mid-1990s, HUD did not track certain types of inquiries or filings that were clearly nonjurisdictional. Nevertheless, some nonmeritorious cases were filed as complaints and thereby tracked. Beginning in 1995, HUD created two categories of cases—"claims" for nonjurisdictional or clearly nonmeritorious inquiries that were summarily dismissed, and "complaints" for those that would proceed to an investigation.

Because of this change in categorization, there is no way to track the entire universe of cases consistently throughout the entire period. Tracking only complaints would result in a higher proportion of nonmeritorious actions in the pre-1995 data. Tracking all cases (claims and complaints) would result in the opposite phenomenon—more nonmeritorious cases in the post-1995 period. In some instances, where this distinction matters, data will be presented both ways—using just complaints and then claims and complaints together.

A second weakness of TEAPOTS is that although the database was created with the intention of tracking cases that are referred over to the HUD ALJs or to the DOJ, the data from the two agencies are unreliable. The DOJ does not report to HUD the outcomes of election cases. Indeed, even if the results of election cases were reported the information would be useless since the definition of what constitutes a "case" is different for the two agencies, and each gives the same case a unique and different docket number.

A Survey of Respondents and Complainants

This failure of HUD to track the outcomes of cases once an investigation is closed required that an integrated database be created to obtain comparable information about the results of Fair Housing cases. This database was created by the author and another researcher in 1999 (Schill and Friedman 1999).

In addition to providing the first and thus far only "cradle-to-grave" picture of the progress of Fair Housing cases, the database was utilized to identify and contact respondents and complainants involved in cases that had received reasonable-cause charges. Creating appropriate sampling frames and contacting complainants and respondents presented a number of challenges. Because each agency had its own method for tracking and defining cases, a uniform definition of a case was created that combined all charges listing the same respondent that were docketed on the same date. From 1989 to 1998, a total of 1,074 cases charged by HUD and docketed with the HUD ALJs were identified using this method. Of these 1,074 cases, 47 were excluded because they had not yet been closed. Because a pretest of the survey instruments indicated that the difficulty of finding complainants and respondents increased tremendously as more time since adjudication elapsed, the potential sample was further limited to cases that were docketed with the HUD ALJs after 1992. After additional adjustments were made to eliminate duplicate cases and cases for which incomplete data existed in the federal databases, the final sampling frame for respondents included 719 cases and for complainants, 704 cases.

Two survey instruments were designed—one to be administered to complainants and one to respondents—in order to gather data about the parties and their experiences. From May 1999 to November 1999, a total of 166 interviews were completed with complainants, representing 161 separate cases. With respect to respondents, a total of 148 interviews were completed with respondents, representing 126 cases. Because the difficulty experienced in locating complainants and respondents necessitated substituting an effort to contact all parties rather than just the originally contemplated random sample,[8] a concern existed about whether the 161 complainants and 126 respondents included in the study were representative of all complainants and respondents.[9] Difference-in-means and difference-in-proportions tests were employed to determine whether the characteristics of the cases in which complainants and respondents were contacted differed from the characteristics of the cases in which complainants and respondents were not contacted.[10] The results indicate that no statistically significant differences exist between the complainants we interviewed and those we could not reach. However, the same is not true for respondents. Respondents in the sample were significantly less likely than their counterparts who were not interviewed to be involved in cases based on race, but significantly more likely to be involved in cases based on family status. Respondents who were interviewed were also significantly less likely to be involved in cases in which an election occurred than respondents who were not interviewed (i.e., 54 percent versus 63.6 percent). With respect to the characteristics referring to the outcome of the cases, sampled respondents were significantly more likely than nonsampled respondents to be involved in a case that resulted in a settlement rather than a decision and in which the complainant received injunctive relief.

Thus, obtaining an accurate picture of how the 1988 Amendments Act has been implemented is made difficult by the absence of appropriate administrative data. By piecing together administrative records from HUD, the HUD ALJs, and the DOJ, a good picture of enforcement efforts emerges. In order to learn more about the experiences of complainants and respondents, however, a survey was fielded. The next two parts contain the analyses of these two sets of data.

HUD'S ENFORCEMENT OF THE FAIR HOUSING ACT, 1989–2003

The Filing of Complaints and Claims

As table 7.1 and figure 7.1 indicate, the number of complaints filed with HUD and FHAP agencies has ranged between 5,800 and 10,200, averaging 7,750 per year. Growth was fairly consistent over the first five years of the period and then dipped with the advent of "claims" in 1994. Since 1997, the number of complaints began to steadily increase, reaching 8,570 in 2003. As might be expected, the share of cases handled by FHAP agencies gradually increased as more states and localities were certified as having substantially equivalent laws. Throughout the first few years of the 1988 act, the federal share of complaints ranged from 54 percent to 69 percent. By 2003, more than two-thirds of all complaints were being handled by state and local FHAP agencies.

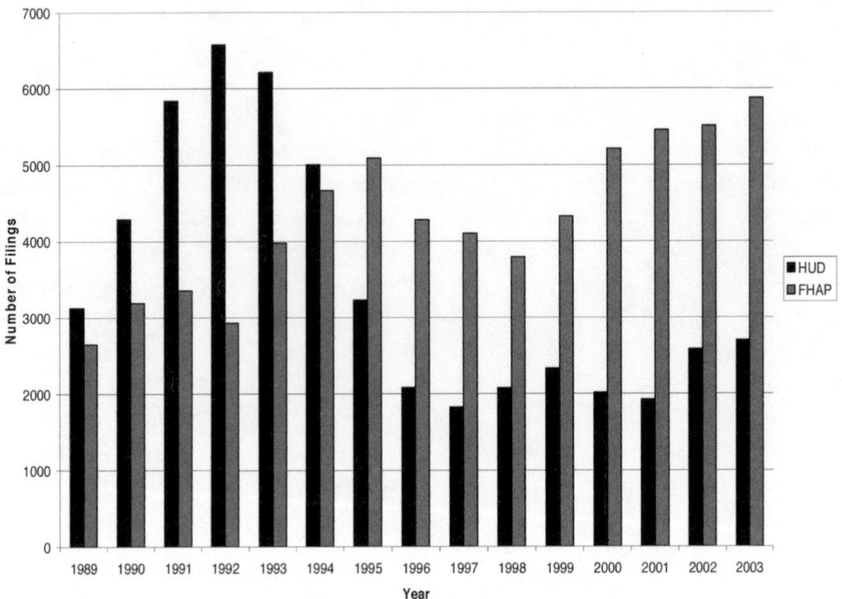

Figure 7.1. Complaints Filed with HUD and FHAP Agencies, 1989–2003.

Table 7.2 shows the protected status of people who filed complaints with HUD since 1989. Although the debates over Fair Housing in 1988 primarily concerned racial discrimination, in most years race-based complaints were not the largest category filed. In the early years of the 1988 act, allegations of familial discrimination (i.e., allegations of discrimination against families with children) were most numerous. Race-related complaints dominated between 1992 and 1998. Since 1999, however, the single largest category of cases was of those filed by persons alleging discrimination based on disability. In 2003, for example, over one-half of all complaints filed alleged discrimination based on disability while only 38.4 percent alleged race discrimination.

Information on the types of prohibited actions alleged in discrimination complaints filed with HUD suggests that the most blatant forms of discrimination are becoming less common. For example, in 1989, 40.9 percent of all complaints alleged that a landlord refused to rent to the complainant or that someone refused to sell someone a home based on a prohibited reason. By 2003, the proportion of filings containing these allegations had declined to only 18.3 percent. As might be expected, the category of discriminatory acts that grew the most over the period were the ones that related to disability (e.g., failure to make reasonable accommodations), which increased from 0 in

Table 7.1. Fair Housing Act Complaint Filings with HUD and FHAP Agencies: 1989–2003

Year Filed	*HUD*	*FHAP*	*Total*
1989	3129	2647	5776
	54.2%	45.8%	
1990	4287	3196	7483
	57.3%	42.7%	
1991	5836	3353	9189
	63.5%	36.5%	
1992	6579	2934	9513
	69.2%	30.8%	
1993	6214	3976	10190
	61.0%	39.0%	
1994	5004	4667	9671
	51.7%	48.3%	
1995	3228	5089	8317
	38.8%	61.2%	
1996	2086	4282	6368
	32.8%	67.2%	
1997	1828	4102	5930
	30.8%	69.2%	
1998	2080	3791	5871
	35.4%	64.6%	
1999	2333	4332	6665
	35.0%	65.0%	
2000	2020	5212	7232
	27.9%	72.1%	
2001	1925	5457	7382
	26.1%	73.9%	
2002	2590	5511	8101
	32.0%	68.0%	
2003	2702	5868	8570
	31.5%	68.5%	
Total	**51,841**	**64,417**	**116,258**
	44.6%	**55.4%**	

1989 to 13.3 percent in 2003. The single most common allegation in 2003 was discrimination in the terms, privileges, and services, which was cited by 39.4 percent of all people who filed complaints.

HUD Dispositions

Table 7.3 shows how HUD disposed of all complaints according to the year in which they were filed. This cohort analysis is not the typical way enforcement

Table 7.2. Filings with HUD by Protected Status

Year Filed	*Sex*	*Race*	*Familial*	*Religion*	*Disability*	*Color*	*National Origin*
1989	11.9%	36.6%	47.8%	1.7%	16.7%	5.8%	6.7%
1990	11.5%	33.5%	45.7%	1.8%	27.6%	3.5%	7.4%
1991	10.6%	37.9%	39.9%	3.4%	28.3%	4.5%	7.8%
1992	14.2%	42.7%	31.5%	2.3%	28.0%	3.4%	9.9%
1993	15.4%	46.1%	26.2%	2.7%	28.3%	1.4%	13.1%
1994	14.8%	46.9%	22.6%	2.9%	32.1%	1.9%	13.2%
1995	16.9%	45.7%	22.6%	2.0%	36.2%	3.1%	12.1%
1996	12.6%	43.2%	23.2%	1.4%	34.4%	6.0%	15.4%
1997	13.3%	43.7%	17.5%	2.2%	42.4%	7.7%	15.6%
1998	13.6%	48.3%	15.2%	1.4%	41.3%	8.2%	13.8%
1999	9.4%	38.0%	20.5%	3.1%	46.6%	7.6%	9.9%
2000	11.0%	41.1%	16.8%	2.0%	48.2%	3.0%	11.1%
2001	13.5%	40.5%	16.3%	1.7%	43.5%	3.7%	10.4%
2002	11.7%	39.2%	14.5%	2.6%	48.6%	1.5%	9.6%
2003	14.8%	38.4%	15.1%	2.6%	51.0%	1.5%	9.9%

data are presented but is thought to be more useful than year-by-year results. The one drawback is that for the most recent year, most cases will necessarily not have progressed as far along in case processing as they would have had more time elapsed. Therefore, caution is advised in interpreting results from 2002 and 2003.

Table 7.3 shows only complaints filed with HUD. Since 1989, 35.6 percent of all complaints were conciliated or settled. The next largest category of cases—comprising just over 30 percent of all complaints—was those that were dismissed or withdrawn for reasons that had nothing to do with the merits of the case, such as allegations that did not fall within the jurisdiction of the Fair Housing Act or HUD or complaints in which the original complainant could not be located or refused to cooperate with the investigation. The third most populated category was the filings that received determinations from HUD that no cause existed to believe discrimination had occurred. Just over 26 percent of all cases had this result. Only 3.3 percent of all complaints (1,720 complaints in total) resulted in reasonable-cause charges being issued.

The single most significant pattern to emerge from these data is the disappearance of reasonable-cause determinations. Figure 7.2 shows graphically how steep this decline has been. For complaints filed in 1993, 318 received reasonable-cause charges from HUD. For complaints filed in 1994 this number declined by 57 percent to 135. By 2000, the number had fallen to only 48.[11]

Table 7.3. Status of HUD Complaints by Year Filed

Year Filed	*Dismissed/ Withdrawn Not on Merits*	*Conciliation/ Settlement*	*No-cause Determination*	*Cause Determination Made*	*Misc.*	*Total*
1989	**1180**	**1199**	**564**	**166**	**20**	**3129**
	37.7%	38.3%	18.0%	5.3%	0.64%	100.0%
1990	**1703**	**1619**	**722**	**175**	**68**	**4287**
	39.7%	37.8%	16.8%	4.1%	1.59%	100.0%
1991	**2560**	**2013**	**892**	**196**	**175**	**5836**
	43.9%	34.5%	15.3%	3.4%	3.00%	100.0%
1992	**3046**	**2038**	**1137**	**200**	**158**	**6579**
	46.3%	31.0%	17.3%	3.0%	2.40%	100.0%
1993	**2503**	**2011**	**1334**	**318**	**48**	**6214**
	40.3%	32.4%	21.5%	5.1%	0.77%	100.0%
1994	**1212**	**2031**	**1576**	**135**	**50**	**5004**
	24.2%	40.6%	31.5%	2.7%	1.00%	100.0%
1995	**714**	**1385**	**1018**	**81**	**30**	**3228**
	22.1%	42.9%	31.5%	2.5%	0.93%	100.0%
1996	**331**	**839**	**812**	**83**	**21**	**2086**
	15.9%	40.2%	38.9%	4.0%	1.01%	100.0%

(continued)

Table 7.3. (*continued*)

Year Filed	*Dismissed/ Withdrawn Not on Merits*	*Conciliation/ Settlement*	*No-cause Determination*	*Cause Determination Made*	*Misc.*	*Total*
1997	**286**	**705**	**706**	**93**	**38**	**1828**
	15.7%	38.6%	38.6%	5.1%	2.08%	100.0%
1998	**416**	**794**	**658**	**99**	**113**	**2080**
	20.0%	38.6%	31.6%	4.8%	5.43%	100.0%
1999	**353**	**925**	**735**	**89**	**231**	**2333**
	15.1%	39.7%	31.5%	3.8%	9.90%	100.0%
2000	**330**	**720**	**805**	**48**	**117**	**2020**
	16.3%	35.6%	39.9%	2.4%	5.79%	100.0%
2001	**313**	**645**	**824**	**20**	**123**	**1925**
	16.3%	33.5%	42.8%	1.0%	6.39%	100.0%
2002	**507**	**789**	**1007**	**17**	**270**	**2590**
	19.6%	30.5%	38.9%	0.7%	10.42%	100.0%
2003	**203**	**741**	**693**	**0**	**1065**	**2702**
	7.5%	27.4%	25.7%	0.0%	39.42%	100.0%
Total	**15657**	**18454**	**13483**	**1720**	**2527**	**51841**
	30.2%	35.6%	26.0%	3.3%	4.87%	100.0%

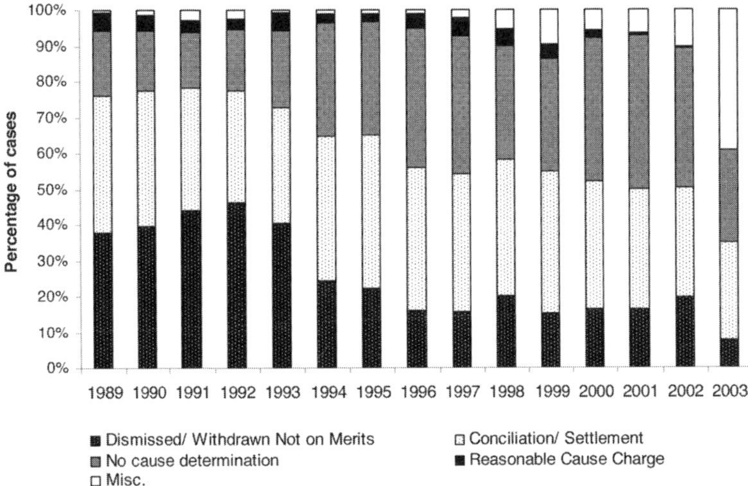

Figure 7.2. Status of Complaints Filed with HUD by Year Filed, 1989–2003.

Elections and Adjudication

Contrary to the hopes and expectations of the framers of the 1988 Amendments Act, most cases in which HUD finds reasonable cause to believe that discrimination has occurred do not get resolved by the HUD ALJs. To the contrary, as figure 7.3 shows, since 1989 in the majority of charged cases (64 percent), one or more of the parties elected to have their cases heard in federal district court. Only for cases filed in 1998 did the majority (53.5 percent) proceed to the HUD ALJs for resolution.

Who was responsible for the decision to elect to proceed in federal district court? Recall that under the 1988 Amendments Act, either party could opt to move the case from the HUD ALJs to court. With respect to each year of filing up to 2000, the respondent was much more likely to have made the election decision than the complainant. Overall, respondents elected to proceed in federal district court in 697 cases, complainants in 330, and both in 39. For complaints filed after 1999, this disparity has narrowed considerably.

The data on outcomes of complaints demonstrate that the single most common resolution of complaints filed with HUD is a settlement or conciliation. Figure 7.4 shows that the median amount of money received by complainants as a result of HUD settlements is extremely modest, ranging from $649 in 1990 to $1,800 in 2000. Although conciliation awards are small, they nonetheless take a significant amount of time to achieve. Since 1989,

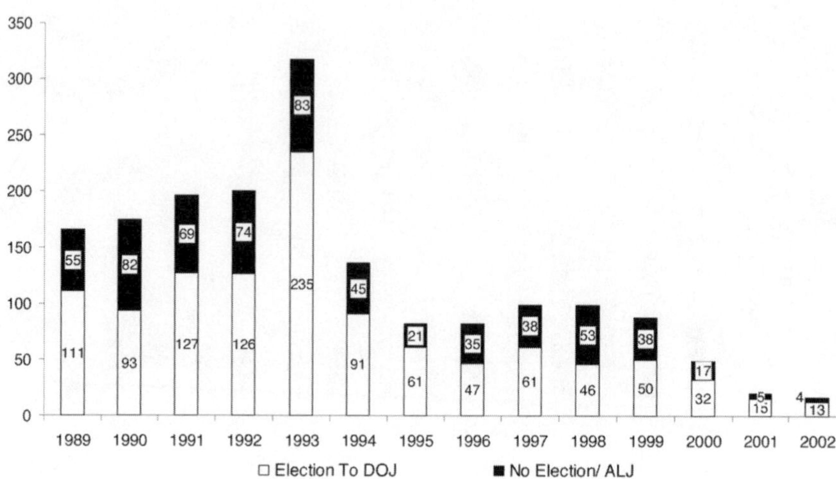

Figure 7.3. Charged Cases and Election Status by Year Filed.

the median number of days to reach a conciliation is 116; no-cause finding cases typically take 311 days. Reasonable-cause charges take even longer—556 days at the median. HUD's record for timeliness has improved substantially in recent years. For cases filed in 2001, the median number of days to achieve a reasonable-cause finding was 476, down from a peak of 709 for cases filed in 1996.

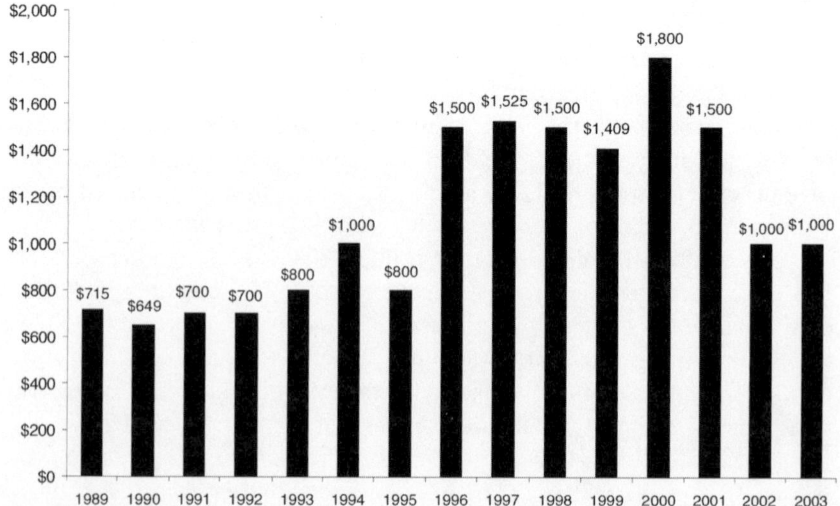

Figure 7.4. Median HUD Conciliation Amounts, 1989–2003.

The analysis of HUD enforcement data shows that only a small number of cases—1,720 cases since the 1988 Amendments Act became law, or only 3.3 percent of all complaints filed with HUD—have proceeded to the point where the complainants and respondents would potentially face each other in a judicial proceeding. Of these, the majority elect to proceed in federal district court. The fact that such a small number of cases utilize the administrative apparatus created by Congress in 1988 underlines the importance of understanding better the experiences of complainants and respondents.

RESULTS FROM THE SURVEY OF COMPLAINANTS AND RESPONDENTS

The rather modest number of cases that receive cause findings by HUD and the relatively small number or complainants and respondents who choose to have their cases heard by the HUD ALJs generate several questions. For example, what are the characteristics of the parties and claims that get this far in the process? What happens to the parties once their cases move to the next step? And does the choice of forum for adjudication have an effect on the ultimate resolution of cases?

Answers to these questions were obtained from the survey of complainants and respondents described above. The survey included responses from 161 complainants and 126 respondents whose cases were closed between 1992 and 1998.

The Filing of Complaints with HUD

Fair Housing complaints may be filed with HUD or with state and local enforcement agencies. However, because there is no administrative exhaustion requirement under Title VIII, complainants may also file directly in either federal or state courts. For a substantial number of the complainants the decision to file with HUD did not appear to be based on a fully informed weighing of the advantages and disadvantages of the two forums—over one-third of the sample (37.3 percent) indicated that they did not know that they could file directly in court. Over 22 percent of the complainants indicated that they had been referred to HUD by a private fair housing advocacy group or by an attorney. One-fifth (19.9 percent) of the complainants said that they had made their decision based on either positive feelings about HUD or their perception of the advantages of filing with the government.

The majority of complainants (87 percent) did not hire a private attorney at any stage of the process. Six percent had private legal representation prior to filing the fair housing complaint and an additional 7 percent employed legal counsel after the filing. Respondents, as expected, had a higher likelihood of being represented; 86.4 percent retained an attorney at some point following the allegation of discrimination.

With respect to the characteristics of the complainants, the complainant and respondent samples were quite similar. The most common basis of complaint was discrimination based on familial status, followed by race and disability. In terms of race, unsurprisingly, patterns vary depending on the nature of the complaint. With respect to complaints alleging racial discrimination, 75 percent of the complainants reported that they were nonwhite. This compared to only 39 percent for familial status complaints and 22 percent for disability complaints. People who filed disability-related complaints tended to have somewhat higher levels of education, were older, less likely to be married, and less likely to have children than those who alleged discrimination on other grounds. With the obvious exceptions of race and children in the household, the characteristics of complainants who filed familial status and race-based claims were roughly similar.

The Slow HUD Investigatory Process: Levels of Satisfaction

After filing a complaint with HUD, three out of five complainants were contacted by the agency within four weeks. However, a substantial number of complainants (38.8 percent) waited over four weeks and 18.2 percent had to wait over ten weeks before being contacted. For almost all complainants in the sample (96.1 percent), it took HUD over six months to reach a cause finding. Indeed, 82.9 percent reported that HUD had taken over one year to make a decision regarding whether to issue a charge.

As might be expected from a group that had successfully received cause findings from HUD, the complainants were significantly more satisfied with HUD's investigatory process than respondents. With respect to whether they believed HUD had thoroughly investigated the complaint, 52 percent of complainants strongly agreed, compared to only 11 percent of respondents. With respect to fairness and impartiality, even more polarized results emerged. Over half of complainants (51.2 percent) strongly agreed that HUD's investigation was fair and impartial, compared to only 6.3 percent of respondents.

The relatively high levels of complainant satisfaction with HUD's investigatory process are also reflected in their responses to a question that asked them whether they would advise a friend or relative to file a complaint with HUD in the event that they had been discriminated against. Over half (55 percent) of complainants strongly agreed with this proposition and an additional 14.2 percent agreed. Fewer than one in ten complainants strongly disagreed.

The Election Decision

In making a decision to proceed before the HUD ALJs or in federal district court, complainants and respondents are likely to be influenced by a number of factors. Some of these considerations are set forth below:

1. *Cost*: The expected cost of proceeding before the HUD ALJ is likely to be lower than in federal district court. Procedures are less formal, and the time to resolution is much shorter.
2. *Time*: The shorter average time period experienced by parties before the HUD ALJs as compared to federal district court is likely to be attractive to complainants. Respondents, on the other hand, may benefit from delay if it discourages complainants from pursuing complaints or encourages complainants to accept settlement offers.
3. *Available Relief*: A successful complainant can receive punitive damages in federal district court, but not in cases before the HUD ALJs. Complainants, particularly those with compelling experiences, may prefer federal district court, while respondents may wish to avoid a large punitive damage award by choosing the administrative adjudication option.
4. *Uncertainty*: Choosing a federal district court may increase uncertainty because of the large number of district court judges, many of whom have had little experience trying fair housing cases. If the parties choose a jury, uncertainty is greater since juries have no prior track record, and a jury may be more sympathetic to certain types of evidence.
5. *The Relationship between HUD and the Office of HUD ALJs in HUD*: Although HUD ALJs are independent from HUD,[12] the parties may not know that. Respondents may feel that they will not get an impartial trial from someone associated with the agency that found reasonable cause to believe that they have engaged in discriminatory conduct. Some complainants may seek to avoid further reliance on HUD enforcement because they are dissatisfied with the way their cases were handled at HUD.[13]
6. *Unfamiliarity with Administrative Enforcement*: For those attorneys who have little litigation experience with Fair Housing Act cases, the HUD ALJ process may be a mystery. They may advise their clients to select the forum with which they are most familiar—the federal district court.

The remainder of this part will examine the election decision and its impact on the outcome of Fair Housing cases. Overall, 19.5 percent of complainants

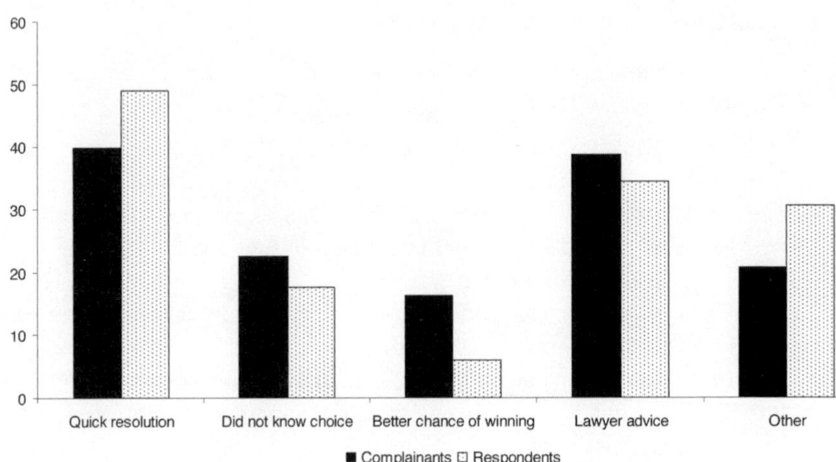

Figure 7.5. Reason for Selecting HUD ALJs.

preferred to have their cases adjudicated in federal district court. Among respondents, 43.3 percent preferred to have their cases proceed in federal district court.

Large proportions of complainants and respondents made their election decisions despite being uninformed about important differences between the two forums.[14] The parties were particularly ill informed about the fact that the HUD ALJs operated independently of HUD. Parties also had relatively low levels of information about the differences in remedies available in the two forums.

Complainants and respondents were asked why they either elected to proceed in federal district court or instead chose the HUD ALJs. Figure 7.5 shows that the most popular reason given by both complainants and respondents for preferring the HUD ALJs was that they wanted a quick resolution of their cases. The second most frequent response was that their lawyer advised them to do so.

As figure 7.6 shows, the role of legal advice in the election decision was also important for parties who elected federal district court.[15] A significant number of complainants and respondents also indicated that they thought they would have a better chance of winning in court or that they wanted a jury trial. Over one-fifth of complainants who elected district court did so because they wanted the opportunity to win punitive damages. Interestingly, among respondents, only 6.5 percent of those who elected district court said they did so because it would take longer and they wanted to wear the complainant down.[16]

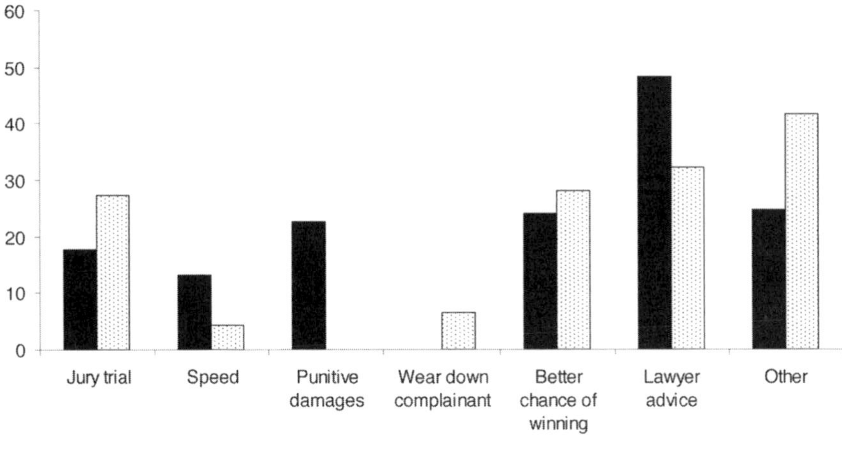

Figure 7.6. Reasons for Selecting Federal District Court.

The Resolution of Cases

Time to Resolve Cases

Cases in which one or more parties elected federal district court took much longer to resolve than cases that proceeded before the HUD ALJs. Comparable disparities exist in the respondent sample. Even more dramatic differences between the two forums exist with respect to cases that took a long time to close; far more cases in district court took more than one year to close.[17]

The large disparities in time required for resolution of complaints between the HUD ALJs and federal district court may be attributable to differences in the nature of the two forums. They may also, however, be attributable to differences in the types of cases that are adjudicated in each forum. To examine whether the choice of forum is independently related to the time to resolution of cases, multivariate methods were employed.[18] The results of the regression, as set forth in Table 7.4, confirm that choice of forum does indeed matter with respect to time to resolution.[19] Controlling for other characteristics of the case and the parties, cases take longer to resolve in federal district court than they do before the HUD ALJs.[20]

Outcomes of Case

Consistent with earlier research (Schill and Friedman 1999), the vast majority of cases in the complainant and respondent samples settled prior to

Table 7.4. Regression Coefficients of Models for Complainants and Respondents Predicting Time until Resolution of Complaints (Weighted)

	Complainants			*Respondents*		
Variables	*(1)*	*(2)*	*(3)*	*(4)*	*(5)*	*(6)*
Case characteristics						
Presence of lawyer	17.7813	22.4953	33.6053	27.3353	49.2077	43.6408
	(47.4221)	(48.0218)	(52.0103)	(50.8583)	(50.7450)	(50.4008)
Forum in which case was adjudicated (1=Federal district court)	228.1171**	223.0581**	224.3602**	186.6673**	182.5261**	177.9947**
	(34.6397)	(35.0690)	(36.7705)	(35.9338)	(36.2031)	(36.1304)
Type of case closure (ref. settlement)						
In favor of the complainant	60.5623	56.3108	50.1027	145.5805	95.5704	84.7318
	(72.6208)	(72.4942)	(76.7551)	(77.9173)	(79.4389)	(78.9763)
In favor of the respondent	222.2503*	201.9237*	310.4248**	−52.0479	−45.4999	−41.1478
	(85.5076)	(85.9391)	(102.9496)	(85.4337)	(84.4421)	(83.7747)
Dismissal/withdrawn	2.0083	8.8682	53.1161	90.7224	72.0896	80.5024
	(56.1313)	(56.1886)	(64.0896)	(57.5726)	(60.4151)	(60.0567)
Complaint characteristics						
Basis of complaint (ref. family status and all but race)						
Race, national origin, and all else (including family status)		60.1024	82.1097		35.6024	35.4630
		(38.2954)	(46.5546)		(40.7676)	(40.4571)
Disability and all but race and family status/ other		-9.1048	13.4863		45.0849	42.6491
		(40.3398)	(44.0799)		(48.1093)	(47.8852)

(continued)

Prohibited action (ref. terms & conditions and anything else but refusal to rent/sell; finance/refusal to sell and anything other than refusal to rent; miscellaneous)						
Refusal to rent and all but refusal to sell		32.2465 (32.6349)	24.0944 (38.0293)		94.3927* (36.8989)	95.8211* (36.7430)
Respondent demographics						
Type of company (1=landlord)	NA	NA	NA			−69.8005* (34.9554)
Complainant demographics						
Education (ref. > high school)						
High school and some college			9.0966 (61.4450)			
College and beyond			−44.1423 (66.9230)			
Total household income (logged)			−26.9092 (21.5153)			
Race (ref. non-Hispanic white)						
Non-Hispanic black			−12.9821 (45.0612)			
Non-Hispanic other			78.0501 (90.6843)			
Hispanic			238.0999** (60.5087)			

(continued)

Table 7.4. *(continued)*

	Complainants			*Respondents*		
Variables	*(1)*	*(2)*	*(3)*	*(4)*	*(5)*	*(6)*
Age			0.8072 (1.6633)			
Intercept	154.5104** (29.9868)	123.9311** (39.9681)	331.0141 (224.4134)	161.2677** (52.8841)	77.2482 (62.2259)	128.3998 (67.0806)
Adjusted R-squared	0.2184	0.2246	0.3090	0.1717	0.2005	0.2172
N	*161*	*161*	*140*	*126*	*126*	*125*

**p<0.01; *p<0.05; ^p<0.10

Table 7.5. Case Outcomes for Complainant Sample by Forum of Adjudication

	Forum of Adjudication	
Outcomes	*HUD ALJs*	*Federal District Court*
Resolution of Case		
Complainant Prevails	13.89	0.94
Respondent Prevails	4.79	3.01
Settlement	73.66	86.36
Other	7.66	9.69
Monetary Relief		
Monetary Award	86.38	71.43
Median Monetary Award	5249.57	5110.43
Median Monetary Award*	5846.40	10385.17
Nonmonetary Relief		
Allow rental of apartment	17.20	12.57
Allow continued rental	5.15	8.18
Allow purchase of home	4.45	0.00
Retrain employees	38.79	31.08
Affirmative action marketing plan	42.26	43.38
Hire non-English-speaking employees	11.23	8.77
Post equal opportunity signs	68.89	62.57
Other	18.16	14.95
N	*57*	*104*

*Based on all cases resolved with monetary awards.

adjudication. As tables 7.5 and 7.6 indicate, the rate of settlement is higher in federal district court than in cases before the HUD ALJs. In the relatively few cases that resulted in a verdict, complainants tended to be more successful in cases adjudicated by the HUD ALJs.[21] In federal district court, however, respondents had a slight edge.[22] Although complainants had a somewhat lower rate of obtaining monetary awards and settlements in federal district court, the amounts received tended to be higher.[23]

Money is not the only form of relief obtained by complainants as a result of the fair housing enforcement process. The most common form of nonmonetary relief is the posting of equal opportunity signs in the places of business of respondents.[24] Other common nonmonetary remedies included affirmative marketing plans and the retraining of employees. Relatively few instances exist where the respondent either agreed to or was required to provide housing.

Satisfaction with Forum

Both complainants and respondents were asked how satisfied they were with the way their cases were resolved. Satisfaction levels among complainants were

Table 7.6. Case Outcomes for Respondent Sample by Forum of Adjudication

	Forum of Adjudication	
Outcomes	*HUD ALJs*	*Federal District Court*
Resolution of Case		
Complainant Prevails	10.51	2.27
Respondent Prevails	3.79	4.55
Settlement	76.02	83.09
Other	9.68	10.09
Monetary Relief		
Monetary Award	82.75	73.15
Median Monetary Award	3187.70	2732.94
Median Monetary Award*	5620.79	6255.87
Nonmonetary Relief		
Allow rental of apartment	3.44	1.91
Allow continued rental	3.01	2.54
Allow purchase of home	0.00	2.86
Retrain employees	25.87	25.48
Affirmative action marketing plan	27.28	29.48
Hire non-English-speaking employees	0.00	7.21
Post equal opportunity signs	27.08	40.79
Other	12.03	11.39
N	*47*	*79*

*Based on all cases resolved with monetary awards.

significantly higher than those among respondents. Among complainants, those whose cases were handled by the HUD ALJs expressed somewhat higher levels of satisfaction than those whose cases were resolved in federal district court. For respondents, as might be expected, the results were very different. Approximately two-thirds of the respondents in each group expressed dissatisfaction, with majorities indicating they were "very dissatisfied."[25]

The complainants and respondents were also asked whether, in the event that they were a party to another Fair Housing dispute in the future, they would elect to have their cases adjudicated in federal district court or by the HUD ALJs. Overall, 58 percent of the complainants would prefer the HUD ALJs but this view was shared by only 38 percent of the respondents surveyed.

IMPLICATIONS AND FURTHER RESEARCH

The Fair Housing Amendments Act was adopted by Congress in 1988 primarily to provide an effective and efficient way for people who felt that they had been unlawfully discriminated against to vindicate their rights. By all accounts, discrimination in housing remains a major problem throughout the metropolitan United States.

Whether the provisions of the 1988 act have achieved the objectives of its sponsors is open to debate. This chapter has shown that while a very large number of complaints are filed annually with HUD, very few ever make it out of the building. Between 1989 and 2003, fewer than 1,800 complaints (or 3 percent) received reasonable-cause findings. While many more cases were settled, the average settlement amounts were exceedingly modest—less than $2,000 per case. Even among the 1,720 cases that were adjudicated in federal district court or by the HUD ALJs, the average compensation and settlement awards were extraordinarily low—less than $10,000. These modest results did not come quickly or cheaply because of bureaucratic inefficiency and because complainants and respondents, themselves, did not, as members of Congress thought they would, make use of the HUD ALJ process.

A law that prohibits the type of activities outlawed by the Fair Housing Act can have a substantial deterrent effect under two sets of conditions. If penalties are low, then enforcement efforts must be intensive so that most lawbreakers will be identified and punished. Alternatively, if intensive identification and prosecution of violators of the law is infeasible, then deterrence would require high penalties for those relatively few who are caught. Current enforcement of the Fair Housing Act shares neither of these characteristics—very few meritorious cases are actually brought (when measured against baseline estimates of the amount of discrimination in the housing market) and the average penalty is exceedingly low.

The inadequacy of current enforcement efforts is hardly surprising. A mode of enforcement that puts the burden on victims to identify when they have encountered discrimination is destined to fail. The average renter or home buyer who is denied housing because of some outlawed reason will not know the reason behind the denial. Indeed, the more sophisticated the violator is, the less likely it is that the victim will successfully identify him or her. Thus the current system of complaint-driven enforcement is likely to miss a large number of meritorious complaints and attract many nonmeritorious ones.

It might be worth considering whether the federal government should shift resources from individual complaint resolution to a more comprehensive strategy to fight housing discrimination. Rather than have their agendas set by people who walk through the doors and file complaints, HUD and the DOJ might better turn their attention to systemic investigations and prosecutions of discrimination in the housing market. In recent years, this strategy has been successfully employed by the two agencies in the areas of mortgage lending and property insurance. Additional pattern and practice cases which seek to root out and eliminate discrimination where it truly exists could be a better use of scarce federal resources than the current system.

Shifting resources away from individual complaints toward pattern and practice cases would not leave individual complainants without any options to vindicate their rights. To the contrary, virtually every state in the nation and most large cities have parallel enforcement mechanisms already in place which, in many instances, duplicate what is done at the federal level. These efforts could continue to be supported by programs such as FHAP. In addition, individuals can always file lawsuits directly in federal and state courts. While direct filing might not be an option for many people who suspect that they have been the victims of discrimination because they either do not know the law or cannot afford an attorney, many meritorious claims could be handled by private attorneys under fee-shifting or contingency fee arrangements.

A move away from individual complaint processing, investigation, and prosecution and toward a greater emphasis on pattern and practice investigations would be most successful if it could engage the energy and expertise of the large number of private Fair Housing enforcement groups throughout the nation. Each year, these groups investigate thousands of suspected acts of discrimination and conduct countless tests. Continued and enhanced support of these efforts under programs such as the Fair Housing Initiatives Program (FHIP) would be vital in any effort to combat housing discrimination.

In the absence of major change in how we enforce the Fair Housing Act, there is still a great need to understand how the current law operates and how existing practices could be improved. This chapter represents the most comprehensive study of federal Fair Housing enforcement that has been conducted to date. Some questions have been answered, but many others remain. Further research might seek to learn more about the determinants of damages in Fair Housing cases. Why are damages and settlement awards higher in federal district court? What characteristics of cases are related to different types of remedies?

In addition, in a sense, the survey of complainants and respondents described in this chapter touched only the tip of the fair housing enforcement iceberg. In recent years, the number of reasonable-cause charges issued by HUD has diminished to negligible levels. Very little is known about the experiences of the vast majority of complainants and respondents who are not part of this very selective group. In addition, as more states and localities have received substantial equivalency certifications, they have taken on preeminent roles in the enforcement of the Fair Housing Act. Despite this, very little is known about the enforcement practices of state and local agencies.

In order to understand better how the Fair Housing Act is being enforced, HUD, the HUD ALJs, DOJ, and FHAP agencies must cooperate with each other to collect *and* share data on cases within their jurisdictions. The agencies must standardize their definitions of what constitutes a case and adopt a uniform docket number system. Finally, the most sophisticated information management system in the world will not take the place of a human commitment to communicate among the agencies as cases proceed through the pipeline.

Despite the passage of more than three decades since the Fair Housing Act was enacted into law, freedom from discrimination in the housing market remains illusory. The Fair Housing Amendments Act of 1988 seems to have fallen short of the hopes of its framers. Policy makers need to consider whether the current federal enforcement mechanism will be sufficient to make future progress. This will not be possible without additional data gathering, research, and analysis.

NOTES

1. In 1974, Congress amended the Fair Housing Act to add sex as a protected status.
2. S. 1358, 90th Cong., 1st Sess. (1967)
3. For example, during the first year of the Reagan administration no Title VIII cases were begun by the DOJ and only two were filed in 1982. According to Massey and Denton (1993: 207), it was not until the last year of the Reagan administration that the total number of filings equaled the yearly average under the Carter administration.
4. For a discussion of this problem see Gaetke and Schwemm (1997).
5. A complainant may file dual complaints in federal or state court as well as with HUD. Once a trial commences in federal or state court, however, HUD may not issue a charge regarding the alleged discrimination and the HUD ALJs may not continue administrative hearings on such matters.
6. In addition to strengthening Title VIII's enforcement provisions, the 1988 Amendments Act also brought within its protective embrace two additional groups. Under the act, it is now illegal to discriminate against families with children and against persons with physical or mental disabilities. In addition, builders of housing must ensure accessibility in certain units, and landlords and condominium associations must make reasonable accommodations to meet the needs of disabled tenants.
7. Indeed, Representative Rodino analogized the federal administrative process to state and local enforcement of antidiscrimination laws by saying, "The highly successful experience of those agencies bears out a prediction made about H.R. 1158—administrative enforcement is effective primarily because it must be used often. Cases before those agencies are almost always settled prior to hearing" (Rodino 1987).
8. A pretest of the survey instruments indicated that the process of locating and contacting complainants and respondents would be very difficult. For most of the cases, the only contact information contained in the federal databases was from the

date the case was filed with HUD. Since a large proportion of the cases filed with HUD were from households who presumably were seeking to move, extraordinary efforts would have to be made to locate them. In addition, even though it might be easier to find respondents, as parties to litigation, their cooperation could not be taken for granted. Therefore, a combination of methods was utilized to locate and obtain completed interviews from both respondents and complainants. To obtain current phone numbers and addresses, postal forwarding addresses, Internet phone books, and the Lexis/Nexis People Finder service were utilized. The Lexis/Nexis People Finder service was one of the most useful methods for identifying potential interviewees. This service was provided without charge by the Reed Elsevier Company. Because most of these sources yielded multiple possibilities, a variety of methods were used to contact the potential interviewees including repeated telephone calls, letters with requests to call back on a toll-free telephone number, and financial incentives.

9. Although both samples were considered fairly representative of the relevant populations, because they were nonrandom it was nonetheless thought to be desirable and prudent to adjust for differences that existed. A standard weighting method for nonresponse (Little and Rubin 1987) was employed to correct for the fact that the parties that were interviewed differed in certain respects from those who were not interviewed. For a complete description of this weighting method as well as the methodology utilized to create the Consolidated Fair Housing Enforcement database and the samples for the surveys see Schill and Friedman (2000).

10. Baseline data about each case were obtained from the Consolidated Fair Housing Database.

11. Because the number of cases with no outcomes is so large for the cohort that was filed in 2003, the last cohort year used to report outcomes will be 2002.

12. The HUD ALJs are, for the most part, independent of HUD. Although they do not have the lifetime tenure of Article III federal district court judges, their independence is protected by the Administrative Procedure Act. The judges can only be removed for good cause established by the Merit Systems Protection Board. See 5 U.S.C. sec. 7521(a). In addition, salaries for ALJs are set by the Office of Personnel Management rather than by HUD.

13. Although the HUD secretary has not done this often, cases exist where he or she has exercised this authority and usually it has been in instances that favor the complainant. See, for example, *HUD v. Mountain Side Mobile Estate*, Fair Housing-Fair Lending (P-H) sec. 25,053, *rev'd* 56 F. 3d 1243 (10th Cir. 1995); In the Matter of Bobby Burris, Fair Housing-Fair Lending (P-H) sec. 25,050, *HUD v. DiCenso*, Fair Housing-Fair Lending (P-H) sec. 25,101, *HUD v. Ocean Sands, Inc.*, Fair Housing-Fair Lending (P-H) sec. 25,056.

14. For example, only 53.2 percent of complainants who chose to proceed before the HUD ALJs knew that the judge would be the trier of the facts in that forum as compared to the jury in federal district court. Among those complainants who selected federal district court, even fewer knew this distinction. Similarly, among respondents preferring the HUD ALJs, 58.8 percent knew the difference between the two forums in terms of the trier of the facts as compared to 62.1 percent of those who selected federal district court.

15. Among complainants who made this decision, 48.2 percent indicated that their lawyer advised them to elect, compared to 32.3 percent of respondents. There appears to be some inconsistency in responses, particularly among complainants, concerning legal counsel. Only 6.4 percent of complainants who elected federal district court were represented by private counsel at the time of the decision. Nevertheless, among complainants who elected, 48.2 percent said their lawyer advised them to do so. This disparity is likely to be explained by the complainant informally obtaining advice from an attorney either at HUD or a private Fair Housing organization rather than from an attorney he or she had retained.

16. A logit regression for complainants that seeks to explain the election decision based on individual characteristics as well as the characteristics of the complaint finds that the sole significant variable is whether the complainant had been represented by an attorney. Those complainants with legal counsel were significantly more likely to elect to have their cases heard in federal district court. For details of the econometric analysis and further results see Schill and Friedman (2000).

17. For example, in the complainant sample, only 5.8 percent of the cases that proceeded before the HUD ALJs took over one year to close compared to 50.5 percent of cases in federal district court. In the respondent survey, only 7.9 percent of cases before the HUD ALJ took over a year to close compared with 46.7 percent of cases in federal district court.

18. Three ordinary least-squares regression models are specified for each sample. The dependent variable represents the number of days between the date a case received a reasonable-cause finding by HUD and the date the case was closed either by the HUD ALJs or by a federal district court judge. The first model includes variables about the litigation including whether the complainant/respondent was represented by an attorney, whether one or both parties elected federal district court, and whether there was a decision in favor of the complainant, the respondent, or a dismissal. The second model includes variables describing the alleged discriminatory act and the protected group of the complainant. The third model introduces demographic characteristics of the relevant party such as income, race, education, and age for complainants or, for respondents, whether the party is a landlord.

19. In the first model for complainants containing only litigation-related variables, two variables were statistically significant. Cases in which one or more of the parties elected federal district court and/or in which the respondent won were likely to take longer to close. The addition of other independent variables in models 2 and 3 does not change this result. In model 3, the variable representing whether the complainant was Hispanic also is positive and statistically significant as was the variable indicating that the claim involved discrimination based on race. The same result for the election variable appears in each of the models for respondents.

20. In addition, in model 3 of the respondent sample, complaints alleging a refusal to rent took significantly longer to resolve than other cases and cases involving a landlord took less time to resolve.

21. In the complainant sample, for cases adjudicated by the HUD ALJs, the complainant prevailed 13.9 percent of the time and the respondent won 4.8 percent of the

time. In the respondent sample, the rates of success before the HUD ALJs were 10.5 percent and 3.8 percent, for complainants and respondents, respectively.

22. In the complainant sample, the complainant won in 0.9 percent of the cases and the respondent succeeded 3.0 percent of the time. In the respondent sample, complainants prevailed 2.3 percent of the time and respondents 4.6 percent of the time.

23. In the complainant sample, the median award (including settlements) among those who received some monetary relief was $5,846 for cases adjudicated by the HUD ALJs and $10,385 in cases that proceeded in federal district court. In the respondent sample, the disparity was somewhat smaller. In the complainant sample, 86.4 percent of complainants whose cases were handled by the HUD ALJs received a monetary award compared to 71.4 percent of those who proceeded in federal district court. In the respondent sample, these figures were 82.8 percent and 73.2 percent, respectively. The median award figures were $5,621 for cases that were handled by the HUD ALJs and $6,256 in federal district court.

24. In the complainant sample, 68.9 percent of complainants who had their cases handled by the HUD ALJs and 62.6 percent who proceeded in federal district court reported this remedy. In the respondent sample, these signs were required in 27.1 percent of the HUD ALJ cases and 40.8 percent of the federal district court cases. The disparity in frequency of equal opportunity signs in the two samples is curious. Unlike monetary awards, the information for this remedy is not taken from the Consolidated Fair Housing Enforcement Database. Thus, the results may be affected by selective memories among the two groups. In addition, it is conceivable that the types of cases in the respondent sample differ from those in the complainant sample. For a discussion about possible sample bias see the second part of this chapter.

25. When asked for the reasons behind their responses, a large number of respondents indicated that they felt the process had been unfair, that the complainants had not told the truth about what had happened, and that HUD had been biased in its investigation, or, most commonly, that "HUD treated us as if we were criminals." In addition, a number of respondents said that they did not do anything wrong, that the complainant knew how to "work" the system and that the process had been long and expensive.

REFERENCES

Curtis v. Loether. 1974. 415 U.S. 189.

Dubofsky, Jean Eberhart. 1969. "Fair Housing: A Legislative History and a Perspective," *Washburn Law Journal* 8(2): 149–66.

Fish, Hamilton. 1988. *Congressional Record*. 100th Cong. 2nd Session, H6498.

Gaetke, Eugene R., and Robert G. Schwemm. 1997. "Government Lawyers and Their Private 'Clients' Under the Fair Housing Act," *George Washington Law Review* 65: 329–78.

Henderson, Wade J. 1987. Testimony. *Fair Housing Amendments Act of 1987*. Hearings Before the Subcommittee on Civil and Constitutional Rights of the Committee on the Judiciary, House of Representatives, 100th Cong. 1st Session.

Kennedy, Edward. 1988. *Congressional Record*. 100th Cong. 2nd Session, S10455.

Ladd, Christine. 1997. Federal Fair Housing Enforcement: The Clinton Record at the End of the First Term. In *The Continuing Struggle: Civil Rights and the Clinton Administration*, ed. Corrine Yu and William Taylor, 221–33. Washington, DC: Citizens' Commission on Civil Rights.

Little, Roderick J. A., and Donald B. Rubin. 1987. *Statistical Analysis with Missing Data*. New York: Wiley.

Long, Larry. *Migration and Residential Mobility in the United States*. New York: Russell Sage, 1988.

Massey, Douglas S., and Nancy Denton. 1993. *American Apartheid: Segregation and the Making of the Underclass*. Cambridge, MA: Harvard University Press.

Munnell, Alicia, et al. 1992. *Mortgage Lending in Boston: Interpreting HMDA Data*. Boston: Federal Reserve Bank of Boston.

National Council on Disability. 2001. *Reconstructing Fair Housing*. Washington, DC: Author.

Pierce, Samuel R. 1987. Testimony. *Fair Housing Amendments Act of 1987*. Hearings Before the Subcommittee on Civil and Constitutional Rights of the Committee on the Judiciary, House of Representatives, 100th Cong. 1st Session.

Relman, John P. 2002. "Federal Fair Housing Enforcement at a Crossroads: The Clinton Legacy and the Challenges Ahead." In *Rights at Risk: Equality in an Age of Terrorism*. Washington, DC: Lawyers' Commission on Civil Rights.

Reynolds, William Bradford. 1987. Testimony. *Fair Housing Amendments Act of 1987*. Hearings Before the Subcommittee on Civil and Constitutional Rights of the Committee on the Judiciary, House of Representatives, 100th Cong. 1st Session.

Rodino, Peter W. 1987. Statement. *Fair Housing Amendments Act of 1987*. Hearings Before the Subcommittee on Civil and Constitutional Rights of the Committee on the Judiciary, House of Representatives, 100th Cong. 1st Session.

Schill, Michael H., and Samantha Friedman. 2000. *Enforcing the Fair Housing Act: A Report to the United States Department of Housing and Urban Development* (unpublished report available from the NYU Furman Center for Real Estate and Urban Policy).

———. 1999. "The Fair Housing Amendments Act of 1988: The First Decade." *Cityscape: A Journal of Policy Development and Research* 4(3): 57–78.

Thurmond, Strom. 1988. *Congressional Record*. 100th Cong. 2nd Session, S10457.

Turner, Margery Austin, Martha Kuhlman, and Aleda Freeman. 1992. *Fair Housing Initiatives Program Complaint Analysis: The Use and Impacts of Testing*. Washington, DC: The Urban Institute.

Turner, Margery Austin, Stephen L. Ross, George C. Galster, and John Yinger. 2002. *Discrimination in Metropolitan Housing Markets Phase 1*. Washington, DC: U.S. Department of Housing and Urban Development.

U.S. Commission on Civil Rights. 1974. *The Federal Civil Rights Enforcement Effort 1974, Volume II: To Provide . . . for Fair Housing*. Washington, DC: Author.

———. 1979. *The Federal Fair Housing Enforcement Effort: A Report of the United States Commission on Civil Rights*. Washington, DC: Author.

——. 1994. *The Fair Housing Amendments Act of 1988: The Enforcement Report*. Washington, DC: Author.

U.S. General Accounting Office. 2004. *Fair Housing: Opportunities to Improve HUD's Oversight and Management of the Enforcement Process*. Washington, DC: Author.

8

Fair Housing Enforcement and Changes in Discrimination between 1989 and 2000

An Exploratory Study

Stephen L. Ross and George C. Galster

The purpose of this chapter is to investigate, for the first time, the variation across metropolitan areas in their changing levels of housing discrimination, with the aim of exploring whether they are "causally" related to corresponding variations in fair housing enforcement activities during the 1990s, controlling for other factors. The specific research questions include: How do changes in the 1989–2000 incidence of racial/ethnic discriminatory behaviors of various sorts correlate with fair housing enforcement activity during the 1990s? Does this answer vary depending on whether one considers the sales or rental housing markets, or discrimination directed against black or Hispanic home seekers?

We now know that, although prohibited by federal statutes since 1968, discrimination by real estate agents and landlords directed against minority home seekers continues to occur throughout America's metropolitan areas (see chapter 2 by Turner, Richardson, and Ross within). Such discrimination can impose substantial psychological as well as economic costs on those who are directly victimized (Yinger 1995). Moreover, housing discrimination has been shown to perpetuate residential segregation (Galster 1986, 1987a, 1988a, 1988b, 1991; Massey, Eggers, and Denton 1994), which in turn has been linked to a variety of negative social and economic outcomes for minority communities.[1]

We now also know that housing discrimination declined substantially in magnitude over the last decade on most measures, with the exception of discrimination against Hispanic renters (Turner et al. 2002; Ross and Turner 2005).[2] This decline has occurred immediately following a substantial strengthening of the federal fair housing law in 1988. There has also been a range of changes and improvements in the enforcement capacity at the governmental and nongovernmental levels during this time period that, arguably, may have been influential in creating the lowered levels of discrimination practiced by the real estate industry. This coincidence raises the provocative issue of how these two occurrences may be causally related.

Our analysis is based on a nationally representative sample of seventeen metropolitan areas where black-white paired tests were conducted and eleven areas where Hispanic-white tests were conducted for both the 1989 and 2000 Housing Discrimination Studies (HDS). We measure the 1989–2000 changes in five different real estate agent behaviors related to differential treatment of minority and white home buyers, and four landlord behaviors related to differential treatment of rental apartment seekers, plus summary indexes of such behaviors in each sector. We use damages awarded in racial-ethnic housing-discrimination lawsuits during the 1990s as a proxy for effectiveness of fair housing efforts. To our knowledge, our work is the first to explore statistically the relationships between fair housing enforcement activities and changes in the incidence of housing discrimination across metropolitan areas.

The remainder of this chapter is organized as follows. In the first section, we highlight key changes in fair housing law and enforcement capacity commencing at the beginning of our study period that could plausibly suggest that law enforcement practices contributed to the reduction of housing discrimination over time. In the next section we review the three earlier studies that have investigated the sources (besides enforcement) for the cross-metropolitan variability of housing discrimination. Following that, we discuss the main methodological challenge in measuring the causal impact of fair housing enforcement on behavior: the likelihood that fair housing resources are targeted to where discrimination is most pervasive. We next present our empirical approach and discuss the data sources and enforcement measures with which we experimented. We conclude by discussing results that are suggestive of deterrence effects and draw a limited set of recommendations for needed research and policy implications about fair housing enforcement efforts.

CHANGES IN FAIR HOUSING LAW AND ENFORCEMENT SINCE 1987

Fair housing enforcement activities in the United States are carried out by numerous agencies, including private, nonprofit organizations, human rights commissions at the state and local levels, and the federal Departments of Justice and Housing and Urban Development. Considerable enhancements to the enforcement system were put into place at about the time of the 1989 HDS, and others appeared in the early 1990s. Thus, it is reasonable to expect that if this expanded fair housing enforcement had its intended impact, it would register as a decline in discrimination observed between the 1989 and 2000 HDS.

The Fair Housing Amendments Act of 1988 created a new administrative adjudication process for more timely resolution of housing discrimination complaints and allowed for stiffer civil penalties (see Schill, chapter 7 within; Mathias and Morris 1999). The 1988 act notably expanded the federal government's role in enforcing fair housing statutes and provided the U.S. Department of Housing and Urban Development (HUD) with the apparatus for a legal, binding resolution of complaints other than conciliation.

The other important legislative initiatives were contained in the 1987 and the 1991 Housing Acts. These acts created the Fair Housing Initiatives and Fair Housing Assistance Programs (FHIP and FHAP) that distribute funds to private fair housing groups and state human rights commissions, respectively, in order to provide education to local communities and conduct investigations of fair housing complaints.

Also noteworthy was the expansion of the U.S. Department of Justice (DOJ) enforcement efforts during the Clinton administration (Galster 1995; Goering and Squires 1999). The Department of Justice (DOJ) manages a civil rights enforcement division and during this period developed its own housing testing division. As a result, the number of DOJ-initiated fair housing cases increased from less than twenty prior to 1988 to well over a hundred during the mid-1990s (Lee 1999).

This listing of enhancements since 1987 does not, of course, suggest that the nation's efforts to combat discrimination have been efficient or sufficient, as there is no reference to staffing or resource levels. Indeed, HUD's implementation of the act has been criticized (see Schill, chapter 7 within) and the adequacy of enforcement capacity nationwide questioned by many (Yinger 1995). More structurally, Galster (1990, 1999) has argued that many enforcement efforts of this period were unlikely to create an effective deterrent against housing discrimination so long as the system relies almost exclusively on individual bona fide home seekers recognizing that they have been victimized and then filing suit. Discrimination is often practiced in a subtle fashion so that victims are typically unaware; even those who are suspicious are unlikely to bear the substantial time, monetary, and psychological costs of pursuing a complaint in light of a protracted process with prospects for minimal compensatory awards.

Thus, we think it is appropriate to investigate empirically the degree to which the strengthening of fair housing law and enforcement capacity beginning in 1987 reduced discrimination over the last decade. Of course, discrimination may well have declined since 1989 for reasons having nothing to do with fair housing activities. We therefore review in the next section studies that have investigated the predictors of housing discrimination in metropolitan areas, so that we may draw upon this work when devising control variables for our own statistical analysis.

PREVIOUS RESEARCH ON CROSS-METROPOLITAN VARIATIONS IN HOUSING DISCRIMINATION

What, besides the intensity of fair housing enforcement, might explain why one metropolitan area has a higher level of housing discrimination than another? Only three studies have examined this question; all utilized cross-metropolitan differences in discrimination as revealed by the national paired-testing studies.[3] They have estimated multiple regression models of the metropolitan level of discrimination, based on metro-wide economic, social, and demographic characteristics, but few robust conclusions have been produced. Perhaps most centrally for the current work, none have tried to model the impact of fair housing enforcement efforts.

Galster and Keeney (1988) investigated the variations in housing discrimination against blacks across forty metropolitan areas that were sampled as part of the HUD-sponsored Housing Market Practices Survey of 1977, the first national study to employ paired testing (Wienk et al. 1979). They created a composite measure of the incidence of rental and sales discrimination in each of these metropolitan areas, based on the results of the paired tests conducted there. They employed this measure (instrumented) as an endogenous variable in a four-simultaneous-equations model of black-white discrimination, segregation, and disparities in occupations and incomes. They found that discrimination was higher in metropolitan areas where: (1) above-median- and below-median-priced, single-family housing was more dissimilarly distributed across space; (2) housing vacancy rates (both tenures combined) were lower; and (3) interracial income disparities were greater. Whites' educational levels and the absolute and relative sizes of the black population in the metropolitan area were not related to the incidence of this composite measure of housing discrimination.

Galster (1991) used data from the aforementioned 1977 Housing Market Practices Survey to explore the geographical differences in discrimination on both the rental and sales sectors. He found that only the metropolitan-wide percentage of whites residing in their current home more than five years provided consistent (inverse) explanatory power for both sectors. In the rental sector, discrimination was more prevalent in metropolitan areas with absolutely larger black populations. In the home sales sector, discrimination was more prevalent in areas with slower-growing black populations and those with lower vacancy rates.

These results could not be replicated by Page (1995) with more recent discrimination data, though it appears likely that her smaller sample of metropolitan areas tested may be the reason. Page could not discern from the 1989 HDS data statistically significant variations in rental discrimination across the twenty-five metropolitan areas sampled. Although such variation was present in the sales sector, her attempts to estimate a multiple regression model of cross-sectional differences in sales discrimination rates revealed no statistically significant predictors.[4]

The research reported above is valuable for our effort because it draws upon the analytic foundations and control variables measuring metropolitan demographic and economic conditions that have proven predictive of underlying discriminatory behavior. None of this earlier work has attempted, however, to relate cross-sectional or historical variations in housing discrimination to variations in fair housing enforcement activities. Our key contribution in this chapter is to introduce for the first time a new set of predictors related to enforcement agency actions in relationship to patterns of discrimination. As we will discuss below, however, there are a number of daunting methodological challenges in attempting this form of causal specification.

THE CHALLENGE OF ESTABLISHING CAUSALITY

The fundamental challenge that any study of the relationship between fair housing enforcement activity and housing market discrimination must face is identifying and measuring unambiguously their causal connections. Ideally, we seek to find out how discrimination will change when enforcement activity changes due to some exogenous force. Under this scenario of causation, a negative correlation between discrimination and enforcement would unambiguously support the notion that the latter deters the former. Unfortunately, causation in the real world cannot be assumed to run in such a simple, unidirectional way. On the contrary, it is likely that metropolitan areas in which discrimination has historically been most severe and resistant to change are precisely where scarce fair housing enforcement resources have been targeted. Thus, we might expect more housing discrimination to cause more enforcement actions, thereby producing a positive correlation between these variables.

We therefore suspect that, in technical terms, enforcement variables are likely to be endogenous, not exogenous. To the degree that they are endogenous there will be a statistical bias toward observing a *positive* correlation between enforcement and discrimination, thus reducing the prospects for concluding that enforcement reduces discrimination. Put simply: the empirical deck is stacked against finding that enforcement matters in the fight against illegal discrimination; thus any observed negative correlation between these two variables offers strong evidence indeed of the efficacy of enforcement. We shall return to this theme later as we describe the particular measures of enforcement activity that we have available to us.

OUR EMPIRICAL APPROACH: REDUCING OMITTED VARIABLES BIAS BY MODELING CHANGES IN DISCRIMINATION

Though causality is the dominant challenge of our research, omitted explanatory variables is another of note. If we are to get the best possible estimate of the relationship between enforcement activity (E) and discrimination (D), we must control statistically for a wide range of other factors that may influence the incidence of discrimination in a metropolitan area. Prior empirical work cited above suggests some feasible control variables to employ. Unfortunately, many of the other control variables are virtually impossible to measure. For example, there are probably a host of metropolitan area-specific historical particulars that have shaped racial attitudes that motivate discriminatory acts. Moreover, other local idiosyncrasies that characterize the real estate brokerage industry in each metropolitan area remain unknown to us. Thus, we consider the potential problem of omitted variables bias a serious one.

Insofar as many of these factors vary inconsequentially over the span of a decade, however, we can minimize their omission by constructing a model of *changes* in discrimination (D), instead of its *level*. Symbolically, the relationships may be specified for a particular metropolitan area j:

$$(1)\ D_{89j} = \alpha + [X_{90ij}]\beta_i + E_{90j}\Phi_i + [C_{kj}]\gamma_k + \epsilon \text{ and}$$

$$(2)\ D_{00j} = \delta + [X_{00ij}]\theta_i + E_{00j}\psi_i + [C_{kj}]\lambda_k + \epsilon$$

where: 89, 90, and 00 subscripts indicate years 1989, 1990, and 2000; Greek letters represent parameters to be estimated by multiple regression; E_j is fair housing enforcement activity; $[X_i]$ is a vector of i measurable metropolitan characteristics that change over time; and $[C_k]$ is a vector of k time-invariant, unmeasurable metropolitan characteristics. Because $[C_k]$ is constant, by taking the *difference* between equations (2) and (1) we can obtain an estimable equation where only measurable variables appear:

$$(3)\ D_{00j} - D_{89j} = [\delta-\alpha] + ([X_{00j}] - [X_{90j}])\,[\theta-\beta] + (E_{00j} - E_{90j})\,[\Phi-\psi] + \epsilon$$

In our model we employ as X the metropolitan statistical area 1990 to 2000 changes in: (1) the proportion of blacks; (2) the proportion of Hispanics; (3) the segregation of blacks; and (4) the ratio of black/white median household incomes. For D we alternately employ the incidence of discrimination against black and Hispanic home seekers, each related to a different sort of discriminatory behavior, to test for the robustness of the patterns we discern. For E we ideally would use changes in enforcement activity by federal, state, and local agencies, but due to data limitations, we were limited to an estimated cumulative value for the period. Details on all these measures follow in the next section.

DATA SOURCES AND MEASUREMENT ISSUES

Measuring Housing Discrimination Consistently Over Time: Key Feature of HDS

We obtained measures of discrimination from the two national Housing Discrimination Studies (HDS), conducted in 1989 and 2000 by the Urban Institute under contract to HUD (Struyk, Turner, and Yinger 1991; Turner et al. 2002). These two HDSs were conducted using consistent sampling and paired-testing protocols in multiple metropolitan areas for both years. Metropolitan areas were chosen to provide a nationally representative sample of housing markets where black and Hispanic home seekers constituted a substantial fraction; the specific areas sampled and the number of rental and sales tests in each are presented in the appendix to this chapter. Because testing was conducted and measures of discrimination were coded in a comparable manner both years, the two HDSs offer a unique opportunity to measure discrimination over time.

A visit with a rental or sales agent is a complex transaction and may include many forms of favorable or unfavorable treatment. We present results for a series of individual treatment indicators that reflect important aspects of the housing transaction. These indicators are identical to those employed by Turner et al. (see chapter 2) and therefore we will not describe them again in detail; they are listed in table 8.1.

We also combine the treatment indicators within each category to create a *composite or consistency measure*, such as "housing availability" or "terms and conditions." Specifically, tests are classified as "white-favored" if the

Table 8.1. Discriminatory Treatment Measures by Category of Agent Behavior

Rental Treatments	*Sales Treatments*
Unit Availability	Unit Availability
Advertised Unit Available	Advertised Unit Available
Similar Unit Available	Similar Unit Available
Number of Units Available	Number of Units Available
Unit Inspection	Unit Inspection
Advertised Unit Inspection	Advertised Unit Inspection
Similar Unit Inspection	Similar Unit Inspection
Number of Units Inspection	Number of Units Inspection
Terms and Conditions	Geographic Steering
Rent for Advertised Unit	Steering on Recommendations
Rental Incentives Offered	Steering on Inspections
Amount of Security Deposit	Financing Assistance
Application Fee Required	Help with Financing Offered
Encouragement	Lender Recommendations
Follow-up Contact	Discuss Down Payment
Asked to Apply	Encouragement
Arrangements for Contact	Follow-up Contact
Told Qualified to Rent	Arrangements for Contact
	Told Qualified to Purchase

white tester was consistently favored, that is, received favorable treatment on one or more individual constituent items, while his or her minority partner received *no* favorable treatment relative to the white tester on any items. Tests are classified as "neutral" if one tester was favored on some individual treatment items and his or her partner was also favored on at least one item. One advantage of this *consistency* composite is that it identifies tests where one partner was unambiguously favored over the other.[5] Finally, we specify an "overall" composite measure, based on the same principles as above, except that consistent favoritism must be demonstrated on one or more of the four (in rental) or five (in sales) behavioral categories, with no countervailing favoritism on any category.

Changes in discriminatory treatment, as measured by the foregoing indicators, has previously been analyzed in detail by Turner et al. (chapter 2), so we will provide only an overview. In the rental market, discrimination persists in 2000 against apartment seekers in both groups in the areas of availability and inspection even though the incidence of such discrimination has declined considerably for blacks since 1989, but not for Hispanics; see table 8.2. Discrimination in the area of encouragement has declined for both groups. However, in fewer types of treatments did discrimination against Hispanic renters decline compared to black renters.

Table 8.2. Incidence of Net Adverse Treatment in the Rental Market

Treatments	*Net 1989*	*Net 2000*	*Change*
Black-White Tests			
Availability	0.144 (0.035)*	0.046 (0.021)*	−0.097 (0.038)*
Inspection	0.148 (0.030)*	0.069 (0.019)*	−0.078 (0.037)*
Terms	0.045 (0.026)#	−0.004 (0.016)	−0.050 (0.030)
Encouragement	0.099 (0.036)*	0.016 (0.022)	−0.083 (0.044)#
Overall	0.098 (0.028)*	0.026 (0.020)	−0.071 (0.034)*
Hispanic-Anglo Tests			
Availability	0.106 (0.038)*	0.111 (0.026)*	0.005 (0.047)
Inspection	0.083 (0.029)*	0.064 (0.022)*	−0.018 (0.038)
Terms	0.014 (0.032)	0.012 (0.023)	−0.001 (0.042)
Encouragement	0.147 (0.037)*	0.035 (0.027)	−0.111 (0.049)*
Overall	0.146 (0.028)*	0.061 (0.025)*	−0.085 (0.039)*

Note: Standard errors are shown parenthetically; * p<.05; # p<.10.

In the sales market, discrimination against black home buyers persists in 2000 in all areas of treatment, but only against Hispanics in financing; see table 8.3. In general, the levels observed in 2000 are substantially lower than they were in 1989, however. The two key exceptions are higher incidences of racial steering of both groups in 2000 and higher incidences of discrimination against Hispanics in the area of financial assistance. For further analysis of steering, see Galster and Godfrey (2005).

Table 8.3. Incidence of Net Adverse Treatment in the Sales Market

Treatments	*Net 1989*	*Net 2000*	*Change*
Black-White Tests			
Availability	0.172 (0.026)*	0.049 (0.022)*	−0.122 (0.034)*
Inspection	0.113 (0.021)*	0.069 (0.025)*	−0.044 (0.033)
Steering	−0.058 (0.016)*	0.049 (0.017)*	0.107 (0.024)*
Financing	0.121 (0.025)*	0.047 (0.023)*	−0.074 (0.034)*
Encouragement	0.130 (0.026)*	0.052 (0.023)*	−0.078 (0.037)*
Overall	0.147 (0.023)*	0.037 (0.018)*	−0.109 (0.030)*
Hispanic-Anglo Tests			
Availability	0.148 (0.027)*	0.028 (0.040)	−0.120 (0.054)*
Inspection	0.127 (0.025)*	−0.029 (0.034)	−0.156 (0.044)*
Steering	0.038 (0.019)	0.034 (0.029)	−0.004 (0.037)
Financing	0.022 (0.025)	0.135 (0.031)*	0.112 (0.043)*
Encouragement	0.164 (0.025)*	0.042 (0.030)	−0.122 (0.044)*
Overall	0.121 (0.023)*	0.067 (0.023)*	−0.054 (0.037)

Note: Standard errors are shown parenthetically; * p<.05; # p<.10.

Table 8.4. HDS Sample Sizes by Metropolitan Area, Year, and Minority Group

	HDS2000		*HDS1989*	
	Black-White Tests	*Hispanic-Anglo Tests*	*Black-White Tests*	*Hispanic-Anglo Tests*
Black-White/Hispanic-Anglo Sites				
Los Angeles	69/68	75/69	75/104	81/120
New York	75/68	66/70	54/87	64/118
Chicago	65/63	65/68	66/103	81/122
Houston	70/78	68/75	42/43	51/53
Miami	74/71	73/70	32/39	58/60
Denver	72/71	73/78	44/51	65/73
Austin	69/75	70/72	32/43	55/63
Black-White Only Sites				
Atlanta	81/78	—	66/94	—
Philadelphia	73/70	—	30/44	—
Detroit	66/71	—	33/48	—
Washington, DC	74/69	—	32/43	—
New Orleans	68/76	—	33/44	—
Pittsburgh	79/75	—	38/46	—
Dayton-Springfield	70/70	—	33/47	—
Orlando	72/76	—	32/43	—
Macon/Warner/Robins	69/73	—	33/45	—
Birmingham	77/66	—	34/48	—
Hispanic-Anglo Only Sites				
San Antonio	—	74/74	—	67/116
Pueblo	—	74/76	—	50/68
San Diego	—	69/74	—	61/76
Tucson	—	75/75	—	59/71
All Sites	1223/1218	782/801	709/972	692/940

Each entry contains two numbers. The first is the number of rental tests and the second is the number of sales tests.

Although the HDS data provide the only reliable measures of housing discrimination over time, we should not fail to note that they have two important limitations for use in estimating statistical models such as equation (3). First, they are measured with error. As shown in table 8.4, the estimated incidence of discrimination in each metropolitan area is based on a finite sample of paired tests and thus has an associated statistical confidence interval. Second, the HDS samples of metropolitan areas are extremely small: seventeen for black-white discrimination and eleven for Hispanic-Anglo discrimination.

This means that multivariate models like (3) must be extremely parsimonious in the variables they employ for controls because of the limited degrees of freedom. In combination, both limitations make it less likely that estimated regression parameters of (3) will pass conventional tests of statistical significance.

Measuring Fair Housing Enforcement Activities

We obtained data from HUD's fair housing complaint database. This is the most comprehensive dataset available, as it records all fair housing cases filed directly with HUD as well as with private, local public, and state agencies that were funded through either HUD's FHIP or FHAP initiatives.[6] For each of the twenty-one sites shown in table 8.4, we extracted from the HUD database all cases filed during the 1990s that involved allegations by black or Hispanic home seekers of discrimination based on race, ethnicity, or color. We also recorded the disposition of the case in terms of findings and awards.

On average in the metropolitan areas where HDS conducted black-white tests, 1,655 race/ethnicity-based complaints were filed with HUD or its affiliated agencies during the decade; the comparable figure for the areas where Hispanic-Anglo tests were conducted (which often were black-white test sites as well) was 1,920. Of these totals, 121 and 163 (or 7 percent and 8 percent, respectively, of the number filed) yielded findings of discrimination.[7] The awards associated with such findings averaged $5,732 and $8,910 for the HDS black-white test sites and Hispanic-Anglo test sites, respectively, though there were wide variations across metropolitan areas and the two sets have seven sites in common.[8] As for the remainder of the cases, HUD and its affiliated agencies closed the bulk of cases with no finding of discrimination (see Schill, chapter 7, for more detail).

As explained above, the central challenge in devising and interpreting a fair housing enforcement variable is endogeneity. We would argue that, given available HUD data, the most likely specification to minimize this problem is a variable that measures the (natural logarithm of) dollar amount of court-ordered awards in each metropolitan area's fair housing cases involving black or Hispanic plaintiffs. First, the dollar amount of awards is influenced by the effectiveness of the local fair housing agency in not only winning cases but doing so in a convincing fashion, which is not likely driven by the overall incidence of discrimination in the area. Second, awards will be exogenously influenced by the practices, precedents, and political leanings of the relevant state and federal court districts. We also would suggest that dollar amount of awards is, in principle, a better measure of deterrence than either numbers of cases filed or won because it comes closer to representing an expected value of loss from discriminating. Moreover, large awards are more likely to get coverage in the local news media than a discrimination finding in a minor case, thus generating a more visible deterrence effect.

In this chapter we therefore employ as our prime explanatory variable the (natural logarithm of) cumulative dollar amount of court-ordered awards in all fair housing cases alleging discrimination on the basis of race, ethnicity, or color in each HDS metropolitan area during the 1990s. We also experiment with an analogous variable specified only for cases in which HUD data allow us to identify the race or ethnicity of the complainant and that complainant is black or Hispanic.[9] Surprisingly, we were able to operationalize this experiment only for cases involving black complainants because the HUD database showed no cases in our HDS sites involving an identified Hispanic complainant where an award was made by the court. The mean award in cases where the complainant was black was $6,448 across our seventeen black-white test sites.

Clearly, the most desirable variable from a conceptual standpoint as a predictor of changes in housing discrimination (our dependent variable) would be one that measures the *effectiveness* of efforts to avoid illegal behaviors that otherwise would have occurred. We recognize that our measure falls short of this ideal in several ways. First, the range of fair housing activities we can measure is circumscribed; we have no information about other activities that may not have yielded cases, such as fair housing education training activities for housing providers. Second, we have no measure of the full set of resources invested in fair housing activities aimed at racial-ethnic discrimination. Even if we were to undertake successfully the daunting task of acquiring budgets of all the relevant agencies, we would still be pressed to measure the budgetary share directed at eradicating discrimination against blacks and Hispanics. Moreover, the budgets would miss the significant in-kind and pro bono resources that they often utilize. Third, this database cannot be used to precisely measure *changes* in the intensity or effectiveness of enforcement activities during the decade, as indicated in equation (3), inasmuch as the data show case numbers varying markedly from year to year. At best it provides indicators of cross-metropolitan variations in the levels of awards against housing discriminators during the period. Fourth, virtually all of the cases tallied alleged violations in the rental, not sales, market. Thus, we are essentially testing whether there were any substantial deterrent effects for real estate sales agents that may have emanated from suits primarily involving the rental sector. All these concerns militate against our observing a statistically significant negative correlation between our enforcement measure and changes in discrimination.

Before leaving the topic of enforcement activity, we should note that we also obtained data from unpublished sources about the fair housing enforcement activities of two additional types of agencies: the U.S. Department of Justice (DOJ) and private, nonprofit fair housing organizations associated with the National Fair Housing Alliance (NFHA).[10] The former activity involved the "pattern and practice" enforcement testing undertaken by the DOJ as part of their enhanced efforts beginning in the early 1990s (Goering and Squires 1999; Lee 1999). Fourteen DOJ cases based on this testing were brought from 1992 to 1999 in our HDS sites. The latter activity involved legal suits resulting from complaints by bona fide home seekers that have been filed with the assistance of NFHA affiliates during the 1990–1999 period. Unfortunately, preliminary experiments with these data did not yield added insights into the causal relationship between local enforcement efforts and changes in discrimination, due primarily to the endogeneity problem but also to a variety of other statistical shortcomings of the data. We emphasize that these statistical issues do not imply anything about the efficacy or cost-effectiveness of these agencies' enforcement efforts.

Measuring Control Variables

Finally, as controls in our regression model of changes in discrimination we employed several changes in demographic and economic characteristics of each metropolitan area that theory and prior research suggest are predictive. Specifically, we included changes in: black and Hispanic metropolitan population shares, income gaps between whites and minorities (black or Hispanic, as appropriate), and black or Hispanic (as appropriate) residential segregation.

These control variables are likely to be related to the intensity of white prejudices that may motivate discriminatory actions in the housing market (Yinger, 1995). The "out-group hostility" theory of prejudice stresses that white prejudice is an antipathy toward members of a minority group, rooted in negative affect and stereotypes. The "group position" theory involves a commitment to relative group position, conditioned by the difference between in-group (white) and out-group (minority) positions that in-group members have socially learned to expect (Blumer 1958; Bobo and Zubrinsky 1996). Following the out-group hostility vein, white prejudice may be abetted in areas where there is a stronger correlation between race and socioeconomic status, as a result of the synergism between race and class prejudices (Bobo, Kruegel, and Smith 1996). Following the group position vein, white prejudice should be intensified in areas where blacks are a more significant share of the population and therefore constitute more of a perceived threat to white neighborhoods, economic status, and political power (Bradburn et al. 1970; Marshall and Jiobu 1975; Giles 1977). This perceived threat to group position may also be greater in areas where the interracial gap in socioeconomic status is less. Residential segregation may also proxy for whites' desires to self-segregate and, by implication, for real estate agents to cater to this desire by discriminating.[11]

We acquired data for measuring the population and economic variables from the 1990 and the 2000 *Censuses of Population and Housing* (U.S. Department of Commerce 1993, 2002). We also obtained segregation index data from the Census Bureau (Iceland, Weinberg, and Steinmetz 2002).

Summary Remarks about the Challenges of Measuring the Effect of Fair Housing Enforcement Activity on Discrimination

The effort to both measure the appropriate concepts and then ferret out their causal connections is extremely challenging on several fronts. First is measurement error: both the dependent variable and the key explanatory variable are unavoidably measured with error. Second is small sample sizes: only a few metropolitan areas had their rates of discrimination comparably measured in the 1989 and 2000 Housing Discrimination Studies. The effect of these two challenges is that reaching conventional standards of statistical significance is difficult. Third is omitted variables: precise measures of the motives of housing discriminators, housing consumer preferences and prejudices, and market and institutional context are not available. Our specification of a change model helps in minimizing this potential bias but does not guarantee its elimination. Fourth—and most importantly—is endogeneity: many potential measures of fair housing efforts may be influenced by the historical levels and intensity of discrimination, creating a reverse causation that obscures the measurement of the desired causal connection. We employ a measure of fair housing effectiveness (dollars awarded by the courts) that tries to avoid this difficulty to the extent possible, but our observed correlations between changes in discrimination and this variable may still be biased in a positive direction.

EMPIRICAL RESULTS

Does More Effective Enforcement Reduce Discrimination?

Our primary finding is that for metropolitan areas whose HUD offices and HUD-supported FHIP and FHAP agencies are more successful in winning larger cumulative monetary awards from their fair housing suits there has been a greater decrease in all sorts of discriminatory behaviors against black apartment and home seekers during the 1990s. The evidence points in this direction in both sales and rental sectors, though it is stronger in the rental market. This is consistent with the claim that in such places there was a stronger enforcement environment that deterred more prospective discriminators against blacks. The explanatory power of monetary awards is considerably weaker in the case of discrimination against Hispanics, which perhaps is explicable due to the smaller sample size and comparatively limited amount of award-generating enforcement efforts directed toward them.

Tables 8.5 and 8.6 present the estimated coefficients for the monetary awards enforcement variable (shown in columns) produced by a multiple regression explaining cross-metropolitan variations in 1989–2000 changes in each of the aforementioned discriminatory treatment indexes (shown in rows). Each regression controls for demographic and economic features noted above; regressions are estimated separately for seventeen black-white sites (columns 1 and 2) and eleven Hispanic-Anglo HDS sites (column 3). Estimates in column 2 differ from others inasmuch as they employ as the enforcement variable the logarithm of the cumulative dollar amount of awards in cases involving complainants who were identified as black.

In interpreting these estimates we compute the standard t-statistics, which are shown parenthetically in tables 8.5 and 8.6. As we expected due to the myriad reasons presented earlier, the majority of the estimated coefficients are not statistically significant, even though many are sizable in magnitude. Therefore, we also conduct an overall test for estimated coefficients for all discriminatory behaviors in both rental and sales for a given black or Hispanic sample. This small sample test is conducted using a sign test. The test can be interpreted as whether there is a consistent pattern of

Table 8.5. Estimated Coefficients of ln (Award Dollars)
Dependent Variable: Changes in Incidence of Discriminatory Behavior in Rental Market

Behavior	*Black-White Tests ($ from race-ethnic cases)*	*Black-White Tests ($ from black cases)*	*Hispanic-Anglo Tests ($ from race-ethnic cases)*
Availability	−0.016	−0.010	0.015
	(1.93)#	(1.26)	(1.38)
Inspection	−0.006	−0.006	−0.002
	(0.38)	(0.45)	(0.30)
Terms	0.011	−0.004	−0.003
	(1.18)	(0.45)	(0.37)
Encouragement	−0.030	−0.029	−0.014
	(2.38)*	(2.75)*	(0.75)
Overall	−0.011	−0.019	−0.003
	(0.09)	(2.07)#	(0.34)

Note: t-statistics shown in parentheses; * = $p < .05$; # = $p < .10$ (two-tailed tests).

Table 8.6. Estimated Coefficients of ln (Award Dollars)
Dependent Variable: Changes in Incidence of Discriminatory Behavior in Sales Market

Behavior	*Black-White Tests ($ from race-ethnic cases)*	*Black-White Tests ($ from black cases)*	*Hispanic-Anglo Tests ($ from race-ethnic cases)*
Availability	0.001	−0.008	0.005
	(0.05)	(0.73)	(0.37)
Inspection	0.014	−0.001	0.014
	(0.75)	(0.04)	(0.93)
Steering	−0.0009	−0.004	0.001
	(1.16)	(0.60)	(0.24)
Financing	−0.010	−0.006	0.010
	(0.73)	(0.52)	(0.47)
Encouragement	−0.027	−0.025	0.031
	(2.09)#	(2.13)#	(2.48)*
Overall	−0.012	−0.013	0.007
	(1.01)	(1.26)	(0.56)

Note: t-statistics shown in parentheses; * = $p<.05$; # = $p<.10$ (two-tailed tests).

positive or negative coefficient signs across the alternative discrimination measures.

Table 8.5 presents results for the rental market. For the apartment availability regression in the sample of sites where black-white HDS tests were conducted, the coefficient for the log of dollars awarded for all race/ethnic/color discrimination cases is -0.016, which is statistically significant at the 10 percent level (using a conservative, two-tailed test). In the case of the encouragement discriminatory behavior, the enforcement variable coefficient is -0.03, which is twice as large and more statistically significant. When considering column 2 of table 8.5 showing results for when only awards in cases involving black complainants are measured, we see that the sizes and magnitudes of the coefficients closely track those in column 1, except that availability becomes insignificant and the overall measure becomes significant (with a magnitude of -0.019). No coefficients of the enforcement variable were statistically significant in the case of discrimination against Hispanic renters (see column 3, table 8.5).

To provide a sense of the magnitude of the implied causal relationships here, we compare the differences in changes in discrimination our estimates would predict between two metropolitan areas that were otherwise identical but one had during the 1990s the mean level of monetary awards and the other had one standard deviation above the mean value of awards. Compared to the metropolitan areas with mean level of awards, the one with higher awards would be expected to evince greater declines in discrimination against black renters by: .075 (availability); .141 (encouragement); and .093 (overall). These are sizable predicted amounts indeed, given that the mean *actual* declines in these three indicators in the HDS black-white sites were .097, .083 and .071, respectively (cf. table 8.2).

Consider next the results for discrimination in the home sales sector, as shown in table 8.6. In the case of blacks, the only statistically significant coefficient for the log of awards occurs for the encouragement behavior. The magnitude and statistical significance of this result is not affected by whether all awards or just awards in cases involving black complainants are considered (cf. columns 1 and 2 in table 8.6). If we conduct the same thought experiment as above, the size of the coefficient here implies that the metropolitan area with one standard deviation higher level of awards would be expected to evince greater declines in encouragement discrimination against black home buyers by 0.061, compared to the metropolitan area with mean level of awards. The mean actual decline in this treatment variable was 0.078. In the case of Hispanics, all coefficients of the awards variable prove positive, one even statistically significantly so; we explore these Hispanic results more below.

Sign tests provide additional insights. When considering the awards enforcement variable coefficients across all eleven discriminatory behaviors against blacks measured in both rental and sales sectors (column 1 in tables 8.5 and 8.6), eight are negative, a result that barely misses statistical significance at the 10 percent level. The comparable test using only awards in cases with black complainants (column 2 in tables 8.5 and 8.6) reveals negative coefficients in all eleven measures, which is significant at the .0005 level. In the case of discrimination against Hispanics, only four of eleven measures evince negative coefficients for the enforcement variable, which is not different from what would be expected by chance.

Taken holistically in the context of the previously described econometric challenges, the evidence in tables 8.5 and 8.6 therefore strongly indicates that metropolitan areas with fair housing efforts yielding larger cumulative monetary damage awards from the court were associated with substantially greater declines in a wide variety of discriminatory behaviors against black renters and, to a somewhat less degree, black home buyers. There were no comparable relationships revealed in the case of discrimination against Hispanics. These intergroup differences in results might be explained as follows. Recall that cases alleging discrimination against Hispanics were few (and monetary awards nonexistent) compared to those alleging discrimination against blacks. With a greater baseline volume of cases, an increase in monetary awards may substantially increase the deterrent effect, but such an increase given a low baseline may have little deterrence effect because it does not change the expected cost of discrimination much.

What Other Factors May Have Influenced the Change in Discrimination?

As it is not the focus of this chapter, we note only briefly the salient findings regarding relationships between control variables and changes in discrimination in our multivariate models. Generalizations are difficult, inasmuch as results often varied depending on which behavior, tenure, and racial-ethnic group was under consideration. We can say with some confidence that metro areas experiencing larger increases in their minority populations evinced smaller declines in discrimination against black renters. Specifically, growth of the Hispanic population's share was associated with smaller declines in discrimination on rental availability and terms, and growth of the black population's share was associated with smaller declines on rental encouragement indicators. Similarly, for discrimination against blacks in the home sales sector, growth in the share of Hispanic population was associated with smaller declines in discrimination on availability, inspection, and encouragement. We could identify no systematically robust relationships for the control variables in equations modeling changes in discrimination against Hispanics in either rental or sales sectors.

DISCUSSION, CONCLUSION, AND DIRECTIONS FOR FURTHER RESEARCH

In this chapter we have attempted for the first time to ascertain if there are statistically detectable relationships between a direct measure of fair housing enforcement effectiveness and corresponding reductions in several directly measured incidences of racial-ethnic discrimination in a metropolitan area's housing market. We used paired-testing data from the 1989 and 2000 national Housing Discrimination Studies and archival data from HUD and HUD-supported fair housing enforcement agencies to operationalize our measures.

This effort proved challenging on several fronts. First is measurement error: both the dependent variables and the key explanatory variable are unavoidably measured with error. Second is small sample sizes: only a few metropolitan areas (seventeen for black-white tests; eleven for Hispanic-Anglo sites) had their rates of discrimination comparably measured in the 1989 and 2000 Housing Discrimination Studies. The effect of these two challenges is that reaching conventional standards of statistical significance is difficult. Third, there is the problem of bias due to reverse causality. If the persistence of discrimination in an area is correlated with its prior level, then it is likely that higher fair housing efforts will be observed where discrimination declines the least. Fourth, variables likely needed as controls in our regressions cannot be measured, creating omitted variables bias. These latter two biases militate against observing a statistically significant inverse relationship between enforcement efforts and corresponding declines in discrimination. There was no feasible way to avoid the first two shortcomings. We tried to avoid the latter two biases, however, by specifying a change in discrimination model that employs monetary awards in discrimination cases as the enforcement variable.

We have found that higher amounts of monetary awards secured during the 1990s in cases brought with the help of HUD and state and local enforcement agencies supported by HUD through its FHIP and FHAP programs are consistently associated with greater declines in discrimination against black apartment seekers and home seekers. The magnitude of our estimates suggests that enforcement effectiveness contributed substantially to the decline in discrimination against black apartment and home seekers observed during the decade. This evidence is consistent with the hypothesis that if these agencies are more successful in raising the expected financial penalties from discriminators in a metropolitan area, the industry will respond by lowering the incidence of such acts. It appears that enforcement in the rental sector may also spill over to create deterrence in the home sales sector, even though few legal cases are brought against sales agents.

We recognize that we cannot be absolutely sure that enhanced deterrence is at work here. The evidence also supports the hypothesis that state and local fair housing agencies that are more effective in securing large monetary awards from the court may also be more effective in, for example, fair housing training of industry operatives and public fair housing education and outreach efforts.

Of course, the general effectiveness of fair housing agencies (for enforcement, education, or agent training) will be strengthened if they receive a more stable base of funding, such as through the FHIP-FHAP federal mechanism. We therefore believe that it is important to note that the federal support for state and local enforcement activities may be an important factor in decreasing discrimination, even if our results are driven by local agency effectiveness in education and agent training, instead of deterrence. While federal dollars tend to be dedicated primarily to support investigation of specific complaints, the reliable funding stream created by the FHIP and FHAP programs may contribute substantially to overall agency effectiveness by increasing the size, professionalism, and stability of agency staff.

We were unable to find any statistical evidence that would support a similar set of conclusions in the case of discrimination against Hispanics. Part of this may be due to the smaller sample of metropolitan areas investigated. But part may also be due to the fact that there appear to be comparatively modest efforts to bring fair housing cases involving Hispanic complainants. In our seven sites where both black-white and Hispanic-Anglo tests were conducted because of their substantial black and Hispanic populations, there were 6,198 cases brought by black complainants and only 1,653 brought by Hispanic complainants, a ratio of nearly 4:1. This fact should be coupled with the observation that there were fewer indicators of discriminatory treatment showing declines from 1989 to 2000 for Hispanic renters than for black renters. These facts suggest that a *lack* of deterrence and/or fair housing agency efforts aimed at educating Hispanics of their fair housing rights may have been important here.

Future research in this field should address itself to the aforementioned empirical challenges. If one were to continue in the vein of multivariate statistical modeling as here, expanding the sample of metropolitan areas where changes in discrimination are consistently measured should be a high priority. If one concedes that the likelihood of an expanded (or even *any*) future HDS seems small, efforts should be directed into alternative means of assessing the intensity and prevalence of discrimination across many metropolitan areas. One notion potentially worth reconsidering was introduced a quarter century ago by Yinger (1979) and Galster (1977, 1981): discrimination should affect the relative prices and rents minorities pay relative to whites in similar neighborhoods. Other investigative approaches that may have merit may involve surveys of white households and housing agents regarding fair housing issues and their racial-ethnic preferences and prejudices.

In closing, we would conclude that more effective enforcement of fair housing laws does have a measurable impact. Indeed, we therefore conclude that a nontrivial part of the observed general reduction in housing market discrimination against blacks 1989–2000 may be attributed to such enhancements. Given the reduction of HUD monetary support for state and local fair housing agencies since the advent of the Bush administration, one is left to wonder whether these favorable trends are continuing into the twenty-first century.

TECHNICAL APPENDIX

The HDS Paired-testing Sample Design

The sample for HDS paired tests consisted of housing units advertised in major metropolitan newspapers, selected randomly each weekend. The study design assured that both tester teammates were equally qualified for the advertised housing unit. Teammates were matched according to gender and age and were assigned similar incomes, occupations, family profiles, and other socioeconomic characteristics. Teammates were trained to behave similarly during the test; neither expressed preferences for certain types of neighborhood. The teammates were sent, in random order over a short period, to visit the real estate agency placing the sampled advertisement and initiated contact by asking to see the advertised home and others similar to it. They often made subsequent phone and in-person contacts with agents, including going on home inspections. After each contact the testers independently filled out common report forms, which recorded the treatment afforded them, locations of the houses discussed or visited, information provided.

Measuring Differences in the Treatment of Testers

From test report forms we constructed various measures of differences in treatment, established to ensure comparably for both 1989 and 2000. A paired test can result in any one of three basic outcomes for each measure of treatment: (1) the white tester is favored over the minority; (2) the minority tester is favored over the white; or (3) both testers receive the same treatment. The simplest measure of adverse treatment is the share of all tests in which the white tester is favored over the minority. This *gross incidence* approach provides very simple and understandable indicators of how often white testers are treated more favorably than their equally qualified minority teammates.

Although *gross measures* of white-favored treatment are straightforward and easy to understand, they may overstate the frequency of what ideally we wish to measure: systematic discrimination. We use the term "systematic discrimination" to mean differences in treatment that are attributable to a customer's race or ethnicity, rather than to any other differences in tester characteristics or test circumstances. This term is not the same as "intentional" discrimination, nor is it intended to mean that these differences would necessarily be ruled as violations of federal fair housing law. Specifically, adverse treatment may occur during a test not only because of differences in race or ethnicity, but also because of random differences between the circumstances of their visits to the real estate agency. For example, in the time between the two testers' visits, an apartment might have been rented, the agent may have been distracted by personal matters and forgotten about an available unit, or one member of a tester pair might meet with an agent who is unaware of some available units. See Yinger (1986), Heckman and Siegelman (1993), Fix, Galster, and Struyk (1993), Heckman (1998), Foster et al. (2002), and Ross (2002) on the methodological issues related to the use of paired testing to measure discrimination.

One strategy for estimating systematic discrimination is to remove the cases where nondiscriminatory random events are responsible for differences in treatment by subtracting the incidence of minority-favored treatment from the incidence of white-favored treatment (*gross measure*) to produce a *net measure*. This approach essentially assumes that all cases of minority-favored treatment are attributable to random factors—that systematic discrimination never favors minorities—and that random white-favored treatment occurs just as frequently as random minority-favored treatment. Based on these assumptions, the net measure subtracts differences due to random factors from the total incidence of white-favored treatment. It is important to note that even when no statistical pattern of race-based differential treatment is observed, individual cases of discrimination may occur.

However, it seems unlikely that all minority-favored treatment is the result of random factors. For example, a minority landlord might prefer to rent to families of his or her own race or a real estate agent might think that minority customers need extra assistance. Other instances of minority-favored treatment might reflect a form of race-based steering, in which white customers are discouraged from considering units in predominantly minority neighborhoods or apartment complexes.

While net measures used in HDS may understate the frequency of systematic discrimination, we have nevertheless employed this measure in order to provide a lower-bound on the level of discrimination. Turner et al. (2002) found that the net and gross measures are fairly robust to controlling for differences in the circumstances faced by testers, differences between the white and minority testers' real-life characteristics, and situations where real estate agents might systematically favor minorities. Ondrich, Ross, and Yinger (2000) use a similar approach to estimate the upper and lower bounds for discrimination and find that the net and gross are typically close to those bounds.

NOTES

The ideas in this chapter do not necessarily represent the views of the U.S. Department of Housing and Urban Development, or any other agency of the federal government. We wish to express gratitude to Fred Freiberg, Todd Richardson, and Cliff Schrupp for their invaluable assistance in obtaining fair housing enforcement data from various sources. Sarah Pratt provided helpful technical assistance regarding the HUD TEAPOTS database. Jackie Cutsinger and Phyllis Seals at Wayne State University and Jason Cutsinger at Compuware Inc. supplied able research and technical assistance.

1. For a wide variety of consequences, as measured through multivariate modeling, see: Galster 1987a, 1991; Galster and Keeney 1988; Massey, Condran, and Denton 1987; Massey and Eggers 1990; Massey and Gross 1991; Cutler and Glaeser 1997; Ellen 2000).

2. The key exceptions to this general decline are discrimination in access to rental housing against Hispanics, racial steering of African Americans, and less assistance in obtaining financing provided to Hispanics.

3. Several theoretical and empirical treatises have probed the motives for housing discrimination: Galster (1987b), Yinger (1995), Ondrich, Ross, and Yinger (2000, 2003).

4. See Page (1995) footnote 7 for details.

5. This consistency composite may incorrectly classify tests as neutral, however, when one tester received favorable treatment on more indicators than his or her partner, or when one tester was favored on the most important indicator. *Hierarchical* composites were constructed by ranking the relative importance of individual treatment measures. The qualitative results are the same using either composite index (Turner et al. 2002).

6. The HUD database, known by its acronym TEAPOTS, records most of the cases noted in the NFHA database. Because of often substantial lags between case filings and ultimate disposition, we included cases that may have been filed as early as 1987 and finally settled as late as 2003.

7. Black complainants filed roughly four times as many cases as Hispanics, though their likelihood of receiving a finding of discrimination was only slightly higher (one to two percentage points).

8. Data were not available about what sorts of dollars might have been involved as part of conciliation agreements.

9. Unfortunately, most of the cases in the HUD fair housing database do not provide this information. We also experimented with a variable based on the number of fair housing cases found in favor of the plaintiff but found this to be a much weaker predictor than awards.

10. We thank Fred Freiberg, the former supervisory equal opportunity specialist for the DOJ during the 1990s, for supplying this information. Cliff Schrupp, executive director of the Fair Housing Center of Metropolitan Detroit, generously shared the accumulated NFHA records. Note that most of the NFHA-affiliated activity is tabulated in the HUD fair housing database, though not the DOJ activity.

11. We recognize that segregation, interracial economic disparities, and housing discrimination may themselves be causally related. To remove these intercorrelations we employ instrumental variables in place of segregation and interracial economic disparities. The identifying exogenous predictors for the former are: the percentages of black and Hispanic populations and the white-black differences in the percentages of respective populations aged forty to fifty-nine years, and for the latter are: white-black differences in the percentage of those aged twenty-five and older who are high school graduates and those who are college graduates.

REFERENCES

Blumer, Herbert. 1958. "Race Prejudice as a Sense of Group Position." *Pacific Sociological Review* 1:3–7.

Bobo, Lawrence, James Kruegel, and Ryan Smith. 1996. "Laissez Faire Racism: The Crystallization of 'Kinder, Gentler' Anti-Black Ideology." Working paper #98 (June). New York: Russell Sage Foundation.

Bobo, Lawrence, and Camille L. Zubrinsky. 1996. "Attitudes on Residential Integration: Perceived Status Differences, Mere In-Group Preference, or Racial Prejudice?" *Social Forces* 74(3): 883–909.

Bradburn, Norman, Seymour Sudman, and Galen Gockel. 1970. *Racial Integration in American Neighborhoods*. Chicago: National Opinion Research Center.

Cutler, David M., and Edward L. Glaeser. 1997. "Are Ghettos Good or Bad?" The *Quarterly Journal of Economics* 112(3): 827–72.

Ellen, Ingrid Gould. 2000. "Is Segregation Bad for Your Health? The Case of Low Birth Weight." In *Brookings-Wharton Papers on Urban Affairs*, ed. William G. Gale and Janet Rothenberg Pack, 203–38. Washington, DC: Brookings Institution Press.

Fix, Michael, George Galster, and Raymond Struyk. 1993. "An Overview of Auditing for Discrimination." In *Clear and Convincing Evidence: Measurement of Discrimination in America*, ed. Michael Fix and Raymond Struyk, 1–68. Washington, DC: Urban Institute Press.

Foster, Angela, Faith Mitchell, and Stephen Fienberg, eds. 2002. *Measuring Discrimination in a National Study*. Washington, DC: National Academy Press.

Galster, George. 1977. "A Bid-Rent Analysis of Housing Market Discrimination," *American Economic Review* 67:144–55.

———. 1981. "Black and White Preferences for Neighborhood Racial Composition," *American Real Estate and Urban Economics Journal* 10:39–66.

———. 1986. "More Than Skin Deep: The Effect of Discrimination on the Extent and Pattern of Racial Residential Segregation." In *Housing Desegregation and Federal Policy*, ed. John Goering, 119–38. Chapel Hill: University of North Carolina Press.

———. 1987a. "Residential Segregation and Interracial Economic Disparities: A Simultaneous-Equations Approach." *Journal of Urban Economics* 21:22–44.

———. 1987b. "The Ecology of Racial Discrimination in Housing: An Exploratory Model." *Urban Affairs Quarterly* 23(1): 84–107.

———. 1988a. "Residential Segregation in American Cities: A Contrary Review." *Population Research and Policy Review* 93(112): 597–614.

———. 1988b. "Assessing the Causes of Residential Segregation." *Journal of Urban Affairs* 10:395–407.

———. 1990. "The Great Misapprehension: Federal Fair Housing Policy in the Eighties." In *Building Foundations: Housing and Federal Policy*, ed. Denise DiPasquale and Langley Keyes, 137–57. Philadelphia: University of Pennsylvania Press.

———. 1991. "Housing Discrimination and Urban Poverty of African-Americans." *Journal of Housing Research* 2(2): 87–122.

———. 1995. "Minority Poverty: The Place-Race Nexus and the Clinton Administration's Civil Rights Policy." In *New Challenges: The Civil Rights Record of the Clinton Administration Mid-Term*, ed. Corinne Yu and William Taylor, 31–56. Washington, DC: Citizens' Commission on Civil Rights.

———. 1999. "The Evolving Challenges of Fair Housing Since 1968: Open Housing, Integration, and the Reduction of Ghettoization." *Cityscape* 4(3): 123–38.

Galster, George, and Erin Godfrey. 2005. "By Words and Deeds: Racial Steering by Real Estate Agents in the U.S. in 2000." *Journal of the American Planning Association* 71:251–68.

Galster, George, and W. Mark Keeney. 1988. "Race, Residence, Discrimination, and Economic Opportunity: Modeling the Nexus of Urban Racial Phenomena." *Urban Affairs Quarterly* 24(1): 87–117.

Giles, M. 1977. "Percentage Black and Racial Hostility." *Social Science Quarterly* 58:412–17.

Goering, John, and Gregory Squires. 1999. "Guest Editors' Introduction: Commemorating the 30th Anniversary of the Fair Housing Act." *Cityscape* 4(3): 1–17.

Iceland, John, Daniel Weinberg, and Erika Steinmetz. 2002. *Racial and Ethnic Residential Segregation in the United States: 1980–2000*. Census Bureau Series CENSR-3. Washington, DC: U.S. Government Printing Office.

Heckman, James. 1998. "Detecting Discrimination." *Journal of Economic Perspectives* 12:101–16.

Heckman, James, and Peter Siegelman. 1993. "The Urban Institute Studies: Their Methods and Findings." In *Clear and Convincing Evidence: Measurement of Discrimination in America*, ed. Michael Fix and Raymond Struyk, 187–258. Washington, DC: Urban Institute Press.

Lee, Bill Lann. 1999. "An Issue of Public Importance: The Justice Department's Enforcement of the Fair Housing Act." *Cityscape* 4(3): 35–56.

Marshall, H., and Robert Jiobu. 1975. "Residential Segregation in U.S. Cities: A Causal Analysis." *Social Forces* 53:449–60.

Massey, Douglas, G. Condran, and Nancy Denton. 1987. "The Effect of Residential Segregation on Black Social and Economic Well-being." *Social Forces* 66:29–56.

Massey, Douglas, and Mitchell Eggers. 1990. "The Ecology of Inequality: Minorities and the Concentration of Poverty, 1970–1980." *American Journal of Sociology* 95: 1153–88.

Massey, Douglas, Mitchell Eggers, and Nancy Denton. 1994. "Disentangling the Causes of Concentrated Urban Poverty." *International Journal of Group Tensions* 24:267–316.

Massey, Douglas, and Andrew Gross. 1991. "Segregation, the Concentration of Poverty, and the Life Chances of Individuals." *Social Science Research* 20:397–420.

Mathias, Charles, and Marion Morris. 1999. "Fair Housing Legislation: Not an Easy Row to Hoe," *Cityscape* 4(3): 21–34.

National Fair Housing Alliance. 2003. *$190,000,000 and Counting: A Summary of Housing Discrimination Lawsuits That Have Been Assisted by the Efforts of Private, Non-Profit Fair Housing Organizational Members of the National Fair Housing Alliance*. Detroit, MI: Fair Housing Center of Metropolitan Detroit.

Ondrich, Jan, Stephen L. Ross, and John Yinger. 2000. "How Common Is Housing Discrimination? Improving on Traditional Measures." *Journal of Urban Economics* 47:470–500.

——. 2003. "Now You See It, Now You Don't: Why Do Real Estate Agents Withhold Available Houses from Black Customers?" *Review of Economics and Statistics* 85(4): 854–73.

O'Reagan, Katherine, and John Quigley. 1996. "Teenage Employment and the Spatial Isolation of Minority and Poverty Households." *Journal of Human Resources* 31:692–702.

Page, Marianne. 1995. "Racial and Ethnic Discrimination in Urban Housing Markets: Evidence from a Recent Audit Study." *Journal of Urban Economics* 2:183–206.

Ross, Stephen L. 2002. "Paired Testing and the 2000 Housing Discrimination Study." In *Measuring Discrimination in a National Study*, ed. Angela Foster, Faith Mitchell, and Stephen Fienberg, 49–66. Washington, DC: National Academy Press.

Ross, Stephen L., and Margery Austin Turner. 2005. "Housing Discrimination in Metropolitan America: Explaining Changes between 1989 and 2000," *Social Problems* 52:152–80.

Schill, Michael, and Samantha Friedman. 1999. "The Fair Housing Amendments Act of 1988: The First Decade." *Cityscape* 4(3): 57–78.

Struyk, Raymond, Margery A. Turner, and John Yinger. 1991. *Housing Discrimination Study: Synthesis*. Washington, DC: U.S. Department of Housing and Urban Development.

Turner, Margery Austin, Stephen L. Ross, George Galster, and John Yinger. 2002. *Discrimination in Metropolitan Housing Markets: Phase I*. Washington, DC: U.S. Department of Housing and Urban Development.

U.S. Department of Commerce. 1993. *The 1990 Census of Population and Housing*. Washington, DC: U.S. Government Printing Office.

——. 2002. *The 2000 Census of Population and Housing*. Washington, DC: U.S. Government Printing Office.

Wienk, Ronald E., Clifford E. Reid, John C. Simonson, and Fred J. Eggers. 1979. *Measuring Discrimination in American Housing Markets: The Housing Market Practices Survey*. Washington, DC: U. S. Department of Housing and Urban Development.

Yinger, John. 1979. "Prejudice and Discrimination in the Urban Housing Market." In *Current Issues in Urban Economics*, ed. Peter Mieszkowski and Mahlon Straszheim, 430–63. Baltimore: Johns Hopkins University Press.

——. 1986. "Measuring Racial Discrimination with Fair Housing Audits." *American Economic Review* 76:881–93.

——. 1995. *Closed Doors, Missed Opportunities*. New York: Russell Sage.

9

National Fair Housing Policy and Its (Perverse) Effects on Local Advocacy

Mara S. Sidney

This chapter examines the relationship between public policy and fair housing organizations. It explores the argument of some scholars and advocates that the fair housing movement in the United States is weak, ineffective, or politically marginalized (Massey and Denton 1993; Smith 1994; Yinger 1995). Such observers typically point to indicators such as inadequate or dwindling governmental and foundation funding, dwindling numbers of complaints, and a seeming endemic lack of political will to seriously address housing discrimination.

I examine the specific proposition that the current characteristics of the local fair housing organizational movement, and the weaknesses that exist, are a product of national fair housing policies that span numerous administrations. The weaknesses of fair housing groups result from identifiable aspects of national fair housing policies. I argue that fair housing policies, rooted in their framing and funding statutes, have produced organizations that are predictably unstable, fragmented, and in constant struggles to either forge or resist alliances. I conclude that policies intended to fight injustice in effect help to sustain it by weakening logical local alliances and by artificially steering fair housing advocacy away from issues associated with such core realities as racial segregation and the production and location of affordable housing. Locally based fair housing advocacy, central to the promotion and execution of civil rights, has become unstable, lacks creative approaches to problems, and relies too heavily on federal as opposed to local resources and support as a result of the very policies that helped create it. Has the fair housing "movement" stopped, for all intents and purposes, moving?

The challenges that federal fair housing policies pose for local grassroots fair housing organizations are not, however, entirely negative. This portrait is therefore not entirely pessimistic. Rather, over the course of a decade of research I have uncovered important examples of fair housing organizations that have found methods to overcome the identified challenges. Such organizations cultivate local community support, including garnering nonfederal resources, and some pursue major fair housing lawsuits that establish the immediacy of threats to fair housing and the benefits that local constituents receive from their work. Such lawsuits also can produce monetary damages that provide a substantial stream of ongoing program funding.

This analysis suggests a different future for fair housing advocacy, in which local advocates both evaluate the constraints that fair housing policy and programs place upon them, and learn how to move beyond them. Without such strategic thinking and locally generated resources, fair housing organizations risk becoming ever weakened captives of uncertain federal fair housing policies and budget restraints. The future of federal civil rights, in an era when many have little awareness of their rights and remedies (see Turner et al., chapter 2 within), requires such strategic repositioning.

Thus I argue that assessing the state of fair housing must go beyond considering whether our laws and programs are up to the task of ending "unfair" housing conditions and practices. It is clear that existing fair housing programs have failed to root out all discriminatory practices, and it is reasonably certain that investing more federal funds in fair housing enforcement would improve policy implementation. But it is also essential to undertake an assessment of how fair housing policies positively and negatively affect the nonprofit local fair housing movement. It is the beginnings of such an assessment that I offer here.

This analysis of fair housing organizations is primarily rooted in qualitative research conducted from 1998 to 2000 in Washington, D.C.; Denver; and Minneapolis.[1] Since that field research ended in 2000, I have continued to meet with local- and national-level advocates at housing and fair housing venues.

A BRIEF HISTORY OF FAIR HOUSING ADVOCACY

Organized advocacy for fair housing dates to the 1940s when the NAACP and Thurgood Marshall developed legal strategies to combat racially restrictive covenants.[2] Advocates next targeted discriminatory underwriting standards used by FHA and fought segregation in public housing. In New York City, for example, advocates launched attacks against the segregative and discriminatory policies of Metropolitan Life's Stuyvesant Town, eventually prompting the company to offer units to blacks as well as to whites beginning in 1952.

Stuyvesant Town advocates founded the first national organization against housing discrimination in 1950. The National Committee Against Discrimination in Housing (NCDH) helped local groups that were lobbying for state and local antidiscrimination laws, many of which targeted discrimination in the real estate industry (Berry 1979; Helper 1969). At the neighborhood level, community groups attempted to quell the panic among white homeowners when African Americans began to move into their neighborhoods, and to fight practices of blockbusting.

The 1960s both energized and complicated the fair housing movement. On the one hand, advocates were energized and empowered by the overall thrust of the civil rights movement. Advocates pursued a major series of lawsuits to end racial segregation in public housing (e.g., the Gautreaux case [Rubinowitz and Rosenbaum 2000]) and to stop the exclusionary zoning and building permit practices that municipalities used to keep affordable housing and racial minorities out.

Within this context, the national Fair Housing Act was enacted in 1968 after years of debate. The law prohibited racial discrimination in housing, establishing a civil right to nondiscriminatory treatment. It specified particular practices that constituted discrimination (for example, by real estate agents or mortgage lenders), and authorized HUD to take and investigate claims. The agency was required to conciliate among the parties rather than to litigate, and the civil penalties for violating the law were quite low. Earlier versions of fair housing legislation gave HUD the power to issue injunctions and restraining orders against alleged violators, but this was removed during the legislative process, as a price of compromise to secure passage. The law gave the Department of Justice authority to intervene where evidence showed a "pattern and practice" of discriminatory treatment, and established the right of individual victims to pursue their claims in court.

The Fair Housing Act was the last of the major civil rights laws of the 1960s to pass. It came at a time when backlash against civil rights was emerging in the context of urban riots, and as the civil rights movement itself was fragmenting with the rise of the Black Power movement. NCDH struggled to survive, as foundation funding dwindled and a backlash against civil rights took stronger hold, exemplified by antibusing crusades and the unsupportive policies of the Reagan administration (Edsall and Edsall 1992). The group eventually disbanded in 1987. But advocates pressed ahead with strengthening amendments to the Fair Housing Act, which were adopted in 1988. The amendments authorized HUD to initiate investigations and to establish an administrative law system to adjudicate claims. HUD now may pursue remedies other than conciliation and judges may award actual damages, civil penalties, injunctive relief, and attorney's fees.

It was at this time that a new nonprofit fair housing enforcement organization emerged—the National Fair Housing Alliance (NFHA). NFHA has been instrumental in advocating for the role of nonprofit groups in fair housing enforcement. In the late 1970s to the early 1980s, a demonstration project at HUD had funded nine local fair housing groups to engage in enforcement testing. Following this, the Fair Housing Initiatives Program (FHIP) was authorized in the 1987 Housing and Community Development Act as a demonstration project, becoming permanent in the 1992 version of the law. This program funds private nonprofit fair housing organizations on an annual, competitive basis to undertake enforcement and education activities. With a congressional appropriation, HUD specifies through an annual Notice of Funding Availability (NOFA) how much funding it will provide and for what purposes.

Today, NFHA is the major umbrella organization for local fair housing organizations and also participates in fair housing enforcement, receiving funding from the FHIP program. As of May 2005, NFHA had eighty operating and forty supporting members in thirty-six states and the District of Columbia. Operating members have voting membership and must engage in fair housing enforcement—taking and investigating claims of discrimination. In 2004, NFHA members received about 18,000 of the 27,319 complaints and claims filed that year (National Fair Housing Alliance 2005).

In addition to such groups, other types of nonprofit organizations also sometimes programmatically address fair housing issues. Legal Aid or equivalent groups, the NAACP, the National Urban League, and other civil rights organizations are intermittently active in lobbying, and litigating both individual and class-action lawsuits in the private and public sector. These groups also help to express and synthesize policy and funding priorities of the country's varying protected classes (e.g., the National Urban League publishes an annual report, *The State of Black America*).

A much smaller, evanescent number of organizations work to achieve racially integrated neighborhoods at times organized through a national organization, the Fund for an Open Society.[3] It has appeared to many observers that such activities are marginal to mainstream "fair housing" enforcement organizations (Keating 1994; Saltman 1990). Despite this seeming national marginalization, advocacy groups in one of the cases I present below have successfully focused on the issue of segregated housing.

Despite the existence of these groups, it seems clear that neither pressing problems of racial inequality nor housing discrimination enjoy a prominent position on national or local policy agendas. Despite the evidence about the absolute level of housing discrimination, there are only 25,000 total cases or charges of housing discrimination filed each year, and many of them are with private and nongovernmental agencies. Only a fraction of those who feel that they have been victims of discrimination ever file a complaint or use the federal or local enforcement machinery (Abravanel 2002). There are undoubtedly many reasons, but part of the reason for this gap may be that fair housing groups do not exist in every state, much less every city, so victims of housing discrimination may not know where to go to seek low-cost or free advice about the maltreatment they feel at the hands of property owners, banks, rental agents, or other parts of the housing industry. Given these indicators, this chapter begins from the premise that local fair housing advocacy can be "stronger" and "more effective." It points to barriers that local groups currently face and then cites examples of how such groups have found methods to overcome them.

STUDYING NONPROFIT CIVIL RIGHTS ORGANIZATIONS: INTERNAL AND EXTERNAL FACTORS

How do we understand the position in which today's local fair housing groups find themselves? Scholars of nonprofit organizations and social movements typically examine both groups' internal resources and their environments or external resources. For example, the influential resource mobilization approach to the study of social movements emphasized that movements arise not simply out of grievances, but because groups are able to generate organizational resources that overcome the costs of individual participation (Edelman 2001; Mueller 1992; Snow et al. 2005). Scholars of interest groups compare resources across groups, such as their membership base, funding levels, and research or technical capacities, to explain whether and how they exert influence (Cigler and Loomis 2002). Scholars of nonprofit organizations also look at the interaction between a group's internal resources and its environment. For example, Stoutland discusses the importance of community development corporations' management capacity, leadership, and internal resources, coupled with the presence of a supportive political and social environment that includes intermediary organizations and willing government officials and public policies (1999).

My research on fair housing groups emphasizes the role of external or structural factors in establishing challenges for these groups. Internal factors such as volunteer base, leadership, and technical skills certainly are critical to the effectiveness of such groups. I argue, however, that these internal resources are heavily, if not primarily, shaped by external factors such as public policies and their funding priorities. That is, weak nonprofit-group resources can be directly linked to component parts of national fair housing policy.

National policy establishes core obstacles and difficulties for groups, whereas locally based resources may offer alternative pathways around these difficulties when they can be effectively cultivated and sustained. The future of the national fair housing movement, I argue, is based on how effectively the latter are recognized and used as a systematic supplement or alternative to dependence on federal priorities and resources.

POLICIES "MAKE" POLITICS

While many assume that policies are created out of political ferment (e.g., Branch 1998), another longstanding body of scholarship conversely suggests that once enacted, policies critically shape subsequent political dynamics. By distributing benefits to some groups while imposing costs on others they create a set of stakeholders with competing interests in federal law (Pierson 1994; Schneider and Ingram 1997; Soss 1999; Wilson 1973). At its simplest, those groups that receive benefits from government programs have an incentive to mobilize politically to maintain and expand them. But relying on one source of funding, especially government funding, can create problems of autonomy for nonprofits, even altering or compromising their initial goals and hindering them from seeking alternative sources of support (Smith and Lipsky 1993). Nonprofits adjust practices to comply with federal rules, and they often shift away from advocacy to service provision. Staff members become caught up in federal funding cycles that require frequent applications and reporting, and they spend time on their own or in professional associations working with government agencies to smooth the mechanics of the government-nonprofit partnership to achieve more efficient grant administration.

Policies do more than foster the mobilization of beneficiaries by allocating resources to them. They articulate a particular definition of a social problem, specify the appropriate solution for it, and specify a mechanism (whether through annual budget appropriations, an entitlement system, etc.) for allocating resources to implement the solution. Statutes typically include statements about their goals and they designate a particular set of instruments intended to move society toward those goals. The Fair Housing Act's major stated goal is "to provide, within constitutional limitations, for fair housing throughout the United States" (P.L. 90-284) and it is implemented nationally through a limited range of civil rights tools intended to eliminate instances of racial discrimination against individuals and institutions such that "equal access" to housing markets would occur. That is, it establishes the right to nondiscrimination in housing, enforceable in agency tribunals and in court. Amendments and subsequent programs have established a set of supplementary rules for accepting and processing claims, for investigations, for punishing perpetrators, and finally for providing relief to victims (see Schill, chapter 7 within, for details of the 1988 amendments).

Politics and knowledge are constraining factors that contribute to the selection of statutory goals and policy tools in that policy makers act on what they "know" to be true about a given problem within a context of political and fiscal contingencies. Because social behavior is complex and changing, policies adopted to address a problem at one point in time—say the later 1960s—are inevitably temporary, partial, or inadequate solutions. The political balance of power at the time a policy is adopted, including necessary compromises, means that lawmakers are seldom likely to adopt the full array of solutions that are known to be "effective." In the 1968 statute, for example, Republicans succeeded in requiring that state and local government agencies be allowed the first opportunity to investigate a complaint even though these agencies had been shown to be a major party to acts of racial intimidation and violence in the past.

Policies and the programs they spawn ideally should shift to address the changing and dynamic nature of a problem they have sought to cure, but they often do not. Choices made at a point in time structure subsequent problem definitions and solutions for decades in part because the very system that has been created has a limited political foundation to generate legislative reform (Baumgartner and Jones 1993; Schneider and Ingram 1997).

This can mean that as a civil rights law prohibits one set of discriminatory acts, it may prompt the development of alternative forms of discrimination as perpetrators adapt to avoid punishment. Current fair housing law, then, will inevitably address some aspects of the evolving societal problem it is said to cure but not others (Jones 1994; Simon 1996; Stone 2001). Advocacy groups will receive federal support for addressing certain forms of recognized discriminatory treatment, but not for newer, adaptive forms of ill treatment. In addition, fair housing policy's original focus on *individual* victims of discrimination and the minimal recognition in the law of the need for more systemic investigations, or affirmative strategies to promote housing integration, has persistently constrained fair housing advocates since the law was enacted in 1968 (Yinger 1995).

Policies and derivative program funding also powerfully shape the prospects for advocacy group coalitions and, conversely, divisions (Schneider and Ingram 1997; see Bowdler and Kamasaki, chapter 10 within). At its simplest, limited federal program funding is bound to direct benefits to one set of groups, giving these constituencies incentives to work together to expand benefits or prompting them to compete with one another for a larger or continuing share. Particular policy tools and program guidelines may encourage or discourage partnerships. Some federal grants require local public-private partnerships as a prerequisite for funding (e.g., Clinton's Enterprise Communities or the ISTEA transportation policy), but fair housing policy has few built-in coordinating incentives. Competitive award programs typically pit local groups against one another. The most obvious example in the fair housing arena is the competition of nonprofits for funding from the Fair Housing Initiatives Program. Advocates of various protected classes (for example, people with disabilities, African Americans, or Latinos) can readily see themselves in direct competition with one another for federal resources (see chapter 10 by Bowdler and Kamasaki within). On a sustained basis, a program of annual competitions predictably reopens the same wounds and issues of "when does my group gets its rightful share." The sense of unfairness ripples annually through the FHIP "fair" housing competition.

Thus by making permanent or institutionalizing a particular problem definition, solution, and funding system, national policies have both positive and perverse "lock-in effects" (Pierson 1994). Once a choice of policy is taken, the cost of adopting alternative solutions increases significantly as constituents are established as beneficiaries and stakeholders. The nation's fair housing problem becomes reified as one of individual case processing rather than broader or alternative, locally driven visions of needs for housing justice and equity. Program investments cumulate over time, representing "sunk costs," and stakeholders become used to a policy's particular way of diagnosing and addressing a problem. The solution adopted by a policy becomes a norm for advocacy activity. As time goes on, actors in a particular policy arena can lose sight of the fact that other possible policy options and programs are feasible, legally permissible, and even necessary.

The lock-in effects of fair housing policies were apparent during the course of my research. At meetings of fair housing organizations, discussion focused on implementing federal fair housing law—discovering and pursuing perpetrators of discrimination in the real estate industry, developing building standards for accessibility for disabled people, reviewing recent court cases. Little or no attention, for example, was devoted to the complex task of achieving racial integration through affirmative strategies or to regional inequities in the provision of affordable housing. The local fair housing problem had become what the law, narrowly constructed in 1968, said it should be.

In what follows, I argue that fair housing policy defines the problem of "unfair" housing by including some goals for housing justice while notably excluding others. In doing so fair housing policy has contributed to the fragmentation of the fair housing movement and has created unnecessary barriers to coalition-building, most notably with those groups pressing for affordable and inclusive housing. Elements of fair housing policy have fostered a low-profile, even invisible, set of advocacy groups that have trouble sustaining their work over the long term.

FAIR HOUSING POLICY RESOURCES FOR NONPROFITS

Moving from the general observation that policies shape politics to a specific analysis of local fair housing organizations requires looking more closely at the resources that national fair housing policy offers to nonprofits. A policy's resources encourage groups to engage in particular kinds of activities, to act in particular arenas, and to adopt particular understandings of a problem. In doing so, groups may neglect aspects of problems that a policy does not address. Drawing on Schneider and Ingram's concept of "policy designs" (1997), I propose a typology of resources to think about how policies influence nonprofits.

First, policies embody and thus offer to groups a particular set of fixed ideas, articulating goals for action. Policies specify the contours of a problem by establishing the tools to attack its causes or to aid its victims. They also may prohibit or establish areas of risky intervention. For example, fair housing policy in conjunction with judicial rulings does not support the promotion of racial quotas in neighborhood integration. Second, policies might offer direct funding to groups. Third, policies specify certain procedures or channels of action that nonprofits can use in their work, establishing which government arenas are used and with which public officials nonprofits interact. Finally, policies and programs can offer information to groups including data or training that groups need to use or enforce the policy.

Fair housing law contains two distinct sets of resources for advocacy groups—a dominant set related to civil rights and a subordinate set related to affordable housing. That is, fair housing law legitimates and supports two kinds of fair housing advocacy, though it encourages one more strongly than the other. Affordable housing has long been interlinked with the pursuit of housing rights for people of color. Higher rates of poverty among African American and Latino households makes them more reliant on subsidized housing than white and Asian households are. Additionally, community opposition to affordable housing is often rooted in racial prejudice, allied with concerns about risk and public costs (but see Emerson, Yancey, and Chai 2001). Securing a right to nondiscrimination in housing markets for people of color thus would entail efforts in the public as well as private housing markets.

Civil Rights Resources

Most resources available from fair housing policy relate to the goal of securing individual civil rights by finding and punishing people engaging in discriminatory practices and then compensating victims. As Schill (chapter 7 within) demonstrates, when handled by the governmental agencies, most of these individual cases typically fail to find reasonable cause or fail to offer a sensible level of relief. Fair housing policy and programs offer funding and technical support to nonprofit groups engaged in this work, which takes place in the form of conciliation, in the courts, or in an administrative law system.[4] Private fair housing groups argue that their work accounts for more than half of the discrimination claims investigated in a given year, and that they play a key role in at least half of the cases in which HUD brings a charge (National Fair Housing Alliance 2004).

HUD's Fair Housing Initiatives Program (FHIP) funds a modest number of nonprofit fair housing organizations on an annual competitive basis to undertake both enforcement as well as education activities. Grants range from $75,000 to $250,000 for these purposes; grants of $1 million over three years fund the creation of two new fair housing groups per year (NFHA 2005). A total of 140 groups have been funded over the past ten years, with about 50 percent of funded groups receiving sustained funding over time. NFHA itself is also a grantee, receiving funds for developing media campaigns promoting fair housing and for starting new fair housing organizations.[5] Groups are funded to receive claims from individuals, to then investigate them possibly through use of fair housing tests, and then to represent those clients in either courts or in the administrative process (see Schill, chapter 7 within). FHIP also offers limited funding for education and outreach activities and HUD holds annual conferences for FHIP grantees to promote information sharing and to provide technical assistance.

Affordable Housing Resources

A second set of more broadly conceived fair housing policy resources is centered on the goal of providing desegregated and affordable housing—all on a nondiscriminatory basis. The Fair Housing Act requires HUD to incorporate "fair housing" into its existing housing and community development programs "in a manner to affirmatively further the purposes of this title" (Sec. 808). This directs attention to the operating procedures and outcomes of federal programs such as public housing, Housing Choice Vouchers or Section 8, and the Community Development Block Grant (CDBG) program.

A wide range of local groups and law firms have filed fair housing related lawsuits against both HUD and local housing authorities or a local government, alleging that their operation of subsidized housing promotes racial or other forms of segregation, thereby illegally discriminating against protected class members, usually African Americans. (For example, in response to advocacy groups, officials in Nassau County on Long Island in New York strengthened its antidiscrimination law in 2004 to prohibit discrimination against Section 8 tenants.) Or groups may try to show that local governments have not "affirmatively furthered" fair housing in their use of federal housing and urban development funds as the Fair Housing Act somewhat ambiguously requires of them. Groups engaged in such work typically have received no direct funding from HUD but quite frequently win damages and fees in successful litigation. There is an undocumented level of such litigation-based financial relief that supports local fair housing and other advocacy groups to promote open and accessible housing. FHIP funding is barred from use in any claims against the government.

Federal fair housing resources, then, are designed to have local fair housing groups develop the legal and investigative expertise to work on individual fair housing cases and not to engage in more complex, broad-scale pattern and practice cases, although a small number of such cases have been pursued at the local level. Most local fair housing work consists of accepting and investigating claims from those persons who believe, rightly or wrongly, that they have been a victim of some form of housing or lending discrimination. They then often conduct one or more fair housing tests, and then use the court and administrative law systems to advocate on behalf of complainants.

Few if any local efforts focus on desegregated or affordable housing. Such efforts exist when there are local pro bono legal resources of support for them or alternative support from foundations or local jurisdictions. Since local contexts vary in their political, social, economic, housing market, and historical characteristics, we need to pay careful attention to groups that leverage local resources in ways that enable broader fair housing work. In the next section I provide case studies of fair housing advocacy in two cities where groups struggled in different ways to adapt federal fair housing resources to their local needs.

TWO MODELS OF FAIR HOUSING ADVOCACY

What does fair housing advocacy look like at the local level? My cases show two models. In one, advocates take nearly full advantage of federal resources, whereas in the other advocates rely more on local resources, using federal resources selectively. In Denver, local advocates secure federal policy resources to pursue civil rights–oriented work against individual instances of housing discrimination. They supplement these with local resources that tend to complement and extend this work, although they extend fair housing work to the arena of schools as well. Nonetheless, their reliance on federal resources means that Denver fair housing advocates are susceptible to the difficulties posed by shifts in federal policy. In the Twin Cities, advocates rely on local resources to address discrimination and the chronic undersupply of affordable housing, using federal fair housing resources to bolster this work. Because affordable-housing resources available from federal policy consist primarily of opportunities to litigate, advocates must have local resources available to launch litigation. In the Twin Cities, such resources exist.

Denver: Federal Resources Sustain and Challenge a Movement

Denver advocates have engaged in fair housing activity from the late 1950s forward. One of the country's largest nonprofit fair housing centers operated there nearly a decade before the 1968 national law was enacted. Although it closed in the early 1970s, a small cadre of advocates retained attention to the issue, keeping it alive in government and industry arenas, and in a neighborhood organization. By the late 1990s, fair housing advocacy focused on fighting individual-level instances of discrimination by traditional fair housing enforcement such as taking and investigating claims, and through partnerships with the local real estate industry focused on educating real estate agents (Sidney 2003: 99–104). An earlier focus on achieving racially integrated neighborhoods had faded from view.

Groups rely on federal policy resources, including problem definitions, funding, procedures, and information. They have cultivated additional funding from industry partnerships. Local innovations include links with the school district, and with a local community development corporation. But at the time of my field research, Denver's fair housing groups had few local allies, were relatively invisible to the general public, and had generally overburdened staff.

After a lull in the late 1970s following the closing of Denver's fair housing center, advocacy revived. When federal funding became available in the late 1980s for fair housing planning, advocates secured a grant and undertook a process that led to the creation in 1987 of a new fair housing center. This center, Housing for All, was joined by two additional fair housing groups—HOME and the local Community Housing Resource Board (CHRB).[6] Housing for All and HOME received FHIP funds to engage in enforcement. They investigated individual claims using fair housing testing, and advocated on behalf of victims spanning the protected classes of racial minorities, families with children, and disabled people. They conducted workshops for home seekers who were members of the protected classes, and they taught real estate professionals about fair housing law and how to abide by it. The CHRB, a relic of a previous federal initiative to start local boards that brought together industry, government, and community members, raised funds from the real estate industry to conduct fair housing training for agents.

Clearly, Denver's fair housing movement uses federal policy's civil rights–related resources, working to decrease discrimination in private housing transactions. Advocates have responded to nearly every opportunity for federal funding, securing money to examine discriminatory practices in home rentals, sales, lending, and insurance. They have conducted special demonstration projects, participated in nationwide housing audits, undertaken fair housing planning projects, and won FHIP grants year after year to support the two fair housing centers. In doing so, fair housing activists in Denver have adapted their strategies to incorporate changes in national law, such as the addition to the protected classes of people with disabilities and families with children. When the national fair housing movement, and HUD, focused on mortgage lending, and insurance, Denver activists also explored these issues.

Denver's advocates began in the 1950s with a focus on fighting segregation, as neighborhoods on the city's east side began to shift from white to black. Although city reports on housing documented poor conditions for black and Latino residents of Denver through the 1940s, it was the movement of black families beyond the "boundaries" of the ghetto in northeast Denver that prompted both white flight and activist efforts to promote fair housing. The city's Latinos, although historically concentrated in northwest Denver, had not experienced levels of segregation from whites as high as those between blacks and whites. Although some of the activists who pioneered these efforts still take part in fair housing organizations, the goal of achieving integration had been set aside by the 1990s.

During the time of my field research, an affordable-housing preservation movement was emerging to protect Section 8 housing in the city. Fair housing advocates were aware of the planning but were not involved in it. One of the city's FHIP grantees was housed inside a community development corporation. Tensions became evident between the CDC staff, who expected the group to serve the CDC's local community, and HOME, whose mandate as a recipient of federal fair housing funds was to engage in metropolitan-wide Fair Housing Act enforcement. In this way, Denver's federally funded fair housing advocates mirror the federal fair housing policy, directing efforts toward individual cases of discrimination and away from local needs, organizational concerns, and the imperatives of coalition building.

But Denver's advocacy did not track uniformly with federal policy, and some important local innovations became evident. There was an attempt to partner with a local community-based nonprofit developer, and there were efforts to link fair housing advocacy to education. These latter initiatives were based upon advocates' opposition to what they saw as an anti-city attitude among Denver-area real estate agents. Their argument was that if real estate agents knew more about Denver schools, for example, they would be less likely to steer middle-class families away from the city and would instead act to promote both economic and racial/ethnic mixing. The local CHRB brought brokers into the schools through its "Yellow School Bus Tours," funded partly with CDBG dollars, and real estate brokers received continuing education credit for the tours.[7] During the fair housing discussion, brokers received data emphasizing the high pupil-achievement levels in Denver schools. These examples illustrate another striking feature of fair housing advocacy in Denver: a proclivity to forge partnerships and work for cooperation rather than to use adversarial strategies such as class-action litigation. In part, this approach reflects advocates' strategic assessment of their context—they lacked the funding to launch such litigation, and they regarded both the state and federal district courts as hostile to their work. They concluded that working cooperatively would enable them to start practical programs to address issues more quickly than would litigation. The antilitigation tendencies of real estate–based CHRBs does not preclude litigation and case processing as a component part of a more comprehensive plan for fair housing but does illustrate that there are circumstances when the more strategic course of action, for a period of time, may be to seek cooperation. The option of moving tactically from forms of cooperation and education to case investigations and legal action should be an inherent right of choice for all fair housing enforcement agencies. Funding should enable and not frustrate such options.

Denver's fair housing advocacy, however, illustrates the difficulties confronting organizations that rely solely or primarily on federal policy resources. First, when they are driven by the federal policy agenda, they may well have trouble adapting this agenda to their local needs and judicial context. Advocates faced tension in addressing affordable housing and community-based approaches with funding that required them to focus on prosecuting cases for all of the Fair Housing Act's protected classes within their region. FHIP grants deprive local groups of the autonomy to control their agenda, require time-consuming annual applications, and present the very real prospect of not receiving funding. When groups receive funding, they must comply with oversight and reporting requirements. There may also be formal or informal HUD pressures to produce a certain *number* of discrimination claims, which staff members believe can reduce the *quality* of their enforcement efforts.

Groups also feel they have to shift their priorities from funding cycle to funding cycle in accordance with HUD's unpredictably changing priorities for fair housing implementation. Thus in one year groups will receive extra "points" for reaching out to new immigrant communities, another year they get credit for focusing on building standards for accessibility to disabled tenants, and yet another year for focusing on fair lending cases. The annual readjustment of priorities driven by grant requirements can frustrate local hiring and investigative planning, and result in a slow start in developing effective investigative protocols for the new federal investigative priority of the year. Note that this is a function of program design—which might instead, for instance, use five-year funding cycles and semipermanent fair housing goals.

Second, advocates did not enjoy a high profile within the city. Using federal policy seemed to keep them in a position of invisibility to local community leaders, elected officials, the media, and the general public. For example, during an interview, a city community-development official explained that few city dollars were allocated to fair housing because of a lack of activity and public demand. Yet a few weeks earlier, one of the local FHIP grantees had won a national award from HUD for an innovative program to improve residential insurance practices that other local housing advocates knew little about. Also during my field research, I attended a meeting of the Colorado Affordable Housing Partnership entitled "Minorities and Affordable Housing." FHIP grantees were neither present nor did participants refer to their work during the program.

As is the case with nonprofit grantees in a range of policy sectors, federal fair housing funds were continually found to be necessary but still insufficient to accomplish all of the tasks. Not only do staff become stretched thin, making maintaining morale difficult, but the mandated private or confidential nature of most case settlements effectively makes them less able to counter their invisibility. Paid staff are extremely busy taking and processing claims, finding testers and coordinating tests, representing clients, and preparing for the next annual proposal competition. While they indicate that they would like to cultivate a diversity of funders to reduce dependence on government and limit their vulnerability to federal budget cuts, they have little time to do so. The terms of their FHIP grants prohibit them from lobbying, which some—out of uncertainty and caution—define quite broadly. Consequently, in Denver, few government officials and local elites were aware of the fair housing group's work. Moreover, as is true in national surveys, many of them were not at all convinced that housing discrimination was a problem in Denver.

Through the FHIP program, HUD has funded local groups to engage in testing. The anonymity of fair housing testers is critical to the success of this method of identifying discrimination. If a leasing agent or broker suspects someone to be a tester, he or she will most likely behave differently during the "simulated" housing transaction. Thus, fair housing groups must keep their testing initiatives and personnel confidential. Confidentiality also arises as an imperative in many fair housing cases settled out of court; it may be a condition for a settlement. The public may never learn the details of the practices a defendant engaged in, or the damages won by the plaintiff and nonprofit group. Nonprofits' work thus remains invisible to most city residents.

Finally, mechanisms of allocating fair housing funds create disincentives for cooperation among fair housing groups in a community. Endemically limited federal funding is awarded on a competitive basis, thus inevitably pitting local groups against one another. Some Denver advocates were unhappy that, with the founding of HOME Inc., the city had two FHIP-funded groups, since they saw federal support in zero-sum terms, fearing that HUD would not maintain adequate funding levels for both groups over time. (By contrast, a local HUD official welcomed the presence of an additional enforcement group, comparing it to having more state troopers on the highways to catch speeding drivers.) Another barrier to cooperation is that legal damages and attorney's fees must be shared among groups if several work together on a successful lawsuit. These aspects of federal enforcement's reliance on testing, and its funding mechanisms, lead some groups to work alone. Doing so, they felt, would help them develop stronger fair housing cases and claims and deter the private real estate industry from some forms of discrimination, while recognizing that this would also keep the problem out of sight and off the official public agenda. The net effect of perfectly logical tactical decisions was to limit or even undermine the possibility of developing longer-term public support.

Although these are serious challenges, federal resources did enable Denver advocates to sustain activity despite several features of the city's context that made it relatively hostile to their work. In Denver advocates relied heavily on federal funding but also had a network of partners in the real estate and insurance industries as well as in state and local government that they had built up over thirty years. Industry funded fair housing training initiatives and partnerships with the insurance industry, for example, to address homeowner insurance redlining. Fair housing groups in Denver kept a low profile because of the nature of legal requirements and their limited resources but also because they worried that in a conservative state greater publicity might spark unpredictable forms of opposition. Lack of resources combined with what they perceived as hostile courts to mean less litigation and more partnership strategies. They then managed their industry and government partners with care.

Minneapolis: Local Resources Leverage National Resources

Twin Cities fair housing advocacy differed dramatically from that in Denver. Fair housing efforts focused on affordable housing provision using a strong base of local resources to leverage the resources that national fair housing policy offers. Indeed, the Twin Cities movement redefined "fair housing" advocacy into the pursuit of regionally dispersed affordable housing. The case of the Twin Cities thus shows another path to an invigorated fair housing advocacy: the entrance of affordable-housing advocates into the fair housing arena. These "new" fair housing advocates brought a strong network of connections to elected officials, experience working in the legislative arena, and educating and mobilizing the public behind affordable housing issues; they were an important resource for those advocates in the Twin Cities who wanted to see more attention paid to reducing racial inequality.

In Denver, fair housing advocacy was restricted to the work of three nonprofits, but in the Twin Cities a wide range of groups had taken up the issue, using a variety of strategies to pursue their goals. In general, these groups relied either on the federal fair housing resources related to affordable housing, or they did not use federal resources at all. As such, they evaded the cycle of invisibility that challenged Denver's activists and other civil rights–oriented fair housing groups, and succeeded at publicly articulating the problem of economic disparities in the metro area, and to a lesser extent, the problem of racial disparities.

State legislator Myron Orfield brought the regional concept of fair housing to the legislative agenda in 1993 when he sponsored a series of bills to reduce concentrated poverty in the Twin Cities. The fair housing movement emerged in those years; a wide range of groups was active, from legal advocates to faith-based organizations to affordable-housing and poor-people's advocacy groups. Legal activists founded two fair housing groups in the early 1990s. The Housing Discrimination Law Project, housed at Legal Services, received FHIP funds to engage in enforcement on behalf of low-income protected classes. The Minnesota Fair Housing Center conducted research it used to influence local policy making. Also in the 1990s, the NAACP, Legal Aid, and a local law firm brought two class-action lawsuits with fair housing dimensions. *Hollman v. Cisneros* charged HUD, the Minneapolis Public Housing Authority, the city, and the state with intentionally segregating African Americans in public housing in the Near North side of the city (Goetz 2003; Orfield 1997). This lawsuit resulted in a negotiated consent decree under which the 770 spatially concentrated public housing units were being replaced with units scattered throughout the metro area, and a community planning process was guiding redevelopment of the North Side public housing. The second lawsuit, against the state, charged that racial and class segregation resulted in inadequate education for Minneapolis children. Plaintiffs sought a metrowide housing-integration policy as part of the relief, although they were not successful. To generate support for this lawsuit, the NAACP founded the Education and Housing Equity Project, which organized and facilitated "community circles" on schools, housing, and race. Citizens formed neighborhood groups throughout the Twin Cities region to discuss patterns of racial and economic segregation and to develop ideas about solutions that their communities would support.

Finally, affordable housing advocates began to undertake fair housing advocacy. Growth in the Twin Cities' minority population converged with the shortage of affordable housing; affordable-housing advocates recognized that their constituency consisted largely of racial minorities, thus they could use fair housing tools to work toward their goal of preserving and increasing the supply of affordable housing. Because of the disparate impact on people of color, lack of affordable housing in a Twin Cities suburb constituted "unfair" housing. As one organizer put it, "You can't organize on housing issues without looking at fair housing issues." Increasing the supply of affordable housing was the solution they most often advocated. The Affordable Housing Stabilization Project formed in 1998 with support from the Family Housing Fund, a local foundation supportive of affordable housing development and research. Affordable-housing activists and lawyers developed fair housing and other litigation strategies to prevent Section 8 prepayment that threatened affordable units throughout the metro area.

Overall, this approach to fair housing focused less on individual cases of discriminatory treatment than on government compliance with fair housing regulation in its use of federal funding for affordable housing. According to one legal activist, "I think that fair housing tools can often be used to preserve affordable housing or to open up doors for affordable housing. Not easily, and never without huge struggles, but affordable housing advocates should look for every tool that they can use to open the doors." Another advocate had begun to examine fair housing requirements of the CDBG program and described a low-rent apartment building in St. Paul that the city was threatening to demolish. Using a fair housing argument helped to preserve the building. She said that "93 families out of 94 were African American. The fair housing angle has been underused [in housing advocacy]."

The Metropolitan Interfaith Coalition on Affordable Housing (MICAH), a faith-based affordable-housing coalition that mobilizes religious congregations on housing issues, won FHIP funds to produce a play on fair housing issues in congregations throughout the metro area. The play was followed by a group discussion during which MICAH passed out postcards to the state legislature, as well as sign-up sheets to identify volunteers for further affordable-housing activities in the congregation's community. Yet another example was Metro Sabbath, the Catholic Archdiocese Office of Social Justice's lobbying campaign to increase state funding for affordable housing; materials sent to congregations throughout the metro area aimed to educate congregations about racial and income residential polarization, and to generate political action.

In this quest for reducing metropolitan inequalities, the problem of racial inequality took a back seat to the problem of economic inequality in the work of many advocates. For example, although Orfield called his proposals "fair housing" bills, and although he and others described the racial and class disparities that existed in the Twin Cities metro area, the compromise legislation focused on encouraging suburbs to develop affordable housing without provisions for reducing racial discrimination or otherwise guaranteeing access to racial minorities (Orfield 1997). Additionally, during interviews with affordable housing activists, they most often described metropolitan inequalities in terms of class rather than race. Those who acknowledged that racial discrimination was part of the problem perceived discussion of it as a political barrier to winning support for affordable housing, and therefore refrained from doing so in public arenas. That is, because of the existence of racial prejudice and discrimination, affordable housing advocates consciously avoided discussing the racial composition of the low-income population when they promoted affordable housing in public arenas; in one advocate's terms, the strategy was to "take the black face out of affordable housing."

In Minneapolis, groups drew on a long tradition of housing advocacy that had built a base of government and foundation support for it. They had the resources (money, skills, and personnel) to mount class-action lawsuits, to build collaborations across groups, and to link fair housing and affordable housing advocacy. Groups engaged in fair housing testing in the private sector, and class-action lawsuits in the public sector. Other groups engaged in fair housing advocacy by congregational-based mobilization drives. An initiative of regional community circles about race and class in housing and schools was meant to coincide with and build support for an NAACP lawsuit on racial segregation and discrimination in education. This range of initiatives was not always tightly coordinated, but together they brought housing to the forefront of the public agenda in the Twin Cities.

THREE CHALLENGES FEDERAL POLICY POSES FOR LOCAL ADVOCATES

Analysis of federal fair housing policy resources and how they are put to use in these two cases suggest that at least three challenges emerge from federal policy. Each of these is evident in the cases. More important, these challenges represent issues that the fair housing community can take up in strategically rethinking the future of fair housing advocacy.

1. Defining Fair Housing Narrowly or Inclusively?

As defined by fair housing policy "fair housing" constitutes a right to equal treatment in the provision of public and private housing. It also suggests that government-supported affordable housing must be provided without regard to race. Although these are the definitions of fair housing that federal policy supports, they are not an exhaustive definition. Fair housing conditions and practices also can be construed as stable racial and ethnic integration in communities; socioeconomic diversity in communities; overcoming uneven development and regional inequities; zoning regulations that promote socioeconomic diversity; working to bring conventional housing services to particular neighborhoods suffering from redlining and predatory lending; and closing racial disparities in housing outcomes, for example, in mortgage denials, where there may not be a single discriminatory practice, but a more structural problem. Advocates engaged in such efforts could be called fair housing advocates, though they often do not label themselves that way.

Current national fair housing programs privilege only some kinds of fair housing activities. Policy fosters fighting individual-level discrimination in the private housing market but limits attention to other kinds of fair housing work essential to a more inclusive and aggressive movement toward housing equity. By directing resources to only one narrow spectrum of fair housing work, national fair housing policy reduces the likelihood that other kinds of fair housing work will thrive. Advocates who want to undertake other sorts of fair housing work need to find alternative sources of funding and support. Additionally, fair housing groups that focus on individual-level claims typically will not engage in efforts to reduce racial segregation or to promote regional equity. As in Denver, if other housing advocates locally work on such issues, fair housing groups may not be at the table.

2. Fragmented Movements and Coalition-Building

Several features of fair housing policy lead to fragmented advocacy. The competitive nature of FHIP funding means that local groups are pitted against one another. In Denver, the funding of a new fair housing group was seen as a cause for concern by the longstanding group, who saw a competitor rather than a potential ally. In the Twin Cities, FHIP funding flowed to two groups for different purposes—for enforcement and for education, thus not spurring concern. In addition, the group engaged in enforcement used its federal grant to hire the services of a research-oriented fair housing group to provide testing services. So collaboration was not completely absent. In Denver, local resources from the real estate industry fostered partnerships between one FHIP grantee and the CHRB to work on fair housing training. Most collaboration in the Twin Cities also emerged from locally based resources rather than federal resources. Local affordable-housing networks could mobilize a loosely connected movement for regional housing equity.

Another way that fair housing policy, and other housing policies, undermine housing advocacy is that groups working to advance housing justice tend to specialize in using one law rather than using many together. To illustrate, take the example of the Community Reinvestment Act (CRA) and the Fair Housing Act. Both laws provide tools to fight housing discrimination, but they have largely given rise to two separate worlds of action even though fair housing and CRA advocates have multiple concerns in common. I would argue that they have complementary needs and skills, but rooting their practices and programs in different legal frameworks serves to drive groups apart more than to propel them toward joint action.

One set of advocates focuses on individuals, the other on patterns of activity. Fair housing groups might pursue litigation against a bank that community reinvestment advocates consider to be a good community lender. Fair housing and CRA advocates have different criteria for judging evidence based on where and how it is to be used. Fair housing groups know what holds up in a court of law; CRA advocates know what gets the public's and lenders' attention. Fair housing and CRA advocates also operate with different time frames. Fair housing claims take longer to pursue, but advocates believe a good ruling in the long run will have powerful effect. CRA advocates want to begin negotiating and to make more immediate changes in lending practices. Fair housing and CRA advocates have different sets of political skills needed to use the laws they use—one more legally oriented, the other oriented toward organizing.

Thus policies themselves foster different kinds of advocacy groups and create obstacles to coalition building. These are not insurmountable, and there are examples of collaboration and overlap, but such examples are not widespread. Recognizing how laws themselves drive advocacy can open up a discussion that could focus on shared issues and complementary skills.

3. Invisible and Unstable Advocacy Groups

In addition to fostering a narrow definition of fair housing, and to posing obstacles to coalition-building, federal fair housing policy fosters low-profile and organizationally unstable advocacy groups. The low profile of most local fair housing organizations contributes to a vicious cycle that keeps fair housing off the local policy agenda: groups that are stretched thin and work in less public arenas bring little public attention to their work. The general public knows little about the work of their local fair housing organizations, and largely fails to consider housing discrimination to be a pressing problem. Fair housing organizations may in turn have difficulty cultivating local resources to support work that the general public sees as irrelevant or unnecessary.

As noted in my discussion of Denver, the nature of the fair housing enforcement process contributes to the low visibility of fair housing work. Anonymity is key to the effectiveness of fair housing tests. Groups have to be sure that local real estate agents do not know much about who, when, where, what is being tested. Court settlements also may require confidentiality. When real estate brokers talk at industry training sessions, it is clear that their sense of the size of a fair housing group's testing program is exaggerated. Nonprofits actually struggle to maintain a qualified pool of volunteer testers and conduct a rather limited number of tests each year, relative to the number of housing transactions that occur. Advocates believe that if housing professionals fear they may be "tested" at any time, they may be more likely to comply with fair housing laws. Nonprofits are thus less likely to publicize the weaknesses of their testing programs as a way of attracting more support for them, and are more likely to work behind the scenes hoping to garner more resources.

The incentive to keep testing results confidential, however, diminishes a fair housing group's ability to convert volunteer testers into public advocates. Because the results of any test may become evidence in litigation, and a tester may be called as a witness to describe his or her experience seeking housing, fair housing groups do not inform testers about the outcome of a test because they fear contaminating the evidence. Volunteer testers rarely know whether they have helped to uncover and punish discrimination or if the tests found no illegal practices at all. These volunteers may gain little sense of the extent of discrimination in their own communities, yet, unlike the nonprofit staffers, whose lobbying activities are restricted by federal funding, volunteers could freely lobby or attempt to mobilize support.

A final reason that fair housing groups tend to be organizationally unstable is that their primary funder, HUD, has proven to be a fragile political partner. On the one hand, HUD has an interest in cultivating strong partnership with FHIP grantees because nonprofits generate the fair housing claims that HUD relies upon to show that it is enforcing the law. But as a federal agency, HUD is especially susceptible to outside influence and pressure from changing presidential administrations, Congress, and the real estate industry (a partner in HUD's own programs). Its orientation and resource emphases typically fluctuate with partisan changes in Congress and the presidency. With each budget cycle, a range of actors has the chance to influence the funding level and direction of fair housing enforcement, and each presidential election brings a change in the agency's top leadership. Federal funds for urban programs began to decline in the late 1970s, and Republicans in Congress and the White House have frequently targeted the agency for cutbacks. This instability has meant that HUD's Office of Fair Housing and Equal Opportunity has been marked by fluctuating goals and program emphases, as well as uneven levels of ever limited resources.

PROSPECTS FOR CHANGE

This chapter has outlined some of the challenges that my research suggests fair housing groups face as a result of fair housing policy. These challenges face individual fair housing groups at the local level, and they confront the national movement that these organizations together comprise. Fair housing groups across the country have had varying levels of success in overcoming these challenges.

It is a truism in studies of politics that government programs create client groups who advocate for the strengthening of their program. Thus we expect FHIP-funded nonprofits to focus attention on improving and expanding the program. My research however suggests that fair housing advocates need to do more. Advocates must work to identify political strategies to overcome the barriers to their own strength that result from dependence on federal policies, and to work to generate locally driven political and social mobilization.

One avenue to explore is to consider what other laws and programs fair housing advocates can use to achieve their goals besides fair housing case processing. Some groups that have successfully litigated class-action lawsuits against insurance companies have won substantial damages that reduce their reliance on FHIP funds and enable them to address fair housing issues beyond the scope of federal law. Housing Opportunities Made Equal (HOME) in Virginia is a notable example (Morris 2001). A third avenue is to focus on cultivating local resources that enable fair housing advocates to move beyond the constraints of federal law while tailoring their advocacy to their local problems. Thus they craft their own model of fair housing advocacy. The Twin Cities case offers one example of this route.

NOTES

1. To study national and local fair housing policy and advocacy, I collected data in several ways. I interviewed participants (government officials, activists, real estate agents); examined archival sources; engaged in participant observation, including attending local and national fair housing meetings, local fair housing trainings, meetings for real estate agents, and other housing events; and I volunteered as a tester for a fair housing group in Denver. For more detail on the methodology, refer to Sidney (2003).

2. This section draws largely on von Hoffman (1998).

3. For their website see: http://www.opensoc.org/aboutus/index.html.

4. Clients and groups may choose (the election process) to litigate on behalf of a client or to use HUD's administrative enforcement process. Either administrative law judges or trial judges/juries may award attorney's fees and damages to local fair housing organizations, although courts have been far more generous (Bensinger 1996; Schill, chapter 7 within).

5. Another program funds state civil rights offices to enforce the law.

6. These boards received small amounts of money as part of HUD's mandated effort to cooperate with the housing industry. Its Voluntary Affirmative Marketing Agreement with the National Association of Realtors in the 1970s led to HUD-sponsored local boards composed of representatives from the real estate industry, the community, and local government. The program ended in 1992, although some CHRBs remained in place without federal funding.

7. The tours consist of riding a school bus to a particular Denver school (often a magnet school), touring the school and meeting the principal, and discussing fair housing issues with a CHRB board member.

REFERENCES

Abravanel, M. D. 2002. "Public Knowledge of Fair Housing Law: Does It Protect against Housing Discrimination?" *Housing Policy Debate* 13:469–504.

Baumgartner, Frank R., and Bryan D. Jones. 1993. *Agendas and Instability in American Politics*. Chicago: University of Chicago Press.

Bensinger, S. R. 1996. "Maximizing Damages for Fair Housing Organizations under the Fair Housing Act." *Journal of Affordable Housing* 5:227–35.

Berry, B. J. L. 1979. *The Open Housing Question: Race and Housing in Chicago, 1966–1976*. Cambridge, MA: Ballinger.

Branch, T. 1998. *Pillar of Fire: America in the King Years 1963–65*. New York: Simon and Schuster.

Cigler, Allan J., and Burdett A. Loomis, eds. 2002. *Interest Group Politics*. Washington, DC: CQ Press.

Edelman, M. 2001. "Social Movements: Changing Paradigms and Forms of Politics." *Annual Review of Anthropology* 30:285–317.

Edsall, T. B., and M. D. Edsall. 1992. *Chain Reaction: The Impact of Race, Rights, and Taxes on American Politics*. New York: W. W. Norton.

Emerson, M. O., G. Yancey, and K. J. Chai. 2001. "Does Race Matter in Residential Segregation? Exploring the Preferences of White Americans." *American Sociological Review* (66)6: 922–35.

Goetz, E. G. 2003. *Clearing the Way: Deconcentrating the Poor in Urban America*. Washington, DC: Urban Institute Press.

Helper, Rose. 1969. *Racial Policies and Practices of Real Estate Brokers*. Minneapolis: University of Minnesota Press.

Jones, B. D. 1994. *Reconceiving Decision-Making in Democratic Politics: Attention, Choice, and Public Policy*. Chicago: University of Chicago Press.

Keating, W. D. 1994. *The Suburban Racial Dilemma: Housing and Neighborhoods*. Philadelphia: Temple University Press.

Massey, D. S., and N. A. Denton. 1993. *American Apartheid: Segregation and the Making of the Underclass*. Cambridge, MA: Harvard University Press.

Morris, P. S. 2001. *Promises Kept: A Study in Organizational Evolution*. Richmond: Housing Opportunities Made Equal of Richmond, Virginia.

Mueller, Carol M. 1992. "Building Social Movement Theory." In *Frontiers in Social Movement Theory*, ed. Aldon D. Morris and Carol McClurg Mueller, 3–25. New Haven, CT: Yale University Press.

National Fair Housing Alliance. 2004. 2004 Fair Housing Trends Report. Washington, D.C.: Author.

National Fair Housing Alliance. 2005. *2005 Fair Housing Trends Report*. Washington, DC: Author.

Orfield, M. 1997. *Metropolitics: A Regional Agenda for Community and Stability (revised edition)*. Washington, DC: Brookings Institution Press.

Pierson, P. 1994. *Dismantling the Welfare State? Reagan, Thatcher, and the Politics of Retrenchment*. Cambridge, MA: Harvard University Press.

Rubinowitz, L. S., and J. E. Rosenbaum. 2000. *Crossing the Class and Color Lines: From Public Housing to White Suburbia*. Chicago: University of Chicago Press.

Saltman, J. 1990. *A Fragile Movement: The Struggle for Neighborhood Stabilization*. New York: Greenwood Press.

Schneider, A. L., and H. Ingram. 1997. *Policy Design for Democracy*. Lawrence: University Press of Kansas.

Sidney, M. S. 2003. *Unfair Housing: How National Policy Shapes Local Action*. Lawrence: University Press of Kansas.

Simon, H. A. 1996. *The Sciences of the Artificial*. Cambridge, MA: MIT Press.

Smith, S. L. 1994. "The National Fair Housing Alliance at Work." In *Residential Apartheid: The American Legacy*, ed. R. D. Bullard, JEG III, and C. Lee, 237–56. Los Angeles: Center for Afro-American Studies, UCLA.

Smith, Steven Rathgeb, and Michael Lipsky. 1993. *Nonprofits for Hire: The Welfare State in the Age of Contracting*. Cambridge: Harvard University Press.

Snow, D. A., S. A. Soule, and D. M. Cress. 2005. "Identifying the Precipitants of Homeless Protest Across 17 U.S. Cities, 1980–1990." *Social Forces* 83(3): 1183–1210.

Soss, J. 1999. "Lessons of Welfare: Policy Design, Political Learning, and Political Action." *American Political Science Review* 93:363–80.

Stone, D. 2001. *Policy Paradox: The Art of Political Decision Making*. New York: W. W. Norton.

Stoutland, S. E. 1999. "Community Development Corporations: Mission, Strategy, and Accomplishments." In *Urban Problems and Community Development*, ed. Ronald F. Ferguson and William T. Dickens, 193–240. Washington, DC: Brookings Institution Press.

Takaki, R. 1993. *A Different Mirror: A History of Multicultural America*. Boston: Little, Brown and Company.

von Hoffman, A. 1998. *Like Fleas on a Tiger? A Brief History of the Open Housing Movement*. Joint Center for Housing Studies. Cambridge, MA: Harvard University.

Wilson, J. Q. 1973. *Political Organizations*. New York: Basic Books.

Yinger J. 1995. *Closed Doors, Opportunities Lost: The Continuing Costs of Housing Discrimination*. New York: Russell Sage.

10

Creating a Fair Housing System That Works for Latinos

Janis Bowdler and Charles Kamasaki

While the Fair Housing Act was passed in 1968 as a method of guaranteeing all persons equal access to housing by barring discrimination based on race, color, national origin, religion, or gender, unfortunately Latinos have not enjoyed the equal access promised by the act. Although some argued in the early years of the act's implementation that the evidence of housing discrimination against Hispanics was sparse, this ceased to be true beginning in the mid-1980s. Indeed, the latest evidence shows that Latinos[1] are now discriminated against more than any African Americans (Turner et al., chapter 2 within).

It is our judgment, based upon the last several decades of federal, state, and local fair housing enforcement, that—notwithstanding this evidence of widespread housing discrimination against Hispanics—the fair housing enforcement system fails to adequately protect the rights of Latinos relative to other groups. We argue in this chapter that the fair housing system is broken from a Hispanic perspective, and presents serious barriers to Latinos who encounter housing discrimination. This is all the more troubling given the dramatic increase of the Hispanic population over the last fifteen years. The release of the 2000 Census documented a 58 percent increase in the Hispanic population between 1990 and 2000 to 12.5 percent of the population, surpassing African Americans as the largest minority population in the United States. As of July 1, 2004, the Census Bureau estimates the population has reached 14 percent of the total U.S. population.

This chapter is divided into three sections. It begins with a summary of studies documenting housing discrimination against Hispanics, discusses how and why the current enforcement system does not protect the rights of Latinos, and concludes with policy options designed to improve enforcement and increase Hispanics' access to affordable housing in neighborhoods of their own choosing.

EVIDENCE OF DISCRIMINATION

The history of discrimination against Latino home seekers is well documented. Previous studies have examined discrimination against Latino home seekers at the local, regional, and national levels. The major studies are described in some detail in Yzaguirre et al. 1999. They include a 1979 study by the Department of Housing and Urban Development (HUD) of discrimination against Mexican Americans in Dallas, which determined that dark-skinned Mexican Americans had a 96 percent chance of experiencing at least one instance of discrimination, and light-skinned Mexican Americans had a 65 percent chance of encountering discrimination in the rental market of Dallas, Texas. Two years later, a 1981 HUD study of selected real estate agents' listings in Boston reported that nearly 74 percent of Hispanic and black callers were informed that no units were available, despite all of these units being available for comparable white callers. During visits to the premises, 49 percent of Hispanic and black inquirers were told that no units were available, despite all white visitors being shown available units. In 1982 HUD funded a Denver study that examined discrimination against Latino families in the home buying market. They found that 60 percent of Hispanic families were told that no homes were available, compared to 31 percent of comparable white families. In 1986 HUD funded a study in Phoenix that found that 13 percent of Hispanic and black renters were charged higher rents than similarly situated whites. Most important, in 1989 HUD released the results of testing research that produced the first national estimate of discrimination against Hispanics in the rental and sales markets of this country's major metropolitan areas. At that time, roughly half of all housing market transactions had some discriminatory content. The study reported an overall discrimination rate of 56 percent for Latino home buyers and 50 percent for Latino renters.

Local studies also reported varying but high levels of differential treatment. In 1995, the Fair Housing Council of Fresno County conducted a study examining northern Fresno County and the City of Clovis. The study found that Hispanic renters encountered a 77 percent rate of discrimination when seeking homes in predominantly white neighborhoods and a 100 percent rate of discrimination for Hispanic families with children. A 1997 San Antonio Fair Housing Council study examined rental units in the San Antonio metropolitan area and found that Latino renters encountered discrimination 52 percent of the time. In a 1997 study, the Washington, D.C., Fair Housing Council found that Hispanic renters faced a 37 percent rate of discrimination and Hispanic home buyers faced a 42 percent discrimination rate. In 2001, the Greater Houston Fair Housing Center found that two out of three Hispanic renters are discriminated against (65 percent). For Latino families with children, the discrimination rate number jumped to more than four out of five (85 percent) (Greater Houston Fair Housing Center 2001).

Lending and Insurance Discrimination

Hispanic families face significant discrimination in the home buying market.[2] We estimate that more than a million Hispanic families are mortgage ready but are either unaware of their home buying options, discriminated against, or otherwise underserved by mainstream financial institutions (NCLR calculations, Joint Center for Housing Studies 2003).[3] Home Mortgage Disclosure Act (HMDA) data for mortgage activity in 2002, for example, reveal that when applying for conventional mortgages, about three out of every five Latinos are approved (61 percent) and nearly one out of five is denied (18 percent) compared to a 12 percent denial rate for whites. The U.S. Department of Justice (DOJ) pursued nine cases between 2000 and 2003 against banks and other financial institutions for using stricter underwriting criteria for Spanish-speaking clients; unfairly denying loans or refusing to loan; harassment based on national origin; charging Latinos higher fees and interest rates for home mortgages; and refusing to lend in Latino neighborhoods (U.S. DOJ 2004).[4]

Evidence of "redlining" by the insurance industry also emerged throughout the 1990s when paired testing revealed that insurance agencies were refusing to insure homes in certain neighborhoods or were offering less coverage for a higher premium to minority families or families living in predominantly minority neighborhoods (NFHA 1995, 2000). Without proper homeowner's insurance, financial institutions cannot guarantee a mortgage and homeowners cannot protect their asset. In the late 1990s, the National Fair Housing Alliance (NFHA) designed and implemented a nationwide paired-testing program to examine instances of insurance discrimination. The tests revealed 100 percent discrimination against Latinos in Chicago and 60 percent in Los Angeles; testers found that Hispanic clients were often screened over the phone using surname and speech accent. While other research studies have offered conflicting conclusions, paired-testing studies have produced enough evidence for advocates to successfully bring suit against several national insurance companies. Cases brought against several major insurers by NFHA have resulted in affirmative relief for Hispanics and African Americans. In a current case (2005) against Prudential Insurance Company, for example, the defendant is alleged to have different underwriting criteria for Hispanic neighborhoods; restricted service to these neighborhoods; discouraged Hispanic homeowners from purchasing homeowner's insurance from their company; and failed to provide antidiscrimination training to agents (*National Fair Housing Alliance, Inc, et al. v. The Prudential Insurance Company of America, et al.*).[5]

On a methodological note, there have been criticisms of the audit studies sponsored by HUD, including the design of the studies, the criteria used for deciding what "discrimination" is, and for other key methodological choices. For example, in HDS2000, consistently unreturned phone calls to nonwhite testers by a sales representative are not counted as discrimination, despite unreturned calls to testers being considered discrimination by legal definitions. For Hispanics, especially first-generation immigrants, unreturned phone calls may be a sign of discrimination based on speech accent or national origin guessed from surnames. Such evidence suggests that the incidence of discrimination may be undercounted.

Discrimination by Municipalities

Both the Department of Justice (DOJ) and private fair housing groups have uncovered significant discrimination against Latinos and other minorities at the local level. Such barriers can make it problematic for Hispanics to have access to entire communities. Municipalities, for example, have used zoning laws, the selective enforcement of occupancy standards, and local building codes to intimidate Latino families, usually in efforts to get them to leave or prevent them from moving into the area. In each case, cities were responding to an increasing Hispanic population and were looking for ways to limit the growth and intimidate families into leaving the area.

There are a few key cases that illustrate this issue. In 1996 the DOJ settled a complaint against the Village of Hatch, New Mexico, for banning mobile homes that were used to house Hispanic farmworkers. The settlement provided injunctive relief, required new housing development, and resulted in a civil penalty against the village. In 1997, DOJ settled with the Village of Addison, a Chicago suburb, for demolishing apartment units primarily occupied by Latinos under the guise of a redevelopment project. The city was ordered to build new housing and compensate the displaced tenants. In a 2002 case against the City of Agawam, Massachusetts, DOJ filed a complaint alleging that the city denied a local farm's plan to extend housing on the basis that it would house too many Jamaicans and Puerto Ricans. DOJ has also settled at least three cases involving a municipality using building codes and ordinances to discriminate against Hispanic families. The town of Cicero, Illinois; the city of Waukegan, Illinois; and the city of Wildwood, New Jersey, each settled their suits through consent decrees. They were ordered to cease their discriminatory practices and to compensate victims. They also were required to pay substantial civil penalties. In March 2004 DOJ settled a case against Bound Brook, New Jersey, that had charged a pattern and practice of discrimination against Hispanics. They had found evidence in an Internet chat room of a local elected official soliciting addresses of Latino-occupied units for selective code enforcement.

In sum, researchers have produced a fairly robust body of evidence demonstrating substantial levels of housing discrimination against Hispanics since the later 1980s.[6] As indicated in the Turner et al. chapter in this book, Hispanics are now encountering more discriminatory treatment in the rental market than are African Americans, the first report that Latinos are now more heavily victimized in renting an apartment.

1989–2000 Housing Discrimination Study Findings

The purpose of this section is to again highlight the findings on housing discrimination that are presented in the two most recent national housing discrimination study audits (see Turner et al., chapter 2 within). In 1989 discrimination rates against black and Hispanic renters were comparable. (See fig. 10.1.)

By 2000, however, discrimination against black renters had declined significantly, whereas Hispanic renters' discrimination rates rose by 1.5 percentage points (which while statistically insignificant nonetheless suggest a possible trend of importance).

In the sales market, while there was a decrease in levels of discrimination for both Hispanic and black home buyers, discrimination against Hispanic home buyers dropped by seven percentage points compared to a twelve-point drop for blacks. Most noteworthy, the levels of discrimination against blacks are now lower than those against Latinos. A closer look at the various elements of adverse treatment reveals additional areas of concern (see tables 10.1 and 10.2). There is also variation in the forms and levels of discrimination experienced. For example, both blacks and Hispanics experienced comparable levels of discrimination when inquiring about the availability of a house but less measured steering (15–18 percent).

Latino home seekers face discrimination in the rental market in the availability of the unit 34 percent of the time; differential agent encouragement happens roughly one-third (32.8 percent) of the time, although for Asians it now appears to happen nearly 40 percent (38.9) of the time. In the sales market Hispanics are discriminated against in looking for a home (46.3 percent),

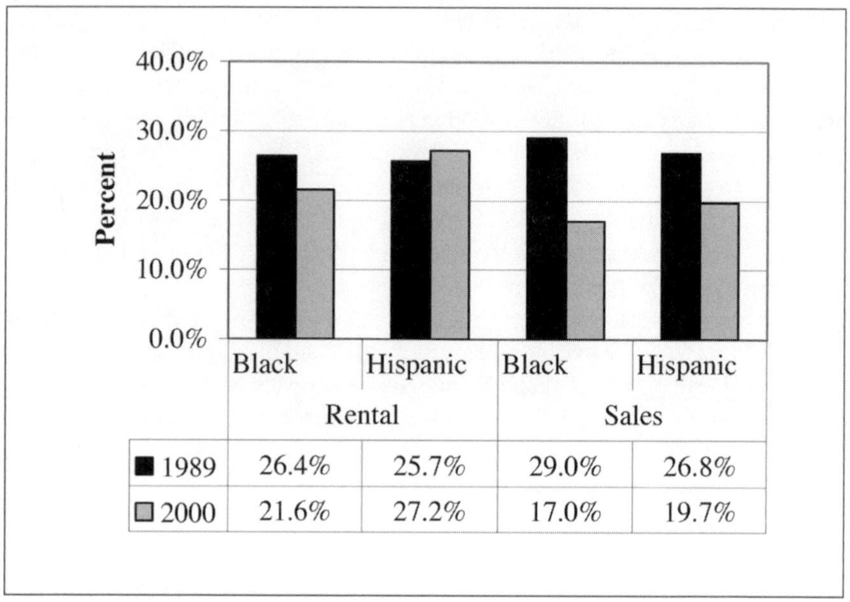

Figure 10.1. Comparable Adverse Treatment against Blacks and Hispanics, 1989 and 2000. Source: *Discrimination in Metropolitan Housing Markets: Phase 1*, 2002.

asking to view an available unit (38.3 percent), being offered less information on financing options (38.6 percent), and agent encouragement (30.6 percent).

Table 10.2 addresses sales market discrimination. This area is critical because of the press of federal tax and program incentives designed to increase the chances of minorities owning their own home. Nonetheless, it is remarkable that on many indicators Hispanics as well as Asians are comparatively worse off than blacks. On average, Asians experience a 20 percent chance of encountering discrimination in buying, which is close to that experienced by blacks, while Hispanics encounter such resistance 17 percent of the time.

Table 10.1. Differential Treatment for Renters by Race and Ethnicity, 2000

Measure	*Hispanic*	*Black*	*Asian/Pacific Islander*
Housing Availability	34.0%	31.5%	28.8%
Inspection of Available Units	24.4%	27.5%	14.1%
Housing Costs	21.7%	21.4%	18.5%
Agent Encouragement	32.8%	31.3%	38.9%
Overall Summary of Measures, Consistency	**25.7%**	**21.6%**	**21.5%**

Source: *Discrimination in Metropolitan Housing Markets: Phase 1 and 2*, 2002.

Table 10.2. Differential Treatment for Home Buyers by Race and Ethnicity, 2000

Measure	*Hispanic*	*Black*	*Asian/Pacific Islander*
Housing Availability	46.3%	46.2%	49.3%
Inspection of Available Units	38.3%	42.9%	50.7%
Geographic Steering	17.1%	15.8%	18.4%
Assistance with Financing	38.6%	36.6%	43.6%
Agent Encouragement	30.6%	31.3%	39.6%
Overall Summary of Measures, Consistency	**19.7%**	**17.0%**	**20.4%**

Source: *Discrimination in Metropolitan Housing Markets: Phase 1 and 2*, 2002.

Nonetheless, each time a Hispanic family goes out to seek to buy a home, they can reasonably anticipate getting treated worse than a comparable white family roughly one out of every five times. On the basic issues of just being told about and seeing the same homes as whites, the discrimination reaches one out of every four times they look at a home. Thus nearly forty years after the enactment of the national Fair Housing Act, one out of every four Hispanics searching to buy a home will be treated unfairly compared to whites who have exactly the same qualifications, resources, and interests.

There is considerable ongoing discussion among researchers regarding how various HD2000 findings should be interpreted. However, the fact that the incidence of housing discrimination against Hispanics now appears consistently as high or higher than that faced by other minority groups is unmistakable.

Why It Matters So Much: Impacts

Discrimination undermines the fundamental American commitment to equal opportunity under the law and for that reason alone society should be committed to its eradication. In the case of housing discrimination, however, there are more tangible harms that result for the victims of discrimination, the neighborhoods and communities in which they wish to reside, and derivatively for the society as a whole.

One inevitable obvious result of housing discrimination is residential segregation (see chapter 5 by Iceland, within). Segregation studies regarding Hispanics point to a trend of modestly rising segregation levels corresponding with the lifting of desegregation orders and the rapid growth in the Latino population, including immigrants. Even where racial isolation declined in certain areas it almost always rose or remained constant for Latino families and school children. Persistent or growing residential segregation of Latinos is associated with a number of related problems. For example: in examining

California's neighborhoods, Sandoval et al. found that while overall segregation declined, as it did for Latinos (74 percent living in segregated neighborhoods in 1990 compared to 66 percent in 2000), Latinos were still more likely to be segregated than blacks (57 percent) or Asians (26 percent) (Sandoval et al. 2002).[7] Schools are also becoming more segregated by both race/ethnicity and socioeconomic status. Latino students, for example, are more likely to attend schools that are underperforming where Latinos are the majority (representing about 57 percent or more of the school population), and where the majority of the students are poor. This situation was especially serious for limited-English Latino school children (Orfield and Lee 2004; Logan, Stowell, and Oakley 2002; Frankenberg, Lee, and Orfield 2003). Families who live in segregated neighborhoods typically have access to fewer city services because of a reduced tax base and miss out on new jobs and investments in new infrastructure compared to families who live in more diverse neighborhoods. Homeowners in segregated neighborhoods suffer economically as well because their homes do not appreciate as much as homes in predominantly white neighborhoods (Orfield 2001; Ware, Redding, and Peuquet 2003).

In short, Latinos arguably experience more discrimination than any other ethnic group in the housing market and encounter discrimination in the mortgage financing and insurance markets. If the fair housing enforcement system were protecting Hispanics' rights effectively, one might expect that formal charges and complaints of discrimination by Latinos would be higher than or equal to those filed by other groups, and that litigation on behalf of Hispanics by government agencies and private groups would be greater than or equal to those on behalf of other groups. Or, if this were not the case, one might expect vigorous, high-profile efforts to reform the system such that discrimination against Latinos could be more effectively addressed in the future.

The following section demonstrates, however, that over the past several decades the fair housing enforcement system itself has barely and often only grudgingly acknowledged the Latino community's status as both the nation's largest ethnic minority and the group that encounters some of the highest incidents of discrimination in housing.

THE CURRENT FAIR HOUSING ENFORCEMENT SYSTEM'S EFFECTIVENESS

Despite the widespread discrimination encountered by Latinos in the housing market, there is, we believe, persuasive evidence that the fair housing enforcement system fails to adequately enforce their rights. As described below, Hispanics are underrepresented in federal fair housing caseloads, including in complaints filed with state and local enforcement agencies and private fair housing groups. Evidence suggests that Latinos face significant barriers to accessing the fair housing enforcement system and may therefore require new policies and programs designed to address these barriers. It is our argument that prior efforts to address the fair housing rights of Hispanics have been sporadic at best and that proposed new efforts have often been resisted by key stakeholders in the process. We further argue that without a major policy intervention, the prospects for improved responsiveness of the fair housing enforcement system to the widespread discrimination experienced by Latinos appear unlikely.

Fair Housing Case Data and Litigation Analysis

In their 2003 report, the National Fair Housing Alliance estimates that Hispanics encounter roughly 440,000 incidents of housing discrimination each year. There were, however, only 600 to 700 complaints of discrimination filed with HUD and all state and local agencies by all those alleging discrimination on the basis of national origin, which includes Hispanics (see table 10.3).[8]

Our analysis of Fair Housing and Equal Opportunity (FHEO) data suggests that Latinos have not benefited equally from the fair housing enforcement system. Complaint data from 1999 to 2003 show a gradual increase in the proportion of complaints from Hispanics, from 7.0 percent to 11.4 percent of all complaints, while complaints from African Americans increased from 36 percent to about 45 percent, except for one "outlier" year when the number jumped to 70 percent (2002). Latinos accounted for only 5 percent of cases for the first quarter of 2004 compared to 23 percent for African Americans.

Given the high levels of discrimination found during audit research, there therefore appears to be a notable discrepancy between the incidence of discrimination and the number of Fair Housing Act complaints reported. A review of the U.S. Department of Justice's publicly available case summaries for

Table 10.3. HUD and FHAP Complaints by Race and Ethnicity, 1999–2004

	1999	*2000*	*2001*	*2002*	*2003*	*First Qtr 2004*
Hispanic	7.0%	8.2%	9.9%	10.4%	11.4%	5.5%
Black	36.1%	41.4%	40.4%	70.9%	45.1%	23.2%
Asian/Pacific Islander	1.1%	1.3%	1.0%	1.5%	1.2%	0.6%
Total Complaints Filed	6,138	6,973	7,009	7,971	8,154	3,392

Source: *Fair Housing,* U.S. Department of Housing and Urban Development.

housing and civil rights enforcement reveals that it has pursued litigation on behalf of Hispanics in less than 13 percent of all of its cases over this period.[9]

Barriers to Effectively Serving Hispanics

There are a number of acknowledged factors that stand in the way of the fair housing system more adequately meeting the needs of the Latino community. We identify three main barriers: lack of knowledge and access, an unmet need for fair housing education and enforcement-capacity building within Hispanic institutions, and the ineffectiveness of the enforcement system.

Knowledge and Access

Because there have historically been so few Latino-focused community-based organizations involved in fair housing outreach, education, and testing, one explanation for the large gap between acts of discrimination and fair housing complaints by Hispanics is a lack of a cultural awareness of the civil rights enforcement system in general and the fair housing system in particular. A general awareness of civil rights is lacking, so that many Hispanics who encounter housing bias may not recognize it when it occurs and not know what to do about it when they do recognize it. This situation is likely exacerbated by the presence of immigrants within the Hispanic population. Many of these foreign-born immigrants come from countries where civil rights laws do not exist. Further, many federal and local civil rights offices lack bilingual staff and materials, which inhibits effective outreach to the Hispanic community. Many Latino families either do not understand their rights, are reluctant to report discrimination, or do not receive information about the federal enforcement housing programs.

Capacity-Building

Latinos have not been welcomed by mainstream stakeholders in the fair housing system. There is a lack of mainstream fair housing agencies that have the capacity to serve the Latino community effectively and even fewer Latino community-based organizations engaged in the field of fair housing. Although anecdotal evidence suggests that a significant number of mainstream fair housing agencies have some capacity to serve the Hispanic community, it is still far from the norm for Latinos or other bicultural or bilingual staff to be proportionately represented in such agencies.

The HUD Fair Housing Initiative Program (FHIP), for example, was designed in part to strengthen the capacity of private fair housing groups. Given

Table 10.4. FHIP Grants Awarded by Focus, 2001–2003

	2001		*2002*		*2003*	
Award Type	*% Latino-Focused*	*Total Awarded*	*% Latino-Focused*	*Total Awarded*	*% Latino-Focused*	*Total Awarded*
Enforcement	11	35	6	48	12	52
Education and Outreach	12	54	13	48	13	66
New Organization	1	5	1	3	1	2
Total	**24**	**94**	**20**	**99**	**26**	**120**

Source: U.S. Department of Housing and Urban Development 2001, 2002, 2003.
Note: "Latino-Focused" includes agencies that targeted Latino and/or Spanish-speaking preferred persons with specific program objectives and deliverables.

recent demographic growth of Hispanics and the documented high incidence of housing discrimination against Hispanics, one might expect a growing portion of FHIP funding to be targeted to agencies building Latino-focused capacity or Hispanic organizations seeking to build fair housing capacity. Our review of data on FHIP grantees, however, reveals that relatively few organizations are targeting the Latino community in a meaningful way. The majority of the FHIP grantees that are targeting Latino, immigrant, or Spanish-speaking preferred clientele are doing education and outreach, and *not enforcement*, suggesting that even highly effective outreach activities could be thwarted by poor enforcement (see table 10.4).

Recently, in 2003, HUD set aside $500,000, or 10 percent of all funds allocated, for a Hispanic education and outreach program, possibly in response to the new discrimination study findings. This award does not encourage Latino-focused enforcement, nor does it promote the needs of the Latino community to the level of priority warranted, given the amount of discrimination it faces.[10]

Ineffective Enforcement

A third possible explanation of the gap between discrimination levels and complaints are weaknesses within the fair housing enforcement system in this country. Endemic to the Fair Housing Act is the fact that filing a complaint does not solve the person's immediate issue of finding a home. Filing a case or pursuing litigation is also typically lengthy and daunting.

Also endemic to the act is that the fair housing system relies almost exclusively on victims themselves reporting the incident of discrimination. This requires victims to know that they have a "civil right," to realize they've been discriminated against, and to be comfortable reporting the incident. While we are unaware of any study comparing the disposition of Hispanic fair housing cases compared to other groups' cases, there is reason to believe that Latinos are given short shrift by the system. First, systematic studies of the Equal Employment Opportunity Commission (EEOC)—a system somewhat analogous to FHEO's—have found that charges filed by Latinos have consistently higher closure rates with no remedy to the charging party, and that remedies awarded to Hispanics are consistently lower than those received by comparable groups (Gonzalez 1993). Also, focus-group participants who have encountered discrimination have made this assertion to us. They have, for example, stated their reluctance to file reports because they believe nothing will come of it (Pérez and Luna 1997).

The situation facing immigrants is of particular concern because an undocumented immigrant family that does file a complaint may face the risk of retaliation, which could end in deportation. Even if one member of a multifamily household is undocumented, a family may be less likely to file a complaint or pursue legal action despite the law being clear that noncitizens are protected from discrimination.

POLICY RECOMMENDATIONS

There is no single shortcoming of the enforcement system that thwarts more effective and inclusive enforcement of fair housing laws for Hispanics. On the contrary, if the authors' analysis is correct, several factors work synergistically to undermine more effective enforcement. These factors include: the relative lack of knowledge within the Hispanic community of the fair housing laws, how to detect discrimination, and how to assert their rights; the lack of capacity within the private fair housing enforcement infrastructure to focus on Latinos, and the relative absence of Hispanic-controlled organizations within that infrastructure; inconsistent, single-year FHIP funding, which presents barriers to the formation of new groups and to the sustainability of positions and skilled staff in private fair housing groups; and the underrepresentation of Latinos within the civil rights enforcement system itself, which is especially clear at HUD's Office of Fair Housing and Equal Opportunity.

These conditions did not spring up overnight. The rapid growth of the Latino population in recent years has not been matched either by a substantial focus on Hispanics within civil rights enforcement agencies or by a commensurate growth in fair housing enforcement resources. Thus, the authors do not believe there is a single "silver bullet" policy option capable of fully addressing the problems we have identified. Furthermore, we believe that the most "effective" remedies are probably the least likely to be implemented in large part because ensuring a systemwide focus would require significant policy shifts and would likely encounter major resistance from status quo stakeholders.

Instead, we propose four sets of policy options to address the endemic ineffectiveness of fair housing enforcement for Latinos. These proposals are not mutually exclusive and are designed such that they could be "mixed and matched," or implemented simultaneously as an entire package. In the sections below, each policy strategy is described.

Strategy One: The Status Quo with Some Enhancements

The first strategy is to rely on the existing fair housing enforcement system with modest "enhancements" designed to improve the system's responsiveness to Hispanics, but with little change to the underlying policy, legal, or political framework undergirding the act. For example, there would be increased outreach to Latinos by public and private fair housing enforcement agencies, preferably including partnerships with Hispanic community-based groups. A pilot project or demonstration program would be carried out in multiple sites or on a small scale, incorporating capacity building and multiyear funding. Modest increases in congressional appropriations for FHIP, FHAP, and HUD/FHEO would be required to ensure that Latino groups are funded and other groups are "held harmless."

While the elements of this strategy option are achievable, they are also likely to be less effective than any of the options listed below for the simple reason that it involves little or no fundamental change, neither building systemwide capacity nor improving overall enforcement effectiveness, despite being politically palatable.

Strategy Two: Capacity Building

The second strategy includes a significant new program to build the capacity of a variety of both mainstream and Latino organizations to enforce the fair housing laws since few public and private fair housing organizations have the capacity and expertise to engage the Latino community to help enforce the fair housing laws. In addition, many in the Hispanic community have expressed a lack of trust in such institutions to equitably enforce the laws on behalf of their members, and Latino community-based groups are typically trusted by the community and have the ability to engage it. However, fewer Latino community-based organizations have the resources or expertise to play a significant role in the fair housing enforcement system, thus this strategy proposes to address such limitations through a multiyear, major funding program for building the capacity of "mainstream" public and private agencies involved in the fair housing system to engage the Hispanic community, combined with targeted support to indigenous Latino organizations and individuals to develop their fair housing expertise. Examples include the designation at HUD and Justice of a special new unit charged with increasing the agencies' responsiveness to Hispanics; the creation of measurable objectives for funding recipients, including the hiring of bilingual staff and the dissemination of appropriate education materials; and "outcome objectives" including significant increases in fair housing complaints and lawsuits filed by or on behalf of Latinos.

Central to the effectiveness of this strategy is the multiyear funding to Latino- and/or immigrant-serving, multipurpose community-based organizations with a proven track record in engaging Hispanics. This capacity-building support should include resources for both outreach and enforcement. Since expertise in engaging the Latino community is minimal or absent at virtually every point in the fair housing enforcement system, this strategy seeks to build Hispanic-focused capacity in most key institutions within the system. While likely to be substantially more effective than the first strategy, it would also be significantly more difficult to establish because it would require major new funding or a major reallocation of existing funds. It is also not clear that the political will exists to elevate Latino concerns to this level of importance. Finally, to the extent that ineffective enforcement may be attributable in part to factors unrelated to lack of capacity, for example, inherent cultural reluctance on the part of Hispanics to file and pursue complaints, or entrenched anti-Latino animus in the civil rights enforcement system itself, then a capacity-building strategy is likely to be of limited effectiveness.

Strategy Three: Proactive Enforcement

The third strategy is to augment the current complaint or charge-based enforcement process with a more proactive testing- and investigation-based enforcement system targeted at Hispanics. Whether due to insufficient outreach, inadequate capacity, poor service once a charge is filed, or even a culturally based predisposition of Latinos against filing and pursuing civil rights complaints, there is a substantial gap between the estimated incidence of housing discrimination and actual enforcement actions. The objective of closing the gap may not be amenable to traditional policy interventions given the size of the overall gap and the unique barriers faced by Hispanics in accessing the system. Viewed through the lens of deterrence theory more commonly applied to the criminal justice system, perpetrators of housing discrimination against all groups, but especially Latinos, face little or no fear of legal sanction. Even those who may engage in discriminatory acts unknowingly have little incentive to educate themselves about the law, given the absence of a credible deterrent. This strategy proposes to address this problem by borrowing from proactive strategies used by criminal law enforcement agencies.

The key elements of this strategy are centered on aggressive law enforcement techniques such as those used in high crime areas in the "war on drugs." Their fair housing counterparts might include: a declaration by the president or HUD secretary of a "zero-tolerance" policy toward housing discrimination, followed by significant levels of agency and private fair housing group paired testing, followed up by immediate enforcement. Such testing could be targeted based on a variety of factors—geography, industrial sector, specific protected class—or be carried out randomly. Either public or private agencies, or both, could conduct the testing and litigation.

The programs would include "whistle blower" protections for industry or government sources who uncover systemic discrimination and for federal systemic "undercover investigations" for particularly egregious and persistent perpetrators of discrimination. Performance would be monitored through a "national discrimination report card," based on testing and market research conducted annually or biannually (or at least more often than once a decade). This would be supplemented by a major "social marketing" campaign to educate the public about the persistence and negative impact of housing discrimination.[11]

This option would provide the certainty that a significant number of enforcement actions—most likely pattern and practice cases—will be brought against major perpetrators of discrimination. Deterrence theory suggests that the likelihood of apprehension—and not necessarily the severity of the penalty—is effective in preventing crime; if this is true in the fair housing context, then the actual number of enforcement actions could be accompanied by a major multiplier effect. Over time, the report card and accompanying social marketing campaign could help build political support for the effort. While undoubtedly the most effective policy option in reducing discrimination, this is also, we judge, the least feasible politically. Anything even remotely resembling this policy package, or for that matter any single element of the package, would likely produce substantial initial resistance and even some persistent political backlash from potential targets of these investigations. This option has the virtue, we believe, of identifying an ideal enforcement regime, given sufficient political will. It also illustrates the distance that proponents of truly effective enforcement have to cover in order to build a political consensus for an effective enforcement regime, not only for Hispanics but for all groups.

Strategy Four: Market Strategy

This final strategy assumes essentially no changes whatsoever are made in public policy. Instead, it asserts that "the market," broadly speaking, particularly if enhanced through focused "corporate responsibility" advocacy by Hispanic advocates and elected officials, may be as, or perhaps more, effective in delivering fair and affordable housing to Latinos in the real market. In this context, the importance of upholding the principle of equal opportunity is given relatively less weight than the practical importance of increasing access to affordable housing. Although mainstream public and private fair housing and subsidized housing infrastructure has been largely indifferent and arguably hostile to the full inclusion of Latino concerns, the Hispanic community's rapid population growth, high labor force participation rate, and increasing purchasing power have attracted substantial private-sector interest. In this context, exclusive or primary reliance by Latino public officials, advocates, and service organizations on a strategy based on government policy and civil rights enforcement to increase fair access to housing seems misplaced. This strategy proposes to augment Hispanic advocates' traditional reliance on a civil rights–based strategy with an equal or perhaps greater reliance on "market" strategies, to channel affordable housing and related resources to the Latino community.

This strategy proposes to leverage Hispanics' growing market power into tangible and measurable improvements in the community's access to affordable housing. This may entail the use of a "carrot-and-stick" strategy to capture an equitable share of private investment for Latino homeownership and rental housing. "Carrots" might include strategies that assist investors in gaining Latino market share, such as prepurchase housing counseling or Community Development Financial Institutions, as well as "softer" approaches such as favorable publicity, cobranding, and comarketing campaigns. For a description of some of these approaches, see Hizel et al. 2002, and Kamasaki and Arce 2000.) Similarly, Hispanic elected and appointed officials would reward cooperating firms with government contracts, deposits for financial institutions, or favorable advertising. "Sticks" might include opposition to financial industry mergers, discrimination litigation, and direct-action campaigns such as boycotts or the threat of such actions by advocates. Hispanic public officials could join such efforts but could also steer procurement, advertising, or deposits away from noncompliant institutions. The creation of new Latino-controlled vehicles, such as community development corporations or housing counseling organizations through which private investment can be channeled, increase capacity for such services as affordable-housing development, homeownership, and other programs that increase equal access to affordable housing.

This "market" approach is of course a flawed mechanism for ensuring equitable distribution of housing to any group, much less to an ethnic minority that experiences substantial discrimination. However, it is far from clear that an "enhanced market" would be any less effective than is the existing fair housing enforcement infrastructure.

One largely market-based approach, supplemented with modest HUD funding, is homeownership–focused housing counseling, which research suggests is producing real, measurable improvements in Latino access to homeownership (Hizel et al. 2002, Hirad and Zorn 2001). The market approach has clear dangers—the potential reduction of support for civil rights enforcement from the nation's largest ethnic minority and heightened tensions between Latinos and other minority groups. Nonetheless, a refocusing or reallocation of Latino advocates' resources away from "traditional" civil rights strategies toward more market-driven approaches arguably has already begun, with no demonstrable negative effect on civil rights enforcement overall.

CONCLUSION

We recognize that both the analysis and recommendations we have offered may appear provocative. Some part of our analytic and policy conclusions are based upon the frustration of the junior author, who has been urging for nearly two decades that the fair housing system become more responsive to Hispanics. We believe that there has been and is little to show for this advocacy in terms of tangible, measurable improvement (Kamasaki 1986; Yzaguirre 1987; Kamasaki 1988a; Kamasaki 1988b; Dolbeare and Canales 1988; Yzaguirre 1989; Yzaguirre 1992; Kamasaki and Yzaguirre 1994; Yzaguirre 1994; Joge 1999).

We feel it therefore useful to frame the issues and policy choices in stark terms. While both we, and the organization we represent, are committed to the principles of equal opportunity embodied in the nation's civil rights laws, we seek improvements in the civil rights enforcement system. We hope that this chapter may serve as a wake-up call to other stakeholders in the system. If the system and its stakeholders are committed to making serious, substantive, measurable improvements with respect to the protection of Hispanic civil rights, then they can expect the vigorous support of NCLR and other Latino advocates. However, NCLR and other Hispanic advocates are obligated to represent their constituents' practical interests and not just the abstract ideals expressed in the Fair Housing Act. For the time being, we must conclude that the Fair Housing Act, as implemented, is incapable of equitably serving the Latino community. Without significant reforms in the civil rights enforcement system in general and the fair housing system in particular, at some point, and we sincerely hope it never comes, Hispanic advocates will be compelled to reconsider their historic support of these enforcement systems and concentrate exclusively on alternative approaches.

APPENDIX

Latinos also face other forms of significant housing discrimination—in the distribution of public housing benefits, access to conventional mortgages, and in the homeowners insurance market. With respect to housing assistance, Latino households accounted for one in six households below poverty, but only one in seven households below poverty living in government-subsidized housing, compared to black households, which accounted for one in four below-poverty households, but one in three below-poverty households living in subsidized housing in 2002. These data drastically understate the degree of underrepresentation of Latinos in assisted housing, especially given the high degree of overcrowding in Hispanic households (about one in eight are overcrowded). For example, in 2002 Latinos constituted nearly one out of every four below-poverty families (23 percent), suggesting that poor Hispanic households contain more than one family.

Two multicity studies examining this issue found that lack of bilingual staff at public housing agencies (PHAs) and government offices and small unit sizes unfairly prevent Latino families from accessing federal housing benefits.

Table 10.5. Households Living in Subsidized Housing by Race/Ethnicity, by Poverty Status, 2002

	Total Households	*Percent of All Households*	*Households in Subsidized Housing*	*Percent of All in Subsidized Housing*
All Households				
Total	109,297	100%	5,006	100%
Hispanic	10,499	9.6%	649	13%
Black	13,315	12.2%	1,717	34.3%
White	80,818	73.9%	2,464	49.2%
Below Poverty Households				
Total	12,754	100%	2,585	100%
Hispanic	2,143	16.8%	368	14.2%
Black	3,022	23.7%	1,014	39.2%
White	7,050	55.3%	1,118	43.2%

Source: *Current Population Survey*, March 2002.

According to a study completed by Lois Athey (2000) for the National Hispanic Housing Council, Latinos were significantly underrepresented on the waitlists for public housing and other subsidies, and were often passed over for units located in Hispanic neighborhoods (Athey 2000). In 1997, NCLR conducted a series of focus groups in Phoenix, Chicago, and Washington, D.C., to identify barriers to improving the poor conditions of Hispanics' housing. Participants continually repeated that they were unable to access federally assisted housing programs, that they felt discriminated against, and that they felt helpless to do anything about it (Pérez and Luna 1997).

NOTES

Lindsay Daniels, policy associate, and Jennifer Kadis, editor, assisted in the preparation of this chapter. The authors also benefited from conversations with Victor Alvarez, assistant director of Latinos United, Shanna Smith, executive director of National Fair Housing Alliance, Kery Nuñez, public policy director at the National Puerto Rican Coalition, and Zixta Martinez, who reviewed earlier drafts of the chapter and provided helpful comments. Preparation of this chapter was supported in part by a contract from Baruch College Fund, City University, New York. NCLR's housing policy analysis work is supported by the Ford Foundation, through its support of the organization's civil rights activity; Bank of America and the Fannie Mae Foundation, through their support of the institution's public policy work on housing and homeownership; and the John D. and Catherine T. MacArthur Foundation and the Rockefeller Foundation, through their support of the NCLR Policy Analysis Center. The opinions cited in this paper are of course the sole responsibility of NCLR, as are any errors of fact or logic, and may not represent the views of the chapter's reviewers, the institution's supporters, or funders.

1. The terms "Hispanic" and "Latino" are used interchangeably throughout this chapter and refer collectively to Mexicans, Puerto Ricans, Cubans, Central and South Americans, Dominicans, and others of Spanish and Latin American descent. Latinos may be of any race; therefore, unless denoted as "non-Hispanic," persons of Hispanic origin may be included in both the "black" and "white" racial categories. Data on Latinos do not include the 2.8 million residents of Puerto Rico.

2. In addition, the introduction of credit scores as a method of measuring risk and pricing insurance products presents a new danger of unintentional discrimination (Rodriguez 2003; Kamasaki 2003; Knutson 2003). Otherwise creditworthy Latino families often have "thin" or no credit histories that translate into low credit scores, and recent research notes that one in four people are likely to have errors on their credit report (Consumer Federation of America 2002). In a case against one major insurer, a court determined that the company's use of credit scores to screen clients unfairly discriminated against Latino homeowners (*Dehoyos v. Allstate Corp.*).

3. Based on NCLR calculations of the data from *State of the Nation's Housing 2003*, Joint Center for Housing of Harvard University, see figure 7.

4. See specifically: *United States v. Associates National Bank*; *United States v. First National Bank of Dona Ana County*; *United States v. Northern Trust Company*; *United States v. Shawmut Mortgage Company*; *United States v. Fidelity Federal Bank*; *United States v. Fleet Mortgage Company*; *United States v. Security State Bank*; *United States v. Long Beach Mortgage Company*; and *United States v. Mid America Bank, fsb.*

5. At the time of this publication, this case was still pending. However, HUD's conciliation shows that Prudential agreed to change some of their underwriting practices as a result of the evidence and case against them. See similar cases brought that did not include Latino testing or plaintiffs: *Nationwide Mutual Insurance Company and Nationwide Mutual Fire Insurance Company v. Henry Cisneros, Secretary of the United States Department of Housing and Urban Development*; and *American Family Insurance v. NAACP*.

6. See: Anti-Discrimination Center of Metro New York, Inc. (2004), a fair housing clearinghouse project; and for a broader perspective on shortcomings of the civil rights enforcement on behalf of Hispanics, see Dolbeare and Canales (1988) and Yzaguirre and Kamasaki 1994.

7. A joint report of Harvard University's Civil Rights Project and the Lewis Mumford Center concluded that segregation is on the rise nationally and links this trend in part to weak enforcement of fair housing laws (Orfield 2001).

8. Overall, twenty-five thousand claims of discrimination were filed on behalf of every protected class member, including Hispanics, during 2002 (NFHA 2003).

9. Further, the Hispanic population grew by 53 percent between 1980 and 1990, and by 58 percent between 1990 and 2000. It is not unreasonable to have expected that this growing population might have been accompanied by increased complaints filed by or on behalf of Latino families, especially given the influx of immigrant families, who almost certainly face increased discrimination based on language barriers and speech accents, particularly in the Southeast and Midwest regions.

10. Further, both public and private fair housing agencies lack a progressive hiring strategy for Latino staff. In part due to funding requirements, agencies often hire one person for education and outreach and another for enforcement responsibilities; all too often, Latinos are hired into the junior and less technical education and outreach positions where their bilingual skills are thought to be best employed.

11. For further elaboration of this idea, see Fix and Turner (1998). See especially Marc Bendick's discussion on the importance and value of "social marketing" in this context.

REFERENCES

Anti-Discrimination Center of Metro New York. 2004. *Fair Housing Bibliography Project*. www.antibiaslaw.com.

Association of Community Organizations for Reform Now (ACORN). 2002. *Separate and Unequal: Predatory Lending in America*. Washington, DC: ACORN.

Athey, Lois E. 2000. *A Comparative Study of the Determinants of Hispanic Participation in Federally Funded Housing Programs in Six Cities and Counties: Chicago, Illinois; El Paso, Texas; City of Miami and Miami-Dade County, Florida; Philadelphia, Pennsylvania; San Juan, Puerto Rico; and Washington, D.C.* National Hispanic Housing Council.

Bradford, Calvin. 2002. *Risk or Race?* Washington, DC: Center for Community Change.

Consumer Federation of America. 2002. *Credit Score Accuracy and Implications for Consumers*. Washington, DC: Consumer Federation of America.

Dehoyos et al. v. Allstate Corporation et al. 345 F3d 290; 2003 U.S. App. Lexis 18172.

Dolbeare, Cushing N., and Judith A. Canales. 1988. *The Hispanic Housing Crisis*. Washington, DC: National Council of La Raza.

Fix, Michael, and Margery Austin Turner. 1998. *A National Report Card on Discrimination in America.* Washington, DC: Urban Institute Press.

Frankenberg, Erica, Chungmei Lee, and Gary Orfield. 2003. *A Multiracial Society with Segregated Schools: Are We Losing the Dream?* Cambridge, MA: Harvard University Civil Rights Project.

Frey, William, and Dowell Myers. 2002. *Neighborhood Segregation in Single-Race and Multirace America: A Census 2000 Study of Cities and Metropolitan Areas*. Working Paper. Washington, DC: Fannie Mae Foundation.

Gonzalez, Claire. 1993. *The Empty Promise: The EEOC and Hispanics*. Washington, DC: National Council of La Raza.

Greater Houston Fair Housing Center. 2001. *Houston Rental Audit*. Washington, DC: National Fair Housing Alliance.

Hirad, Abdighani, and Peter Zorn. 2001. *A Little Knowledge Is a Good Thing: Empirical Evidence of the Effectiveness of Pre-Purchase Homeownership Counseling*. Washington, DC: Freddie Mac Corporation.

Hizel, Erika, Charles Kamasaki, and Geraldine Schafer. 2002. *Increasing Hispanic Homeownership: Strategies for Programs and Public Policy*. Issue Brief No. 7. Washington, DC: National Council of La Raza.

Home Mortgage Disclosure Act. 2002. *National Aggregate Table 4-2: Disposition of Applications for Conventional Home-Purchase Loans, 1 to 4 Family Homes, by Race*. www.ffiec.gov/hmda_rpt/natagg_welcome.htm.

Joge, Carmen. 1999. Testimony on Latinos and the Equal Employment Opportunity Commission. U.S. Equal Employment Opportunity Commission.

Joint Center for Housing Studies. 2002. *State of America's Housing: 2002*. Cambridge, MA: Harvard University Press.

———. 2003. *State of America's Housing: 2003*. Cambridge, MA: Harvard University Press.

Kamasaki, Charles. 1986. Testimony on the Fair Housing Amendments Act (H.R. 4119). Subcommittee on Civil and Constitutional Rights of the House Committee on the Judiciary.

——. 1988a. Testimony on Segregation and Housing Discrimination in the Hispanic Community. Subcommittee on Housing and Community Development of the House Committee on Banking, Finance, and Urban Affairs.

——. 1988b. Testimony on the National Affordable Housing Act. Subcommittee on Housing and Urban Affairs of the Senate Committee on Banking, Housing, and Urban Affairs.

——. 2003. *Credit Scoring in Underwriting: Value and Concerns.* Presented to State Farm Insurance Company.

Kamasaki, Charles, and Laura Arce. 2000. *Financial Services and Hispanic Americans*. Issue Brief No. 2. Washington, DC: National Council of La Raza.

Kamasaki, Charles, and Raul Yzaguirre. 1994. "Black-Hispanic Tensions: One Perspective." *Journal of Intergroup Relations.* 21(4): 1994–95.

Knutson, J. Haakon. 2003. "Credit Scoring in the Insurance Industry: Discrimination or Good Business?" *Loyola Consumer Law Review* 15:315–29.

Latinos United. 1996. *Latinos United: History of the Lawsuit*. Chicago: Latinos United.

Logan, John R. 2002. *Separate and Unequal: The Neighborhood Gap for Blacks and Hispanics in Metropolitan America*. Lewis Mumford Center for Comparative Urban and Regional Research. Albany: State University of New York.

Logan, John, Jacob Stowell, and Deirdre Oakley. 2002. *Choosing Segregation: Racial Imbalance in American Public Schools, 1990–2000*. Lewis Mumford Center for Comparative Urban and Regional Research. Albany: State University of New York.

Mayor's Office of Housing. 2003. *Analysis of Impediments to Fair Housing*. San Francisco, CA: City and County of San Francisco.

National Fair Housing Alliance. 2004. *National Fair Housing Alliance: 2004 Fair Housing Trends Report*. Washington, DC: National Fair Housing Alliance.

——. 2003. *National Fair Housing Alliance: 2003 Fair Housing Trends Report*. Washington, DC: National Fair Housing Alliance.

——. 2000. *Six Fair Housing Groups Sue Citigroup, Travelers and Aetna Alleging Discrimination Against African American and Latino Homeowners*. Press Release. Washington, DC: National Fair Housing Alliance.

——. 1995. *Fair Housing Act Under Siege by Insurance Lobbyists.* Press Release. Washington, DC: National Fair Housing Alliance.

National Fair Housing Alliance, Inc. et al. v. The Prudential Insurance Company of America et al. 208 F. Supp 2d; 2002 U.S. Dist. Lexis 12597.

National Housing Law Project. 1999. "HUD's Fair Housing Duties and the Loss of Public and Assisted Housing." *Housing Law Bulletin* [online] www.nhlp.org/html/hlb/199/199fairhsg.htm.

Orfield, Gary. 2001. *Housing Segregation: Causes, Effects, Possible Cure*. Cambridge, MA: Harvard University Civil Rights Project.

Orfield, Gary, and Chungmei Lee. 2004. *Brown at 50: King's Dream or Plessy's Nightmare?* Cambridge, MA: Harvard University Civil Rights Project.

Orfield, Gary, and Joyn T. Yun. 1999. *Resegregation in American Schools*. Cambridge, MA: Harvard University Civil Rights Project.

Pérez, Sonia M., and Victoria Luna. 1997. *Locked Out: Hispanic Underrepresentation in Federally Assisted Housing Programs*. Washington, DC: National Council of La Raza Office of Research, Advocacy, and Legislation.

Rodriguez, Eric. 2003. *Credit Scoring in Underwriting: Value and Concerns*. Presented to State Farm Insurance Company.

Sandoval, Juan Onésimo, Hans P. Johnson, and Sonya M. Tafoya. 2002. "Who's Your Neighbor: Residential Segregation and Diversityin California." *California Counts*. Public Policy Institute of California. http://www.ppic.org/main/publication.asp?i=163.

Santiago, Anna M. 1996. "Trends in Black and Latino Segregation in the Post-Fair Housing Era: Implication for Housing Policy." *La Raza Law Journal* 9(2): 131.

Turner, M. A., S. L. Ross, G. C. Galster, and J. Yinger. 2002. *Discrimination in Metropolitan Housing Markets: Phase 1*. Washington, DC: U.S. Department of Housing and Urban Development.

U.S. Department of Housing and Urban Development. 2001. *FY 2001 Fair Housing Initiatives Program (FHIP): Projects Selected for Funding*. http://www.nmhc.org/Content/ServeFile.cfm?FileID=1678.

———. 2002. *FY 2002 Fair Housing Initiatives Program (FHIP) Awards*. http://www.hud.gov/news/releasedocs/fhip/index.cfm.

———. 2003. *FY 2003 Fair Housing Initiatives Program (FHIP) Awards*. http://www.hud.gov/offices/fheo/partners/FHIP/FY20003FHIP.cfm.

U.S. Department of Justice. 2004. *Case Summaries*. www.usdoj.gov/crt/housing/documents/casesummary.htm.

Ware, Leland, Louis L. Redding, and Steven W. Peuquet. 2003. *Delaware Analysis of Impediments to Fair Housing Choice*. Center for Community Research and Service. Newark: University of Delaware.

Wissoker, Douglas A., Wendy Zimmermann, and George Galster. 1997. *Testing for Discrimination in Home Insurance*. Washington, DC: The Urban Institute.

Yzaguirre, Raul. 1987. Testimony on the Fair Housing Act of 1987 (S. 558). Subcommittee on the Constitution of the Senate Committee on the Judiciary.

———. 1989. Testimony on the Housing and Community Development Act of 1989. Subcommittee on Housing and Community Development of the House Committee on Banking, Finance, and Urban Affairs.

———. 1992. Testimony on Fair Lending and the Home Mortgage Disclosure Act. Subcommittee on Housing and Community Development and Subcommittee on Consumer Affairs and Coinage of the House of Representatives.

———. 1994. Testimony for Oversight Hearing on Fair Housing. Subcommittee on Civil and Constitutional Rights of the House Committee on Judiciary.

Yzaguirre, Raul, Laura Arce, and Charles Kamasaki. 1999. "The Fair Housing Act: A Latino Perspective." *Cityscape* 4(3): 161–70.

Yzaguirre, Raul, and Charles Kamasaki. 1997. *Comment on The Latino Civil Rights Crisis*. Presented to The Latino Civil Rights Crisis Research Conference, Washington, DC.

11

The Effectiveness of Fair Housing Programs and Policy Options

John Goering

The core questions for this chapter are straightforward: Has the Fair Housing Act worked as Congress intended? And if it has not worked well, what, if anything, should be done to more reasonably and effectively provide fair housing rights in the United States? I offer an overview below of how much we know about whether programs and policies in the arena of open housing have succeeded, failed, or merely gotten by at some middling level of accomplishment.

There are two issues to focus upon in answering the question about whether the open-housing law has worked. The first concerns how well the law is administered. Does it educate citizens about how to use the fair housing legal system? Does it efficiently process those cases that have merit and provide relief to those who complained? Typically such questions are answered in a process evaluation. The material reported in the chapters within by Schill, Sidney, and Bowdler and Kamasaki each offer critical parts of such process or administrative assessments. The second focus is on whether we know if the law has changed outcomes. Is the law, for example, a clear and measurable cause of the reduction in housing discrimination over the last decade? Such questions are typically answered in an outcome evaluation, of which chapter 8 by Ross and Galster is among the first since the law's enactment. We do not, however, have anything like a definitive process and impact evaluation of the nation's fair housing laws.

In its most perfect condition, real evidence of effectiveness would show that the law worked to noticeably improve the lives of those it was designed to benefit, that the benefits were achieved cost effectively, and that the effects of the program have lasted a long time (Rossi 1987; Crane 1998). For civil rights enforcement programs, real changes in behavioral outcomes would mean most, if not all, people believed in and supported the objectives of open-housing laws, the level of discrimination dropped steadily for all protected groups, and such improvements were caused by the existence of the law and its enforcers (Hochschild 1996; Leonard 1990; Sparrow 2000). It is quite hard, however, to assemble the evidence of these interrelated changes.

PROBLEMS IN ESTABLISHING CAUSALITY

Knowing whether any housing justice improvements have been *caused* by open-housing programs is complicated by the limited data available and the cost and complexity of a comprehensive evaluation, including the difficulty of distinguishing longer-term underlying shifts in "race relations" from the direct role of governmental civil rights programs. The chapters by Schill and Ross and Galster suggest some of the major data reasons why it is hard to fully understand the operation and effects of fair housing law enforcement programs and funding systems.

A related reason why it is hard to establish causality is that we lack a usable theory of behavioral change in housing markets. There are no good analytic guideposts or models to help us separate the impacts of public policies from non-policy-driven social forces (Loewen 2005: 177–91). For real changes in outcomes or behavior to occur through programmatic change, we should know how well federal laws, such as those affecting civil rights, are embedded within the structure of costs and ethical requirements in major housing and mortgage market institutions. We would need insights into the collateral community-based social norms regarding acceptance of protected classes that are integral to the operation of housing markets. This would include knowing how well the law's prohibitions and penalties are understood and endorsed and how to best develop programs of education and information. What is required to make the chance of being caught and punished a key behavioral motivator, and how are such calculations judged in the light of local community biases? How has the denial or restriction of housing options been adopted and embraced within communities, including this country's newest immigrants and among the minorities? What would they need to learn, from what sources, in order for them to take seriously their right to file complaints? Given that we know that roughly 20 percent of Americans disapprove of open-housing laws, how do such opponents leverage other occasional or limited supporters of discrimination? How does such open and tacit opposition to civil rights become translated into codes of conduct for local real estate actors? Can programs in support of tolerance and openness find means to contain or reduce such opposition?

We know, therefore, little about the sociological and economic foundations for breaching civil rights laws in return for compensating strong community (including financial) support for such bias. We do not know how clustered the supporters of open housing are in contrast to those who oppose the law's objectives, nor how to tip the balance of local support in favor of active enforcement. Such evidence needs to be understood, of course, within the trajectory of substantial improvements in support for civil rights that have occurred over the last half century (Light 2002). We are seeking evidence of impacts and changes that will reduce discrimination to less than its current role in 20 to 30 percent of all transactions.

Another part of the frustration in evaluating how well a law regulating housing market behavior works is that there is little uniformity as to how property is regulated, rented, sold, financed, foreclosed, or advertised. A plethora of individual, neighborhood, citywide, regional, and occasionally national actors and institutions decide who gets to rent an apartment, sell or buy a home, or get a reasonably priced mortgage. Local governments often complicate the question of knowing how well government is regulating housing markets by the enactment of an uneven and often overlapping range of regulatory, code-enforcement, and other legal requirements that affect how property is owned, managed, and transferred (Schill 2005). For the disabled, for example, local building codes are often the crucial standard according to which buildings are constructed or adapted and these codes may not incorporate all the requirements of the fair housing act (Steven Winter 2003). A national program of open-housing enforcement has to be superimposed, therefore, on fragmented markets, localized regulatory interventions, and unexamined market behavior (Schuck 2003: 205–6; Schill 2005).

Basic information about the performance and operation of each of the component parts of a housing transaction is also scant, even to the members of the real estate industry. In New York, for example, there is no single, comprehensive list of all available housing units for rent or sale; no single multiple-listing service.[1] No housing agency, real estate firm, fair housing enforcer, or a person in search of an apartment can know all the choices there are at any given time. If such relatively simple information is unavailable, it is impossible to estimate when denials of such opportunities may occur, by and against whom, and why. Information about what mortgage type and price is best for any individual household is additionally complicated by the invisibility of the credit rating systems, by the use of statistical forms of discrimination, by the wide and confusing range of mortgage products, and also by the intention to conceal fraudulent lending practices (Ross and Yinger 2002; Squires 2004).

In addition to the fragmentation and opaqueness of housing markets, there is the added problem that government has not gotten better at creating centralized, nationally driven solutions to social problems but has, for some decades now, been withdrawing into a more passive, nonproactive regulatory posture (Rossi and Freeman 1989). Laws have increasingly not been aggressively enforced when voluntary approaches could be substituted (Sparrow 2000).

Many argue, both within and outside of government, that we should simply stop expecting the federal government to be the solution of first or even last resort (Schuck 2003). And the longer this expectation—and argument—of a minimalist role for the federal government persists, the more likely it will become a politically self-fulfilled prophecy. A September 2005 Pew Research Center poll, for example, reports that 56 percent of Americans feel that "government is almost always wasteful and inefficient," up from 51 percent in 1999.[2] With such popular sentiments in play, agencies are likely to continue to lose qualified staff and expertise and soon will only function to maintain minimal services and programs (Smith 2005: 41).[3]

Two additional factors impinge on the question of whether and how fair housing legislation can be effective. The first concerns the overall structure of rights enforcement in the United States as it has been established by Congress. The second addresses the particular role or niche that fair housing has been assigned within its parent agency, the U.S. Department of Housing and Urban Development.

The Balkanization of Civil Rights

Congress has delegated to separate administering bodies the obligation to enforce specific individual civil rights claims in isolation from other agencies and from the community context within which discrimination occurs.[4] Civil rights laws as congressionally constructed assume that bias is divisible into claims that are recognized and treated in separate offices and by separated teams of investigators, lawyers, administrative law judges, funding agents, and—most notably—by divisible remedial strategies or plans. The sociological foundations for viable antidiscrimination campaigns at the local level are handicapped by such administrative balkanization.

It is a system constructed to be indifferent to issues of cumulative causality in which, for example, segregated schools might lead to mistreatment in the labor market or to denial of housing and credit (refer to chapter 3 by Massey and Blank). It is a system in which the legal divisibility and management of rights is preferred over the sociologically inclined administration of conjoint biases that accumulate and affect entire markets and communities. The latter assumes that communities differ in their contextualized biases and levels of intolerance applied to protected class members across a range of economic and social activities. Voting rights would potentially more likely be denied in a town where schools are segregated, where housing is denied or segregated, where restaurants shun minorities, and where jobs are rationed by race. There would be a legitimacy to race denial and bias that would not exist in a community composed largely of race liberals.[5] The right to appear intolerant across human and civil rights domains is locally fostered and sustained and might be, conversely, minimized if conjoint antidiscrimination social systems were in place with socially constructed legitimacy and salience.

Within the system of balkanized rights administration there is no umbrella of rights promotion and education that could reduce the high levels of indifference to open-housing rights reported on in the chapter by Abravanel and in chapter 1. It would also be sociologically imprudent to assume that it is only in the arena of housing where the majority of Americans will say they know relatively little about the law and would "do nothing" even when confronted with an act of discrimination. Such resentment or indifference would plausibly appear in surveys that asked if people believe that if discriminated against in getting a job they would file a grievance with the Equal Employment Opportunity Commission or when they are denied access to a restaurant they would file a grievance with the Justice Department. No such surveys have, however, been conducted, and their absence balkanizes our appreciation of the limits of civil rights support throughout the country.

The fundamental failure of current forms of federal civil rights is that the balkanization and legalization of rights fail to address the social systems that support continuing forms of denial and mistreatment as a matter of societal norms and institutional treatment. They are too passive and fragmented to foster effective appreciation and utilization of a sociologically realized set of integrated rights.

The Marginalization of Open Housing at HUD

There is another central reason to worry about the effectiveness of the nation's fair housing laws. Historians (Freund 2004: 22) help us understand the conditions for making the fair housing laws become effective by looking back to the foundations of equal justice programs within HUD and its predecessor agencies. They have pointed out that the federal fair housing enforcement system has been rooted in the belief of key administrators that racial discrimination was simply not a pressing issue. Despite efforts by the first HUD secretary, Robert Weaver, open-housing programs and bureaucratic systems at the national level had little leverage. These weak and marginalized roots for the open-housing enforcement programs set the platform for the subsequent limits of national fair housing programs (Bonastia 2000; von Hoffman 1998).

HUD, it is argued, is politically compromised by its commitment to both develop cities and housing for the poor while also trying to help those protected by fair housing laws get an apartment or home, regardless of how much they earn. The first part of the mandate is to assist low- and moderate-income persons, while the latter assumes income is not relevant but race or another protected class is. HUD pays builders and apartment managers to build and rent apartments to those of modest means, while it also seeks apartments using legal sanctions and offering no subsidies. Efforts to ban discrimination against some of the same groups by some of the same providers are often tactically compromised. The agency is preoccupied by issues of production, building conditions, and rents, so that the goal is often getting housing built no matter where it is located, segregated or not (Jackson 1985: 219–30; Suttles 1990: 51–75; Bratt and Keating 1993; Vale 2000; Goetz 2003). It was within HUD's own subsidized housing stock, for example, that the implementation of fair housing laws were first and most immediately fought over because of illegal segregation and discrimination (Goering 1986; Schuck 2003; Vale 2000: 266–307; Goetz 2003).

HUD administers, then, a structurally and congressionally embedded conflicted message: we care principally about bricks, mortar, and rents and are therefore like most local landlords and lenders—but we also exist to police the biases with which you may administer access to your houses and mortgages. Human rights are, to put it starkly, an anomalous obligation for real estate developers and managers, just as being the agency that is the bearer of a mandate to create truly balanced and integrated living means that HUD would be the central unending target of community opposition (NIMBYism) to affordable housing and to minorities. HUD tries to do sociologically incompatible things within the same market, with the result that its supporters are often fragmented or in conflict (see chapter 9 by Sidney; Sidney 2003).

HUD offices are necessarily preoccupied by huge and costly issues of urban housing need that can be illustrated by the need in winter 2006 for rehousing hundreds of thousands of residents of New Orleans and the Gulf Coast, including roughly 150,000 minority poor families (Nutting and Watts 2005; DeParle 2005). Such need can overwhelm the question of whether one unit rather than another has been fairly opened to a white, black, Hispanic, disabled, or Asian family. Often the housing needy will insist on speedy remedies whose very funding and construction serve to reinforce the racially or ethnically divided character of our cities. Briggs (2005: 249), notes that HUD's institutional civil rights enforcement tasks have long been handicapped; "administrative agencies entrusted to collect, process, investigate, and in some cases adjudicate claims are notoriously under funded, backlogged, and *conflicted* about how to best pursue their policy mandates" (emphasis added). Elizabeth Julian, a former assistant secretary for fair housing issues at HUD, for example, makes the case that "the structure of HUD doesn't lend itself to fair housing ever getting the national attention and having the clout necessary for effective enforcement" (Julian n.d.). It is these incompatible choices and programmatic norms that suggest the necessary severance of HUD and fair housing.

HUD's conflicted missions are not the only concern. Over a decade ago, Bratt and Keating (1993: 3) reminded us that HUD had become "synonymous with all that is wrong with federal domestic social policies and programs." A former HUD secretary also testified that the agency was (in 1998) "the poster child for failed government" (Bovard 2000).[6] In 2001, HUD's inspector general (Gaffney 2001) again noted HUD's performance deficit in which there was a notable gap between what HUD was supposed to do and what it had "the ability to accomplish." Periodic internal and program reforms, which have often been accompanied by staffing and budget cuts, have meant that even best-intentioned administrators have had little time before new "reforms" or cuts limit their ability to institutionalize program change.[7] As HUD has confronted the dilemmas of worst-case housing need and neighborhood rebuilding priorities, along with budget reductions, it has been able to only marginally attend to complaints about unfair treatment. Given the bipartisan nature of this short-changing, it appears essential to plan for the future for fair housing enforcement outside of HUD. We return to this recommendation in the concluding section.

The Law, Causality, and Performance: The Effectiveness of the Federal Fair Housing Enforcement Mechanism

Knowing what legal and program changes would work best or better is complicated by the lack of evidence that the law has impacts upon the discriminatory behavior it was intended to change.[8] While there is general public support for the broad principle of open housing (see chapter 4 by Abravanel), we nonetheless know that unobtrusive forms of mistreatment continue to occur in housing transactions. In order to know why there is not a better connection between popular support for antidiscrimination measures and actual treatment, we need to have an appreciation for what the federal enforcement process actually does once a person decides to bring a complaint. We are aided in this analysis not only by the chapters in this collection but by recent evaluations of the manner in which enforcement of the nation's open-housing laws is carried out (GAO 2004; GAO 2005).

Implementing a law—like fair housing enforcement—requires rules and regulations, personnel hired in sufficient numbers, offices opened, flyers and other promotional material announcing the availability of the new federal service, procedures to handle the requests and complaints of citizen-clients, some criteria to judge whether the services are being provided satisfactorily as required in the statute, and the necessary funding to pay for the smooth and efficient functioning of this entire system. Below we briefly describe how the procedural parts of the fair housing law should work. This typological assessment builds on the six procedural requirements for individuals and fair housing system managers listed in chapter 1, table 1.2. A discussion of the first three was undertaken in chapter 1, and we focus here on the final three stages, which include:

- The individual's ability and patience to pursue the claim; manager's provision of support and information.
- Individual's satisfaction; manager's success in obtaining satisfaction.
- Individual as the source of information to others about successful fair housing case settlement; manager as promoter of law's benefit.

Both official government and nongovernmental reports indicate that fewer than 3,000 cases of housing discrimination are filed annually with HUD, and this number declined from 1992 (see chapter 7 by Schill; GAO 2004: 24; GAO 2005: 12; NCD 2001; Walton 1988: 96). This compares with the roughly 75,000 to 80,000 charges of employment discrimination received annually by the EEOC.[9] In 2003, while the number of cases filed was more than 8,000, the majority (two-thirds) were handled by state and local agencies (GAO 2004: 25). HUD took in an average of only 2,200 cases a year (GAO 2004: 72) while for 2004 it received 2,800 complaints (GAO 2005: 12). Yet even with such small numbers, HUD had a "substantial backlog" of cases, which curiously enough also existed early on as well (Walton 1988: 96). The bulk of complaints alleging housing discrimination in the United States are reported to nonprofit, local agencies: roughly another 18,000 in 2004 (National Fair Housing Alliance 2005).[10] This asymmetry is central to the issue of deciding what agencies are best situated to handle individual complaints.

Receiving a case or complaint is just the opening step in a process leading to an investigation to decide whether the complaint has merit. If it does, there is some form of adjudication leading to getting relief for the victim. To appreciate how well this part of the enforcement process works, a recent Government Accounting Office (GAO) study used telephone testers to see how they were treated at HUD and FHAP agencies (GAO 2005: 16). They found evidence of poor performance including the fact that 10 percent of those who wished to complain could never get a callback even after three attempts. In roughly a third of these test calls, over a third said they "had difficulty contacting staff" after the first callback. When they did reach a person at an agency, over half of the time the personnel required them to wait a week or more to fill out an intake form that would be mailed to them "during which the caller could lose a housing opportunity" (GAO 2005: 17). One test caller who stressed how urgent her situation was nevertheless was told that filling a complaint was "'a slow process' and that her complaint would not be acted on for some time" (GAO 2005: 17). The GAO report summarizes the evidence: "the time it takes to receive the form can delay the enforcement process potentially resulting not only in the loss of a housing opportunity but also in complainants becoming frustrated with the process and deciding not to pursue their complaint" (GAO 2005: 21–22).

Out of the total number of cases filed with HUD, roughly one-quarter are closed before the agency proves that discrimination has actually occurred so that penalties might be imposed. In addition, one of every five cases is typically closed "administratively," or for the convenience of the agency.[11] In nearly half of all cases that are investigated, the agency decides there is no legal basis to proceed; this is called a determination of no reasonable cause (GAO 2004: 33). GAO, however, could find no explanation as to why out of a sample of 2,000 complaints that appeared at intake to potentially involve a fair housing violation, only 306 ever became a real or "perfected" complaint (GAO 2005: 250). Large numbers of complaints that enter HUD's door are therefore ended, without an investigation that might show whether discrimination actually occurred.

There are, then, typically only a small number of cases where HUD feels there has been real discrimination. Fewer than two dozen cases led to the decision, or determination, that there was "reasonable cause" to proceed. Schill (chapter 7 within) reports that only 3.3 percent of all cases filed since 1989 resulted in such a reasonable-cause charge being issued. It is important to note that GAO investigators could not prove that there was a legitimate claim for the rest of the cases. There are, nonetheless, only 3 to 5 percent of all cases where government agencies have both investigated and then been convinced that discrimination actually occurred (GAO 2004: 34).[12] This "disappearance of reasonable cause charges from HUD" is among the major findings reported by Schill and is among the fundamental reasons to wonder whether the average person for whom the fair housing laws were enacted already knows that they will not likely receive any help.[13]

Another measure of effectiveness in enforcing the law is whether or not the agencies investigate cases promptly, as Congress in 1988 mandated. Although Congress instructed HUD to investigate cases in 100 days, it took over 470 days to close a case, or more than five times longer than the time mandated (see Schill chapter). A GAO study (2004: 38) reported that in 2000 only 14 percent of cases were investigated on time.[14] The average time for investigating their cases was, according to GAO, nearly 260 days. In their 2005 GAO report, they find that 98 percent of cases, other than those with reasonable cause, did not meet the required time frame (GAO 2005: 35). When asked, the people who administer the law say that there is a perverse tradeoff between meeting this timetable and investigating cases carefully and thoroughly. Key enforcement staff told GAO investigators that there is a "tension between the need to meet the 100-day benchmark and the simultaneous need to conduct a thorough investigation and said that at times one goal cannot be achieved without some cost to the other" (GAO 2004: 56). Again, if the average person knew that nearly a year or more of their lives could be used up and there would be little to show for it, it would appear rational not to complain.

If a person sticks it out through the enforcement process, and the case is won, what do they get in terms of dollar payout? At the conclusion of cases, we learn, the average monetary award or payment victims have gotten is an average of roughly $800 for black complainants and $600 for those who are Hispanic (Schill and Friedman 1999; Schill suggests an average of $2,000 in this volume). This represents in inflation-adjusted terms little increase from the 1970s and 1980s, when the median level of monetary relief ranged from $390 to $500 per case (Goering 1986: 209). Despite the fact that the law has higher authorized ceilings for monetary payments, they have not been provided even for cases where proof of a legal violation has been found.

Another outcome of this process should be that the people who stayed with it until the end were pleased with the result. However, the results from Schill's nonrandom sample of people who filed cases and stayed with them until a final decision was reached shows us that roughly a third are not. Even though penalties are slight for those who have been charged with a violation, almost 70 percent of real estate actors leave the enforcement process convinced that the adjudicating agency, HUD, is unfair and biased.[15] The GAO (2005: 56) also conducted a sample of complainants and report that "half of all complainants were somewhat or very dissatisfied with the fair housing enforcement process." And 40 percent of those who did complain said they "would be unlikely to file a complaint in the future." GAO (2005: 72) summarizes their evaluation by commenting that people's negative views towards the fair housing investigative process diminishes "the Act's effectiveness in deterring acts of housing discrimination or otherwise promoting fair housing practices."

Finally, for successful cases, virtually no evidence of their outcome is ever announced, since agencies frequently agree as part of the settlement not to publicize the results. This is done, it is argued, to help ensure speedier and more ready cooperation of defendants. However, it appears to be a major social cost, since it leaves those few successful cases invisible to all except the immediate parties. No other individuals, believing themselves victimized, will learn of the successful result and thereby potentially feel encouraged to similarly apply.

The answer, then, to the first evaluation question is that the law as administered does not meet the intended standards set by Congress. Fair housing has not caught on as a viable right, it works too slowly, dismisses far too many cases based on testing evidence, offers tiny levels of relief or payoff, is unsatisfying to many of those who do participate in the full process, and is invisible by design from those who need it. This is not a credible record for an agency that has had nearly forty years to get it right.

Have There Been Any Impacts?

The evidence in this collection reveals that if we ask whether the law has been effective at *ending* discrimination, the answer is no. There is still differential treatment in 20 to 30 percent of transactions, and in the case of the disabled even higher. If the question is, has discrimination declined? the answer is yes, for African Americans, although this is only one of the two groups for which comparable time-series audit data are available.

More central is the question of whether fair housing enforcement may have caused these reductions. The research in chapter 8 by Ross and Galster suggests that the reductions appear to have been influenced by the enforcement process—no matter its weaknesses. They report that HUD's two major funding programs—the Fair Housing Assistance Program (FHAP), for state and local governments, and the Fair Housing Initiatives Program (FHIP), for private, nonprofit groups—had a statistically significant effect in causing the reduction in discrimination faced by blacks from 1989 through 2001. "The magnitude of our estimates suggests that enforcement effectiveness contributed substantially to the decline in discrimination that black apartment and home seekers observed during the decade." The authors use program dollars as the measure of program activity, recognizing that it is annually readjusted to account for the actual levels of complaints, which is possibly the same thing as the real-world level of real discrimination. They acknowledge the statistical problem of endogeneity that affects this area of outcome research, meaning that both program dollars and the measure of discrimination used are tapping into the same thing and are statistically interwoven. It is nonetheless of importance to know that a rise in funding levels is associated with a decline in discrimination faced by blacks.[16]

For the first time, we have evidence, even though it is limited by the nature of data available, of a modest positive impact of part of the government's enforcement activities. Missing is any information on whether the Justice Department's systemic efforts or HUD's own direct efforts may have helped, although such cases are often selectively targeted only at areas with the highest levels of discrimination, where change may take longer to occur or where results may be harder to detect.

In addition to the decline in the level of discrimination against blacks, there is also the positive news, cited earlier, that a sizable number of Americans agree with the principles of the open-housing law. While they do not fully understand the coverage of the actual law, the principled support of the law is now at a high point, even though a steadfast minority does not support the law's goals. Given the rapid increase in the size of the Hispanic and Asian populations (Alba and Nee 2003; Portes and Rumbaut 2001; 2005) and their low levels of interest in filing complaints, there is reason to worry that the existing configuration of programs and policies will overcome the bureaucratic inertia and ineptness that has been documented at HUD. The chapter by Bowdler and Kamasaki, for example, takes critical note of the negligence of Hispanics' fair housing concerns.

SUMMARY OF PERFORMANCE ISSUES

Forty years after its enactment, large proportions of Americans are simultaneously supportive of an open-housing law but vague to quite skeptical about what the actual fair housing law offers them by way of legal entitlement. One-fifth, after years of educational campaigns, remain opposed to the law, and in both national samples and in a New York survey, over 80 percent of those who believe they have been discriminated against do not believe they can turn to fair housing enforcement systems for assistance with their housing equity concerns. The right to fair housing appears largely abandoned and certainly disused by those for whom it was intended (Barry 2002). Even though respondents to a 2005 survey (Abravanel, chapter 4) report greater willingness to file complaints in the future, it is not clear what programmatically may have altered their inclination to use a system they have otherwise judged irrelevant.

The assumption that the beneficiaries of a law are its natural supporters is then, at best, uncertainly founded. We found little evidence in New York for active campaigns to address fair housing equity issues. Indeed, it is the 20 to

30 percent of people who state their open opposition to fair housing that could more probably coalesce to form the core of active neighborhood opposition to integrative or antidiscriminatory programs. Equally worrying, minority attitudes in support of racial mixing and enforcement may be weakening as blacks become further disengaged and as immigrants learn the benefits of our existing system of race prerogatives. Recent opposition to immigrants, in the United States and in other countries, appears another likely foundation for a core of resistance to further benefits and rights to newcomers that cannot be effectively counterbalanced by a broadly based antiracist political campaign.[17]

The typological labels that social scientists have applied to race, housing markets, and discrimination are, therefore, analytically unhelpful. By focusing almost entirely on the opinions of average American citizens, they have lost sight of the role and power of real estate institutions and actors in deciding whether any such opinions matter in actual housing decisions. Social scientists have typically restricted their methodological choices, from a comprehensive set of causes suggested by analysts of social exclusion (Hills, Le Grand, and Piachaud 2002), to a narrow range of individually or personally focused decisions. As a result, both researchers and policy makers have lost sight of the roles of government agency and institutional constraints.

The evidence in this collection suggests that neither housing market institutions nor consumers have fully embedded civil rights laws into their core decision making. Open housing has not become an essential civic entitlement which Americans count upon in housing transactions. Since government agencies are not seen as helpful, there is then both a "lack of recognition of basic rights" by the public as well as a "lack of access to political and legal systems necessary to make those rights a reality" (Burchardt, Le Grand, and Piachaud 2002: 3). We do not then live in anything resembling a post–civil rights reality.

Whether the United States ever intended to take civil rights seriously, it has in fact only allocated limited funding, staff, and leadership to the statutory obligation to address the root causes of housing mistreatment and racial separation. It has permitted a system of enforcement shortcomings to continue for decades without major attention to alternatives and necessary systemic redesign. The progress that has occurred needs to be noted for what it is. It has been largely the result of tiny numbers of individuals who felt it important enough to stick with an enforcement system that has discouraged or rejected the complaints of most others.

A recent national survey of Americans' reactions to the racial implications of Hurricane Katrina highlights the racially and ethnically polarized reactions of people to such events and to the issue of racial injustice. The results highlight how even such major trauma has only marginally altered preexisting popular views of the issues of race, poverty, and justice. In the context of a series of questions addressing people's reactions to the aftermath of the hurricane, they were asked if they agreed that there is a lot more racism in the United States than they ever imagined. While only 42 percent of whites felt this way, roughly three-quarters (76 percent) of blacks and two-thirds (66 percent) of Hispanics agreed that they now saw more of an issue (New America Media 2005). They were also asked whether they agreed that "life is a lot more difficult for Blacks in the United States than I ever imagined." Again the replies were racially polarized: whites agreed only one-third of the time, while nearly three-quarters (73 percent) of blacks said they agreed. Roughly half, or 47 percent, of Hispanics and Asians also agreed. As an example of citizens' views about the chances of getting help in dealing effectively with such crises, they were asked whether they agreed that: "I cannot rely on the American system and its institutions to protect my family in a crisis." Roughly 60 (59) percent of blacks and 43 percent of whites agreed, as did half (50 percent) of sampled Hispanics. Given the relative lack of confidence in American institutions, however vaguely they are defined in this question, it is nonetheless striking that many in this country no longer expect much from the existing federal system of supports. Given the continuation of substantially different worldviews of whites and blacks, along with considerable disaffection from government agencies, there is support for those who argue that our form of "racism" remains more or less untouched at its core. There has been change for the better, but the fundamental policy problem remains quite similar in many of its core dimensions to that which existed four decades ago.

Given this, what are the reasonable policy options that confront us after this intensive look into the issue of fairness in housing? Below we sketch out hypothetical policy choices as a means of thinking through what should be done in the face of evidence that the existing system does not work well for the people it was intended to serve. The first two options help set the stage, as straw-persons, for the concluding two options.

POLICY CHOICES FOR THE TWENTY-FIRST CENTURY

Repeal the Federal Fair Housing Act

One not unrealistic choice would be to stop throwing good money after bad and terminate the federal government's largely ineffective and frustrating efforts to address housing discrimination. If after four decades, hundreds of millions of federal dollars and the efforts of both political parties have failed to increase the number of Americans using their housing rights, or even knowing much about them, we should give up. We should as a nation abandon the rhetoric of equal justice, since it is fictive, and terminate the programs as wasteful and largely pointless. No amount of hectoring or bargaining can, under the existing intractable rules of political change, substantially improve the way in which the federal government addresses the shortage of fair housing and the lack of interest in such rights. This argument would be supported by those who argue that the central government continues to be a constrained and suspect instrument for establishing racial justice through the use of race-based programs (Schuck 2003: 329).[18]

Central to this view of the government's failure is that there has never been adequate funding made available to address the measured level of actual discrimination and the needs of protected class members for information and case processing help. The current conservative policy frame only reinforces this as an ongoing worry since in such a worldview, "personal failure stems not from economic or social inequalities but from the moral failings of thriftless, heedless, lawless, libertine and lazy individuals—precisely the sorts of people (conservatives charge) liberals want to coddle with needless destructive spending" (Wilentz 2005: 20).

Too little funding has for so long been made available that arguments can now be floated by nonconservatives, if only gingerly, about triage (Swarns 2006). Are blacks the neediest and therefore most deserving of a higher priority when scarce resources are handed out? Or are Bowdler and Kamasaki (see chapter 10 within) correct in highlighting the deep frustrations within the Latino community about getting a fair share of attention and funding for the growing needs of their constituents? Having far too little to plan with has meant that such triage considerations become paralytic of effective political mobilization and, at the local level, limit groups' ability to tap into local support for a more energized view of housing needs and rights (see Sidney, chapter 9 within). A fair housing enforcement and funding system has been created that feeds on itself instead of creating new alliances and strategies to deal with the changing problems.

If the law does not work as intended, and if the American public has no intention of providing the funding needed to provide a fully effective rights-enforcement system, then one option is to end it. The executive branch would act to rescind and repeal the Fair Housing Act and terminate all funding effective the following year. Individuals seeking relief could turn to private attorneys or to private groups that could find the funding privately to continue their efforts. States and localities would be free to decide whether they need their own local laws and find the funds to administer them. Those feeling aggrieved could also make use of an older generation of statutes and the Constitution around which to frame their complaints. The real estate industry, banks, insurance companies, banking regulators, and others would still be subject to other consumer protection laws. They would now, however, be free of federal agencies, to allow market realties to determine who best to serve, how well, and where.[19]

But would not the moral cost of abdicating all federal commitments to this central civil right not cause a reinforcing backlash of comparable rejections at the local level? Not only would federal offices close but so too would many state and local enforcement agencies long accustomed to federal grants under the Fair Housing Assistance Program (see Sidney, chapter 9). A national renunciation of the federal government's ability to care and provide for open housing would cause an insuperable tear in the fabric of the country's platform of civic commitments. It is also reasonable to suppose that local and state governments could not find the taxing authority to supplant the vanished federal dollars, no matter how inadequately and poorly targeted they have been. Local resisters of fair housing could more readily accumulate enough neighborhood influence to shift the balance against any new local open-housing ordinances requiring funding. Battles at the local level over which groups would deserve more would potentially cripple local alliances needed for other equity issues, and paralyze those who would then have to become dependent on more mercurial foundation and private funding.

It is also a fairly rash response to the limited evidence we have at hand. We have found and offered no evidence about the potential utility and power of the federal government's role in housing justice should the leadership be there to seriously undertake systemic or pattern and practice investigations. Changes in executive branch leadership are inevitable, and the marginal impact of having federal authority to back a case is far better than relying solely upon local governments, which are often more susceptible to real estate interests and community opposition to racial change.

Do Nothing

The second choice would be to leave well enough alone. The system we have is acknowledged to be imperfect but any legislative alternative could be far worse. Since policy analysts tell us that virtually no federal government program gets 100 percent of what it sets out to accomplish, we should count our blessings, namely the accomplishments we have achieved, and not solely look into a glass that only appears unduly empty. Work with what you have and do not count on unrealistic reforms, especially when attempts to open the Pandora's box of legislative reform may be used to impose unwanted legislative restraints. Opposition forces will attempt to extract their pound of flesh once they see the opportunity to press home an antirace, antiquota, or anti–big government message. Attempts at reform will likely yield losses rather than gains in enforcement capability, and funding is a familiar part of pragmatists' concerns over major reform.[20] Schuck (2003), for example, has already proposed that minorities learn to get along better by growing "thicker skins" as his version of a policy choice.

Such policy and political caution has become a standard part of policy discourse over the last decade or more, suggesting any other view would be concurrently Pollyannaish and risky. However, it fails to account for the misadministration of even basic requirements of the law's mandates. Moreover, if this is the policy conclusion, it is logically no different in effect from option one, since there is clear evidence that the current fair housing rights option is unused and potentially evaporating. It would, then, be wiser and cleaner to elect option one and abandon any pretense that a real—as opposed to formal and largely fictive—right has been provided to the country. There is no point in stringing people along in some vain hope that a thin gruel of protection is better than nothing, since the very rights being so inadequately offered are withering away in the minds of those who are supposed to be empowered and helped. The status quo is a policy choice that actually also ensures that rights will disappear just as surely as they would under the first choice. It would occur only more slowly, less visibly, but with damage done to the only remaining political constituents for major reform. Fair housing as an actual right would be eviscerated.

Reshape HUD Programs

The third logical choice would be to systemically rethink the manner in which federal equal opportunity in housing is provided within HUD. Evaluation evidence and performance data should help reshape or completely overhaul those programs that promise but have not delivered the fair and diverse housing intended in 1968 (Tranel 2003; Glover and Bell 2005). A central assumption, strongly suggested by decades of congressional appropriations, is that we have been funding our civil rights open-housing duties on the cheap. Some part of this parsimony may be due to Congress's belief that HUD could do no more, and no doubt an additional part is due to the more fundamental political marginalization of rights. It is my argument, then, that justice, when administered in half measures, results in the ultimate atrophy of the very foundations of citizen support. Without justice and rights competently administered, the apathy and cynicism that is suggested in the survey data shown in part one are the inevitable dead end for civil rights enforcement. If not done well, it appears that the first option returns as the actual as opposed to a putative policy decision.

What, then, is it about the existing structure of fair housing law enforcement regulations, programs, and funding that needs most to be changed to demonstrate that fair housing is a meaningful part of everyone's sense of citizenship and civic entitlement? Four of the clearest findings within this collection are that, first, fair housing is not ably or evenly administered throughout the United States, even though the administering agency, HUD, has had decades to perfect the delivery mechanisms.

Second, existing levels of ignorance of housing rights recommends a dramatically new sustained national campaign aimed at the real estate industry, local communities, and citizens. If Americans know so little and rely even less on an enforcement system in place for decades, then major change in the manner in which educational and enforcement campaigns are run is essential. These new programs must be redesigned and based upon an assessment of the social construction and meaning of rights, and rights opposition, in local areas. There is no one-size-fits-all for educational programs, any more than there is for an investigative program. It is, however, hard to guess what part of the norms and preferences Americans use in searching for housing, mortgages, and neighborhoods needs to be changed to create a new, proactive, popular foundation in support of grassroots-driven rights enforcement. We do not yet know enough about willing and unwilling supporters of fair housing, but recent surveys show us the beginnings of a new program of rights promotion. A period of sustained experimentation and evaluation is most needed to learn, from a range of demonstration efforts conducted over several years, what can best affect the indifference to rights, and what can best produce an increased willingness to use new forms of storefront-like intake systems.[21]

Third, based upon decades of testing evidence, culminating in the most recent set of audits, it is indispensable to systemically offer all complainants the option of testing to accompany their complaints. Given the proven difficulty of detecting most forms of discrimination without testing data, including most especially in uncovering evidence of steering, it should become a legislatively mandated right for all complainants.[22]

Fourth, if Ross and Galster are proven correct and some programs have an effect in reducing discrimination, there should be a much more targeted focus on appreciating what parts of the complex federal enforcement system are likely to have the greatest impact upon levels of segregation and discrimination and then to pursue them vigorously. This is not idle social science curiosity but rather a practical search for what works and why and at what cost. If they are correct that FHIP has an effect, then there should be continued reliance on the existing system of private fair housing groups as well as state and local agencies as the major intake and investigative arm of the open-housing pledge.

An open, unanswered question is whether systemic investigations, whose broad reach can theoretically cover major parts of an industry, might be the most effective use of federal, rather than state and local, resources. It is my assumption, as well as that of several of the contributors to this collection, that this is the case. It is time, at last, to test whether and to what extent this is accurate. Systemic investigations can be initiated making use of either a pattern of individual complaint data or additional evidence such as that provided by large-scale testing.[23]

Create a New Federal Open-Housing Commission

Without better answers to core questions about program effectiveness at HUD, and without evidence of any major change over the last decades in the will to innovate, it would be imprudent to continue to permit HUD to continue to administer a set of rights it has proven incapable of either effectively promoting or protecting. The recommendation is, then, to transfer open housing enforcement authority to a new independent commission focused only on fair housing rights and remedies. It would be an agency with trained investigators and testers whose primary goal is systemic change and that administers a wide ranging network of private nonprofit organizations (Ellen and Voicu 2006).

This would end HUD's complicated, conflicted role as housing provider, mortgage guarantor, and legal arbiter of what housing treatment is fair and equal. Even if periodically the HUD cabinet accepts equal opportunity as a core program goal, it has proven impossible to translate such commitments into the sustained investigative energy and programs needed to reduce current levels of housing inequity. With one-fifth to one-quarter of all housing transactions still discriminatory, and the multiple flaws in administration noted above, a new beginning could only be an improvement.

The new agency would have the benefit of being single-minded in its program actions. A fresh start also would mean that new staff could be employed with new ideas. HUD fair housing offices have been long demoralized and poorly managed in handling their statutory obligations. As noted by many, equal housing has been and remains a marginalized HUD program. At the new agency, ideas and innovations would not have to be approved by a cabinet distracted by other duties. Experimentation would help in the design of a better set of funding solutions and program ideas suited to the needs identified in this collection. A central part of the success of this reform would require increased funding; without such increases we would essentially be returned to the first option identified above.[24]

Taking Initiative at the Local Level

New York City is a useful example of one major metropolitan area that has begun innovative local community group actions aimed at revitalizing fair housing enforcement. After the collapse of a local open-housing group that had operated for over three decades (Chen 2004), at least two major new groups began to establish different sets of programs and policy options for the city and region. These initiatives, while at their beginning stages, suggest a model for more energized and aggressive local actions to reduce housing disparities rooted in both older and newer civil rights protections. The programs suggest that locally inspired actions and funding can breathe life into what at the federal level appears moribund or intransigent. A new Fair Housing Justice Center was established in New York in spring 2004 with funding from the Ford Foundation, FHIP, and other local sources. Diane Houk, a former Justice Department fair housing attorney with over twenty years of experience, serves as the executive director. In addition, Fred Freiberg, a former local private fair housing group director and Justice Department testing coordinator, serves as the field services director. There is, in addition in New York, the Anti-Discrimination Center of Metro New York.

The Fair Housing Justice Center is incorporated as part of an older organization, HELP USA.[25] The central goal of this new local program is to plan and implement a series of systemic housing discrimination investigations using both testing and nontesting evidence. Their specific goals are, in their words, to examine systemic discrimination that restricts access to housing opportunities or fosters segregation; advocate public policies that reduce inequality and promote open and inclusive communities; and, finally and interestingly, to upgrade and strengthen local, state, and national fair housing enforcement. They intend to address the housing equity needs of all protected classes, including those of newer and growing immigrant populations, those with limited English proficiency, and those with physical and mental disabilities.

Their goal is not just law enforcement but is integrally connected to the objective of creating mixed-income housing opportunities. They intend to develop prototypes for the development of mixed-income housing in low-poverty/high-opportunity areas, including gentrifying neighborhoods, with part of the funding for this derived from the monetary relief obtained from fair housing litigation aimed at repairing "the harm caused to the New York community by systemic housing discrimination." They argue that:

> With few exceptions, enforcement of fair housing laws at the local, state, and national level is uneven, unsophisticated, and under-funded. At the federal level, HUD is issuing fewer housing discrimination charges and there has been a diminution of fair housing enforcement activity by the Civil Rights Division of

> the Department of Justice. Unfortunately, this conspicuous decrease in federal fair housing enforcement activity has not occurred in response to a corresponding reduction in housing discrimination, but instead stems from a shift in national priorities. Likewise, many public agencies at the state and local level charged with enforcing fair housing and fair lending laws lack training and resources, fail to complete investigations in a timely manner, and seldom achieve an outcome or remedy favorable to victims of discrimination or the community. Housing discrimination often remains unreported when individuals and groups lack confidence that government enforcement agencies will act to enforce their rights. In 2002, the City of New York Division of Human Rights received only 82 housing discrimination complaints from a city of more than 8 million people.[26]

Many private fair housing groups, they argue, are now entirely dependent upon HUD for their program funding, and this reliance has resulted in less independence and a reduction in fair housing litigation, particularly against government entities that may be engaged in discrimination. In New York City, for example, the Open Housing Center closed in 2003, after thirty-two years of providing fair housing services to the community, partly due to their inability to find alternative means to fund their programs. The lackluster track record of most government enforcement agencies including the New York State and City human rights agencies means, they assert, that undertaking only individually based complaint enforcement will yield little in the way of either short-term or lasting results. More importantly, they say, while a complaint-responsive enforcement strategy may provide some relief to individual victims of discrimination, it typically will do nothing to repair any damage that discrimination may have caused to the community.

There is, then, a need, they argue, for systemic responses to housing discrimination that can lead to community-based remedies. Where individuals may be unaware of persistent and insidious inequalities of treatment, proactive fair housing testing can, Houk and Freiberg argue, identify the patterns of discrimination that limit segments of the population from gaining access to housing opportunities. They have also found over the last year that discrimination in New York is often so blatant and pervasive that there is no need to test. Landlords have openly told their tenants, for example, to stop allowing Hispanic and black guests to come to their apartment or face eviction, leading to an immediate case being successfully filed and won.

In addition to counseling, investigative assistance, legal referrals, and "testing" investigations, they also propose to develop initiatives to expand residential housing choice, increase the supply and variety of affordable housing options, and foster "inclusive residential living patterns." They are proposing to do what Sidney in her chapter has said is so hard, including investing in development of mixed-income housing opportunities in low-poverty or "high-opportunity" areas. They finally have also proposed to develop new technology applications and other investigative resources for public and private fair housing and civil rights enforcement agencies "to improve the quality and effectiveness of fair housing law enforcement activities."

The second nonprofit organization operating within the New York region is the Anti-Discrimination Center of Metro New York. It has, for the last several years, been operating a range of programs including testing, research, litigation, and a campaign addressing the effects of racial and ethnic segregation.[27] In 2005, they led an effort that resulted in changing New York City's civil rights law to make it easier for cases to be filed by increasing coverage to include domestic partners.[28] The intent was to make it possible that changes or reductions in federal legal protection would not imperil rights for residents of the city. They have also been engaged with housing advocates throughout the region to establish a more active campaign of both litigation and policy development with the goal of broadening housing opportunities outside the narrow, traditional confines of most enforcement-only organizations. The principle or motto of the organization is areawide in its thrust: "one community, no exclusion." Significantly, they insist on seeing their only role as eliminating discrimination and segregation, and not organizational continuation or survival. "When will we go out of business?" is the way the executive director of the organization, Craig Gurian, puts it.[29]

These programs and plans constitute novel and important new strategies for making fair housing enforcement come alive within one of this country's global cities. Ford Foundation funding will, it can be hoped, be provided over several years to test out the Fair Housing Justice Center model for linking systemic enforcement and affordable housing. Even if only a portion of what they hope to accomplish in fact occurs, New York City—at least—will have a far more legally and programmatically effective platform with which to undertake the next generation of programs and ideas. There may also be a model of best practices that other private groups might embrace. Because they are dependent for most of their work on nonfederal funding, they will also likely have to struggle to grow their programs and services.

CONCLUSION

It is encouraging that new ideas and energy are being applied to the dormant fair housing movement by the new programs started in New York. While such efforts are being undertaken, it also appears critical to attempt a new approach at the federal level. Since a continually passive posture toward major reforms is ultimately corrosive of the interests that are supposed to be protected, my recommendation is that federal fair housing enforcement functions be transferred to a new independent agency, an Equal Housing Commission, just as employment discrimination is handled by the independent Equal Employment Opportunity Commission (EEOC) (Burstein 1985; Abelson 2001).[30] Such a new agency should more likely be able to breathe new life into the statutory promises left untended by HUD by overcoming the accumulated institutional entropy. The hypothesis is that they could only do better, given the accumulated evidence presented above.

The proposal would be to separate the private market antidiscrimination programs now at HUD from its program compliance, or Title VI, tasks associated with reviewing the compliance of government programs with civil rights duties. The latter would remain at HUD. Fair housing enforcement at the individual and systemic level would be free of HUD's endemically countervailing weights and pressures. It would be relaunched as a new federal civil rights enforcement agency, the Equal Housing Commission. The private sector housing duties would begin with establishing a larger number of intake offices administered by private fair housing groups. This would necessarily include extensive new forms of outreach to Hispanics, Asians, and the disabled. The new agency would also have to take a more aggressive role in correcting the high levels of misinformation about discrimination in housing and credit. Also, since the bulk of Americans say they are unwilling to use this civil right, they would engage in systematically planning for a long-term program to promote awareness of these rights.

Also at the local level, regionwide equal housing commissions would be created that would include representatives of the major affected groups, including civil rights advocates, housing providers, and major nonprofit agencies committed to enforcing equal rights and equal housing opportunity. When such nonprofit centers do not exist, funding should be provided for their establishment and operations. They would be required to establish a biannual and five-year plan for the allocation of enforcement and education resources that would then be funded by the commission, making use of community-development funding as well as matching funds from local sources.[31]

But will a new Equal Housing Commission really work better than the current flawed system? Such a seemingly simple "change-the-box" solution, critics will argue, merely will expose the vulnerabilities of this now politically isolated, pure-law-enforcement agency. It would become as inert and inept as the EEOC. It would likely be subject to intensified acts of political control, manipulation, and budget squeezes after each new big successful case alienated another powerful member of the real estate industry, Congress, or the White House. It is not really possible, critics will argue, to design a better enforcement processes, given what we know of the sociological foundations of housing inequality, including the political contours of the prior and current executive branch. There is little point at present of proposing reforms for an administration undermined and distracted by other crises and management failures. Perhaps this is true.

However, having examined evidence and programs on race, housing, and enforcement for decades, the evidence within this book provides as strong an impetus for change as we have had during that time period. Evidence of some progress and local initiative also suggests that programs can be changed and can have positive, even if incomplete, impacts. Most notably, research shows us for the first time that much of the public has withdrawn from its willingness to see their fair housing rights as a credible part of their civic entitlements. This paralysis of rights is central to the analysis of a need to change policies, since if we do not, then, as a country, we will have lost a central foundation for viable civil and human rights. The withering of fair housing is potentially emblematic of the atrophy of larger commitments to human rights and the protection of our civil liberties. The American Dilemma of sixty years ago will have become an American paradox: a country ostensibly committed to fair housing whose sociological and administrative expressions of this choice are frail, marginal, and substantially ineffective.

There has been progress, we can report, in that we are now better aware of the shape, trends, processes, and even causes operating within the world of race, justice, and housing. We can also report credible signs of local innovations that could provide alternative methods for addressing the shortcomings in the federally established fair housing system. Perhaps this is the best that can be expected for a country seemingly unknowingly committed to priorities and practices that ensure the ongoing fragility of civil rights in housing for another generation. But undertaking change is necessary and not incidental. Not in a generation have we had the evidence and argument accumulated herein that the law's promises have become hollowed out and are in urgent need of reform.

APPENDIX: METHODOLOGICAL DESIGN FOR THE "WHAT DO WE KNOW ABOUT FAIR HOUSING" NEW YORK CITY SURVEY

This appendix summarizes the design for the 2005 New York City Fair Housing Survey. The survey was conducted by the Baruch Survey Research Unit (SRU). A total of 372 interviews were completed by SRU interviewers between July 15 and August 14, 2005.

Table 11.1. Household Strata for the Five Boroughs of New York City

Borough	*Households*	*% of HHs*	*Expected*	*Interviews Completed*	*Weighted*
Bronx	463,212	15.3 %	57	51	57
Brooklyn	880,727	29.2	109	107	109
Manhattan	738,644	24.5	91	88	91
Queens	782,664	25.9	96	105	96
Staten Island	156,341	5.2	19	21	19
TOTAL	3,021,588	100%	372	372	372

Sample Design

The sample design used a RDD (random digit dialing) sample generated by MSG-Genesys Sampling Inc., drawn from the five boroughs of New York City, proportionate to the number of households in each borough. Strata were used to help approximate the distribution of household interviews in each of the five boroughs. The household strata are as shown in table 11.1.

Telephone Calling Procedure

Probability methods were used within each household to select one adult as the designated respondent. (This replicates the design of the 2002 U.S. Housing and Urban Development study on housing discrimination awareness, *How Much Do We Know*). Six attempts were made on all live numbers (excluding numbers that were nonworking or nonresidential numbers). Refusal conversion was attempted, where households or individuals who initially refused to participate were recontacted and asked a second time to participate. Interviewing was conducted at the SRU's computer-assisted telephone-interviewing lab in both English and Spanish.

Survey Error

The margin of error for this survey, based on sample size alone, is ± 5.1 percent at the 95 percent confidence level. The sample is subject to a small amount of noncoverage error, because household telephone samples fail to include the small proportion of New York City households that are not telephone subscribers (which includes both those without any telephone service and those who only have cell phones). As not all selected respondents agree to participate in a survey, nonresponse errors may also be present. In addition, factors such as question wording and the ability of respondents to recall factual details and articulate answers and opinions can also affect the accuracy of survey findings.

Weighting of Data

The data were weighted for the probability of selection on a borough level and on a household level by using the inverse of the number of adults in the household. The weights were calculated so that the weighted total is identical to the initial sample size, to reduce the possibility of distorting the variance estimates.

NOTES

1. In September 2005, the U.S. Justice Department sued the National Association of Realtors for their refusal to allow some Internet providers of information about listings of houses for sale, access to their members' MLS listings of other units (*Newsday* 2005).

2. Pew Research Center (2005).

3. A survey of employee morale in federal government agencies, conducted in 2004, reveals that HUD has the fifth-lowest staff morale of the thirty agencies for which data were reported. The agency with the lowest staff morale was Homeland Security, where analysts commented that "there is something fundamentally wrong at the organization" (Rosenbaum 2005).

4. Each civil rights law operates in isolated silos of regulations, applications, funding, personnel exigencies, evaluation and performance concerns, and other requirements. There is no one office of civil rights with local outreach stations throughout the country where claims of bias can be brought. Voting rights are handled by the Department of Justice, employment discrimination by the Equal Employment Opportunity Commission, school desegregation by the Department of Education, and housing rights by the Department of Housing and Urban Development (Walton 1988).

5. I acknowledge my debt to the work of Robert K. Merton (1948a; 1948b), who pioneered the analysis of structural underpinnings of racial disadvantage.

6. See Bovard (2000).

7. To illustrate the inability of fair housing issues to attain attention in an agency affected with multiple serious management and performance crises, we can cite the number of personnel or staff assigned to all of the country's fair housing duties. Despite the growing number of immigrants and minorities, there were only 750 people at HUD in 1994 who were employed full-time to work on all of the country's fair housing issues, including public sector Title VI and private market cases. This number dropped to 589 by 1998 and was still below the 1994 threshold in 2005 when there were only 650 people overall (GAO 2004: 47; GAO 2005: 11). What remained consistent was that the federal fair housing staffing levels remained at roughly 5 to 6 percent of HUD's overall staffing from 1994 up through 2005. There appears to be a limit

to this level of staff support and no more—despite increased responsibilities, evidence of poor performance, and national testing and survey data revealing large gaps in serving those experiencing discrimination. Recent mandatory staff cutbacks have resulted in senior fair housing staff worrying that they will "lose many of their best staff" because of these reductions (GAO 2004: 48).

8. Barbara Bergmann (1996: 169) reminds us of some of the impediments to the law having its intended effects. "Laws alone are ineffective when the behavior they forbid is not confined to a small part of the population, when the behavior goes on behind closed doors, when the violations are difficult and expensive to prove, and when the penalties are not easy to apply."

9. See: http://www.eeoc.gov/stats/charges.html.

10. Thirty-seven percent of Schill's survey informants did not even know they had the right to file in federal court, which suggests that FHIP agencies may be/are being rewarded/encouraged to send cases to HUD rather than allowing clients to make their own choice. Another 10 percent said they could not afford federal court, meaning that FHIP agencies are either unsupportive of or unable to cover the cost of pro bono legal services for those who might like to file in federal court. That is, roughly half of the cases that did come to HUD might not have, had the complainants been aware of their rights and options.

11. In state and local enforcement agencies, the administrative, or no-cause, closure rate as of 1997 was nearly 45 percent (Schill and Friedman 1999: 66).

12. State and local agencies have reported reasonable cause in 7 percent of their cases (GAO 2004: 36).

13. GAO (2005: 48) reports that over half of complainants were not offered any of the help required for conciliation, and in a quarter of cases (26 percent) agency "staff suggested that the parties work out their differences on their own."

14. This proportion rose to roughly 40 percent of the cases in 2002 but only after a major but temporary initiative.

15. In our sample of the opinions of New Yorkers about fair housing enforcement, we learned that many felt that stronger penalties would be appropriate. When asked the question, "Do current laws generally provide severe enough penalties, like fines, for people who are found guilty of discriminating against renters or homebuyers?" roughly 30 percent said they were strong enough, another 35 percent stated they should be stronger, but the remaining 35 percent did not know how to answer the question. Possibly because of inadequate information about the nature of the penalties that are in fact imposed, large numbers of people in New York City simply do not know what to say when asked about how to improve the law's operation. There is, then, for those few who remain through the final stages of legal review, a nontrivial number of unhappy participants—both those who complained and those who were defendants.

16. It is important to note that the source of enforcement data for them to use was a HUD database called TEAPOTS, which GAO has recently reported is seriously limited in recording current and complete data on cases (GAO 2005: 22). Ross and Galster were unable to detect an impact of antidiscrimination funding on the treatment of Hispanics, suggesting differences in the volume and nature of Hispanic complaints, the

attention paid to them by the FHAP and the FHIP, or the sources of discrimination. The analysis of the situation facing Hispanics by Janis Bowdler and Charles Kamasaki (chapter 10) adds another concern, as a major national Hispanic nonprofit organization appears impatient with being second place in this arena of civil rights.

17. See for example: Confessore (2006); Shurka et al. (2004); Swarns (2006).

18. Shuck (2003: 332–33) continues: "Government should not interfere with people's freedom except in unusual circumstances. . . . People should (instead) cultivate an interest in and sympathy for those who are different, trying by an act of moral imagination to put themselves in the shoes of strangers before judging them." He recommends that, instead of taking offense and filing civil rights complaints, people instead just develop "thicker skins." The evidence presented earlier demonstrates that minorities have had, of necessity, to harden themselves. They already file trivially too few complaints. Justice on behalf of those denied is buttressed by whites whose skins have hardened against evidence of bias and steering. Schuck stands the civil rights problem, incorrectly in my view, on its head on behalf of an ideological commitment to free market solutions. Many complaints, he continues (335), "make a mockery of the law when the law is brandished to penalize what often is only just ignorance, boorishness, interpretive confusion, ill-considered speech, clumsy provocation, misjudgment, rough or poor humor, and other unfortunate infelicities." I find his dismissal of this country's centuries of racial insults to be at best sociologically and empirically ill-considered.

19. Americans would be free of the pretense of being two-faced: saying we believe in equal justice but never really offering it to any but a tiny handful. Foreign countries would no longer have to laugh behind our backs at our hypocrisy when we say we are a country of equals while staring, rather directly, into palpable signs of racial injustice and inequality. No one would need any longer to be surprised by the concomitant evidence of racial neglect and impoverishment as appeared in the aftermath of Hurricane Katrina or that is documented in this volume. The United States would be just another advanced, market-based economy offering explicitly limited social benefits and safety-net protections, with no more distinguished or ostensible a record of ensuring human and civil rights than dozens of other countries. The nation would join other nation-states struggling to advance their economic and world political interests while allowing human rights interests to fall officially into a familiar distant second or third place. We would appear less honorable as a nation, but we could credit ourselves with being more open and honest about our inequalities. We could not be criticized for our unwillingness to eliminate them, since our pledges and promises of decades ago have been de jure—as well as de facto—rescinded and canceled. People could live their lives knowing and becoming resigned to the fact that there would be no federal relief, ever.

20. One analyst's view is succinct: "With less at stake than in 1964, it should come as no surprise if Congress continues to temporize in the hope that someone else will somehow make this issue go away" (Lund 2002: 332).

21. HUD has recently initiated a research contract aimed at systematically rethinking many of the obstacles to more effective internal HUD case processing. It will, however, take up to two years before the results from this project will be avail-

able for program redesign consideration (interview with Todd Richardson, PD&R/HUD on December 15, 2005).

22. The logical mechanism for the provision of such testing evidence is the existing system of private, nonprofit fair housing groups. They frequently have access to trained pools of volunteer or staff testers or can get the training needed to recruit additional staff.

23. The critical choice is to enable federal agencies, including DOJ, to concentrate their skills and resources on such major cases while enabling local groups and agencies to handle the current bulk of the twenty thousand or so individual complaints that are filed, with that number expected to grow following major outreach and education initiatives mentioned earlier. Reforms might at more distant points in time take into account suggestions such as those by Loewen (2005), who proposes a new "Residents' Rights Act" that would mandate regional sharing of minority households, linked to penalties tied to the withdrawal of federal program funds or the mortgage property deduction. Cashin (2004) and Maly (2005) also propose grassroots organizing at a large scale and not a federal government campaign aimed at the target of housing mixing. Fiss (2003) and Polikoff (2004) also each propose national programs relying upon federal powers to relocate the black poor out of the worst segregated ghettos so that the mix of poverty and racial isolation can be definitively ended. A federal effort to address housing integration would, however, represent a major transformation of the prior passivity and reluctance on this issue. Regional fair-share allocations have been the dream or goal of fair housing advocates for decades. Each proposal has, however, encountered resistance, indifference, or fear by state government, Congress, and the executive branch (French 2004). It remains likely that in the short run, of the next decade and more, only grass-roots action will be available to actively promote the integration of minorities and other protected classes.

24. Under any reform scenario, funding from the federal government needs to increase if the law is to be both better understood and used, and that it will "perform" better by reducing existing levels of differential treatment to substantially lower levels. But should funding go from $20 million for private groups to $100 or $200 million? What is the most sensible and efficient use of scarce resources with competing domestic needs? Central to any broadening of services are the underserved needs of Hispanics and the disabled, which appear notable in the evidence presented in this collection. It would also be easy to imagine a campaign of rights promotion at high schools and colleges aimed at children of immigrants who are, for the first time, experiencing the disillusionment of being treated unfairly and unjustly because of their "protected" ascriptions. But caution is needed in deciding on a sensible plan for funding federal and local initiatives; how much law enforcement with how much innovation is necessary to break out of the box of currently stagnant enforcement mechanisms? Who should be given funding to create a new way for the average American to visualize and value the set of rights that are now largely unused? It is too simple to argue that the funding previously made available was simultaneously too little and misdirected, without a clear evaluation of what we can learn from the shortcomings of all that funding. From 1989 through FY 1996, for example, HUD allocated a total of $105 million through all facets of its nonprofit FHIP program. Nearly $43 million of this sum was

slated for enforcement and $27 million for education and training (GAO 1997: table II: 1; 19). Recently, the Office of Management and Budget estimated the budget outlays for both FHAP and FHIP fair housing programs to have been $50 million in 2003, $44 million for 2005, and, for 2006, a budget of only $39 million, with $23 million for state and local agencies under the FHAP program and only $16 million for nonprofits, under the FHIP program. While it is clear that these sums were and will be inadequate to the tasks and shortcomings outlined in this book, what more should be allocated, for what purposes, and to what entities? For intake, testing, and case investigations, funding is moving in the wrong direction. More rather than less funding should be provided at the local, nonprofit level for those groups that have the capacity to manage intake and testing, including bringing more complex or resistant cases to the federal level (Rogers 2005). Central to any argument about what agencies or who will get more over the next several years should be that it will be allocated based on unmet need. The federal government needs to do its own analysis of impediments to affirmatively further the purposes of the fair housing act aimed at helping those who are being neglected and most harmed. Included in this needs assessment, as had been done in New York (see above), is to think of needs regionally and in terms of how to use existing housing programs to more proactively reduce both discrimination and segregation.

25. HELP USA is a not-for-profit organization that has been developing housing and providing social services and employment assistance for roughly eighteen years. It developed 2,300 residential housing units and assists 11,000 individuals nationwide. Its central focus is helping homeless families, survivors of domestic violence, persons recovering from substance abuse, people living with AIDS, and ex-offenders. http://www.helpusa.org/advocacy/.

26. This material is derived from e-mails and interviews with Diane Houk and Fred Freiberg; interview on December 5, 2005. They also provided access to funding proposals, parts of which are referenced and cited in this section.

27. For more detail on this organization see their website: http://www.antibiaslaw.com/about/about.html.

28. The statute is the local Civil Rights Restoration Act and was signed into law by the mayor in October 2005.

29. Interview with Mr. Craig Gurian on December 19, 2005.

30. On the EEOC see Abelson (2001) and http://www.eeoc.gov/.

31. Local commissions would process individual cases in conjunction with private fair housing groups. Serious and larger-scale cases would be designed by or referred to the Federal Equal Housing Commission and to the Justice Department. Issues of the denial of housing to individuals would be treated at the local level by a single intake office with common services and systems for getting cases examined and resolved in a timely manner. Complicated cases would be investigated by joint, federally supervised teams. Federal resources should be concentrated at the final stage when large-scale or systemic cases are readied for court or trial before administrative law judges or federal courts. It can be hoped that new initiatives, like the one begun in New York City, will demonstrate that alternative methods for handling cases can be found and that they can be shown to be flexible, innovative, and ultimately effective.

REFERENCES

Abelson, Reed. 2001. "Anti-Bias Agency is Short of Will and Cash: Can The E.E.O.C. Be More Aggressive?" *New York Times*, July 1 (Section 3): 1, 12.

Abravanel, Martin, and Mary Cunningham. 2002. *How Much Do We Know? Public Awareness of the Nation's Fair Housing Laws*. Washington, DC: The Urban Institute. http://www.huduser.org/publications/fairhsg/hmwk.html.

Alba, Richard, and Victor Nee. 2003. *Remaking the American Mainstream: Assimilation and Contemporary Immigration*. Cambridge, MA: Harvard University Press.

Banton, Michael. 1987. "The Beginning and End of the Racial Issue in British Politics." *Policy and Politics* 15(1): 39–47.

Barry, Brian. 2002. "Social Exclusion, Social Isolation, and the Distribution of Income." In *Understanding Social Exclusion*, ed. John Hills, Julian Le Grand, and David Piachaud, 13–29. New York: Oxford.

Bergmann, Barbara. 1996. *In Defense of Affirmative Action*. New York: Basic Books.

Bonastia, Chris. 2000. "Why Did Affirmative Action in Housing Fail during the Nixon Era? Exploring 'Institutional Homes' of Social Policies." *Social Problems* 47:523–42.

Bovard, James. 2000. "HUD's Biggest Farce." *The Free Market* 18(1). http://www.mises.org/freemarket_detail.asp?control=328&sortorder=articledate.

Bratt, Rachel, and W. Dennis Keating. 1993. "Federal Housing Policy and HUD: Past Problems and Future Prospects of a Beleaguered Bureaucracy." *Urban Affairs Quarterly* 29(1): 3–27.

Briggs, Xavier de Souza. 2005. "Conclusion: Desegregating the City." In *Desegregating the City: Ghettos, Enclaves, and Inequality*, ed. David Varady, 233–57. Albany: State University of New York Press.

Burchardt, Tania, Julian Le Grand, and David Piachaud. 2002. "Introduction." In *Understanding Social Exclusion*, ed. John Hills, Julian Le Grand, and David Piachaud, 1–12. New York: Oxford.

Burstein, Paul. 1985. *Race, Jobs, and Politics: The Struggle for Equal Opportunity in the United States since the New Deal*. Chicago: University of Chicago Press.

Cashin, Sheryll. 2004. *The Failures of Integration: How Race and Class Undermine the American Dream*. New York: Public Affairs.

Chen, David. 2004. "Fair-Housing Groups Say New York City Is Falling Behind." *New York Times*, June 14.

Confessore, Nicholas. 2006. "Thousands Rally in New York in Support of Immigrants' Rights." *New York Times*, April 2.

Crane, Jonathan, ed. 1998. *Social Programs that Work*. New York: Russell Sage.

DeParle, Jason. 2005. "What Happens to a Race Deferred." *New York Times*, September 4.

Ellen, Ingrid Gould, and Ioan Voicu. 2006. "Nonprofit Housing and Neighborhood Spillovers." *Journal of Policy Analysis and Management* 25(1): 31–52.

Fiss, Owen. 2003. *A Way Out: America's Ghettos and the Legacy of Racism*. Princeton, NJ: Princeton University Press.

French, Chanin. 2004. "New Jersey Court Requires Good Faith Negotiations Prior to Bringing Mt. Laurel Litigation." *Practicing Planner* (Winter). American Planning Association. http://www.planning.org/affordablereader/pracplanner/MtLaurelvol2no4.htm.

Freund, David. 2004. *Democracy's Unfinished Business: Federal Policy and the Search for Fair Housing, 1961–1968*. Washington, DC: Poverty Research and Action Council.

Gaffney, Susan. 2001. "Testimony of the Inspector General, HUD." U.S. Senate Hearing on HUD's Program, Budget and Management Priorities for FY-2002. See http://banking.senate.gov/01_04hrg/042501/gaffney.htm.

GAO. 1997. "Fair Housing: Funding and Activities under the Fair Housing Initiatives Program." (March) GAO/RCED-97-67. Washington, DC: GAO.

———. 2004. "Fair Housing: Opportunities to Improve HUD's Oversight and Management of the Enforcement Process." (April) GAO-04-463. Washington, DC: GAO.

———. 2005. "Fair Housing: HUD Needs Better Assurance That Intake and Investigation Processes Are Consistently Thorough." (October) GAO-06-79. Washington, DC: GAO. http://www.gao.gov/docsearch/repandtest.html.

Glover, Angela, and Judith Bell. 2005. "Equitable Development for a Stronger Nation: Lessons from the Field." In *The Geography of Opportunity: Race and Housing Choice in Metropolitan America*, ed. Xavier de Souza Briggs, 289–309. Washington, DC: Brookings Institution Press.

Goering, John. 1986. "Minority Housing Needs and Civil Rights Enforcement." In *Race, Ethnicity, and Minority Housing in the United States*, ed. Jamshid Momeni, 194–215. New York: Greenwood Press.

Goetz, Edward. 2003. *Clearing the Way*. Washington, DC: Urban Institute Press.

Hills, John, Julian Le Grand, and David Piachaud, eds. 2002. *Understanding Social Exclusion*. New York: Oxford.

Hochschild, Jennifer. 1996. "You Win Some, You Lose Some . . . : Explaining the Patterns of Success and Failure in the Second Reconstruction." Paper Presented at the annual meetings of the American Sociological Association, New York, August 19.

Jackson, Kenneth. 1985. *Crabgrass Frontier: The Suburbanization of the United States*. New York: Oxford.

Julian, Elizabeth. N.d. "Where Should Fair Housing Enforcement Go From Here?" Unpublished report.

Leonard, Jonathan. 1990. "The Impact of Affirmative Action Regulation and Equal Employment Law on Black Employment." *Journal of Economic Perspectives* 4: 47–63.

Light, Paul. 2002. *Government's Greatest Achievements: From Civil Rights to Homeland Security*. Washington, DC: Brookings Institution Press.

Loewen, James. 2005. *Sundown Towns: A Hidden Dimension of American Racism.* New York: The New Press.

Lund, Nelson. 2002. "Illusions of Antidiscrimination Law." In *Beyond the Color Line: New Perspectives on Race and Ethnicity in America*, ed. Abigail and Stephan Thernstrom, 319–39. Stanford, CA: Hoover Institution Press.

Maly, Michael. 2005. *Beyond Segregation: Multiracial and Multiethnic Neighborhoods in the United States*. Philadelphia: Temple University Press.

Merton, Robert K. 1948a. "What Do We Know about Prejudice?" University of Chicago Round Table, May 2: 1–10.

———. 1948b. "Discrimination and the American Creed." In *Discrimination and National welfare*, ed. R. M. MacIver. New York: Harpers.

NCD. 2001. *Reconstructing Fair Housing*. November 6. Washington, DC: National Council on Disability. http://www.ncd.gov/newsroom/publications/fairhousing.html.

National Fair Housing Alliance. 2005. *2005 Fair Housing Trends Report*. April 5. Washington, DC: National Fair Housing Alliance.

New America Media. 2005. "Lessons of Katrina: America's Major Racial and Ethnic Groups Find Common Ground after the Storm." October 27. http://news.ncmonline.com/news/view_article.html?article_id=c6db092735d6fb5f21886d716cdf2464.

Newsday. 2005. "Feds Sue Realtor Group over Internet Policy." September 9. http://www.usdoj.gov/atr/public/press_releases/2005/211008.htm.

Nutting, Rex, and William Watts. 2005. "Nation Faces Unprecedented Choices: How Far Should the U.S. Go in Making New Orleans Whole?" *Market Watch*, September 9.

Pew Research Center. 2005. "Katrina Has Only Modest Impact on Basic Public Values," September 22, press release. Washington, DC: Pew Research Center.

Polikoff, Alexander. 2004. "Race Inequality and the Black Ghetto." November/December. Washington, DC: Poverty and Race Action Council.

Portes, Alejandro, and Ruben Rumbaut. 2001. *Legacies: The Story of the Immigrant Second Generation*. New York: Russell Sage.

———. 2005. "Introduction: The Second Generation and the Children of Immigrants Longitudinal Survey." *Ethnic and Racial Studies* 28:983–99.

Rogers, David. 2005. "White House to Trim Katrina Spending Request." *Wall Street Journal*, October 19: A8.

Rosenbaum, David. 2005. "Study Ranks Homeland Security Dept. Lowest in Morale." *New York Times*, October 16: 14.

Ross, Stephen, and John Yinger. 2002. *The Color of Credit: Mortgage Discrimination, Research Methodology, and Fair-Lending Enforcement*. Cambridge, MA: MIT Press.

Rossi, Peter. 1987. "The Iron Law of Evaluation and other Metallic Rules." In *Research in Social Problems and Public Policy*, ed. Joann Miller and Michael Lewis. Greenwich, CT: JAI Press.

Rossi, Peter, and Howard Freeman. 1989. *Evaluation: A Systematic Approach*. Newbury Park, CA: Sage.

Schill, Michael. 2005. "Regulations and Housing Development: What We Know." *Cityscape* 8(1): 5–19.

Schill, Michael, and Samantha Friedman. 1999. "The Fair Housing Amendments Act of 1988: The First Decade." *Cityscape* 4(3): 57–78. http://www.huduser.org/periodicals/cityscpe/vol4num3/current.html.

Schuck, Peter. 2003. *Diversity in America: Keeping Government at a Safe Distance.* Cambridge, MA: Belknap Press.

Sidney, Mara. 2001. "Images of Race, Class, and Markets: Rethinking the Origins of U.S. Fair Housing Policy." *The Journal of Policy History* 13(2): 181–214.

———. 2003. *Unfair Housing: How National Policy Shapes Community Action.* Lawrence: University of Kansas Press.

Shurka, Kalbir, et al. 2004. "Race, Social Cohesion, and the Changing Politics of Citizenship." *London Review of Education* 2(3): 187–95.

Smith, Daniel. 2005. "Political Science: Is the Bush Administration Anti-Science?" *New York Times Magazine*, September 4: 37–41.

Sparrow, Malcolm. 2000. *The Regulatory Craft: Controlling Risks, Solving Problems, and Managing Compliance*. Washington, DC: Brookings Institution.

Squires, Gregory. 2004. *Why the Poor Pay More: How to Stop Predatory Lending.* Westport, CT: Greenwood.

Steven Winter Associates. 2003. *Multifamily Building Conformance with Fair Housing Accessibility Guidelines*. February. Washington, DC: HUDUSER. http://www.huduser.org/publications/fairhsg/multifamily.html.

Suttles, Gerald. 1990. *The Man-Made City: The Land Use Confidence Game in Chicago*. Chicago: University of Chicago Press.

Swarns, Rachel. 2006. "Growing Unease for Some Blacks on Immigration." *New York Times*, May 4.

Tranel, Mark. 2003. "Enforcement of Fair Housing Law: A Complex Task Managed by a Complex System." Paper presented at the Association for Public Policy Analysis and Management Conference, Washington, DC, November 8.

Vale, Lawrence. 2000. *From the Puritans to the Projects: Public Housing and Public Neighbors*. Cambridge, MA: Harvard University Press.

von Hoffman, Alexander. 1998. *Like Fleas on a Tiger? A Brief History of the Open Housing Movement*. W98-3, August. Cambridge, MA: Joint Center for Housing Studies.

Walton, Hanes. 1988. *When the Marching Stopped: The Politics of Civil Rights Regulatory Agencies*. Albany: State University of New York Press.

Wilentz, Sean. 2005. "Bush's Ancestors: What Contemporary Conservatism's Ties to the American Past Tell Us about Its Future." *New York Times Magazine*, October 16: 18–22.

Index

Page locators in italics refer to figure and tables

About the Editor and Contributors

Martin D. Abravanel is a senior research associate at the Urban Institute, where he directs program evaluation, performance measurement, and survey research studies of low-income housing programs, community and economic development programs, and fair housing initiatives. From 1979 to 1997, he was the director of the Division of Policy Studies in the Office of Policy Development and Research at the U.S. Department of Housing and Urban Development.

Rebecca M. Blank is Joan and Sanford Weill Dean of Public Policy at the Gerald R. Ford School of Public Policy at the University of Michigan, Henry Carter Adams Collegiate Professor of Public Policy, and professor of economics. She is also the codirector of the National Poverty Center at the Ford School. Prior to coming to Michigan, she served as a member of President Clinton's Council of Economic Advisers. She chaired the panel for the National Research Council that produced the report *Measuring Racial Discrimination*.

Janis Bowdler is a senior policy analyst for the National Council of La Raza (NCLR). She is responsible for coordinating policy analysis and legislative and advocacy activities related to increasing and maintaining Latino homeownership. In addition, she provides technical assistance to the NCLR Homeownership Network. She has written and published on such topics as housing discrimination, housing counseling, housing conditions, predatory lending, and barriers to homeownership in the Latino community.

Ingrid Gould Ellen is associate professor of public policy and urban planning at the Wagner Graduate School of Public Service at New York University and codirector of NYU's Furman Center for Real Estate and Urban Policy. Professor Ellen's research interests center on urban social and economic policy, with a particular focus on housing and community development. She has published several papers on racial integration in neighborhoods and schools and is author of *Sharing America's Neighborhoods: The Prospects for Stable Racial Integration* (2000).

George C. Galster is the Clarence Hilberry Professor of Urban Affairs at the Department of Geography and Urban Planning, Wayne State University–Detroit. Since earning his PhD in economics from M.I.T., he has published over 100 scholarly articles. His latest book (coauthored) is *Why NOT in My Back Yard? The Neighborhood Impacts of Assisted Housing* (2003).

John Goering is professor of public affairs and in political science at Baruch College and the Graduate Center of the City University of New York. He is the author of several dozen articles as well as editor or author of several housing- and race-related books. Previously he directed evaluation and research on housing, neighborhood change, and civil rights issues at HUD, and served on the staff of the Clinton White House Initiative on Race.

John Iceland is an associate professor of sociology at the University of Maryland–College Park and a faculty associate of the Maryland Population Research Center. He was chief of the Poverty and Health Statistics branch at the U.S. Census Bureau before joining the Maryland faculty in 2003. Professor Iceland's research focuses on poverty and residential segregation issues. His current work on segregation looks at the residential patterns of immigrants.

Charles Kamasaki is senior vice president at the National Council of La Raza (NCLR), where he has headed the Office of Research, Advocacy and Legislation since 1989. He is responsible for managing NCLR's research, policy analysis, and advocacy activity on a wide range of issues, including civil rights, education, economic mobility, housing and community development, immigration, and other issues. He has authored and supervised the preparation of several dozen policy and research reports, articles, and editorials. He also serves as a director of the Raza Development Fund, one of the nation's largest Community Development Financial Institutions (CDFIs).

Douglas S. Massey is the Henry G. Bryant Professor of Sociology and Public Affairs at Princeton University. He is a past president of the American Sociological Association and the Population Association of America and current president of the American Academy of Political and Social Science.

Todd M. Richardson is deputy director of the Program Evaluation Division Office of Policy Development and Research at the U.S. Department of Housing and Urban Development. He has managed numerous program evaluations, including the long-running Moving To Opportunity evaluation and the national Housing Discrimination Study. He has been a HUD field economist in Detroit and developed scattered site public housing. He has a master's in public policy from the University of Michigan.

Stephen L. Ross is an associate professor at the University of Connecticut. He has devoted the bulk of his academic career to studying discrimination and other issues related to the general welfare of minorities in U.S. cities. His research has been published in the *Review of Economics and Statistics*, the *Economic Journal*, *Social Problems*, *Journal of Urban Economics*, and other related journals, as well as in a book on mortgage lending discrimination.

Michael H. Schill is dean and professor of law at the UCLA School of Law. From 1994 to 2004, Dean Schill was director of the Furman Center for Real Estate and Urban Policy at NYU School of Law. He is the author of three books and over forty articles on issues of housing and urban affairs.

Mara S. Sidney is associate professor of political science at Rutgers University–Newark. She studies public policy and advocacy against racial inequality, particularly with regard to housing and education. She is the author of *Unfair Housing: How National Policy Shapes Local Action* (2003), and her work has appeared in the *Urban Affairs Review*, the *Journal of Urban Affairs*, and the *Journal of Policy History*.

Margery Austin Turner directs the Urban Institute's Metropolitan Housing and Communities policy center. She examines issues of residential location, racial and ethnic discrimination and its contribution to neighborhood segregation and inequality, and the role of housing policies in promoting residential mobility and location choice. She served as deputy assistant secretary for research at the Department of Housing and Urban Development from 1993 through 1996, focusing HUD's research agenda on the problems of racial discrimination, concentrated poverty, and economic opportunity.